D0392433

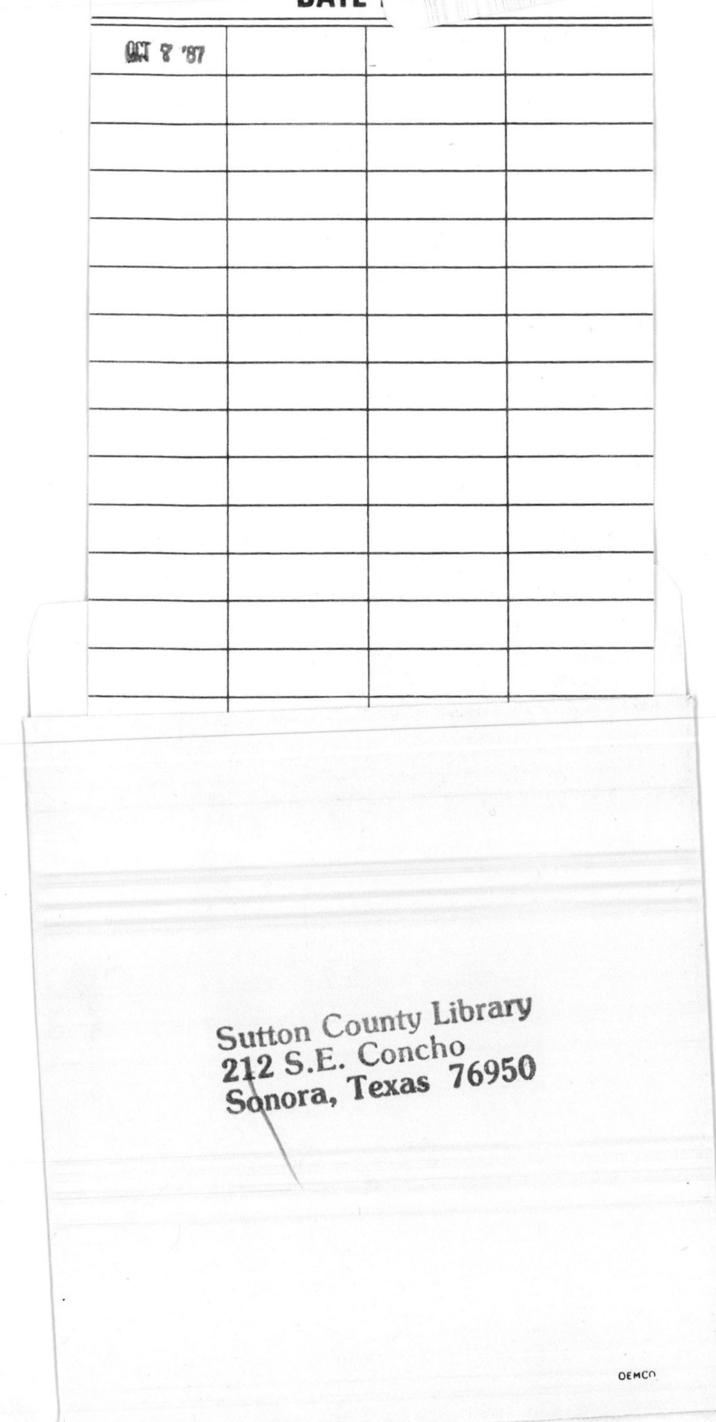
DATE
OCT 8 '87
Sutton County Library
212 S.E. Concho
Sonora, Texas 76950
DEMCO

Developments in the Study of Criminal Behaviour

Developments in the Study of Criminal Behaviour

Volume 2

Violence

Edited by
Philip Feldman
University of Birmingham

JOHN WILEY & SONS

Chichester · New York · Brisbane · Toronto · Singapore

Library of Congress Cataloging in Publication Data (Revised):
Main entry under title:

Developments in the study of criminal behavior.
Includes index.
Contents: v. 1. The prevention and control of offending—v. 2. Violence
1. Criminal behavior, Prediction of—Collected works. 2. Juvenile delinquency—Collected works. 3. Violence—Collected works. I. Feldman, Philip.
HV6035.D48 364.3
81-21946
AACR2

ISBN 0 471 10176 1 (vol. 1)
ISBN 0 471 10373 X (vol. 2)

British Library Cataloguing in Publication Data:

Developments in the study of criminal behaviour.
Vol. 2: Violence
1. Criminal psychology
I. Feldman, Philip
364.3 HV6080

ISBN 0 471 10373 X

Photosetting by Thomson Press (India) Limited, New Delhi and Printed in the United States of America

The Contributors

Ron Clarke	*Senior Principal Research Officer, Home Office Research Unit, London.*
William Davies	*Senior Psychologist, Her Majesty's Prison, Birmingham.*
Jonquil Drinkwater	*Research Associate, Department of Psychology, University of Birmingham.*
Philip Feldman	*Reader in Clinical Psychology, Department of Psychology, University of Birmingham.*
John Gardner	*Senior Clinical Psychologist, Walsall Area Health Authority.*
Moira Gray	*Research Clinical Psychologist, Department of Psychology, University of Birmingham.*
Kevin Howells	*Lecturer, Department of Psychology, University of Leicester.*
Patricia Mayhew	*Principal Research Officer, Home Office Reserach Unit, London.*
Lyn Minchin	*Senior Clinical Psychologist, Selly Oak Hospital, Birmingham.*
Jill Peay	*Research Officer, Centre for Criminological Research, University of Oxford.*
Kate Osborne	*Lecturer, Department of Psychology, University of Wales Institute of Science and Technology.*

Contents

Preface

There can be no doubt of the large scale personal distress and the heavy financial cost which result from violence whether in public or private settings. This book contains eight chapters reviewing various aspects of violence, under the broad heads of description, explanation and control, followed by a final overview chapter. It is the second of two volumes on recent developments in the study of criminal behaviour. The contributors concentrate on areas of violence which have attracted recent public concern and have stimulated much research activity, rather than on more traditional issues. The topics represented here tend to have been studied and reported in relative isolation from each other and this volume is one of the first to bring them together under one roof.

A continuing theme of this book is that the situational emphasis of social learning theory is likely to be much more helpful in both the explanation and the control of violence than the personality or social stress approaches. Advances in both intervention and prevention will be assisted by public policy developments, but these must be specific and practicable, rather than vague nostrums such as an improvement in the status of women.

The first three chapters deal with violence between individuals. Chapter 1, by John Gardner and Moira Gray, reviews the extensive but often seriously inadequate work on violence by parents against their children and sets out some possibilities for helping parents to become more skilled. In the second chapter Lyn Minchin stays in the home and discusses violence between couples, almost always by males against their female partner. Chapter 3, by Kate Osborne, deals with sexual violence against women, another topic concerning which public anxiety is growing, and debunks several widely held myths.

The next three chapters are concerned with violence in more public settings. Chapter 4, by Patricia Mayhew and Ron Clarke, reviews recent studies of vandalism—or property damage—many from the Home Office Research Unit. This form of violence is apparently trivial so far as each individual act is concerned, but the total effects are considerable, both in financial terms and on the quality of life, for example in large housing developments. Chapter 5, by Jonquil Drinkwater, deals with psychiatric hospitals, the subject of many scandals and subsequent public enquiries. There are some important implications for general management practices and for staff training both from this chapter and from the next one by Will Davies. This deals with several aspects of violence in prison, including riots and hostage taking.

The last two substantive chapters cover different aspects of the 'mentally abnormal violent offender'. Chapter 7, by Kevin Howells, considers the evidence for a special link between violence and mental disorder and in Chapter 8 Jill Peay reviews assumptions concerning 'dangerousness' which underlie public policy as represented by current and proposed legislation.

In a final chapter I bring together some of the key themes represented throughout and, in particular, implications for both accurate explanations and effective social action.

I hope that this book will be of interest to social science researchers and students, to policy planners and to professionals concerned with the control of violence in its many settings. I am most grateful to all the contributors for their helpful responses to my editorial efforts and to my secretary, Marie Chalmers, for her skill and patience throughout the preparation of both volumes.

PHILIP FELDMAN, 1981

Developments in the Study of Criminal Behaviour. Volume 2: Violence
Edited by Philip Feldman

1

Violence Towards Children

John Gardner and Moira Gray

'It is a sad fact that there is a better government policy to protect animals than children from experimentation'

Marion Wright Edelman, Director of Children's Defence Fund

Introduction

Violence between parents and children has become a major social problem in the last 20 years. It is not a new phenomenon; instances of the barbarous treatment of children, flogging and mutilation abound (Oliver, 1978). As early as 1660 in the USA the need for child protection was recognized in common law (Morris, 1979) and it is now well recognized that no country, culture or population is innocent of child abuse. What has changed in recent years is public and professional concern for the abused child, resulting in an impressive body of research literature. Data have been collected by research workers in numerous disciplines reflecting the complexity of the problem and the range of professionals involved, including social workers, psychologists, paediatricians, psychiatrists and lawyers. The consequences have been twofold: the rapid development in the field in response to the urgency of the problem has led to many methodologically weak studies and, secondly, a multiplicity of models and practices arising from the diverse perspectives of workers in the field. Several aspects of the problem, such as the identification of abuse, have received considerable research attention while little has been written about ways of helping families where abuse occurs.

This chapter will describe some of the problems in the existing research that have retarded the development of our understanding of the origins of child abuse. A brief critique of alternative models and treatments based upon them will be compared with a social interactional model derived from social learning theory. The advantages of this model will be discussed, together with recent behavioural interventions with abusing families. Some speculations concerning prevention of child abuse will be described, particularly those relating to parent training and education. We shall restrict our discussion to physical and psychological abuse and shall not consider sexual abuse of children, which we believe to be a different problem.

Incidence of abuse

Although estimates of incidence vary, numerous studies indicate a problem of considerable proportion. In the United States, Gil (1970) estimated that there were between 2.5 and 4.1 million cases of child abuse per year. Later investigators suggested lower figures of 1.5 million (Fontana, 1973) to 50 000 (Light, 1973), while Gelles (1977) reported that approximately 500 000 American children were either threatened with a gun or a knife or actually attacked by their parents in 1975. In a memorandum of evidence to the Parliamentary Select Committee on Violence in the Family, Scott (1977) reports data from several British studies indicating that between one and 12 children per 1000 are abused by their parents or guardians. Estimates vary according to the age of the children included in studies and the definition of abuse adopted (e.g. serious physical injury or psychological abuse). Herrenkohl *et al.* (1979) confirmed the generally held view that abuse frequently recurs but indicated that recurrence involved more than one perpetrator of abuse, more than one target and more than one type of abuse.

The use of official figures to compile the above estimates has undoubtedly led to under-estimation of the problem and over-representation of certain social groups in the figures. Several studies have reported a higher proportion of child abusers from lower SES classes (e.g. Smith, 1975; Garbarino, 1977), although some reported child abuse cases from higher SES families (Steele and Pollock, 1968; Helfer and Kempe, 1968). Apparently conflicting results on incidence and SES status arise from several areas of bias. Over-representation of lower SES groups in the official figures is not because they are necessarily more likely to abuse children but because of the response of official agencies with whom they are more likely to be in contact than higher SES families. Instead of focusing on a defined population of child abusers, an alternative research strategy could be employed to yield better epidemiological data. Self-report studies of 'normal' parents in representative national samples are needed to counter the biased picture of reality shown by official figures. This would also raise certain problems, some subjects may under-report and others may over-report. However, carefully conducted self-report studies are likely to yield samples less subject to bias than those from official statistics. Gil (1970) conducted a national survey to determine public awareness of child abuse, making the assumption that members of the community know of cases of child abuse even though they are not reflected in official figures. He estimated that between 2 and 4 million adults in the United States knew families involved in child abuse incidents in one year. This was a good attempt to obtain normative data but it does not go far enough. Information about 'other families' moves further away from actual incidents of abuse and is therefore more subject to distortion and subjective judgements.

Gelles (1977) did conduct a study employing a national probability sample, looking at all forms of domestic violence, but no information was available on families with babies under age 3. However, extrapolating from the results to the United States population of 3–17 year olds, Gelles concluded that between 1 and 2 million children had been killed, beaten or punched by their parents during 1975. Researchers may have been reluctant to conduct studies of this type in case people were reticent to report abusing incidents. However, Feldman (1977) cites many examples of good self-report studies of offending from the field of criminal behaviour, where greater reticence might have been expected. Obtaining a true epidemiological picture is vital, otherwise research and social policy actions may inevitably fail because they are based on incomplete and biased data.

Developments in research

Since Kempe highlighted the problem of 'battered children' (Kempe *et al.*, 1962) many developments have taken place both in understanding the nature of child abuse and in prevention. Several excellent reviews reflect the process of research development over the years (Spinetta and Rigler, 1972; Parke and Collmer, 1975; Friedrich and Boriskin, 1976; Burgess, 1979; Gambrill, 1981). A shift has taken place from looking for simple, unitary causes of abuse, either psychological or social, to a recognition that abuse has multiple determinants which must also be viewed in a social context.

Multiple causality

The first framework adopted by early researchers was the psychiatric model (Kempe *et al.*, 1962; Steele and Pollock, 1968). Following the medical tradition, attempts were made to locate psychopathology within the parents. Traits such as rigid, domineering, immature and self-centred were cited, although agreement across studies was difficult to find. In a comprehensive review of the literature on personality characteristics, Spinetta and Rigler (1972) were unable to draw any definite conclusions from research other than that abusive parents 'allowed aggressive impulses to be expressed too freely', which is merely restating the description of their abusive behaviour. Disillusionment with this approach led to the adoption of the sociological model, based on the assumption that external forces within the society caused child abuse. Many variables have been investigated within this model and linked to child abuse in varying proportions: social class (Gil, 1970), unemployment (Light, 1973), family size (Gil, 1970) and social isolation (Garbarino, 1977). In addition the cultural acceptance of violence to resolve conflict has been seen as a pervasive background setting precipitating the occurrence of child abuse (Steinmetz and Straus, 1974). One of the major problems in deriving a causal explanation of abuse from the sociological model is that it is unable to account for the finding that, given the same set of deprivation or adverse conditions, many parents do not abuse their children.

A conceptual problem which has dogged the child abuse field has been the persistent attempt to find one or two 'causes' of child abuse as though they offered the key and fit this into what Kaplan (1964) calls a hierarchical theory. A hierarchical theory is organized like a 'deductive pyramid in which we rise to few and more general laws as we move from conclusions to premises which entail them'. The very diversity of explanations for child abuse shows the need for a concatenated theory. In this model component laws typically converge at a central point with each one specifying one of the factors which plays a part in the phenomenon which the theory is to explain. For example, Straus (1979) relates 25 different factors to child abuse which individually account for a small proportion of the variance. A second complication making it difficult to pinpoint the causes of child abuse is that these factors do not operate in isolation from each other. A number of stresses impinging upon families have been isolated as predisposing factors in child abuse. They include such factors as unemployment, inadequate housing conditions, social isolation and large families. However, the mere existence of these factors is insufficient, the crucial element is the individual's *perception* of a particular condition. An overview of research suggests that individual psychological characteristics are implicated as well as a number of social stress factors and a model which takes an interactional perspective is clearly needed. Unfortunately the importance of recognizing both social and psychological variables has only recently been accepted. A number of writers began to recognize the limitations of earlier models and attempted to conceptualize child abuse in multidimensional terms (Garbarino, 1977; Belsky, 1978). Burgess (1979) gives the clearest and most comprehensive description of interactions between social and psychological variables in his social interactional model. Only an interactional model can adequately explain results from studies such as Empson and McGlaughlin (1979). In a longitudinal study of 60 disadvantaged families, the authors found that families with high stress tended to have a less well developing child than families under little stress, but the study also showed that despite highly stressful conditions in families, some children develop well.

A social interactional model takes account of the multifaceted nature of child abuse and permits analysis of the conditions which may elicit and maintain abusive behaviour. The pattern of interactions between family members becomes an important source of information regarding antecedent and maintaining variables in abuse. The potential role of the child in provoking abuse is also acknowledged. The conditions under which the child is reared and the methods used by the parents, particularly their punitive methods, may help to explain why some adults are predisposed to abusive behaviour given certain setting conditions. Lastly, there is an emphasis on the learned nature of parenting and an acceptance that many parents have insufficient knowledge and skill to equip them to carry out the highly complex task of child rearing. Not only may they lack fundamental skills, there may also be an absence of coping strategies to deal with stress, giving rise to a spiralling effect of increased stress and less effective coping.

The application of social learning principles to child abuse will be considered in more detail later.

Methodological problems

The volume of research on child abuse has been impressive. It arose out of pressing social needs over the past 20 years and, while this response on the part of the workers in the field is admirable, concurrent problems have developed, probably as a consequence of the urgency of the problem. Much of the research in the area is methodologically inadequate, thus questioning the validity and interpretation of the results obtained.

The most basic problem lies in the definition of child abuse. Some studies limit the term to children who have received serious physical injury in circumstances that indicated that the injury was caused wilfully rather than by accident. But ambiguities can arise over interpretations of 'serious' and diversity exists even within physical injury which includes lacerations, head injuries, limb injuries, burns, fractures and bruises. For other researchers, child abuse covers the total spectrum of abuse beginning with parents who have the potential to abuse children through emotional abuse to serious physical and sexual abuse. Lack of clarity over the term child abuse has led to confusion in the literature and makes comparisons across studies difficult. Parke and Collmer (1975) restrict their definition to physical injury, modifying the definition of Kempe and Helfer (1972): 'any child who receives non-accidental physical injury (or injuries) as a result of acts (or omissions) on the part of his parents or guardians that violate the community standards concerning the treatment of children'.

The concept of intentionality rather than accident is crucial to a definition, although ascribing intent is problematic for it is an unobservable occurrence. The recognition that child abuse is a community-defined phenomenon is important, but implicit in the definition is an assumption that community standards can somehow be measured in order to know when a violation has occurred. This is very unlikely. Burgess (1979) widens his definition to include 'non-accidental physical and *psychological* injury and omits the reference to community standards. The approach to child abuse taken in this chapter is a continuum one. Child abuse is viewed as lying at one extreme of a continuum of child management problems. The underlying assumption is that there exists a quantitative rather than a qualitative difference between child abusers and non-abusers. This still leaves the problem of which particular behaviours are to be labelled child abuse, requiring psychological, medical or legal intervention. In some cases this is relatively clear-cut if the child's injuries require hospital treatment, such as scalding by hot water. However, such dramatic incidents, although highly publicized, are among the minority of abusive incidents. The more insidious forms of abuse may involve continuous verbal abuse, threats of physical violence and excessive physical punishment which does not require medical attention. There is no clearly accepted definition of abuse in such cases. Because research and treatment efforts have concentrated on the extremes of physical punishment, often resulting in serious injury or death, we lack knowledge of more subtle and perhaps more psychologically damaging forms of abuse which affect considerably larger numbers of children. In a study of random, 'non-problem' families with children under 5 years old (Gray, 1980), it was found that 30% experienced difficulties severe enough to be labelled child management problems. The parents' typical response was to attempt to control children by physical punishment, usually smacking with a hand, either alone or in conjunction with other methods of control, such as reasoning.

In addition to problems of definition, very few studies have set out to test specific hypotheses and many start and end as broad studies with relatively untested common-sense assumptions. Finding representative samples is difficult and often studies have used samples which are easily available yet failed to resist the temptation to generalize results to wider samples. A further common problem is the failure to provide comparison data of non-abusing families in order to evaluate whether certain characteristics such as social isolation apply only to abusing families or may be accounted for by an intervening variable such as social class.

Research questions

We believe that the most widely used models for an understanding of child abuse, upon which are based the vast majority of existing attempts to intervene, suffer from serious deficiences. Before considering these models, it is worth noting that, with the exception of a small but promising body of research based on social learning theory, many of the most important questions to ask in the field of child abuse have simply not been posed in the existing literature. The first area in which much research is needed would focus upon a functional analysis of incidents that have led directly to injury to the child. Investigation would attempt to determine setting events that have led to injury, including the precise behaviours of the child prior to the offence. The behaviour and cognitions of parents at this time should also be a central focus of research, as indeed would be the consequences of battering both for the child and the parent. Determination of the contingencies controlling and maintaining abusing behaviour have certainly been carried out with individual families and some excellent published reports of behavioural interventions with abusing families have recently appeared in the literature. It must, however, be stressed that such reports are extremely scarce in comparison with the vast majority of published work in the field of child abuse. Equally, very few published reports have asked the following questions: Precisely what do abusing parents understand of child management? How have abusing parents attempted to cope with problem behaviour in their child, and what strategies do they use in their attempts to control the behaviour of the child who has been abused?

Research into the use of both punishment and reward procedures by abusing parents would also be a central area of inquiry for behavioural psychologists. These questions can only be answered by empirical research involving observational studies and clearly defined intervention procedures. One of the fundamental premises of social learning theory is that such questions must be asked by both researcher and practitioner before a proper understanding of the nature of child abuse can be achieved. Parent and child must both be the object of investigation, and it is the interaction between the two which we believe should be the major focus of attention.

Models of child abuse

Psychiatric model

The great majority of clinical practice and intervention from statutory agencies derives from three models for understanding child abuse. It is against this background that the social learning theory-based approach may be viewed. The first approach may be called the psychiatric model. This rests on two assumptions. First, that child abuse may be understood almost entirely by detailed psychiatric examination of the parents and the child is considered to have a minimal role in the development of the pattern of abuse. Secondly, the parents of abused children suffer from some kind of disease process which is reflected in their abnormal personalities. Therefore, we may observe repeated attempts to demonstrate that these parents display pathological personality characteristics that will distinguish them from non-abusing parents. Often this involves listing of personality traits that may be derived either from clinical interviews and diagnoses or from a set of standardized test instruments (Parke and Collmer, 1975). Scott (1978) typifies the dismissal of the role of the abused child by asserting that in the great majority of cases the stimulus offered by the child is quite trivial. Nonetheless, reviews of the published opinions and research based on the psychiatric model (e.g. Spinetta and Rigler, 1972; Parke and Collmer, 1975) reveal little agreement on the nature of any proposed personality disorder. Many of the investigations use a variety of psychiatric assessment procedures and semi-structured interviews of questionable validity. Parke and Collmer (1975) note that in most studies there are no control groups of non-abusers drawn from other types of clinical populations, or from normal populations. They also note the limited relationship between personality traits and overt behaviour.

Spinetta and Rigler (1972), in a detailed examination of hypothesized personality defects in the literature, can only conclude that the single common feature was that abusing parents allowed aggressive impulses to be expressed too freely. It is self-evident that this is a tautological statement and, as Kellmer-Pringle (1978) concludes, it is unlikely that parents of abused children will be homogeneous or that there will be common specific factors to account for their behaviour. The one consistent finding in the psychiatric literature has been that investigators have reported that many abusing parents were very frequently abused or neglected as children. The effect that this might have upon the development of abusive behaviour may be best understood within the framework of social learning theory.

One of the most regrettable aspects of the psychiatric model is that where there have been extensive, controlled studies the opportunity to ask many of the most crucial questions, noted earlier, has been missed. One such example in the UK was a large controlled study carried out in Birmingham (Smith *et al.*, 1973; Smith, 1975). Data were collected from the families of 134 battered children in the West Midlands over a 2 year period. These children were all under 5 years old and the parents had either admitted physical abuse of their child or could give no other adequate explanation for injuries which were entirely consistent with physical abuse. They were compared with a control group consisting of 53 children who had incurred injury for which there was no question of parental abuse. Psychiatric interviews were conducted, together with some psychometric assessments of both parents and children. The abusing parents were more frequently from lower social class groupings, attained lower scores on intellectual assessment, and were significantly more neurotic on personality inventory scales when compared with the control group. Non-blind psychiatric interview ratings yielded higher mean scores for hostility for the abusing parents. Similarly, a high percentage of the abusing parents received a psychiatric diagnosis of personality disorder (76% of mothers, 64% of fathers). A high percentage of mothers of the abused children were pregnant before marriage (87%) and were more frequently unmarried and younger at the birth of their first child in comparison with the control group. The data from the Smith study revealed no significant differences in the sex of the abused child, but they were significantly younger than the controls and achieved lower scores on the Griffiths Developmental Scale (Smith *et al.*, 1973). Smith (1975) rather poignantly noted that for the under-5 age group in Birmingham, non-accidental injury was the second highest cause of fatality in 1972.

The study certainly yielded an impressive series of data, some of which might have offered important implications for practitioners and agencies attempting to detect, predict and help abusing families. However, there are a number of criticisms that must be offered. The first was the failure to match the index and control groups on measures of social class. It is known that the incidence of many of the variables under review (e.g. aggression, psychiatric illness and intelligence) may vary with the level of social class of the population studied. Smith's attempt to balance his figures by using a *post hoc* statistical method involving the conversion of raw scores to percentages may be questioned when there were so few abusing parents falling into some of these social class groupings. The validity of abnormal personality diagnosis on the basis of non-blind interviews may also be questioned. Having gained access to such a large number of abusing families and elicited their co-operation in an intensive study only adds to the disappointment that quite fundamental questions concerning the incidences of abuse and circumstances surrounding them were not asked with anything like the degree of structure with which other variables were examined. Parental understanding of child management and acquisition of child care skills, together with information about the use of punishment to control their child's behaviour, were also areas neglected. With the exception of gross measures of development the children, and in particular their behaviour in relation to incidents of abuse, were largely ignored in this study. Verbal reporting by parents that some of the battered children were more difficult, and that abusing parents used smacking and withdrawal of love more frequently to control their children, simply draws to the attention of the reader the missed opportunities of this study. Behavioural assessments and observational data on such a large sample of abused children might well have yielded extremely interesting results. Instead there seems to be preoccupation with a search for psychopathology in the parents, and even this assumed psychopathology was present in such a way that it bore little tangible relationship to parental behaviour in the interactions with the child. The result was that at the end of the day, although an extensive and time-consuming study had been carried out, there were very few data to aid either the identification of parents who abused their children or the design of intervention programmes, even of an experimental nature.

The diversity of explanations for child abuse hypothesized within the psychiatric model is reflected in the wide range of attempts to devise treatment programmes based upon the model. As Parke and Collmer (1975, p. 556) note: 'Choice among therapies are probably as much a function of the prior theoretical orientation of the therapist as a function of an examination of the dynamics of the child abuse'. A wide range of individual psychotherapies and group therapies are reported in the literature. Many last for months and several for a matter of years. As Parke and Collmer point out, the amount of therapist time and cost place severe limitations on the type of individuals to whom this range of techniques can be offered. The failure to report the details of intervention in any way that would enable either replication or evaluation must also seriously restrict the development of psychiatric approaches to therapy. One typical example involved 74 mothers who had received treatment entitled 'open relationship therapy' (Ounstead *et al.*, 1974). These abusing mothers, all diagnosed as suffering from mental illness, psychopathology and inadequate personality, were encouraged to regress via a series of role-reversal exercises. Empirical evaluation of the effects of this intervention was rejected, since the authors considered statistical analysis of results to be meaningless as ideas and practice are both in a state of evolution. To report that in most cases there had been a notable improvement in the interfamilial dynamics is little solace for practitioners seeking guidelines from published literature.

To summarise: the psychiatric model of child abuse has little empirical validity. The assumptions that the parents of abused children are all suffering from a psychiatric disorder and that the child has a minimal role to play, together with the data presented being at best based on verbal reports of overt behaviour by abusing family members and at worst professional opinions or assertions, combine to place serious limitations on the acceptability of this model to any neutral observer wishing to understand child abuse.

Social welfare model

The social welfare model forms the basis for much of the practice of those professionals who are employed to provide statutory services in the UK and the United States. The model implicates a wide and heterogeneous collection of variables in the ontogeny of child abuse. One of the most fundamental premises of the model is that abusing families live under extreme conditions of environmental stress, frequently being socially disadvantaged and deprived. It is assumed that high levels of stress will lead to violence within the family and that in some cases this is directed towards children. Indeed one of the major proponents of this model has defined child abuse in terms of inflicted deficits between a child's actual circumstances and those that would ensure optimal development (Gil, 1970). Attribution for abusive behaviour is therefore assigned to injustices and inequality within society as a whole and many of its institutions, e.g. schools, day care centres and courts, follow policies that result in insufficient promotion or a failure in provision of the means needed for optimal development that may be defined in Gil's terms as child abuse. As we have already discussed, stress factors are often present in abusing families but these are correlational data.

The social welfare model, however, assumes that violence will be a direct result of the degree of stress experienced by families who abuse their children and that this stress is related to the social disadvantage of the individual family. Much of the data produced to support this model has been generated by surveys carried out by various social service agencies. Whilst the model has been predominantly shaped by surveys and official statistics, its efficacy may be more clearly evaluated by looking at the effects of attempts to reduce the stress factors in abusing families.

Attempts to intervene, based on the social welfare model, are as varied as the factors that have been found to correlate with child abuse. Gil has proposed the most ambitious and far-reaching attempts to alleviate stress factors. He proposes that ideally it would require the elimination of poverty, the elimination of the use of force as a means of achieving societal ends when dealing with children, and the elimination of psychological illness. The implications are the provision of employment for all parents, comprehensive health care and social services, improved standards of housing and education. In practice, social welfare procedures range from the placement of foster 'grandparents' in the homes of children who have been battered, 24 hour lifeline services, crisis nurseries and self-help groups such as Parents Anonymous. The effects of supervision and regular home visits from social service and state agency workers are also attempts to prevent further abuse, although they offer less tangible variables for research. Sim (1978) and Noble (1978) have both strongly criticized the practice of many social workers in the UK because of their continued commitment to follow the views espoused by Bowlby (1951; Bowlby *et al.*, 1956) concerning the hypothesized disastrous effects of mother–infant separation. Noble expresses extreme concern that the critical reappraisal of Bowlby's research has not been reflected in social welfare practice. Whilst this might have led to extreme risk of further abuse to children in families because protection of the child by removal from the home has been considered an anathema, Sutton (1981*a*) has also emphasized the serious danger of false positives in attempts to screen for child abuse and the major psychological consequences of such 'identification'.

The overriding difficulty when attempting to appraise the validity and utility of the social welfare model is that, despite it being the basis for so much practice of the helping professions, so little has been systematically evaluated. Sutton (1981*a*), in a critical review of existing services, has noted that when provision in the United Kingdom by the Department of Health and Social Services and the National Society for the Prevention of Cruelty to Children (NSPCC) was being rapidly expanded to deal with an increasingly recognized problem of child abuse over the past decade, there was a total lack of any evaluation of the various explanations, identification procedures or treatment programmes that were advocated on the basis of professional intervention. As Seebohm (1968) states:

'The personal social services are large-scale experiments in helping those in need. It is both wasteful and irresponsible to set experiments in motion and omit to record and analyse what happens. It makes no sense in terms of administrative efficiency, and however little intended, indicates a careless attitude to human welfare' (p. 142).

Skinner and Castle (1969) reported for the NSPCC that in the UK an alarmingly high percentage of children that they had studied and who had been battered were returned home to be subsequently re-battered, despite quite extensive input from social service agencies to these families. Gil (1970) in the United States has also reported that over 50% of children may be re-battered after they have been clearly identified as abused children. Such figures simply underline the crucial importance of conducting evaluative research into existing services, but unlike the social interactional model the social welfare model does not lend itself easily to component analyses or cost-effectiveness research.

In the United States the first wide-scale evaluation of intervention programmes is under way. Preliminary findings (cited in Cohn and Miller, 1977) suggest that multidisciplinary approaches to intervention have not demonstrated their effectiveness or justified their cost. In most programmes it has been clear that the parents have been the exclusive focus of intervention and, as will be argued later, this may reflect a serious shortcoming in the vast majority of current attempts at behaviour change. On a much smaller scale, evaluation of a current provision for abusing families, in the UK, has shown that such research is quite feasible. It is also possible to evaluate existing service on indices that reflect cost-effectiveness and will therefore be particularly acceptable to those managers and administrators responsible for developing and maintaining social welfare services to abusing families. This study (Sutton and Nanton, 1978; Sutton and Roberts, 1981) consisted of an evaluation of the effectiveness of what was termed 'developmental day care' and involved 20 children who had been admitted to a social services day care centre with a history of physical abuse and neglect. These children were compared with a control group of 20 abused children who had been admitted into local authority residential care during the same period. They were matched on age, area of the city, year of admission, sex, culture of upbringing and reason for admission. The important measures taken included admission to residential care, any change in the child's legal status (i.e. whether the child was the responsibility of the local authority or whether parental rights had been assumed) and contact at follow-up with social services departments (i.e. whether or not the family were still considered to be an open case with social services departments). These measures have the advantage of offering a possible direct index of the relative cost-effectiveness of day care services in comparison with residential care. At follow-up 2 years later, the children who had been receiving developmental day care were still at home living with their parents, whereas only seven of the control children were living at home. All of the day care children had remained the legal responsibility of their parents whereas 12 of the control children were under care orders from the local authority. Of the day care group, only five were still an 'open case' with social services departments at follow-up, in comparison with 15 of the control children.

Whilst this study involved retrospective data collection and did not attempt component analyses of the intervention offered in either the day care centre or residential care, even on these relatively crude measures it is possible to question the far more costly placement of children into residential homes in comparison with an existing day care service. This study illustrates the type of evaluative research which is essential to an understanding of the effectiveness of existing services based on the social welfare model. The validity of the model itself may be questioned until empirical data are produced that will indicate the effectiveness of stress reduction procedures already being offered on a widespread scale to abusing families. Whilst interventions based on the broad social welfare model are undoubtedly most laudable, and the quality of lives of many recipient families will undoubtedly have improved, it does seem unlikely that cultural tolerance of aggressive behaviour and high degrees of environmental stress are of themselves necessary or sufficient to account for specific physical abuse to children.

The legal model

Abusive behaviour towards the child does, of course, contravene state and national legislation and there is a legal model for child abuse that is relevant to our discussion. This model takes as its first premise the assumption that individuals are responsible for their own actions and must be held accountable for their behaviour. By adulthood, it is assumed that a distinction has been made between acceptable and non-acceptable behaviours in terms of society's norms and that there will be predictable consequences for abusive behaviour towards children. The notion that individuals are free to choose and that by contravening the law of the land we can anticipate legally sanctioned attempts to punish our behaviour is, however, inconsistent with a behavioural model of human behaviour. It might be suggested that responsibility for behaviour lies with the environment rather than some hypothetical fixed attribute of the individual. But, leaving this aside, the legal model attempts to deter individuals from engaging in abusive behaviour because of the assumed punishing consequences that would follow, whether in the form of imprisonment, fines, or the child being taken into care, for example. Equally, these consequences are intended to punish abusive behaviour that has already occurred in order to deter parents from abusing in the future or to prevent such abuse by physically separating child and parents.

The legal model does not give us a clear understanding of why parents abuse their children. It may describe their behaviour—that they have chosen to harm their child, despite the predictable risk of society's attempts to punish them. However, quite drastic attempts to intervene are implied. In England, two sets of consequences may follow abusive behaviour. The first involves criminal proceedings brought against parents on the grounds of cruelty, with the prosecution attempting to gain a conviction for murder, attempted murder, infanticide, manslaughter, actual bodily harm or neglect. The defence may typically suggest that the behaviour was accidental, or that parents had been under extreme provocation or suffered from diminished responsibility. Typically, lack of any witness results in the courts attempting to make decisions on the basis of professional 'experts', and this presents serious problems which we shall return to a little later. The local authority in England is required by the Children and Young Persons Act (1969) to inquire into any cases where there might be grounds for bringing care proceedings in respect of a child. Here, consideration is given to the child's physical and psychological development in terms of neglect or ill-treatment. The child may be considered to be beyond the control of the parent or guardian or he might be considered to be at risk of exposure to moral danger. As Francis and Sutton (1977) note, the local authority has a duty to bring such cases to court unless it is satisfied that it is in the interests neither of the child nor of the public to do so. They also note that the pressure of the legal system and public opinion may well act as an aversive consequence for parents admitting battering or neglecting their children and yet to seek help with their management of the child may risk the child being removed from them. The legal model then inadvertently may arrange for contingencies to be highly aversive for admitting battering. Thus, the major obstacle in the treatment of child abuse may be the lack of willingness of parents to admit their problems because of the highly aversive consequences that may follow. Social workers may therefore run into serious difficulties if parents perceive them as investigators acting as agents of the local authority.

A second difficulty that may arise with attempts to prevent or to punish abusive behaviour follows from the intensity and scheduling of punishing consequences from state and national laws. The probability of the child being taken into care or placed under a supervision order, together with the severity of fines or imprisonment imposed on parents, is likely to be directly related to the history of abuse. Thus those parents who can demonstrate that this was their first offence against the child, or that it occurred under atypical circumstances that are unlikely to arise in the future, may anticipate a low probability of the child being taken into care or that criminal proceedings will be successfully brought against them. Those with a long history of abusive behaviour towards their child may anticipate more severe punishing consequences from the legal model. The basic maxim is that the punishment that will follow is directly proportional to the severity of the crime and the history of previous suspected or proven abusive behaviour. Experimental studies on punishment contingencies have shown that punishment is most effective when it is delivered very shortly after the occurrence of the target behaviour and is very strong. Punishing consequences that increase gradually in intensity following repeated emission of the target behaviour will be far less effective in reducing that behaviour (e.g. Johnson, 1972). In other words, research in the field of experimental psychology has suggested that the most effective form of punishment in terms of reducing abusive behaviour would be to punish abusing parents severely as soon as the abuse is first detected. The current legal model does quite the opposite.

If a parent is considered to be suffering from a form of mental illness, then an exception is made to the notion of responsibility for one's own behaviour. The individual is no longer deemed responsible and instead intervention follows the pathway prescribed by the medical model. In some cases, therefore, there may be some pressure on the part of the defence, perhaps when faced with daunting evidence from the prosecution, to avoid the punishing consequences from the legal model by pleading diminished responsibility on the grounds of mental illness. As Francis and Sutton (1977) comment, it may be possible to understand why the medical profession have been keen to find a cause for battering, in order that they might exempt parents from punitive retribution for their actions. Smith (1975), while following the outcome of 134 families who took part in his study, listed other difficulties inherent in the present legal structure. He noted that if parents freely acknowledge a fault but claim it to be a single regrettable 'lapse', then the courts often have little choice but to dismiss the case, and he expresses little surprise at the high rates of re-battering reported by the NSPCC. Juvenile courts in England, which consider the needs of the child, have no absolute authority to require psychiatric or other 'expert' reports on the parents. In some cases, therefore, they may be required to make decisions about the needs of the child in relation to the natural home on the basis of limited data. Smith (1975) also notes wide regional variations in local authority care orders, again questioning the consistency of criteria used by courts to place such orders and take children into care. Finally, he observed that care and supervision orders made by courts are made quite frequently in the form of a probation order. In practice, many children are returned to their parents with insufficient consultation made by social service agencies with either the courts or physicians. He noted that in his study almost half of the families received voluntary supervision orders.

In court, the legal, social welfare and medical models become closely interrelated. It is the decision of social services departments in England as to whether care proceedings should be brought on the basis of investigations carried out by social workers in conjunction with medical reports. Multidisciplinary case conferences are held to come to joint decisions. The decision to remove the child into the care of the local authority rests not only on an assessment of parental care facilities and abilities, but also on what alternative placements may be provided by the state. A good foster home is preferable to an inadequate natural home for the child, but the likelihood of providing a good foster home needs to be considered very carefully (Francis and Sutton, 1977). The widely held view that separation of the child from its natural parents may have disastrous psychological consequences (based on highly questionable views expressed by Bowlby) is likely to influence decisions relating to placement in local authority care. The legal model may provide punishment in the form of fines or imprisonment, but it may direct the case into the social welfare model in the form of supervision orders carried out by social workers, or into the psychiatric model by accepting that parents are mentally ill and in need of some form of psychotherapy. Thus, not only is the legal model vulnerable to criticisms of its own sanctions noted earlier, but is contaminated by the weaknesses of both the psychiatric and the social welfare models.

A final deficiency of the legal model may be found in an area that we believe will become an increasing focus of critical attention in the future. This concerns the use of reports and evidence presented by experts in Court. Sutton (1981*a*, *b*), has published excellent critiques of some of the traditional practices in the field of child abuse and a thoughtful discussion of issues involved in decision-making in the courts. He warns against the dangers of courts relying on and accepting at face value the 'professional expertise' of many professionals who present opinions on the needs of children and their families. He also questions the validity of much of the evidence presented by 'experts' in terms of making predictions about the child's behaviour and development. Sutton believes that there is often a very weak basis to what is routinely presented as expert evidence by representatives of all the child care professions. In relation to social workers he suggests that

> 'social workers and those that associate with them in offering expertise on matters of child care to the Courts presently have little or no empirical data to support a professionalism that claims knowledge of why a child acts as he does, what is likely to follow this or that intervention, etc.' (Sutton, 1981*a*, p. 89).

Much that is related as fact and unequivocal professional expertise is often simply theory with no experimentation or real data as its basis but is presented as highly empirical and therefore respectable evidence. Sutton concludes with some very practical guidelines for lawyers and magistrates who deal with assumed experts in child care in the courts. These would help lawyers to discriminate between professional opinion and scientific data, to understand the bases upon which opinions are offered, and the nature and known efficacy of interventions and treatments that may be offered. He suggests that a more critical appraisal of the evidence presented by experts in court will follow only if they take the initiative in this respect:

> 'If the Courts are to find relevant expertise in child development significantly higher than that presently offered them, they will have to make an *active* contribution of their own towards creating the conditions and the demand for such an advance. They have the power and the duty to control or protect the juveniles before them, and they have the potential to exercise these in such a way that they provide a visible check on some at least of the activities of the institutions that intervene in the lives of these children and their families. There are various approaches which, though far from new, might be more widely adopted by magistrates and judges, solicitors and barristers, to increase the accountability of the various child care agencies routinely represented in Court. The characteristic form taken by professional evidence is the written report. Wider adoption might be made of the practice of allowing the parents the opportunity (and the time) to check its contents. Further, if a "specialist", an educational psychologist, a psychiatrist, the head of an assessment centre, feels able to sign a report giving a recommendation (often in effect a judgment) on a child's needs for treatment of this kind or that, then he should be routinely expected to appear before the Court so that the evidence should be open to the normal means of proof through cross-examination under oath or affirmation. And in such cross-examination the expert should be challenged to state the basis for the particular formulation of the child's needs or for the precise goals and expectations of the treatment recommended. An "opinion" alone should be clearly stated as such, and its basis made explicit. In both written and oral evidence it should be made quite clear what is fact and

what is interpretation or supposition, why the information presented to explain present circumstances is regarded uniquely to do so, and how the recommended intervention is supposed to achieve its promised outcome. It should also be asked what indications there are that the treatment proposed actually works. There is no final test of what is an adequate explanation in such a context, but the most honest criterion is surely to apply the same standards of credulity as you would if such conclusions were being urged for you or your child, and not just in a Court of Law' (Sutton, 1981*a*, pp. 99–100).

The vast majority of existing services to abusing families are based upon the psychiatric, the social welfare or the legal models. We can only agree with Sutton (1981*a*) when he asserts that the most pressing problem in establishing a system that links theory and practice in child care is the general failure in existing practice to recognize that a research strategy is needed to determine the relative worth of different approaches. Without a research strategy there can be no evaluation of the validity of theories and the theories themselves cannot be modified or developed on the basis of how effective they turn out to be in practice. Practice alone is not enough and the opinion of those involved in a given project cannot itself be accepted as an index of outcome. One of the most important strengths of the social interactional model of child abuse is that research, in terms of scientific evaluation, is an integral part of the model.

Social learning theory

Social learning theory offers a framework for a detailed analysis of child abuse at a theoretical level and in addition allows for intervention strategies to be devised from an empirical base. Bandura (1969, 1977*a, b*) has taken learning theory beyond the narrow S-R conceptions of human behaviour into a cognitive conception of social learning. A distinctive feature of social learning theory is the acknowledgment that people are not passive recipients of environmental stimuli nor driven by inner forces. Rather, psychological functioning is explained in terms of a continuous reciprocal interaction of personal and environmental determinants.

There are a number of important principles derived from the theory which lead to a new view of child abuse. Social learning theory emphasizes the acquisition of response through observation or modelling. Psychological theories have traditionally assumed that learning can occur only by performing responses and experiencing their effects. Social learning theory argues that nearly the whole range of learned behaviours can be acquired or modified through observational learning. The principle of reinforcement has also been reconceptualized to encompass a fuller picture of humans with their cognitive capacities to construct and interpret their own reality. A broader range of reinforcement influences are covered. Anticipation of reinforcement is one of several factors that can influence what is observed. By observing a behaviour vicariously, people can learn how it is done and the consequences of its performance. This capacity to learn by observation enables people to acquire behaviour patterns without having to form them gradually by trial and error. One of the most important propositions of the theory is the distinction between acquisition and performance of behaviour. Behaviour can be observed without any immediate acting out. This learned behaviour is stored and may be acted out later *if appropriate circumstances arise.* The latter phrase is crucial for it helps to explain the finding that many child-abusing parents were themselves abused as children, but it highlights the need to analyse in detail the situational circumstances surrounding a particular child abuse incident. Social learning theory suggests two factors of importance:

(1) The behaviour must be in the person's repertoire. Even after extensive observation of physical abuse the person must be capable of carrying it out.
(2) The opportunity must be present to enact the behaviour, e.g. if other people are constantly around, the possiblity of abuse may be reduced.

The work of the Family Violence Research Programme at the University of New Hampshire over the past 10 years has accumulated evidence that the family is probably the most violent setting people are likely to encounter (Straus, 1978, 1979). Ample opportunity exists to observe how violence is conducted and the consequences for both perpetrator and victim. Children learn that physical force often achieves desired objectives but the victim must be physically weaker. Added to behavioural know-how is an attitudinal component supplied by an implicit cultural norm which sanctions the use of physical force to discipline children and resolve conflict. Each individual also has access to aggressive encounters through the media, constantly reinforcing the message that physical force is effective and legitimizing its use.

Unlike violence, physical punishment as a form of discipline is normatively approved and in addition is generally assumed to stem from altruistic motivation, 'for the child's own good'. Several studies of punishment practices show a high percentage of use. Korsch *et al.* (1965) found that one-third of mothers attending a mother and baby clinic spanked their children by the age of 1 year. In a representative national sample of American adults, Stark and McEvoy (1970) reported that 93% of parents used physical punishment. Within the context of such a high rate of physical punishment it is not surprising that a small proportion of extreme incidents occur. Gil (1970) concludes, 'most incidents of child abuse involve normal individuals exercising discipline against behaviour which in their view needs correction'. Such an analysis does not explain all incidents of child abuse but emphasizes how societal acceptance of force clouds the issue between 'acceptable' and 'unacceptable' force.

Antecedents

The role of the child in the development of abuse. A serious shortcoming in both the psychiatric and sociological models is their failure to give adequate recognition to the role of the child in incidents of abuse.

In contrast, the social interactional model for child abuse allows for the possibility that the child himself may contribute towards his own abuse in a variety of ways. Thus child abuse is seen as the result of a particular match between parents with certain characteristics and behavioural deficits and children with behaviours that present severe management difficulties. If we are to challenge the assumption inherent in the traditional models for child abuse that a study of the parents alone will lead to an understanding of abuse, then we must describe how the child may contribute towards his own abuse and present some clear evidence that he may be implicated.

There is now an ample literature that demonstrates individual differences between children from birth (Dunn, 1979; Sameroff, 1979). A number of methods have been used to assess these individual differences and to evaluate their continuity into later childhood. One of the most well known longitudinal studies was carried out by Thomas and co-workers in New York (Thomas *et al.*, 1963; Thomas and Chess, 1977). Thomas attempted to classify children from birth in terms of different aspects of temperament, such as activity levels, rhythmicity of biological functions, adaptability, mood, distractability and sensory threshold. He identified three major groups of children that could be classified according to their behavioural temperaments and styles which he labelled as 'difficult', 'easy' and 'slow to warm up' children. The 'difficult' children were characterized by low arousal thresholds, intense reactions when aroused, and irregular and unpredictable biological functions, such as their sleep and feeding patterns. Although this group constituted only 10% of the children studied, at subsequent follow-ups on the development of these children he reported that they constituted 25% of those children who presented with conduct disorders and behavioural problems in later childhood. He noted that the development of subsequent behavioural disorder related to the ability of the parents to adjust to admittedly difficult temperament and behaviour presented by the child. At birth there were no differences in the attitude towards child rearing of mothers with different types of child but subsequently differences in attitude became apparent as a function of their experience with their own child. As Sameroff and Chandler (1975) noted, knowledge of the characteristics of the child alone, or of the characteristics of the parents alone, will not enable us to make accurate predictions about subsequent parent–child interactions. It is the character of the specific transaction between child and parents which will determine subsequent development. They arrived at these conclusions on the basis of a review of a wide range of longitudinal studies of children born with a variety of reproductive complications.

Dunn (1979) has published an excellent review of research looking at continuities in individual differences. She notes that some of the more recent work on individual differences has attempted to focus on more detailed and reliable measures of behaviour than ratings of broad traits of style and temperament. Levels of attention, activity and intensity of response have all been investigated but have presented problems for measurement. Very few studies have followed children beyond the early months of life and it is very rare to find longitudinal studies as extensive as that published by Thomas and his colleagues. Nonetheless, 'The wealth of recent research on infancy has amply confirmed what parents and those who care for babies know so well—that young babies differ markedly from one another' (Dunn, 1979, p. 69).

If individual differences between children from birth are to have any role to play in contributing to our understanding of child abuse, then it must lie with the shaping and influencing of the behaviour of parents. Both Bell and Harper (1977) and Osofsky and Danziger (1974) have demonstrated that newborn infant behaviour may influence the care-taking and socialization behaviour of mothers. Sameroff (1979) has outlined how difficult child temperaments will place more demands on parents' adaptive ability and care-taking skills and may impair strong attachments between parent and child. However, he stresses the importance of studying the child in the context of his own environment because only when development is seen as a complex interaction between the child's changing competencies and temperaments and the attitudes and behaviour of parents, can predictions about subsequent development be made.

If we accept that from birth there are important individual differences between children and that these might be more accurately defined in terms of indices such as the infant's ability to modify his state (Packer and Rosenblatt, 1979) rather than earlier concepts involving temperament and trait classifications, we may then ask whether there is evidence that the abused child is likely to contribute to his subsequent suffering by behaviour that he has shown from birth or early childhood. Friedrich and Boriskin (1976) argue that particular types of children may produce parental stress reactions, some of which might stimulate abuse. They considered the correlation between abused children and prematurity. The studies reviewed suggest that a significant proportion of low birthweight infants are present in populations of children who are subsequently abused. The figures are often in excess of 20% and they argue that since it is known that prematurity correlates with some degree of difficult behaviour in childhood, such as distractability, restlessness, sleeping and feeding difficulties, the child's behaviour as a function of premature birth may relate directly to child abuse. Some data, suggesting a correlation between abused children and mental and physical handicap are also reviewed by Friedrich and Boriskin (1976) with a similar argument that such factors may lead to a range of difficult behaviours in the child that might stimulate stressed parents to abuse their child. Sandgrund *et al.* (1974) compared neglected, abused and control children in terms of mental retardation and found a significantly higher percentage of mental handicap in the abused and neglected groups. Soeffing (1975) also argues that many abused children have 'special characteristics', including premature births, chronic illness and mental retardation.

Parke and Collmer (1975) speculate on the pathway from reproductive causality to child abuse by noting that low birthweight infants place greater demands on their parents than normal infants, they may disappoint their parents due to developmental retardation in early life, and note some experimental evidence (Stevens-Long, 1973) suggesting that highly active children may elicit more extreme forms of discipline from their care-takers. There is certainly recent experimental evidence that labelling a child as atypical can exert a significant effect upon autonomic measures of parental reaction to selected behaviours of the child. Frodi (1981) described how 96 parents watched a videotape recording of a baby who was either smiling or crying. Groups of parents were told that the infant was 'normal', or 'difficult', or premature. In fact the infant was identical throughout. The pattern of autonomic responses, and emotions reported, revealed that the 'premature' infant triggered greater autonomic arousal when it was crying than did other infants and the 'premature' and 'difficult' infants elicited less sympathy when crying than did the 'normal' infant. In a second study, videotape recordings of real premature or term infants were shown and the cry of a premature infant elicited greater autonomic arousal and more self-reported negative emotions than did the cry of a term infant. By using dubbed sound over the video recordings, it was possible to demonstrate that the way the infant sounded had a greater impact than the way it looked, although the most marked difference occurred when both the cry and the face were those of premature infants. These two studies suggest that atypical babies (premature) or infants labelled as atypical triggered a response pattern that was consistent with patterns seen after exposure to anger-provoking scenes or noxious stimuli. In a third study, Frodi and her colleagues compared 16 mothers of term babies and 16 mothers of premature babies whilst looking at video recordings of other premature and full-term infants. The mothers of the premature infants responded with a particularly pronounced arousal to the infants' cries, whereas those mothers whose own babies had been described as 'easy' exhibited less physiological arousal and were more willing to interact with the stimulus babies. This suggests that mothers who interact daily with premature babies, or those whom they perceive as difficult, have become sensitized to their aversive features and therefore exhibit exaggerated negative responses to the stimulus babies in the experiments.

If we accept that current research does demonstrate that prematurity, mental retardation, physical handicaps and perinatal complications are over-represented in abused populations, then we must of course ensure that we do not conclude that the correlation implies causality. As Friedrich and Boriskin (1976) note, it would be fanciful to conclude that the special child is the sole contributor to abuse. The vast majority of children who are born with pre- or perinatal difficulties, or with a degree of handicap, are not abused by their parents. But we cannot ignore such correlations since figures cited in many studies are in excess of norms we may derive from the most severely socially disadvantaged populations.

However, we must guard against the simplistic conclusions that might be drawn from these data. For example, Solomons (1979) hypothesizes that impaired mother–infant bonding due to the lack of responsiveness of the infant to the mother will be the result of immaturity or birth trauma in the abused child. Sameroff (1979), in a particularly careful critique of published research in the field of reproductive complications and subsequent behaviour, stresses throughout that no reliable predictions can be made about cognitive and behaviour competence following pre- and perinatal difficulties without a thorough examination of the behavioural environment in which the child will be reared. He found that environmental factors have generally been ignored in research efforts aimed at finding links between early pregnancy and delivery complications and later deviant behavioural development. Yet even in the early Chess and Birch study (Thomas *et al.*, 1968) it was noticed that parental reaction to what was labelled 'colicky' behaviour on the part of the child will be the most important determinant of the fate of these difficult infants.

'As long as one conceptually isolates these children from their environments, the inefficiencies will continue. Only when development is appreciated as a complex interplay between the child's changing competencies and temperament and the changing attitudes and behaviour of the important socialising agents in the environment can the prediction problem be squarely faced' (Sameroff, 1979, p. 147).

We may conclude at this stage that at least some abused children started life with some degree of biological disadvantage. As we have stressed, how this may relate to their subsequent behaviour and in turn to the provocation of abusive behaviour from parents cannot be answered without an investigation of the behavioural environment in which they are reared. There are other sources of evidence, however, that suggest that the abused child may present with particular problems of management for parents. Gil's survey data (Gil, 1970) revealed that 29% of his sample of identified abused children exhibited some deviations in social interaction and functioning prior to abuse. Johnson and Morse (1968), cited in Burgess (1979), found that in a large sample of abused children 70% of them presented welfare workers with difficulties of control and management, such as continual crying or whining, stubbornness, negativism and infrequent smiling. The problem is that while such reports are of great interest to researchers and clinicians alike in this field, their status is little more than that of anecdotal reports. One of the biggest problems in research in this field has been a tendency to rely upon indirect measures of behaviour such as clinical assessments, rating scales and questionnaires. We require observational studies carried out on abused children or those at risk before a stronger light can be shed upon the question of the role of the child in abuse. Whilst we may speculate that certain characteristics of the child may make it more likely that he will be abused, it can also be suggested that as a result of abuse the child may develop behaviour patterns which will in turn elicit further abuse from parents. Abuse may therefore shape behaviour which will increase the probability of further abuse. Not only may aggressive behaviours be modelled directly by parents but if physical punishment is used in any consistent fashion, is delivered with a pattern of slow acceleration after the first appearance of target behaviours, and occasionally the child is actually reinforced instead of punished for a particular behaviour, then parental attempts at elimination of aversive behaviour will be ineffective. The result might be that the child continues to display behaviour that ultimately invites physical abuse. Patterson's description of the development of coercive control between parent and child (Patterson, 1979) provides a highly relevant framework for an understanding of how aggressive behaviour may be shaped and maintained by negative reinforcement contingencies. A number of authors have suggested that this model of coercive interaction might be particularly relevant to an understanding of family interaction in the field of child abuse (Hutchings, 1980*a, b*; Gambrill, 1981).

Parental perceptions of the child's behaviour. Behaviour displayed by the child is undoubtedly important but it is unlikely to be the only factor. The perception of that behaviour is also crucial. Crozier and Katz (1979) noted during data collection that the child labelled as a problem by the parents showed little difference behaviourally from other children. The way the parents reacted to the behaviour was different. In fatal cases Scott (1978) states that the immediate stimuli included refusal of food, vomiting, crying and refusal to smile. The parents' interpretation of the stimuli was all important: 'She was playing up', 'A battle of wills', 'He defied me' are samples of the parents' comments afterwards. A commonly noted observation has been that abusive parents are ignorant of normal child development and perceive age-appropriate behaviour of their children as wilful defiance or negativism (e.g. Tracy and Clark, 1974; Kempe and Kempe, 1978). Other historical factors may influence the parents' perception of the child. He or she may be the result of a premaritally conceived pregnancy, or come too soon after the birth of a previous child. Perhaps the child is a boy when the parents wanted a girl.

Social isolation. Lack of community involvement and social isolation has been shown to be characteristic of abuse-prone families (Young, 1964; Garbarino, 1977). Young (1964) reported that 95% of severely abusive families had no stable continuing relationship outside the family. Leonski (1974), cited by Parke and Collmer (1975), in a large and careful study found that 89% of abusive parents who had telephones had unlisted numbers; in contrast, only 12% of the non-abusive parents had unlisted telephone numbers. Parke and Collmer (1975) suggest that abusive parents may lack the social skills that are necessary to form and maintain friendships and community ties.

Parental self-efficacy. The strength of people's convictions in their own effectiveness determines whether they will even try to cope with difficult situations. Bandura (1977*b*) makes the distinction between outcome expectations, which are estimates that a given behaviour will lead to certain outcomes, and efficacy expectations, beliefs that the person can produce the necessary behaviour. Several studies have indicated that abusive parents have less education than non-abusive parents (Gil, 1970; Smith and Hanson, 1975; Garbarino, 1977) and this factor may contribute to reported unrealistic expectations of the child on the part of abusive parents. Spinetta and Rigler (1972) report that abusive mothers expect adult behaviour and interaction from their children. The need to educate parents about child development and child rearing is a relatively new idea and one which is not universally accepted (Giurguis, 1978). If formal information of this type is not available many young women may reach motherhood with little contact and knowledge about children other than what is available through the media. Often the stereotype of motherhood is one of romantic bliss showing the link between mother and baby as one of absolute beauty and trust. The babies in advertisements are never dirty and screaming and the mothers nothing less than glamorous. When reality falls short of romance it requires a considerable amount of maturity and confidence on the part of the mother to cope with a child who does not behave as the little cherub in the magazine. It is not hard to see how mothers could develop unrealistically high expectations about what is required from a good mother and because of lack of knowledge and experience have low efficacy expectations of their ability to produce the necessary behaviour. Successes raise mastery expectations and repeated failures lower them, especially if the mishaps occur early in the course of events. The relationship between self-efficacy and child abuse has not received a great deal of research attention. However, several treatment reports indicate the abusing parents' feeling of inadequacy in relation to caring for the child (Reavley and Gilbert, 1976; Crozier and Katz, 1979; Gambrill, 1981). But our understanding of the link between child abuse and self-efficacy could be further developed.

Family interactions. A final factor which must be considered is the nature of the family itself. For most people living in a family entails both physical and emotional closeness. Conflicts of interest inevitably develop in such surroundings and in many families solutions to problems are handled by aggressive physical means. In an observational study, Reid and Taplin (1977) showed higher rates of overall aversive behaviour for the mother and child in the abusive families. The abusive mothers and their children were also more likely to issue negative commands and to strike each other. Given that these families are poorly skilled in managing conflict and that additional stress may be present in the form of large families, unemployment and mental conflict, it is understandable how an escalating cycle of conflict and aggression can result. Patterson (1977) suggests the maintaining mechanism in aggressive behaviour is not positive reinforcement

Table 1 Examples of the antecedents involved in child abuse

Historical and social	Isolated from family and friends Marital conflict Wanted a child of the opposite sex Deprived social conditions
Immediate	Crying; refusal of food
Overt	Close proximity to the child Demanding child Family conflict of interests
Cognitive	Perception of child's behaviour (e.g. refusal to smile) Unrealistic expectations of the child Unrealistic expectations of parenthood

but negative reinforcement. Abusive behaviour on the part of parents would therefore serve to terminate aversive behaviour in their children.

Behaviour

We have already noted the confusion which exists in the literature because of the lack of clarity in the definition of child abuse. Within the term physical injury a range of behaviours are subsumed, from a slap which is administered instantaneously to burns from scalding water which take place over a longer time scale. Medically, distinctions are made in terms of severity but behaviourally the time involved in carrying out the behaviour is vital. Treatment by response prevention has a better chance of success in a behaviour which takes minutes to perform, the time it takes to run a bath of hot water, than in a beating which immediately follows the stimulus. What is needed is a description of the actual behaviour involved. Incidents of physical abuse are difficult to study for two reasons. They tend to be low frequency behaviours which take place typically within the privacy of the home. Burgess (1979) recommends the study of family interaction patterns as an alternative high fequency behaviour on the assumption that daily repetitive negative interactions have a more detrimental effect on the child's development than one or two serious physical assaults.

For a more extensive description of behaviour it is necessary to consider the parent's cognitions as an integral part of the chain of events leading to abuse which the parent emits prior to, accompanying and following the abusive behaviour. A person's appraisals, attributions, expectations and self-evaluations have become a legitimate area of inquiry by behaviour therapists in recent years.

Unfortunately, most child-abuse research has not collected the kind of data to enable us to judge the importance of internal dialogue and its relationship to abusing behaviour. Only through a careful assessment of all aspects, emotional, behavioural and cognitive, can specific intervention strategies be devised. Lazarus's (1976) multimodal assessment of the BASIC ID (Behavioural, Affect, Sensations, Images, Cognitions, Interpersonal and Drugs) is an example of a comprehensive framework which precludes too narrow a focus during initial assessment. In specific cases attention to all parameters is unnecessary but in a multifaceted problem like child abuse a wide range of factors should be considered initially. An important feature of behavioural approaches has been to encourage a move away from global and anecdotal investigations and instead to develop a solid base for making interpretations based on empirical data. By acknowledging that humans can be affected by observation as well as direct experience, new research channels were opened and workers such as Reid and Patterson have conducted many good observational studies of behaviour. At the Oregon Social Learning Centre over 10 years they have developed the Family Interaction Coding System which provides a sequential account of family interaction in the home. However, over all there have been few attempts to collect detailed observational data of parent–child interactions in abusive and comparison families. Those that have been made indicate that children in abusive families display high rates of aversive behaviour and abusive parents lack behaviour management skills (e.g. Reid and Taplin, 1977; Burgess and Conger, 1978). Clearly there is a need for observational studies to continue and expand. At the same time researchers should recognize the potential importance of cognitions in developing and maintaining abusive behaviour, particularly in treatment studies. Bandura's work on self-efficacy suggests that checks should be made on the parents' view of their contribution to treatment and how adequate they consider their performance. Let us consider a treatment goal which states that the parent is to comfort the child adequately. The behaviours leading to that goal could be performed satisfactorily according to the therapist's criteria, but if the parents had extremely high performance expectations they may still feel as if they cannot comfort the baby properly. Perhaps they managed to succeed because the therapist was there, it was just a good day and tomorrow will be different, or the baby was good-tempered for a change. Negative statements in this vein are common in treatment and deserve systematic investigation. In particular we need to know what is the content of the parents' cognitions that are predisposing to abusive behaviour and, secondly, what is the parent failing to say which would lead to alternative coping behaviours other than abuse?

Consequences

Identifying the contingencies which maintain abusive behaviour is a vital part of the analysis. In normal circumstances if a baby cries and the parent is able to stop the crying by feeding or comforting he or she will be reinforced and the caring behaviour maintained. If an abuse-prone parent fails to stop the baby crying, he or she may feel worthless and inadequate at a cognitive level and may avoid the child or physically abuse it at a behavioural level. This is very much an oversimplification to illustrate what may happen; the individual controlling contingencies may be extremely complex and difficult to identify. Equally, there may be an interaction between the child who is very demanding, making reinforcement difficult for the mother to obtain, and lack of knowledge and skills of how to handle the baby on the part of the mother. The fact that physical coercion is effective in the short term should not be underestimated as an important consequence for abusing parents – it produces compliance. However, evidence from experimental animal literature and clinical observation points to physical punishment alone as an ineffective means of control (Gambrill, 1977). Apart from anything else the child is not taught an alternative way of behaving, merely to stop a current behaviour, and therefore new learning fails to take place. In a survey of maternal methods of control, Gray (1980) found that although all mothers used physical punishment on some occasions, two-thirds expressed negative feelings after its use and in addition a discrepancy was found between how mothers actually disciplined their children and their preference for discipline. This suggests that either mothers are not aware of alternative methods of child rearing or lack knowledge about implementing alternatives. Psychologists may know theoretically that punishment is less effective than rewarding desired behaviour but this idea goes against cultural norms. Many mothers expressed fears about being 'too soft' or not showing the child 'who was boss'. Any change in the pattern of child rearing from punishment to reward cannot solely be based on empirical evidence and education programmes should take into account those parental attitudes which may initially be against such change. Any alternative to physical punishment must be acceptable and *effective* for parents.

Public and media stereotypes of parents who abuse children contain judgements about inhuman monsters who are cruel and abnormal – showing no concern about the consequences of their abusive behaviour. In a paper on compassion and ethics in the care of the retardate Skinner (1972) illustrates how physical abuse need not be 'cruel' or 'uncaring' in the normative sense of these words. He argues that abuse in children's homes is well documented throughout history and that the trouble arises because those who exert control are subject to little or no counter-control. The same argument applies equally to child abuse. Children are too small and weak to protest and in most cases of abuse reciprocal action is weak or absent. Feldman (1977) cites several studies which support the notion that aggression is most sharply reduced in the face of an opponent who has a greater retaliatory capacity. The dimension of counter-control has unfortunately not received direct attention but it should be recognized as important, especially in intervention programmes, and counter-control built into treatment if it is absent.

Treatment implications

Treatments based on social learning theory basically aim to help parents develop a wider behavioural repertoire for dealing with problem situations and enable them to manipulate the environment more adaptively. The majority of studies describing treatment of child-abusing families have suffered from common problems. Because treatment techniques were reported in general terms replication of studies was virtually impossible. An urgent need exists for carefully designed and evaluated treatment programmes. One of the advantages of the social interaction model lies in the fact that the theory gives rise to predictions which can be tested and evaluated in treatment programmes. There is an emphasis on individual differences which helps to formulate the most appropriate form of intervention in a particular case. Gambrill (1981, p. 6) outlines the unique characteristics of a behavioural approach to assessment:

'1. a preference for descriptive data rather than inference
2. supplementary verbal report with observational data collected in the natural environment
3. identification of specific desired outcomes to be achieved
4. collection of baseline information
5. identification of immediate antecedents and consequences related to child maltreatment
6. a careful search for personal and environmental resources.'

Only when such a careful assessment is made can specific interventions be implemented. The methods employed are wide ranging and varied, as would be expected to deal with a multidimensional problem. They include, for example, social skills training, instruction in more effective methods of child management, problem-solving training and anxiety management.

If abusing parents react to their child's aversive behaviour by attempting to terminate it through physical coercion, this could be seen as a coping strategy, albeit an undesirable one. Little work has been undertaken on the notion of coping in social science generally, although some research has been conducted largely within a sociological framework with particular reference to life events and stress (e.g. Pearlin and Schooler, 1978; Andrews *et al.*, 1978). However, Straus (1979) directly relates life events and stress to child abuse and, using a modified version of the Holmes and Rahe Stressful Life Events Scale (Holmes and Rahe, 1967), was able to show that abusing families showed high levels of stress. They also looked at how people coped with stress and discovered that some responded with violence and some did not. Cochrane (1978) argues that people have a more or less extended hierarchy of coping mechanisms available to them which is used sequentially to deal with stress. All responses are aimed at neutralizing the stress. In this framework abusive behaviour is seen as a coping attempt to deal with perceived stress, but at the bottom end of the hierarchy of adaptiveness. The model requires empirical validation but is a useful starting point to examine the relationship between coping and abusing behaviour. We need to know whether there is a hierarchy of coping responses which are invoked sequentially for everyone in the same order or if there are patterns of coping responses which start at different points in the hierarchy for individuals with perhaps several levels used at the same time. The degree of stress giving rise to coping responses may also be important in determining the nature and extent of the coping repertoire. We know that some people suffering the same objective stresses do not batter their children.

In a preliminary investigation of the coping strategies normal mothers use, Gray (1980) found that there are common coping strategies in crisis situations. Usually several coping strategies were employed, e.g. leaving the room and making a cup of tea or giving the child to the father and then going to see a friend. Generally most mothers managed to recognize the point when they were about to lose control and hit the child and were able to break the connection between how they were feeling and the next step of hitting the child. This was most commonly accomplished by putting a physical distance between themselves and the child. Not all mothers were able to do this and continued to stay with the child, while shouting, hitting or kicking doors and walls to prevent them hitting the child. All are attempts to develop alternative behaviours to abuse and we need further systematic investigation of the effectiveness of different coping strategies.

One of the difficulties in measuring a behaviour such as coping is the need to assess its effectiveness not just in terms of dealing with immediate problems but also for reducing the likelihood of future occurrences of the problem, and this must be taken into account. Perhaps the results from this study are surprising when it is remembered that the mothers were drawn at random from general practitioners' lists and were not referred as problems. They were socially stable, had been in the neighbourhood on average for 5 years, had reasonable social support, had few financial problems and were predominantly from social classes 2 and 3. Yet 86% of these 'normal' mothers said they had reached the stage when they were about to lose control and most added a rider that this had happened on several occasions. To the question, 'Are you ever worried you might hit your child harder than you meant to?', 61% answered 'Yes'. Not only might further research in this area suggest new treatment tactics for abusing parents, it might also suggest ways of helping non-abusing parents to cope more effectively.

We have criticized many of the attempts to research child abuse which assume from the outset that the focus of attention must be a search for abnormality in offending parents. In contrast, the social interactional model, based on social learning theory, implies that both child and adult have a role to play. However, when looking in the literature for empirical data to evaluate the precise role of the parent, the same difficulties present themselves as with the search for the role of the child. There are few observational studies but many hypotheses and opinions. Spinetta and Rigler (1972) reviewed what amounted to published professional opinions on the characteristics of abusing parents, but they did suggest that some parents may have mistaken notions of child rearing and may be deficient in certain parenting skills. A number of practitioners who have conducted behavioural training programmes with abusing families have noted that child management skills deficits are frequent and important components in their intervention programmes (e.g. Reavley and Gilbert, 1976; Hutchings, 1980*a*,*b*; Gambrill, 1981). These programmes will be reviewed later in this chapter but it is worth nothing that parental skill deficits, in terms of both competency and knowledge, were in many cases directly observed by clinicians implementing behavioural procedures. In many parts of the UK a voluntary 'phone-in support and advice service is offered and a recent annual report documented that in the majority of telephone calls received, the caller asked for advice on child management (Parents Anonymous, 1980). Parents who lack a wide and flexible range of effective caretaking and disciplinary techniques would certainly be at risk for becoming involved in coercive procedures since alternative effective means of terminating the child's undesirable behaviour would be absent.

Burgess and Conger (1978) reported a family interaction study that utilized direct behaviour observation methods. They compared 17 abusing families with 17 who had neglected their child and 19 controls. Three types of experimental task were introduced for all families, consisting of a co-operative task, a competitive one and a discussion period. They used a detailed behavioural coding system and found a large number of statistically significant differences between the families. First, abusing mothers were found to be less verbal than controls and they also initiated less positive physical interaction (e.g. cuddles) with their children. Negative interactions (typically consisting of threats, criticisms, statements of disapproval and negative emotional affect) were significantly more frequent from abusing parents. A much larger proportion of the total verbal and physical contacts by abusing parents, therefore, were aversive when compared with controls. The children themselves were more negative and less verbal in the abused group and one may speculate as to whether they were already learning patterns of coercive control themselves or whether it simply reflects extinction of attempts to behave in more positive terms. Reid and Taplin (1971), cited in Gambrill (1981), reported a greater engagement of aversive interactions by abusing parents and Frodi and Lamb (1980) also report differences in the way abusing parents and controls respond to infant cries and smiles. The latter compare 15 abusing mothers with 15 non-abusers when exposed to a crying infant. Whilst both groups evidenced physiological arousal, this was more pronounced with the abusers, who also demonstrated more annoyance and less sympathy than the non-abusers. When presented with a smiling infant, non-abusers responded with little change in physiological indices but the abusers, however, responded in a fashion that was almost indistiguishable from that displayed when presented with crying infants. Thus, abusers responded as if *any* elicitation of social interaction were aversive. Frodi and Lamb naturally draw attention to the interactive nature of the relationship between the behaviour of the abused child and his or her parents. Thus, atypical children may elicit abusive behaviour from their care-takers but the abuse itself may also lead its victims to acquire atypical and aversive behaviours.

It has also been suggested that abusing parents may set unrealistic standards and have distorted perceptions of age-related behaviour in their child. Similarly, the child may become labelled because of early difficulties in development and management and once that child is labelled as difficult or bad, for example, the perceptions and reactions of parents may continue to be dominated by the original label. Such speculations are certainly interesting and worthy of study, but at present there is little evidence to support the notion that these features are specific to abusing families.

Burgess and Conger (1978) advocate detailed research into family interaction patterns and attention to the reciprocal nature of interactions between parent and child. Such research would parallel the work of Patterson in Oregon on a wide range of families with marked behavioural difficulties. This would seem to us to be the only sensible line of inquiry if we are to unravel the complex factors that undoubtedly interact along the pathway that eventually results in physical abuse. Cause–effect relationships will never be conclusively identified without interactional analyses. One example of this may be seen in the work of Reidy, who has investigated the aggressive, cognitive and social characteristics of abused and neglected children (Reidy, 1977; Reidy *et al.*, 1980). Using ratings of behavioural problems by teachers, psychometric assessment and questionnaire data, Reidy concluded that abused and neglected children attained lower intellectual levels, yielded lower self-esteem scores and displayed more aggressive behaviour and a range of behavioural problems than non-abused, control children. Although Reidy suggests that his data are consistent with social learning theory formulations that children exposed to highly aggressive models will display more aggressive behaviour themselves, others may suggest that the behaviour of the abused children may not reflect parental child rearing but instead may determine such behaviour in their parents.

To summarize, the social interactional model of child abuse includes three major assumptions:

(1) Abusing parents present with a range of social and parenting skill deficits which may result in punitive and coercive patterns of child management. An absence of coping skills to deal with stress resulting from aversive behaviour on the part of the child, and in some cases an adverse physical environment, may also be characteristics.

(2) Abused children may well contribute to the abusive behaviour displayed by their parents.

(3) Both research and intervention should focus directly upon family interactions before the pattern of child abuse can be understood and extinguished.

It may be suggested, therefore, that child abuse is the result of a particular mis-match between a child in terms of his needs arising from his particular characteristics and behaviour and parents who also have needs and expectations about their child arising from deficits in parental competency and child rearing skills. The specific nature of the child's behaviour will vary widely from one family to another and, equally, parental skills and competency will differ between families. The one common factor is that the child's needs are not met by the parents and that the parents have been unable to cope with their individual child without recourse to excessive physical punishment or gross neglect.

Sameroff (1979) has suggested that rather than a continuum of reproductive casualty being the determinant of poor developmental outcome, it is the environmental risk factors which are crucial and he suggests a continuum of care-taking casualty. He believes that although reproductive casualties may be the starting point for the production of later problems, it is the care-taking environment that will determine the ultimate outcome. The abused child might be placed at one extreme end of this continuum of care-taking casualty providing that we accept that it is likely that he may also contribute significantly to the problem of mis-match between parent and child.

Behavioural interventions with abusing families

The critical test of any model of child abuse follows from an evaluation of the efficacy of treatment programmes derived from the model. With social learning theory as their basis a number of behavioural programmes have been conducted with abusing families. Published reports of these programmes are relatively few in number in comparison with interventions based on other models. They are also of recent origin and differ in terms of the components included within them and the targets set and achieved. This is consistent with theory, however, since the specific deficits of parents will naturally vary and target behaviours for change in the child will also differ. Factors that are maintaining abusive behaviour within families will also be idiosyncratic.

Two recent and important literature reviews, summarizing the behavioural approach towards child abuse, have been published (Hutchings, 1980*a*; Gambrill, 1981). Both emphasize the importance of detailed and careful behavioural analyses with abusing families and Hutchings warns against the danger of concluding that behavioural approaches are easy to apply to an extremely complex clinical problem; she also points out that the complexity of the determinants of child abuse must not be underestimated. Gambrill's review is directed primarily towards social workers and, whilst encouraging them to adopt behavioural approaches towards their intervention work with abusing families, she also takes care to describe the detailed components of assessment and intervention that may be necessary and stresses the wide range of specific techniques and targets which may be important for effective intervention with any individual family.

Some published treatment studies have focused upon training parents in more effective ways of managing their child's behaviour and in teaching them new child-care skills. Denicola and Sandler (1980) describe training programmes with two abusing families which included a coping skills component. They used videotape recordings of problem situations for discussion by parents and focused on teaching them the use of positive reinforcement skills rather than punitive punishment techniques. The coping skills component included relaxation training, the use of self-instruction and some problem-solving skills. Data collected showed a reduction in the amount of disapproval show by parents towards their child and an increase in the amount of positive reinforcement directed towards the child. During treatment and at follow-up the children also showed an increase in pro-social behaviour and a reduction in behaviour that had been aversive for parents. This illustrates the importance of the reciprocal nature of interactions between parent and child which is fundamental to interventions based on social learning theory and the social interactional model of child abuse.

Sandler *et al.* (1978) also reported that baseline recordings of mother–child interactions with two abusing families revealed low and inconsistent patterns of social reinforcement of the child by parents. The training was directed at increasing the rate of approval and positive physical contact between mothers and children. Over nine treatment sessions intervention included reading assignments, practice of skills taught between sessions and role play of the use of positive reinforcement. Tangible reinforcers were given to parents for compliance and progress made during treatment.

The use of role play to practise relevant child management skills was also an important component in the interventions reported by Crozier and Katz (1979) with two abusing families. Social learning principles were applied in these home-based treatments aimed at improving child management skills and eliminating aversive control procedures used by the parents. Results demonstrated large reductions in the rate of aversive parent and child behaviours and corresponding increases in constructive behaviour of most family members. These changes were maintained at follow-up with no re-occurrence of child abuse.

Jeffrey (1976) described one family in which parents' attempts to use aversive control procedures outweighed their use of positive reinforcement with their child. A programme was established to increase the use of positive comments for which parents received tokens which could be traded in for tangible rewards. An increase in positive interactions and reduction in negative and aversive procedures was reported during treatment. Gambrill (1981) makes the important observation that there is a need to explore not just the knowledge that parents have about child management but also their competences. In other words, parents may possess quite effective rewarding skills but rarely use them, or do so in an inconsistent fashion. They must learn not only how to reward and how to avoid the use of physical punishment but also to control their own anxiety and in some cases develop more realistic expectations of their child's behaviour.

Reducing excessive anxiety levels about parent–child interaction has been an important feature of some of the interventions described by Reavley and Gilbert (Reavley and Gilbert, 1976; Reavley *et al.*, 1978). Interventions described by these therapists often place particular emphasis upon participant modelling as a teaching technique, and in two single case studies (Reavley and Gilbert, 1976) an anxiety hierarchy relating to a range of mother–child interactions was drawn up and graded exposure carried out. In addition, mothers were taught a number of coping skills and cognitive strategies to help reduce anxiety levels. Reavley and Gilbert have conducted behavioural programmes with over 30 families who were referred for inappropriate child handling, of which many cases included physical abuse. A wide range of techniques based on social learning theory have been used in packaged programmes which makes component analysis difficult. Similarly, Hutchings (1980*b*) has reported promising outcome data after applied behavioural interventions with a range of families with child management difficulties, some of whom have physically abused their children. Both Reavley and Hutchings stress that although the behavioural outcome might be similar, the determinants of abuse often varied and required treatment programmes designed for the individual family. Both have also attempted to train professionals other than psychologists in the use of a range of behavioural techniques for intervention with abusing families (nurses and health visitors respectively) and together with Gambrill's teaching directed at social welfare workers it is to be hoped that we can see the beginnings of an attempt to penetrate traditional agency practice with the skills of applied behaviour therapy based on social learning theory.

Whilst there has been an increasing number of published reports of the application of behavioural procedures to abusing families (and outcome data are extremely promising) it is still an extremely rare form of agency practice. Much research remains to be done. The majority of published work consists of very small samples or single case studies and there are few component analyses of treatment packages that have been implemented. Gambrill (1981) lists some of the advantages of this approach, including the collection of empirical baseline data against which intervention effects can be evaluated; targeting is more precise and specific than with other forms of intervention and the duration of treatment is relatively short. She notes that the scientific nature of behavioural approaches should enable more objective decision-making in multidisciplinary case reviews. The broad educational approach towards intervention applied by the social interactional model may help clients accept treatment in a way that the more traditional interventions do not because of their pejorative implications. A final advantage that we might note arising from the behavioural approach rests with their home-based site for intervention. Note only does this facilitate generalization effects which can be confounded when treatment is based in a hospital or residential care setting, but the goal of intervention is to enable the child to live safely and happily with his natural parents rather than being taken into care, with resultant high financial and psychological costs to those involved.

We believe that ultimately the most rapid way to change traditional practice with abusing families will be to produce comparative study data in which traditional methods of intervention are compared with behavioural approaches based on social learning theory. If, as is quite probable, the behavioural approaches are demonstrably more effective in reducing abuse and certainly more cost effective than alternative forms of intervention, then the social interactional model of child abuse will become more widely accepted and in time will become the basis for intervention practice rather than the psychiatric, social welfare or legal models.

As we have discussed earlier, many of the existing interventions based on traditional models of child abuse are not conducted in such a way that they can be empirically evaluated, still less that they can be compared with recent developments in the field. As scientific practitioners become more widespread and active in the field of child abuse, this state of affairs will become increasingly untenable. We have described one attempt at a comparative study (Sutton and Nanton, 1978) and Gambrill has summarized a small number of studies that have compared the effects of behavioural programmes with the traditional services provided by child welfare agencies in America (e.g. Wolfe *et al* (1980) and Stein *et al.* (1978), cited in Gambrill (1981)). It is to be hoped that the favourable outcomes from the behavioural approaches will herald further research and development of these approaches as well as more critical and objective evaluation of traditional treatments and agency practices.

Prevention

It is a salutory thought that in the long term primary prevention is the only answer to the problem of child abuse. Children who are abused by their parents have observed and learned a violent model of parenting and sometimes go on to abuse their own children, thereby perpetuating the generation cycle of abuse. We must find a way to break the pattern and prevent future abuse. This chapter has concentrated on tertiary prevention, i.e. treatments designed to help parents once abuse has occurred, and realistically in the short term this is where the contribution of the behavioural approach lies. However, it is primarily an educational approach which involves parents as participants and encourages them to learn new self-management skills. There is no reason why the same principles could not be extended to educate parents in a broader sense. The best possible defence against problems is to build resources and adaptive strengths in people from the start. If skills could be effectively implanted this provides an attractive pathway to primary prevention. For primary prevention to work it means ensuring that grandparents provide good parenting. It is a colossal task which will involve many professions including politicians, teachers, psychologists and sociologists.

In the UK parent training is not a generally accepted idea. Mothers themselves assume that parenting is a 'natural' skill rather than one which can be learned, and professionals have yet to discover appropriate delivery systems to appeal to parents. An attempt to set up the British Association for Parent Education in 1973 failed (Pugh, 1980), although it was criticized for its restricted appeal to the educated middle classes. A Department of Health and Social Security report in 1973 concluded that the most common view was that the majority of parents would not participate in parent education classes and a less formal approach was needed. New initiatives are under way at the antenatal stage (Birch and Chambers, 1979); in schools with adolescents (Hutchinson and Devine, 1978; Burns, 1979) and with parents (Hardy, 1979). The National Children's Bureau in London has started a 3 year project to set up a national clearing house for the dissemination and interchange of ideas and information on schemes and services in the field of preparation and support for parents with young children.

The situation in the United States is somewhat different. Many schools are assuming the responsibility of backing up parents in providing young people with the knowledge and skills of parenting. In 1972 the Office of Education joined with the Office of Child Development in developing a major programme—Education for Parenthood. Its purpose was to improve the competence of teenage boys and girls for becoming parents (Bell, 1975). Many states have developed parenthood programmes for use in schools (e.g. Silverman, 1979; Dubanoski and Tanabe, 1980) and in the home (e.g. Gotts, 1977; Truitt, 1979) backed up by media packages (Bjorklund and Briggs, 1977). Evaluation of parent training programmes is vital, in terms of their overall effectiveness, with which groups of people, and the effectiveness of the components of the packages.

The idea of parent training programmes suggests that there are a set of identifiable skills we know about, can measure objectively and impart to others. In reality this is not true. Parent education is hampered by a lack of consensus about what we are training children for, and amongst professionals there is a great deal of uncertainty and confusion about what is good practice in child rearing. Two basic issues must be dealt with:

(1) *What to teach parents about child rearing*. One attempt was made to find an answer to this problem involving a panel of experts which in 1973 met under the auspices of the Office of Child Development (Anderson and Messick, 1974) in an attempt to define the meaning of 'social competency' in young children. They arrived at 29 statements that represent facets of social competency in youngsters and recommended that these serve as goals of early intervention programmes. Obviously there are difficulties in defining concepts such as social compentency, and many statements reflect inadequacies in both our theoretical and empirical knowledge of young children. However, any attempt systematically to investigate and determine the goals of childrearing must be applauded. It should also be acknowledged that there is no single 'right' kind of parenting and that good parenting skills come in a variety of styles.

(2) *How to teach parenting skills*. Many management techniques are available and have been researched but less attention has been spent on methods of service delivery. This is particularly important in the light of parental attitudes which see parenting as a natural rather than a learned skill and where physical punishment is considered an effective method of control, albeit an undesirable one.

Training parents in new methods of child rearing might be more appropriately labelled secondary prevention, where potential problems are dealt with before they escalate. The real targets for primary prevention are children themselves, to teach them to grow up as competent and effective parents. Shure and Spivak (1974, 1978, 1979) have developed an elaborate research and training package for teaching cognitive problem-solving skills to young children. The assumption behind their approach is that there are a group of interpersonal cognitive problem-solving (ICPS) skills that mediate social adjustment and their effort since 1968 has been to identify and measure ICPS skills over a broad age span and to explore how intervention programmes may enhance their operation. Their hypothesized skills include alternative solution thinking, consequential thought and means–end thinking. The emphasis lies in teaching the child *how* to think and not what to think. The results from the project are promising; for example, in a study with 4 year old, black, inner city children, the shy, anxious ones gained the most in social problem-solving skills. This gain correlated directly with a decrease in maladjustment ratings. The programme children also improved significantly on such dimensions as concern for others, ability to take initiative and autonomy, whereas the controls failed to show this improvement. However, several important questions remain to be addressed: whether stress in children affects the programme's effectiveness, under what circumstances skills are not applied, and the effectiveness of various elements in the package. Other approaches to primary prevention have been attempted. For example, Allen *et al*. (1976) as part of a comprehensive 18 month, three-tiered, preventive school mental health programme used social problem-solving training with fourth grade children as their primary prevention component.

We have already seen that abusing parents and many non-abusing parents lack problem-solving skills and adaptive coping strategies, D'Zurilla and Goldfried (1971) argue that 'our daily lives are replete with situational problems which we must solve in order to maintain an adequate level of effective functioning'. If rearing children adds to already existing stress, then equipping children with life skills of problem solving is of crucial importance.

Conclusions

Violence towards children is a highly emotive subject that has become the subject of increasing concern to society in recent years. The media, the public and professional agencies are becoming more aware of the tragic consequences of child abuse. We have argued, however, that the traditional, and widely held, theoretical models forwarded to account for abusing behaviour suffer from major deficiencies despite the fact that the vast majority of attempts by professional agencies to intervene are based upon these models. We have also suggested that until very recently the abusing parents have been the sole focus of concern and research and until the balance is redressed, when we can have a greater understanding of the role of the child and how this interacts with the role of the parent, then both models and interventions will often be inadequate.

Social learning theory offers a comprehensive framework for an understanding of violence towards children and recent research has suggested that interventions based upon social learning theory have yielded promising data. Whilst we believe that a behavioural approach to intervention, based upon social learning theory, may be the most effective path to follow for those involved in crisis intervention, much effort must be directed towards prevention. Parental education, in terms of child management skills and also personal effectiveness, will in the long term be the only real solution to society's apparently insatiable appetite for violence towards children.

References

Allen, G. J., Chimsky, J. M., Larcen, S. W., Lochman, J. E., and Sellinger, H. E. (1976). *Community Psychology and the Schools*. Hillsdale, N. J: Lawrence Erlbaum.

Anderson, S., and Messick, S. (1974). Social competency in young children. *Developmental Psychology*, **10**, 282–293.

Andrews, G., Tennant, C., Hewson, D. M., and Vaillant, G. E. (1978). Life events stress, social support, coping style and risk of psychological impairment. *Journal of Nervous and Mental Disease*, **166**, 307–316.

Bandura, A. (1969). *Principles of Behaviour Modification*. New York: Holt, Rinehart and Winston.

Bandura, A. (1977*a*). *Social Learning Theory*. Englewood Cliffs, N. J.: Prentice-Hall.

Bandura, A. (1977*b*). Self-efficacy: towards a unifying theory of behavioural change. *Psychological Review*, **84**, 191–215.

Bell, R. Q., and Harper, L. V. (1977). *Child Effects on Adults*. Hillsdale, N. J.: Lawrence Erlbaum.

Bell, T. H. (1975). The child's right to have a trained parent. *Elementary School Guidance and Counselling*, **9**, 271–276.

Belsky, J. (1978). Three theoretical models of child abuse: a critical review. *International Journal of Child Abuse and Neglect*, **2**, 37–49.

Birch, K., and Chambers, M. (1979). Preparation for parenthood. *Health Visitor*, **59**, 507–510.

Bjorklund, G., and Briggs, A. (1977). Selecting media for parent education programmes. *Young Children*, **32**, 14–18.

Bowlby, J. (1951). *Maternal Care and Mental Health*. Geneva: World Health Organization.

Bowlby, J., Ainsworth, M. D., Boston, M., and Rosenbluth, D. (1956). The effects of mother-child separation: a follow-up study. *British Journal of Medical Psychology*, **29**, 211–247.

Burgess, R. L. (1979). Child abuse: a social interactional analysis, in *Advances in Clinical Child Psychology*, Vol. 2 (Eds B. B. Lahey and A. E. Kazdin). New York: Plenum Press, pp. 141–172.

Burgess, R. L., and Conger, R. D. (1978). Family interaction in abusive, neglectful and normal families. *Child Development*, **49**, 1163–1173.

Burns, E. K. (1979). Parents of tomorrow: involvement of secondary school pupils in pre-school playgroups in Scotland. *International Journal of Child Abuse and Neglect,* **3**, 975–984.

Cochrane, R. (1978). Psychological aspects of life events: a tentative model. Paper read at British Psychology Society Clinical Division Joint Meeting, University of Sheffield, June 1978.

Cohn, A. H., Miller, M. K. (1977). Evaluating new motive treatment for child abuse and neglectors: the experience of federally founded demonstration projects in the USA, *Internal. Journal of Child Abuse and Neglect*, **1**, 2–4, 453–458.

Crozier, J., and Katz, R. C. (1979). Social learning treatment of child abuse. *Journal of Behavioural Therapy and Experimental Psychiatry*, **10**, 213–220.

Denicola, J., and Sandler, J. (1980). Training abusive parents in child management and self-control skills. *Behaviour Therapy,* **11**, 263–270.

Dubanoski, R., and Tanabe, G. (1980). A classroom programme on social learning principles. *Family Relations*, **29**, 15–20.

Dunne, J. (1979). The first year of life: continuities in individual differences, in *The First Year of Life: Psychological and Medical Implications of Early Experience* (Eds D. Shaffer and J. Dunn). Chichester John Wiley, pp. 69–90.

D'Zurilla, T. J. and Goldfried, M. R. (1971) 'Problem solving and behaviour modification'. *Journal of Abnormal Psychology*, **78**, 107–126.

Empson, J., and McGlaughlin, A. (1979). Stress factors in the lives of disadvantaged children. Paper presented to the annual conference of the British Psychology Society, April 1979.

Feldman, M.P. (1977). *Criminal Behaviour: A Psychological Analysis.* Chichester: John Wiley.

Fontana, V. (1973). *Somewhere a Child is Crying: Maltreatment—its Causes and Prevention*. New York: Macmillan.

Francis, J., and Sutton, A. (1977). The battered child and his parents: can we help?'. *Social Work To-day*, **4**, 16–17.

Friedrich, W. N., and Boriskin, J. A. (1976). The role of the child in abuse: a review of the literature. *American Journal of Orthopsychiatry*, **46**, 580–590.

Frodi, A. M., and Lamb, M. E. (1980). Child abusers' responses to infants' smiles and cries. *Child Development*, **51**, 238–241.

Frodi, A. M. (1981). Contributions of infant characteristics to child abuse. *American Journal of Mental Deficiency*, **85**, 341–349.

Gambrill, E. (1977). *Behaviour Modification: Handbook of Assessment, Intervention and Evaluation*, San Francisco, Jossey-Bass.

Gambrill, E. (1981). The use of behavioural procedures in cases of child abuse and neglect. *The International Journal of Behavioural Social Work and Abstracts*, **1**, 3–26.

Garbarino, J. (1977). The human ecology of child maltreatment: a conceptual model for research. Journal of Marriage and the Family, **39**, 721–735.

Gelles, R. J. (1977). Violence towards children in the United States. Paper presented at the annual meeting of the American Association for the Advancement of Science.

Gil, D. C. (1970). *Violence against Children: Physical Child Abuse in the United States.* Cambridge, Mass. Harvard University Press.

Giurguis, W. R. (1978). Is parenthood teachable?. *British Journal of Psychiatry,* **133**, 282–288.

Gotts, E. (1977). Instructional television products for effective parenthood: a national assessment of parent education needs. Paper presented at the American Educational Research Association, New York City.

Gray, M. A. (1980). A questionnaire study of maternal methods of control. MSc thesis, University of Birmingham.

Hardy, M., (1979). Prevention of baby battering. *The Practitioner*, **222**, 243–247.

Helfer, R. E., and Kempe, C. H. (Eds) (1968). *The Battered Child Syndrome*. Chicago: The University of Chicago Press.

Herrenkohl, R. C., Herrenkohl, E. C., Egolf, B., and Seech, M. (1979). The repetition of child abuse: how frequently does it occur? *International Journal of Child Abuse and Neglect*, **3**, 67–72.

Holmes, T. H., and Rahe, R.H. (1967). The social readjustment rating scale. *Journal of Psychomatic Research*, **11**, 213–218.

Hutchings, J. (1980*a*). The behavioural approach to child abuse: a review of the literature, in *The Understanding and Prevention of Child Abuse: Psychological Approaches* (Ed. N. Frude). London Batsford, pp. 181–191.

Hutchings, J. (1980*b*). Behavioural Work With Families Where Children are 'At Risk'. Paper presented to the First World Congress on Behaviour Therapy, Tel-Aviv University, Israel.

Hutchinson, E. D., and Devine, D. C. (1978). *Understanding Children. A Course in Preparation for Parenthood for Senior Pupils. Teachers' Handbook*. Paisley: Strathclyde Regional Council, Department of Education, Renfrew Division.

Jeffrey, M. (1976). Practical ways to change parent–child interactions and families of children at risk, in *Child Abuse and Neglect* (Eds I. Helfer and R. E. Kempe). Cambridge, Mass.: Ballinger, pp. 209–223.

Johnston, J. M. (1972). Punishment of human behaviour. *American Psychologist*, **27**, 1033–1054.

Kaplan, A. (1964). *The Conduct of Inquiry: Methodology for Behavioural Science*. San Francisco: Chandler.

Kellmer-Pringle, M. (1978). The needs of children, in *The Maltreatment of Children* (Ed. S. M. Smith). Lancaster, England: Medical and Technical Press, pp. 221–243.

Kempe, C. H., and Helfer, R. E. (1972). *Helping the Battered Child and His Family*. Philadelphia: Lippincott.

Kempe, C. H., Silverman, F. N., Steele, B. B., Droegemueller, N., and Silver, H. K. (1962). The battered child syndrome. *Journal of the American Medical Association*, **181**, 17–24.

Kempe, R. S., and Kempe, C. H. (1978). *Child Abuse*. London: Fontana.

Korsch, M., Christian, J., Gozzie, E., and Carlson, P. (1965). Infant care and punishment: a pilot study. *American Journal of Public Health*, **55**, 1180–1880.

Lazarus, A. (1976). *Multi-modal Behaviour Therapy*. New York: Springer.

Light, R. J. (1973). Abused and neglected children in America: a study of alternative policies. *Harvard Educational Review*, **43**, 556–598.

Morris, B. (1979). Value differences in definitions of child abuse and neglect. Jehovah's Witnesses: a case example. *International Journal of Child Abuse and Neglect*, **3**, 651–655.

Noble, S. M. (1978). The contributions of the social agencies and the social worker, in *The Maltreatment of Children* (Ed. S. M. Smith). Lancaster, England: Medical and Technical Press, pp. 351–391.

Oliver, J. E. (1978). The epidemiology of child abuse, in *The Maltreatment of Children* (Ed. S. M. Smith), Lancaster, England: Medical and Technical Press, pp. 95–119.

Ounsted, C., Oppenheimer, R., and Lindsay, J. (1974). Aspects of bonding failure: the psychopathology and psychotherapeutic treatment of families of battered children. *Developmental Medicine and Child Neurology*, **16**, 447–456.

Osofsky, J. D., and Danziger, B. (1974). Relationships between neonatal characteristics and mother–infant interaction. *Developmental Psychology*, **10**, 124–130.

Packer, M., and Rosenblatt, D. (1979). Issues in the study of social behaviour in the first week of life, in *The First Year of Life: Psychological and Medical Implications of Early Experience* (Eds D. Shaffer and J. Dunn). Chichester: John Wiley, pp. 7–35.

Parents Anonymous (1980). Parents Anonymous Lifeline, Birmingham. Second Report.

Parke, R., and Collmer, C. (1975). Child abuse: an interdisciplinary analysis, In *Review of Child Development Research*, Vol. 5, (Ed. E. M. Hetherington). Chicago: University of Chicago Press, pp. 509–589.

Patterson, G. R. (1979). *Families: Applications of Social Learning to Family Life*. Champaign, Illinois: Research Press.

Pearlin, L., and Schooler, C. (1978). The structure of coping. *Journal of Health and Social Behaviour*, **19**, 2–21.

Pugh, G. (1980).*Preparation for Parenthood*. London: National Children's Bureau.

Reavley, W., and Gilbert, M. T. (1976). The behavioural treatment approach to potential child abuse—two illustrative case reports' *Social Work Today*, **7**, 166–168.

Reavley, W., Gilbert, M. T., and Carver, V. (1978). The behavioural approach to child abuse, in *Child Abuse: A Study Text* (Ed. V. Carver). Milton Keynes: The Open University, pp. 223–232.

Reid, J. B., and Taplin, P. S. (1977). A social interactional approach to the treatment of abusive families. Unpublished manuscript, Oregon Research Institute.

Reidy, T. J. (1977). The aggressive characteristics of abused and neglected children. *Journal of Clinical Psychology*, **23**, 1140–1145.

Reidy, T. J., Anderegy, T., Tracy, T., and Cotler, S. (1980). Abused and neglected children: the cognitive social and behavioral correlates, in G. J. Williams and J. Money (Eds), *Traumatic Abuse and Neglect of Children at Home*. Baltimore: Johns Hopkins University Press, 284–290.

Sameroff, A. J. (1979). The etiology of cognitive competence: a systems perspective, in *Infants at Risk: Assessment of cognitive Functioning* (Eds R. B. Kearsley and I. E. Siegel). Hillside, N. J.: Lawrence Erlbaum, 115–151.

Sameroff, A. J., and Chandler, M. J. (1975). Reproductive risk and the continuum of caretaking casualty, in *Review of Child Development Research*, Vol 4 (Eds F. D. Horowitz, M. Hetherington, S. Scarr-Salapatea and G. Siegel). Chicago: University of Chicago Press, pp. 187–244.

Sanders, R. W. (1978). Systematic desensitization in the treatment of child abuse. *American Journal of Psychiatry*, **135**, 483–484.

Sandgrund, A., Gaines, R., and Green, A. (1974). Child abuse and mental retardation: a problem of cause and effect. *American Journal of Mental Deficiency*, **79**, 327–330.

Sandler, J., Van Dercar, C., and Milhoan, M. (1978). Training child abusers in the use of positive reinforcement techniques. *Behaviour Research and Therapy*, **16**, 169–175.

Scott, P. D. (1977). Non-accidental injury to children. *British Journal of Psychiatry*, **131**, 366–380.

Scott, P. D. (1978). The psychiatrist's viewpoint, in *The Maltreatment of Children* (Ed. S. M. Smith). Lancaster, England: Medical and Technical Press, pp. 175–203.

Seebohm (1968). Report of the Committee on Local Authority and Allied Personal Services (The Seebohm report). Comnd. No. 3703. London: HMSO.

Shure, M. B., and Spivak, G. (1974). *Social Adjustment of Young Children: A Cognitive Approach*. San Francisco: Jossey-Bass.

Shure, M. B., and Spivak, G. (1978). *Problem-solving Techniques in Child-rearing*. San Francisco: Jossey-Bass.

Shure, M. B., and Spivak, G. (1979). Interpersonal problem solving and primary prevention: programming for pre-school and kindergarten children. *Journal of Clinical Child Psychology*, **1979**, 89–94.

Skinner, B. F. (1972). Compassion and ethics in the care of the retardate, in *Cumulative Record*, 3rd Edn (Ed. B. F. Skinner). New York: Appleton-Century-Crofts, pp. 3–37.

Silverman, M. (1979). A synthesis of behavioural and communication approaches to child rearing for parenting skills classes. Practicum II. Nova University.

Sim, M. (1978). Introduction—a child speaks, in *The Maltreatment of Children* (Ed.

S. M. Smith). Lancaster, England: Medical and Technical Press, pp. 1–8.

Skinner, A. E., and Castle, R. L. (1969). *78 Battered Children:A Retrospective Study*. London: NSPCC.

Smith, S. M. (1975). *The Battered Child Syndrome*. Butterworth: London.

Smith, S. M., Hanson, R., and Noble, S. (1973). Parents of battered babies: a controlled study. *British Medical Journal*, **4**, 388–391.

Smith, S. S., and Hanson, R. (1975). Interpersonal relationships and child-rearing practices in 214 parents of battered children'. *British Journal of Psychiatry*, **127**, 513–525.

Soeffing, M. (1975) Abused children are exceptional children. *Exceptional Children*, **42**, 126–133.

Solomons, G. (1979). Child abuse and developmental disabilities. *Developmental Medicine and Child Neurology*, **21**, 101–108.

Spinetta, J. J., and Rigler, D. (1972). The child-abusing parent: a psychological review. *Psychological Bulletin*, **77**, 296–304.

Spivak, G., and Shure, M.B. (1976). *The Problem-solving Approach to Adjustment*. San Francisco: Jossey-Bass.

Stark, R., and McEvoy, J. (1970). Middle class violence. *Psychology Today*, **4**, 52–65.

Steele, B. F., and Pollock, C. B. (1968). A psychiatric study of parents who abuse infants and small children, in *The Battered Child* (Eds R. E. Helfer and C. H. Kempe). Chicago: University of Chicago Press, pp. 93–116.

Steinmetz, S. K., and Straus, M. A. (Eds) (1974). *Violence in the Family*. New York: Dodd, Mead.

Stevens-Long, J. (1973). The effects of the behavioral context on some aspects of adult disciplinary practice and affect. *Child Development*, **44**, 476–484.

Straus, M. A. (1978). The social causes of interpersonal violence: the example of family violence and Odyssey House non-violence. Paper read at the American Psychological Association Conference, Toronto.

Straus, M. A. (1979). Family patterns and child abuse in a nationally representative American sample. *International Journal of Child Abuse and Neglect*, **3**. 213–225.

Sutton, A. (1981*a*). Science in court, in *Childhood, Welfare and Future* (Ed. M. King). London: Batsford, pp. 45–104.

Sutton, A. (1981*b*). Sorting the wheat from the chaff: the examination of expert evidence on child care matters, in *Reports to the Court: Guidance for Independent Reporters in Child Care Cases* (Ed. J. Tunnard). London: Family Rights Group, pp. 21–32.

Sutton, A., and Nanton, V. (1978). The effectiveness of developmental day care in certain cases of physical abuse and serious neglect. Unpublished Research Report, Birmingham Parent and Child Centre.

Sutton, A., and Roberts, E. (1981). Day care for young children who are abused or neglected. *Social Work Service*, **25**, 29–33.

Thomas, A., and Chess, S. (1977). *Temperament and Development*. Brunner/Mazel, New York.

Thomas, A., Chess, S., and Birch, H. G. (1968). *Temperament and Behavior Disorders in Children*. New York: New York University Press.

Thomas, A., Chess, S., Birch, H. G., Hartzig, M. E., and Koi, S. (1963). *Behavioral Individuality in Early Childhood*. New York: New York University Press.

Tracy, J. J., and Clark, E. H. (1974). Treatment for child abusers. *Social Work USA* **19**, 338–342.

Truitt, J. (1979). The family education association of west-centre Indiana: a grassroots prevention programme for mental health. *Contemporary Education*, **50**, 72–76.

Young, L. (1964). *Wednesday's children. A Study of Child Neglect and Abuse*. New York: McGraw-Hill.

Developments in the Study of Criminal Behaviour. Volume 2: Violence
Edited by Philip Feldman

2

Violence Between Couples

LYN MINCHIN

Introduction

In many homes a certain amount of violence is regarded as natural, acceptable and even desirable. Little brothers may be expected to fight each other and considered unmasculine if they do not; parents may be expected to smack disobedient children; love-making may involve violence of various degrees for some couples. Of course extreme violence—murder or torture—receives general condemnation, except perhaps in the unusual and controversial example of abortion, where the measure of human status accorded the victim may determine one's attitude. Disregarding abortion, the helplessness of the victim and the bullying element involved help to make baby battering and granny bashing seem reprehensible. On the other hand husband battering may be seen as a joke since our stereotypes make it difficult for us to imagine a husband the helpless victim of his wife.

There is a grey area between extreme violence which no society would tolerate and milder forms of violence which some families would consider normal. Wife battering lies in this area, being less accepted now than in former times (Davidson, 1977; May, 1978) and apparently less accepted in some communities than others (Loizos, 1978; Scott, 1974). However, in the UK there is still more violence between couples than many would be prepared to condone. Knowledge of the laws against cruelty here and in other societies gives some indication of how far we have come and how far we still must go in order to eliminate this form of cruelty. For example, rape of wife by husband has been made an indictable offence in some North American states, in South Australia and in Israel, yet in the UK there is as yet little public debate on revising the Criminal Law to make rape in marriage a crime.

Violence against wives was noted as a social problem in the mid-nineteenth century with police, magistrates and law reformists deploring the lack of legal protection offered to abused wives. Public disquiet about this matter and the suggestion that family violence was increasing, led in 1853 to the passing of the Act for the Better Prevention and Punishment of Aggravated Assaults upon Women and Children. This Act, known as the 'Good Wives' Rod', provided for 6 months imprisonment or a £20 fine for those convicted of aggravated assault on a female or on a male younger than 14, and offenders could also be bound over to keep the peace for 6 months following release.

In 1878 divorce was made easier for working-class wives by the passing of the Matrimonial Causes Act, enabling abused wives to separate from their husbands legally and allowing them maintenance and custody of children under 10. However, these rights were restricted to those wives who had never committed adultery.

Public concern about wife beating waxed and waned in the following years. Only within the last decade has public anxiety about battered wives been sufficiently aroused for some measures to be take to provide for the safety of victims rather than focusing on increasing provisions for punishing offending husbands. This recent wave of interest with its emphasis on protection for the victims was kindled by the developing Womens' Liberation Movement and by publicity surrounding Erin Pizzey, the founder of the first refuge for battered women (see Pizzey, 1974).

Given this historical perspective, it is clear why the bulk of the sociological, psychological and criminological literature on violence between couples, as well as media interest in the subject, has concentrated on female partners as victims. Virtually no attention has been paid to the matter of violence between homosexual partners of either sex; nor has there been much discussion about husbands or male partners as victims.

Transcripts of interviews with battered wives indicate that violence is two-way in some of these families (Straus, 1977*b*) and there is some evidence that husband-battering occurs in other partnerships as well (Straus, 1977*b*; McClintock, 1978). Steinmetz (1977*a,b,c*) in the United States has claimed that wives resort to violence more than husbands. However, her interpretations of battering statistics have been questioned (Pleck *et al.*, 1977; Fields and Kirchner, 1978). It is clear from these and other sources (Gibson and Klein, 1969; Gibson, 1975) that serious violence, that which results in serious injury or death, by husbands against wives is more prevalent than serious violence by wives against husbands. A number of researchers suggest that women who assault their husbands tend to be acting in self-defence rather than initiating violence (Wolfgang, 1958; Flynn, 1977; Straus, 1977*b*) but there is insufficient empirical evidence to substantiate this.

Theoretically we should be concerned with the study and prevention of violence against both female and male victims. However, there are practical reasons for giving priority to female rather than male victims. First, as mentioned above, male assailants in general cause more serious injuries through their greater physical strength, their tendency to attack when their victims are pregnant (Straus, 1977*b*; Fields and Kirchner, 1978; Dobash and Dobash, 1979) and their greater tendency to use dangerous weapons (Straus, 1977*b*; Fields and Kirchner, 1978). Secondly, women victims, particularly those with children, are more likely than male victims to be trapped with their assailants by economic and social constraints (Gelles, 1977; Straus, 1977*a*).

In summary then, this chapter is concerned with violence between cohabiting couples (or ex-cohabitees), with an emphasis on women as the victims. 'Violence' here refers to the intentional infliction of personal injury, the use of force to harm one's partner. In legal terms this includes battery, assault, wounding with intent, murder and manslaughter.

It is not clear whether rape should be included or not. Neither rape nor any other type of sexual assault receives much attention in the literature on spouse abuse. Gayford's information based on interviews with battered women (Gayford, 1978) suggests that it is rare to find a sexual component in an attack. However, it may be that sexual assault is seen by many wives as legitimate violence and not as battering, a view supported by anecdotal material from Prescott and Letko (1977). Alternatively it is possible that researchers in this area are defining their concept of violence to exclude sexual assault, and future investigations should make it clear whether this is the case.

The following discussion will be restricted to physical violence. In family matters mental cruelty is an important subject in its own right. One aspect, verbal abuse, is sometimes mentioned in the professional literature on violence as 'verbal violence'. Anecdotal material, such as that of Dobash and Dobash (1979), suggests that verbal abuse, and mental cruelty in general, may precede or accompany physical violence. However, there is insufficient published research on 'verbal violence' as a separate issue for it to be considered in any detail in this chapter.

The incidence of violence between partners

The research literature to be discussed in this chapter gives some indication of the distress battering causes to many women, children and men, its psychological, physical, social and economic effects on individual victims. However, without an estimate of the incidence of battering we have little idea of the effects on the community, for example, in terms of general practitioner, hospital and prescription expenses, police and court costs, working days lost, Social Security payments for maintenance and housing, and social workers' time and expenses. Unfortunately there are no reliable sources of information on the incidence of violence between partners.

In England at any one time there are approximately one thousand battered women in the refuges affiliated to the National Women's Aid Federation. In 1979 a total of nearly 7000 women accompanied by 13 000 children passed through these refuges. However, this number does not include the many battered women in areas without refuges nor those who do not need or do not choose to use refuges.

Details from divorce petitions are sometimes cited as giving an indication of the prevalence of battering but this information is often unreliable and again seriously underestimates the actual incidence.

Failing other sources, police and crime records can be used but again it must be assumed that these will not reflect the true incidence of marital violence. Crime statistics indicate that approximately 300 people a year are convicted of murder or manslaughter in English and Welsh courts, with the figures remaining relatively constant over the last 10 years. In Scotland the number of people convicted of murder or culpable homicide has risen from 44 in 1968 to 69 in 1978. Analysis of records for the years 1957–71 by Gibson and Klein shows that the recorded murderers were predominantly male and that of the female victims over half were murdered by their husbands or lovers (Gibson and Klein, 1969; Gibson, 1975).

Looking at the statistics for all crimes of violence against the person McClintock (1978) reports that approximately one in five cases in England and Wales involve members of the same family. In Scotland the proportion is one in seven, possibly because of the slightly different police recording system used there by which some violence is classed as 'a breach of the peace' (McClintock, 1978).

Detailed analysis of police records for 1970 for four areas of England indicate that in the cases of family violence listed almost three-quarters of the victims were females and of these the majority were women attacked by their partners (McClintock, 1978). Similarly, in Scotland, Dobash and Dobash (1979) studied court records for 1974 for Edinburgh and part of Glasgow and found that, of the 1044 cases of family violence listed there, three-quarters of the cases were 'wife assault' or 'alleged wife assault'.

The extent of wife battering in England and Wales is also suggested by the number of court injunctions granted to wives against husbands who have assaulted them: 2267 injunctions granted with power of arrest and 6558 without power of arrest during the 18 months up to December 1978, according to provisional figures reported by Coote and Gill (1979).

It has been suggested that information from police and court records may not provide a clear picture of the true extent of violence between partners. In-depth interviews with victims indicate that in general they report to the police only a small proportion of the violent incidents in which they are involved (Straus, 1977*b*; Dobash and Dobash, 1979). Similarly, interviews with people sampled from the general population suggest that they frequently do not report the violent domestic incidents in which they are involved (Gelles, 1974; Gaquin, 1977).

Crimes carried out in the privacy of the home are not easily detected unless the victim or a witness reports them. There may be no witness, or the only witness may be a child. The victim may be unable to complain because he or she is too ill, of low intelligence, ignorant of the law, involved in breaking the law him or herself, or because he or she accepts such violence as normal in the home. He or she may be unwilling to complain because of fear of retribution from the offender, shame in admitting that something is wrong in the marriage or the family, embarrassment at discussing family matters or sexual matters with the police or in court, reluctance to have weakness or lack of masculinity revealed (in the case of husband battering), affection for the offender, previous unhelpful or unpleasant experience of police or court action or inaction, or fear of causing the break up of the marriage (with associated worries about children, housing, security, finance or status). Witnesses related to offenders or victims may have similar reasons for keeping quiet about offences. In some cases professionals—doctors, social workers, health visitors—may be aware of or suspect offences but fail to report them through reluctance to breakup a family, because of a poor opinion of the police or because of lack of faith in legal measures (Renvoize, 1978).

A crime may be bought to the notice of the police or courts by victims, witness or other concerned person but no further action taken. This may be the victim's choice: he or she may decide against legal involvement. According to Renvoize (1978) so many women victims refuse to testify in court against their husbands that police often feel they are wasting their time doing anything for them. Alternatively, the victim or family member may want the police to intervene as an outside authority to frighten the offender rather than to arrest him. In other cases police inaction may be due to a view that domestic incidents are trivial, taking up time which would be better spent attending to 'serious' crime, or that domestic violence is normal rather than criminal. Whatever the reason, police inaction has been well documented by the National Women's Aid Federation in the UK, as well as in the United States by Bard (1971) and in West Germany by Haffner (1977). The failure of some judges and magistrates to take family violence seriously has also been noted (Renvoize, 1978; Coote and Gill, 1979).

One actual or imagined characteristic of much family violence makes the victim less inclined to complain and outsiders less inclined to take notice if he or she does complain: in some cases the offender is, or is believed to be, reacting to provocation from the victim and the crime is seen as natural justice. A development from this idea is reflected in the literature concerning supposed masochistic characteristics of battered wives (Waites, 1977; Price and Armstrong, 1978) and in treatment programmes aimed only at the victims. However, although some women may provoke their partners, research (admittedly biased to the women's point of view) suggests that this happens only in a minority of cases (Gelles, 1974; Dobash and Dobash, 1977; Hilberman and Munson, 1977). In those cases which do involve provocation, only in unusual circumstances would a violent reaction appear to be justified; for example, the provocation may be no more than criticizing heavy drinking (Hanks and Rosenbaum, 1977; Price and Armstrong, 1978).

Ideally, to estimate the prevalence of violence between couples one should survey a representative sample of the general population. However, there are ethical and procedural difficulties in carrying out surveys on such private and potentially embarrassing subjects, and no such information is available as yet for Britain.

In the United States several surveys have been reported; for example, that of Prescott and Letko (1977), who advertised in *Ms* magazine for readers who had experienced marital violence, and that of Roy (1977) who collected data from women contacting a Women's Aid crisis centre. However, the women in these surveys cannot be assumed to be representative of the general population: battered women who know about crisis centres and who seek help from them may differ in significant ways from other battered women. Similarly, battered women who read magazines concerned with feminist issues may differ from battered women in general.

Less biased information is available from the National Crime Survey (Gaquin, 1977), with data from interviews with members of 60 000 households selected to match the 1970 census data. The results of this survey suggest that 3.9 in every 1000 women are assaulted by their husbands or ex-husbands per year while only 0.9 in every 1000 men are assaulted by their partners or ex-partners. Unfortunately separate figures were not obtained for couples living together and for separated couples. Of the assaults, 56.8% resulted in injury, 23.7% required medical care, 14.3% caused a need for hospital treatment, and 21.2% resulted in 1 day or more lost from work.

Steinmetz (1977*a*) studied domestic violence in a sample of 49 families in Delaware, using interviews, questionnaires and daily conflict-recording sheets. Over a recording period of 1 week there were no incidents of physical aggression between spouses. However, the questionnaire data suggested that physical aggression had been used to resolve conflict at least once in the past in 60% of the families. In 10% of the families, physical aggression was 'almost always' used to resolve arguments. Unfortunately the families may not have been representative of the general population since the sample only included households with telephones and intact families with at least two children aged between 3 and 18. Out of 217 families selected, only 125 were contacted, 25 of these refused to participate, and of the remainder only 49 completed the recording sheets. Of the participating families only 35% of the husbands took part. Steinmetz also mentions a Hawthorn effect in daily recording with some participants made more aware of family interactions and avoiding overt conflict to a greater extent than usual.

In a larger research programme, Straus, Gelles and Steinmetz studied violence between 2143 couples selected as representative of American families with respect to age, race and socioeconomic status (Straus, 1977*b*; Gelles, 1978). During the year prior to being interviewed 3.8% of these couples reported that there had been one or more incidents of wife beating, with an average frequency of 1.7 beatings per year, although this covered a wide variation in frequency. Since higher rates were found in a number of pilot studies, Straus (1977*b*) suggests that there may have been under-reporting in the larger programme because violence is so normal in some families that minor incidents were easily unnoticed or forgotten, because the victim was too ashamed or the attacker too guilty to admit to severely violent incidents, or because possibly more violent separated and divorced couples were omitted from the sample. Alternatively, the sampling or the research methods used in the pilot studies may have biased their results and the larger study may have been more accurate.

It is possible that these surveys are not revealing the true extent of the problem. However, the figures as they stand do indicate that violence between partners in the United States is widespread and that a significant proportion of incidents of domestic violence result in physical injury and time lost from work. One cannot assume that a similar amount of violence occurs (or does not occur) in the United Kingdom. The American experience highlights the difficulties of research in this area but without surveys of the general population like the American National Crime Survey it is impossible to estimate the size of the problem.

Characteristics of violence between partners

Some of the information on characteristics of spouse abuse comes only from interviews with battered wives in refuges. Such information is inevitably biased to the victims' point of view. In addition it is possible that there are features in the violence they have experienced not typical of spouse abuse in the general population. Unfortunately, as yet there are no comparative studies involving victims who have gone to refuges and victims from the same population who have not sought this assistance. Bearing this in mind, however, the patterns of violence revealed from this limited source are important in their own right for helping our understanding of spouse abuse.

Types of violence

According to the data obtained from women in Scottish refuges by Dobash and Dobash (1979) violent incidents most commonly took the form of 'punching the face or body', with 'kicking, kneeing or butting' being the second most typical form. 'Slapping, pushing or pulling' were also very frequent, with 'hitting with an object or weapon' and 'attempts to drown, smother or strangle' much less common.

In the American general population survey reported by Straus (1977*b*) 'pushing, shoving or grabbing' was rated as the most common form of violence committed by both husbands and wives. For husbands 'slapping' had the next highest incidence, but for wives 'throwing' was more common. Use of a weapon did not figure prominently in either of these surveys, although in the US National Crime Survey (Gaquin, 1977) weapons were listed as having been used in 29.7% of spouse abuse incidents with 'use of guns' accounting for 11.3% of incidents and 'use of knives' 10.6%.

The differences between these figures may reflect cultural differences in choice of violence, differences between violence experienced by women in refuges as against other women, or sex differences in choice of violence. Further investigation is needed to explore the bases of these differences. Valid comparisons would be easier if investigators gave fuller details of the types of violence found, without combining data into a small number of categories—unless there could be general agreement on what categories to use.

'Rape' is listed as 'other' violence together with 'bite' and 'stand on' by Dobash and Dobash (1979) but neither rape nor any other form of sexual abuse is mentioned by Straus (1977*b*). Gaquin (1977) excluded information on marital rape because of the low incidence recorded. However, as mentioned previously, it is possible that sexual assaults occur but are not classed as violence by some of the women concerned.

Severity of violence

The homicide rates already mentioned provide one index of severity. Further indications come from the National Crime Survey data: 56.8% of spouse abuse incidents resulted in injury, 23.7% requiring medical care and 14.3% hospital treatment (Gaquin, 1977). Rounsaville (1978*a*, *b*) interviewed women in a hospital casualty room and found that with the women he was able to identify as battered the main injuries were contusions, lacerations and broken bones (even broken toes in one case). Of the battered women interviewed in Scottish refuges in the study by Dobash and Dobash (1979), 70% reported that the latest violence against them resulted in bruises, 13% in cuts, 5% in hair pulled out, 4% in fractured bones.

Serious injuries were also reported by many of the battered women interviewed at Chiswick by Gayford (1978). He lists physical damage ranging from bruises to retinal damage (in two cases) and in one case epilepsy resulting from injuries.

Again there is insufficient comparative data to show whether there is a difference in the severity of the violence experienced by those victims who go to refuges and those victims who do not.

In psychological terms the severity of this violence is unmeasurable. However, anecdotal information from those who have worked with battered women bears witness to the severity of the psychological damage, inflicted both on the victims and on children involved (Lion, 1977; NSPCC School of Social Work, 1977; Melville, 1978; Renvoize, 1978; Dobash and Dobash, 1979).

Frequency of violent incidents

The data reported by Straus (1977*b*) indicate a wide variation in the frequency of assaults. One-third of the couples who admitted violent episodes reported only one assault per year; another third reported five or more assaults per year, including some who experienced violence weekly.

History of violence within the relationship

The Scottish women interviewed in refuges for the Dobash and Dobash study (1979) were questioned about the onset of violence. Twenty-three per cent reported violent incidents before marriage; 84% had experienced one or more assaults within the first 3 years of marriage. Only 8% were not assaulted until after 5 years of marriage. Gayford (1978) reported a similar proportion of battered women—one-quarter—experiencing violence before marriage or cohabitation.

We do not know how many relationships end in the very early stages because of violence by either partner.

Precipitating factors

In the United States National Crime Survey, 70.3% of incidents of spouse abuse occurred between 6 p.m. and 6 a.m. Similarly, Gelles (1977) reported that in the violent families he studied 78% of assaults took place between 5 p.m. and 7 a.m. For Gelles' families, weekends were much more dangerous than other days of the week with 69% of respondents reporting violent incidents on weekends, predominantly on Sundays.

Not surprisingly, since these are the times when most couples are together, the Scottish women in the survey by Dobash and Dobash (1979) also reported that evenings and nights were worse than the day-time, but for them Friday and Saturday nights were more violent than Sundays.

This difference may reflect the influence of drinking patterns in the different populations. The disinhibiting effect of alcohol in contributing to marital violence has been suggested by several researchers, e.g. Martin (1978) and Shainess (1977). Gayford (1978) reported that 44 of the 100 women he interviewed at Chiswick were only battered when their husbands had been drinking. From the survey by Roy (1977) it appeared that 80% of the men who drank occasionally only beat their wives when they were drunk. However, this was not true of the heavy drinkers, who tended not to restrict their assaults to those times. The relationship between drinking and marital violence needs more detailed investigation, particularly in view of recent findings concerning the effects of different amounts and types of alcohol on aggressive behaviour (Taylor and Gammon, 1975). In addition, it is relevant to consider the results of a study reported by Lang *et al.* (1975) that male subjects who believed that they had drunk alcohol were more aggressive than those who had the same drink but who believed it to be non-alcoholic.

Gerson (1978), studying police records on alcohol-related acts of violence in Ontario, Canada, found a difference between marital assaults and non-marital assaults. In the latter, in 75% of cases the victim was drinking but not the offender. This was very rare for marital assaults: only 13% of these occurred after the victim had been drinking but not the assailant. Half of the remaining incidents followed drinking by both assailant and victim, and half followed drinking by the offender only.

Drinking also features as a subject of arguments, often leading to violence. Almost all of the violent incidents described by battered women were preceded by a confrontation. Commonly conflicts centred on expectations about domestic work, often with the husband demanding immediate attention to his needs and the wife not prepared to comply. As well as drinking, other sources of conflict were sexual jealousy, usually unfounded according to the women, and problems regarding allocation of money. (Flynn, 1977; Roy, 1977; Dobash and Dobash, 1979).

Possessiveness and sexual jealousy were also found to be major sources of conflict leading to violence in a survey of battered women attending a mental health centre and a hospital emergency room in Connecticut (Rounsaville, 1978*a*). Rounsaville commented that the degree of possessiveness often seemed extreme and involved preventing wives from going on errands or from visiting or having visits even from female relatives and friends.

In Steinmetz's survey of a sample of Delaware families (Steinmetz, 1977*a*), she divided the conflicts leading to violence into two categories: those concerned with 'major' issues such as child discipline and sex role problems, and those concerned with 'minor' irritations, idiosyncratic to the couple concerned, such as clashes over untidiness. She admits that what she might classify as a minor and trival complaint could be a major issue to the couple concerned.

The confrontation preceding violence is not necessarily verbal according to Dobash and Dobash (1979).However, Flynn (1979) and Gelles (1977) stressed the importance of verbal aggression as a factor leading to physical aggression. It is suggested that the less articulate partner compensates by using physical violence to resolve conflicts. As yet there is no hard evidence to support this suggestion. This and other aspects of the relationship between verbal and physical aggression obviously need further investigation.

Avoiding violence

When threatened by a violent husband only eight of the Chiswick women seen by Gayford (1975) tried to hit back; 19 attempted to escape when they thought violence was imminent, but 42 could see no way of avoiding the violence.

Of the women interviewed by Dobash and Dobash (1979) only four of the 109 tried to retaliate. Most responded by remaining passive to avoid aggravating the violence. Many could see when violence threatened but reported that they were unable to prevent it whatever action they took.

Theories of spouse abuse

A variety of theories concerning the origins of marital violence have been presented in the literature, and some authors (Stahley, 1977; Rounsaville, 1978*b*) have tried to test hypotheses arising from some of these theories against what facts are now available. Unfortunately, not all speculation on this subject lends itself to empirical testing, and even when testable hypotheses can be drawn from a theory the facts needed may be too difficult to obtain. The hidden nature of spouse abuse and the biased state of our information concerning it limit what hypotheses can be checked.

Psychological or pathological explanations

Implicit in much of the theoretical literature and in media commentary on spouse abuse is an assumption that marital abuse is caused by mental disorder on the part of the batterer or his or her victim.

In some cases marital violence is apparently related to the abnormal mental state of the battering spouse. Psychosis may be implicated although this appears to be a rare cause: for example, Faulk (1977) assessed the mental state of 23 men charged with seriously assaulting their wives and found only two suffering from psychosis.

Alternatively, poor temper control and violent outbursts may be attributed to the effects of organic conditions or of metabolic disorders, particularly those resulting in hypoglycaemia. Elliott (1977) discusses the role of the limbic system in controlling violent behaviour and cites examples of clients whose violence resulted from damage or disease to the limbic system. Amongst these were some whose temporal lobe epilepsy had led to sclerosis of part of the temporal lobe, those with minor head injury leading to contusion of the temporal lobes, and those in whom tumours or operations to remove tumours had affected the limbic system. Others had temporal lobe damage following infection such as viral encephalitis, or as a result of stroke, Huntington's chorea or brain abscess.

Very little research has been carried out on characteristics of husband or wife batterers so we cannot know what proportion of batterers suffer from problems such as the above. On the other hand it appears that only a minority of sufferers from these disorders do become violent (Elliott, 1977), which suggests that even for this minority additional causes of violence should be sought beyond disease or brain damage.

With regard to violent women, some investigators have blamed premenstrual tension for violent behaviour (e.g. Morton *et al.*, 1953; Dalton, 1964). However, more recent researchers throw doubt on this conclusion, querying the validity of figures obtained in the earlier investigations and stressing that relationships found between menstrual phases and crime are correlational and not necessarily causal (e.g. Parlee, 1973).

There has been some speculation about the personalities of wife and husband batterers. Symonds (1978) classifies violent husbands into three types: the immature, impulsive, irritable individual; the dependent, highly anxious, resentful, guilt-ridden individual whose violence follows drinking; and the overly controlled, compulsively hostile, arrogant, vindictive individual. He offers only limited explanation for the origins of these characteristics and no reason for the association with violence. How many non-battering husbands have similar personalities and how do they differ from these individuals? In addition Symonds' speculation derives from work with a small (but unspecified) number of clients who cannot be assumed to be representative of wife beaters in general.

Similarly, Shainess (1977) describes certain personality types characteristic of wife beaters: the passive-aggressive individual whose helplessness and vulnerability lead to violence when triggered by conflict with his wife; the obsessive-compulsive individual who attacks when his defences are threatened; the sadistic type who attacks his wife primarily because she is the closest person to prey on. Shainess offers no data to substantiate this typology.

Psychoanalytic explanations of spouse abuse tend to focus on the victim rather than the batterer, although some writers do speculate on the psychodynamics of the assailant. Lesse (1979), for example, suggests that wife beating represents to the violent husband punishment of his symbolically loved–hated mother. This is clearly untestable and contributes nothing to an understanding of the roots of marital violence.

The frustration–aggression hypothesis of the Yale group (Dollard *et al.*, 1939) is sometimes invoked as an explanation of domestic violence. Dollard *et al.* contended that frustrations inevitably and innately lead to aggression. Later experimental evidence caused the Yale group to broaden this hypothesis to admit that reactions other than aggression could also follow frustration (Miller, 1941). Despite the attraction of the hypothesis in terms of its apparent ability to account for everyday experience, it has severe limitations due to individual differences in what constitutes frustration.

Both Flynn (1977) and Gayford (1978) found that a substantial proportion of the battered wives whom they interviewed had husbands with criminal records for violent offences, including cases of armed robbery and attempted murder. Other researchers in this area have neglected to check whether and to what degree the battering spouse is or has been violent to people other than his or her spouse. It would seem that these are fundamental questions for research. Without information on these points one cannot assume that marital violence is a distinct problem, separate from violence in general. Until this information is obtained it would seem sensible to defer speculation about the causes of spouse abuse, particularly speculation which implies that the origins of marital violence reside solely in the victim or in properties of the marriage interaction.

Those theories which focus on characteristics of the battered spouse as a cause of violence apparently start from one of two assumptions: that he or she consciously or unconsciously precipitates the violence by provoking the batterer, or that he or she chooses a violent partner to live with. The first possibility, suggested by Gayford (1978), Price and Armstrong (1978) and others, has been discussed earlier in this chapter. The point was then made that there is little evidence of provocation sufficient to justify violence. However, the information available on this is biased, coming almost exclusively from the victims rather than their assailants, so that further research is needed in order to clarify this issue.

The second possibility, that the victim seeks a partner known to be violent, also lack empirical support. Although Dobash and Dobash (1979) found that almost one-quarter of the women they interviewed had been assaulted by their partner before marriage, there is no proof that they married these men because of the violence. They may have married them despite their violence.

Following the above assumptions, some theorists have suggested that the victims seek violence to satisfy masochistic needs (e.g. Shainess, 1977, 1979; Waites, 1977). This view is criticized by Rounsaville (1978*b*), whose interviews with battered women suggested that few had experienced violence in previous relationships or as children, and that few felt that they deserved to be assaulted or approved of any violence between husband and wife. Other researchers critical of the masochism hypothesis include Dobash and Dobash (1979), Marsden (1978), Melville (1978) and Symonds (1979).

That some women remain with their battering husbands or leave only for short periods is taken by some writers to provide evidence of their masochistic tendencies. A number of points can be made which argue against this suggestion. Information from battered wives indicates that many would have left earlier if they had known of somewhere to go (Gelles, 1977; Roy, 1977; Gayford, 1978; Rounsaville, 1978*b*; Dobash and Dobash, 1979). Refuges have only recently appeared on the scene and are still not widely available; there may be no provision of public housing, such as local authority accommodation in Britain, for women who are officially regarded to have made themselves homeless; some may have no friends or relatives with whom they can stay; where the husbands have been possessive and jealous the wives may have lost contact with friends and relatives (Rounsaville, 1978*a*; Dobash and Dobash, 1979). Even when accommodation can be found women may be trapped in the relationship by economic need, particularly if they have young children or poor employment prospects (Gelles, 1977; Prescott and Letko, 1977; Straus, 1977*a*; Star, 1978).

As Rounsaville (1978*b*) comments, battered women may stay with their partner in spite of the violence rather than because of it as the masochism hypothesis would imply. There may be positive features in the relationship which override the negative aspect, the violence. This is particularly likely where the violence is not severe, is infrequent, or if the wife believes the partner's promise to reform.

Another possibility is that the women stays because of fear of what her husband will do if she leaves. It is not unusual for the battering spouse to threaten to kill the wife, their children or himself if she leaves him (Roy, 1977; Rounsaville, 1978*b*; Dobash and Dobash, 1979).

To explain why women stay when there is no apparent reason for them to do so the concept of 'learned helplessness' is sometimes invoked (Walker, 1977). This suggests that when she is unable to control her partner's violence, the battered woman becomes depressed and helpless, lacking the motivational, emotional and cognitive attributes and the self-esteem necessary for her to initiate action to escape from the situation. There is partial support for this hypothesis in that many battered women report being depressed (Prescott and Letko, 1977; Gayford, 1978; Rounsaville, 1978*b*) and that they tend to have low coping abilities (Star, 1978). However, a proper test of the hypothesis should start with comparison of battered and non-battered women and women before and after experiencing battering with respect to the characteristcs such as depression and poor coping ability that are predicted by the theory.

Explanations focusing on social interactions

The preceding discussion considered theories in which the causes of marital violence were sought within characteristics of individuals. Alternative approaches have focused on interpersonal or interactional processes as the source of violence.

Following from the resources theory of Blood and Wolfe (1960), Goode (1971) has developed a social exchange theory to explain family violence. He describes the family (like society) as a power system in which four sets of resources are in operation to maintain stability: economic variables, prestige or respect, love or friendship, and force or threat of force. As a child the batterer, murderer or child abuser learns to use force or the threat of force by example from his parents and others in authority. As an adult he will resort to force if he feels there is an imbalance in family transactions, if for example he feels he is missing out on respect or love he is owed, and if force is the only resource he has at his command. Goode (1971) suggests that force is used more by those in the poorer classes partly because they have less alternative resources and partly because their socialization experiences teach them to depend more on force. Not all researchers would agree that the poorer classes do use more force, however. Although criminal statistics show more marital abuse in the lower classes (Gaquin, 1977; McClintock, 1978), this may reflect the fact that a greater proportion of the population belongs to the lower classes, or it may be that the middle classes are more skilled, have more resources, or have greater motivation to hide their offences.

Equity theory (Walster, *et al.*, 1978) is similarly concerned with what individuals feel they contribute to a relationship and what they receive in return. If one partner perceives an inequality in the exchange he (or she) may react with anger or resentment before seeking ways to increase his (or her) benefits. However, if the partner perceives himself as the exploiter, rather than attempting to make the exchange more equitable he may restore equity psychologically, reducing shame or guilt for exploitation by convincing himself that the victim deserves to be exploited. As in the theory of cognitive dissonance (Davis and

Jones, 1960), the exploiter may begin to denigrate his victim. Under the terms of this theory the assaulting husband may either be reacting to perceived exploitation by his wife or may be justifying his own exploitation of her by debasing her psychologically and physically.

Palmer (1972) and Henry and Short (1954) use role interference theories to explain violence, suggesting that an individual becomes violent towards the person he (or she) perceives to be frustrating his (or her) attempts satisfactorily to play out competing roles. An example given by Humphrey (1978) is that of the alcoholic whose drinking interferes with performance of his occupational role and consequently also his performance in the role of husband. He then behaves aggressively towards the person whom he perceives as making demands and having expectations he cannot meet—his wife.

Straus (1973, 1977*a*) and Gelles (1974) propose a general systems theory of domestic violence, incorporating many of the causative factors suggested by other theorists. Straus (1973) puts forward a circular model with the scene set for violence within the family by antecedents such as cultural and social attitudes (towards violence, towards wives and towards women), by family structure, and by individual characteristics of the family members. Violence may be precipitated by factors such as stress and inter-individual conflict and may be followed by consequences which maintain or escalate violence in the family and in society.

This model emphasizes the importance of the family as a training ground for physical aggression, with violent behaviour being learned through modelling and reinforcement, from parents and other authority figures, from siblings and peers and through the media (following Bandura and Ross, 1961).

Overall the theoretical model put forward by Straus and Gelles can be criticized for being too broad, with too many non-specific determinants suggested, and with no pointers to the most important determinants. There is sound empirical evidence that aggressive behaviour can be learned through modelling from live and filmed models (e.g. Bandura and Walters, 1963). It would, therefore, be parsimonious to suggest that social learning may provide sufficient explanation for marital violence without recourse to the additional determinants postulated by Straus and Gelles. However, there has been little research specifically concerned with the learning of marital violence.

Although some data are available on battered wives' experiences of violence, both as abused children or by witnessing violence between their parents (Gelles, 1977; Gayford, 1978), unfortunately, the few researchers who have checked on batterers' childhood experiences of violence have relied on indirect information from the wives (Roy, 1977; Gayford, 1978). Without further investigation of batterers' experiences of violence in childhood and in later life it is difficult to assess the validity of the social learning explanation of marital violence.

In general, theorizing about marital violence seems to have moved to quickly for the information available. The priorities now should be to obtain more adequate data on spouse abuse, particularly data on batterers rather than victims, and on the setting and precipitating events, maintaining factors and other social learning variables, and to formulate and test hypotheses more closely related to available evidence as a prelude to further model building.

Intervention and prevention

The preceding discussion highlights some significant gaps in our understanding of the factors causing and maintaining violence between couples. Because of these gaps general policies for the reduction or elimination of marital violence put forward in the literature must be considered as measures worth trying experimentally or measures called for on other grounds rather than as clear guidelines for lessening violence.

Into this category fall suggestions to the effect that improving the status of women as wives and as members of society will reduce marital violence (Lesse, 1979; Straus, 1977*a*). There are strong humanitarian and egalitarian reasons for improving the status of women and for changing situations in which men have authority over women purely on the basis of their gender, as for example in some business and insurance dealings, some taxation laws, some religious mores and in some employment and housing practices. However, as yet we have no proof that removal of these abuses will result in a lessening of marital violence.

Similarly, although there are ethical and humanitarian (and possibly aesthetic) reasons for censoring violence against women in the mass media, we have no evidence that such a move will necessarily lead to a reduction in violence between partners, as hoped by London (1977), Steinmetz (1977*b*) and Straus (1977*a*). The same is true of banning physical punishment in schools or by parents in the home, the stopping of violent sports such as boxing, and the lessening of life stresses, for example by making contraception more easily available or by improving housing standards. All of these measures may be desirable for humanitarian reasons but we cannot be certain that any or all or them will lessen marital violence to any extent.

While there is a lack of research evidence to identify which general policies deserve priority, there are nevertheless a number of specific measures which should be adopted to help couples who are already in a battering relationship. The first essential, and one that is already receiving attention from many women's groups, is to meet the needs of victims. On the basis of research with battered women at Canterbury's Women's Centre, Pahl (1978) sums up these needs as medical treatment if the victim has been injured, followed by protection, accommodation, support and advice.

In addition, one can consider what courses of action are open to victims at present and how services could be improved to provide better help to victims, whichever course they choose. In broad terms, victims may leave home temporarily or permanently, seek outside help to restrain the violent partner or to force him (or her) to leave, or remain in the situation and attempt to introduce changes to limit the amount and the effects of the partner's violence.

Leaving home

A number of researchers have reported that many women living with violent partners would leave them if they had somewhere to go and that many women living in refuges would have left their partners earlier if the refuges had been available (Gelles, 1977; Roy, 1977; Gayford, 1978; Dobash and Dobash, 1979). The publicity surrounding the founding of the first refuge for battered women by Erin Pizzey in 1972 in Chiswick, London, made it obvious that there was a considerable demand for accommodation for these women. This led to the formation of Women's Aid centres in many British towns and to the founding of refuges throuhgout Britain as well as in the United States, in Australia and some parts of western Europe (Fojtik, 1977; Haffner, 1977; Karl, 1977; Novak and Meisner, 1977). However, it is clear that provision is not meeting demand in that the present refuges are often overcrowded, and the position is being made worse by the closure of some refuges through failure to meet health or safety regulations or through lack of financial support.

The women's groups who have founded and helped to run these refuges have made an impressive contribution to the alleviation of the distress suffered by battered women, not only by providing short term accommodation but additionally in many cases by helping with finding permanent housing, by advice on divorce and other legal measures, by assistance in finding employment and child-minding facilities, and by providing mutual support.

The major handicaps under which many of the refuges function arise from lack of community and state support so that finance is a problem, there are difficulties in establishing working relationships with government agencies for assistance in finding more permanent housing, welfare assistance and legal aid, and in some cases there is community or local government opposition to the use of buildings as sheltered accommodation. To some extent this lack of support, or even active opposition, may be the result of dislike of the refuges' links with the Women's Movement or disapproval of the way some refuges are run. Even amongst the groups managing shelters there are disagreements over issues such as whether counselling should be mandatory or not, whether any one-to-one or group counselling should be provided, whether the organizational structure should be completely democratic to encourage self-help or whether this leads to inefficiency, whether men helpers or professionals should be allowed in or all males banned, and whether or not there should be restrictions on the number of times women can come back to refuges and on their length of stay (Lynch and Norris, 1977; Naples and Janes, 1977; Ridington, 1977; Leghorn, 1978; Melville, 1978; Pahl, 1978). It is possible that in some areas some battered women may be reluctant to use a refuge because of its policies.

It is clear that more short term accommodation is needed for battered women, particularly for those with children. However, there is also an urgent need to evaluate and compare the different types of short term accommodation that could be provided, to consider what is appropriate as long term accommodation for single parents, and how to ensure easy transition between the two.

As mentioned earlier in this chapter, finding accommodation is not the only problem deterring battered women from leaving their partners. Information or assistance is frequently needed on matters such as obtaining welfare assistance and other financial problems, on finding employment or on retraining opportunities, on legal matters such as divorce and separation, and on finding child-minding facilities. Such problems are not peculiar to battered women and although it is useful for advice centres to be connected with refuges this sort of help should also be provided for battered women who do not want to separate even temporarily as well as for non-battered women who are considering separation. There are advantages in having such centres located centrally and away from refuges so that they can be well advertised without affecting the safety of women in refuges.

Seeking help to change, restrain or remove the violent partner

If the violent partner accepts that he (or she) has a problem and is prepared to seek help, some form of treatment may be possible depending on the cause of his violent behaviour. If the violence is associated with organic or metabolic disorder, medication or dietary changes may be helpful (Elliott, 1977). Similarly, if alcoholism is a contributory factor, psychological treatment or referral to Alcoholics Anonymous may be appropriate. Where loss of control or inappropriate reaction to frustration are involved there are some psychological treatments which may be beneficial, e.g. behavioural self-control training (Kauffman and Wagner, 1972). This type of treatment is likely only to be available through professionals, such as some clinical psychologists, psychiatrists or social workers. If the violent partner is clearly psychologically disturbed it may be possible to have him (or her) committed to a psychiatric hospital where treatment such as the above can be attempted. However, there is obviously a greater chance of any treatment being successful if the individual accepts it voluntarily.

Little has been published on the use of group treatment with violent partners, although this would seem a promising and cost-effective treatment approach. Malville (1978) reports that group therapy is offered to battering husbands through the Chiswick refuge and that some men, usually the less brutal ones, attend group discussion sessions there. She suspects that some attend as a way of getting their wives back, although this should not matter provided some improvement in their bahaviour results.

Marital therapy is another alternative provided that both partners are prepared to take part. Therapy based on a social learning approach (e.g. Jacobson and Margolin, 1979) may be helpful in teaching both partners to recognize the antecedents of violence in their relationship and in assisting them to develop more constructive methods of resolving disagreements.

If the violent partner cannot be persuaded to seek treatment it may be possible to deter him (or her) from violence by the threat of police involvement or by actually calling the police or taking legal action. As discussed earlier in this chapter there has been criticism of police handling of domestic incidents. However, research in the United States shows that given appropriate training the police can intervene effectively (International Association of Chiefs of Police, 1977; Stephens, 1977). In one study, Bard (1971) set up a training scheme for selected policemen to specialize in domestic problems. They were trained to act as mediators and to make appropriate referrals to social service and mental health agencies rather than to arrest or ignore incidents. One incidental spin-off from this scheme was a big drop in injuries to police. Dobash and Dobash (1979) and Renvoize (1978) suggest that clearer guidelines from their chief officers could help the British police deal more effectively with marital violence.

In some American states and in England and Wales an alternative to police involvement and criminal law proceedings is provided by the civil law (Dellapa, 1977; Coote and Gill, 1979). Under the Domestic Violence and Matrimonial Proceedings Act of 1976 and the Domestic Proceedings and Magistrates Court Act of 1978 in England and Wales, victims can ask for injunctions prohibiting the violent spouse from the matrimonial home. A power of arrest can be attached to the injunction so that police can arrest the spouse if he or she re-offends. Married people can seek this protection through the county courts or the High Court and also through the cheaper, less formal and more private magistrates' courts. Coote and Gill (1979) claim that certain improvements in the law are still necessary, such as ensuring that proceedings are heard from beginning to end by the same judge or magistrate and extension of these laws to Scotland and Northern Ireland. The establishment of family courts with judges, magistrates and lawyers chosen for their knowledge and interest in family matters, as in some American states and in Australia, would also be an improvement, as would an increase in the number of women entering the legal profession. To many women the courts and the laws would seem less frightening and more approachable if they were less dominated by men. Female judges and lawyers may not differ significantly from their male counterparts in their attitudes and beliefs; however, female victims might be happier to appear before other females in the expectation that they would be more understanding about the problems faced by women.

Social workers and general medical practitioners are often approached for help following incidents of marital violence. It would seem from comments in the literature that there is room for considerable improvement in providing them with appropriate training to handle these incidents (Jordan and Packman, 1978;

North West Region of the National Women's Aid Federation, 1978; Renvoize, 1978).

Remaining in the situation

For a variety of reasons some victims may prefer to remain with a battering spouse and to take no action leading to intervention by outsiders. For these people there are still some measures that can be taken to improve the situation. Geller and Walsh (1977) suggest looking for the antecedents of impending violence and planning ways to avoid it. When violence is inevitable certain practical measures may be helpful, e.g. having spare car keys available, having a room with a lock on the inside, keeping some money hidden for escape purposes, ensuring that there is always an easy exit from the house. Geller and Walsh (1977) and Ball and Wyman (1977) also suggest that self-defence lessons or martial arts training might be useful.

Conclusions

The demand for refuge places and the use made of women's aid centres are evidence that present resources for helping the victims of marital violence need to be expanded. As a matter of urgency ways need to be found to make assistance available to a greater number of victims and alternative methods of helping should be investigated.

However, helping victims cope or escape is not a long term solution to the problem of violence between couples. At the individual level the aim should be to change the behaviour of the violent partner so that he (or she) no longer physically abuses the same or a new victim, and following the social learning model he must be stopped from teaching his violent behaviour to his children. At present, although there are methods available for helping violent individuals to learn alternative and more acceptable ways of behaving, there are not sufficient resources for doing this on a large scale, and there is no legal framework by which training could be made compulsory.

We do not know the size of the problem we are dealing with, nor have we sufficient information to predict what general measures should be effective for reducing violence between partners in furture generations. Research in this area could now usefully focus on the following:

(1) An in-depth study of couples in a battering relationship, looking specifically at what factors cause and maintain the violence, and looking in detail at the batterers' experience of violence—what violence they have observed, what violence they have suffered and what violence they have inflicted on victims other than the current partner. It is important that this information be obtained from the batterer and the victim, not from the victim only, as in most previous research.

(2) Detailed surveys of the general population to give a clearer idea of the extent of the problem and its distribution in the population. Information should be obtained about violence against partners in homosexual as well as heterosexual relationships, and again details of their experience of violence should be obtained from both partners.

References

Ball, P. G., and Wyman, E. (1977). Battered wives and powerlessness. *Victimology*, **2**, 545–552.

Bandura, A., and Ross, S. (1961). Transmission of aggression through imitation of aggressive models. *Journal of Abnormal Psychology*, **63**, 575–582.

Bandura, A., and Walters, R. H. (1963). *Social Learning and Personality Development*. New York: Holt, Rinehart and Winston.

Bard, M. (1971). The study and modification of intra-familial violence, in *The Control of Aggression and Violence* (Ed. J. L. Singer). New York: Academic Press, pp. 154–164.

Bard, M. (1977). Family crisis intervention: from concept to implementation, in *Battered Women* (Ed. M. Roy). New York: Van Nostrand Reinhold, pp. 172–192.

Blood, R. O., and Wolfe, E. M. (1960). *Husbands and Wives: The Dynamics of Married Living*. New York: The Free Press.

Coote, A., and Gill, T. (1979). *Battered Women and the New Law*. London: Inter-Action Inprint.

Dalton, K. (1964). *The Premenstrual Syndrome*. London: Heinemann.

Davidson, T. (1977). Wife beating, in *Battered Women* (Ed. M. Roy), New York: Van Nostrand Reinhold, pp. 2–23.

Davis, K. E., and Jones, E. E. (1960). Changes in interpersonal perception as a means of reducing cognitive dissonance. *Journal of Abnormal and Social Psychology*, **61**, 402–410.

Dellapa, F. (1977). Mediation and the community dispute centre. In *Battered Women* (Ed. M. Roy). New York: Van Nostrand Reinhold, pp. 239–249.

DHSS(Department of Health and Social Security), Department of the Environment, Scottish Office, Welsh Office (1976) *Observations on the Report from the Select Committee on Marriage*. London: HMSO.

Dobash, R. E., and Dobash, R. P. (1977). Wives: the appropriate victims of marital violence. *Victimology*, **2**, 426–442.

Dobash, R. E., and Dobash, R. P. (1979). *Violence against Wives*. New York: The Free Press.

Dobash, R. E., Dobash, R. P., Cavanah, C., and Wilson, M. (1977). Wife beating: the victims speak. *Victimology*, **2**, 608–622.

Dollard, J., Dobb, L., Miller, N. E., Mowrer, O., and Sears, R. R. (1939). *Frustration and Aggression*. New Haven, Conn.: Yale University Press.

Elliott, F. A. (1977). The neurology of explosive rage: the dyscontrol syndrome, reprinted in *Battered Women* (Ed. M. Roy) New York: Van Nostrand Reinhold, pp. 98–109.

Faulk, M. (1977). Men who assault their wives, in *Battered Women* (Ed. M. Roy). New York: Van Nostrand Reinhold, pp. 119–126.

Fields, M. (1977). Wife beating: facts and figures. *Victimology*, **2**, 643–646.

Fields, M., and Kirchner, R. M. (1978). Battered women are still in need. *Victimology*, **3**, 216–226.

Flynn, J. P. (1977). Recent findings related to wife abuse. *Social Casework*, **1977**, 13–21.

Fojtik, K. M. (1977). The NOW Domestic Violence and Spouse Assault Project. *Victimology*, **2**, 653–657.

Gaquin, D. A. (1977). Spouse abuse; data from the National Crime Survey. *Victimology*, **2**, 632–657.

Gayford, J. (1975). Wife battery. *British Medical Journal*, **i**, 194–197.

Gayford, J. (1978). Battered wives, in *Violence and the Family* (Ed. J. P. Martin). Chichester: John Wiley, pp. 19–39.

Geller, J., and Walsh, J. (1977). A treatment model for the abused spouse. *Victimology*, **2**, 627–628.

Gelles, R. J. (1974). *The Violent Home*. Beverly Hills, Calif.: Sage Publications.

Gelles, R. J. (1977). No place to go: the social dynamics of marital violence, in *Battered Women* (Ed. M. Roy). New York: Van Nostrand Reinhold, pp. 46–63.

Gelles, R. J. (1978). Family violence and social policy, in *Violence and the Family* (Ed. J. P. Martin). Chichester: John Wiley, pp. 169–182.

Gerson, L. W. (1978). Alcohol-related acts of violence. *Journal of Studies on Alcohol*, **39**, 1294–1296.

Gibson, E. (1975). *Homicide in England and Wales, 1967–1971*. Home Office Research Study No. 31. London: HMSO.

Gibson, E., and Klein, S. (1969). *Murder 1957–1968*. Home Office Statistical Division Report. London: HMSO.

Goode, W. J. (1964). *The Family*. Englewood Cliffs, N. J.: Prentice-Hall.

Goode, W. J. (1971). Force and violence in the family. *Journal of Marriage and the Family*, **33**, 624–636.

Haffner, S. (1977). Wife abuse in West Germany. *Victimology*, **2**, 472–476.

Hanks, S. E., and Rosenbaum, C. P. (1977). Battered women. *American Journal of Orthopsychiatry*, **47**, 291–306.

Henry, A., and Short, J. (1954). *Suicide and Homicide*. Glencoe, Ill.: Free Press.

Hilberman, E., and Munson, K. (1977). Sixty battered women. *Victimology*, **2**, 460–471.

Humphrey, J. A. (1978). Role interference: An analysis of suicide victims, homicide offenders, and non-violent individuals. *Journal of Clinical Psychiatry*, **26**, 652–655.

International Association of Chiefs of Police (1977). Training keys 245 and 246, reprinted in *Battered Women* (Ed. M. Roy). New York: Van Nostrand Reinhold, pp. 144–164.

Jacobson, N. S., and Margolin, G. (1979). *Marital Therapy*. New York: Brunner/Mazel.

Jordan, B., and Packman, J. (1978). Training for social work with violent families, in *Violence and the Family* (Ed. J. P. Martin). Chichester: John Wiley, pp. 325–343.

Karl, M. (1977). Refuges in Europe. *Victimology*, **2**, 657–666.

Kauffman, L. M., and Wagner, B. R. (1972). Barb: a systematic treatment technology for temper control disorders. *Behavior Therapy*, **3**, 84–90.

Kutun, B. (1977). Legislative needs and solutions, in *Battered Women* (Ed. M. Roy). New York: Van Nostrand Reinhold, pp. 277–287.

Lang, A. R., Goechner, D. J., Adesso, U. J., and Mariatt, A. (1975). Effects of alcohol on aggression in male social drinkers. *Journal of Abnormal Psychology*, **84**, 508–518.

Leghorn, L. (1978). Working with battered women. *Victimology*, **3**, 91–107.

Lesse, S. (1979). The status of violence against women. *American Journal of Psychotherapy*, **33**, 190–200.

Lion, J. R. (1977). Clinical aspects of wife battering, in *Battered Women* (Ed. M. Roy). New York: van Nostrand Reinhold, pp. 126–136.

Loizos, P. (1978). Violence and the family: some Mediterranean examples, in *Violence and the Family* (Ed. J. P. Martin). Chichester: John Wiley, pp. 183–196.

London, J. (1977). Images of violence against women. *Victimology*, **2**, 510–524.

Lynch, C. G., and Norris, T. L. (1977). Services for battered women. *Victimology*, **2**, 553–562.

McClintock, F. H. (1978). Criminological aspects of family violence, in *Violence and the Family* (Ed. J. P. Martin). Chichester: John Wiley, pp. 81–101.

Marsden, D. (1978). Sociological perspectives on family violence, in *Violence and the Family* (Ed. J. P. Martin). Chichester: John Wiley, pp. 103–133.
Martin, J. P. (Ed.) (1978). *Violence and the Family*. Chichester: John Wiley.
May, M. (1978). Violence and the family: a historical perspective, in *Violence and the Family*. (Ed. J. P. Martin). Chichester: John Wiley, pp. 135–167.
Melville, J. (1978). A note on 'Men's Aid', in *Violence and the Family*. (Ed. J. P. Martin). Chichester: John Wiley, pp. 311–313.
Miller, N. E. (1941). The frustration–aggression hypothesis. *Psychological Review*, **38**, 337–342.
Morton, J. H., Additon, H., Addison, R., and Hunt, L. (1953). A clinical study of premenstrual tension. *Ammerican Journal of Obstetrics and Gynecology*, **65**, 1182–1191.
Mushange, T. mwene. (1977). Wife victimization in East and Central Africa. *Victimology*, **2**, 479–485.
Naples, S., and Janes, S. (1977). Letter to the editors. *Victimology*, **2**, 422–423.
North West Region of the National Women's Aid Federation (1978). Battered women and social work, in *Violence and the Family* (Ed. J. P. Martin). Chichester: John Wiley, pp. 315–324.
Novak, D. G., and Meismer, D. T. (1977). A plea for help: one community's response. *Victimology*, **2**, 647–653.
NSPCC School of Social Work (1977). Yo yo children, in *Battered Women* (Ed. M. Roy). New York: Van Nostrand Reinhold, pp. 249–263.
Pahl, J. (1978). *A Refuge for Battered Women*. London: HMSO.
Palmer, S. (1972). *The Violent Society*. New Haven, Conn.: College and University Press.
Parlee, M. B. (1973). The premenstrual syndrome. *Psychological Bulletin*, **80**, 454–465.
Pizzey, E. (1974). *Scream Quietly of the Neighbours will Hear*. Harmonsworth: Penguin Books.
Pleck, E., Pleck, J. H., Grossman, M., and Bart, P. (1977). The battered data syndrome. *Victimology*, **2**, 680–683.
Prescott, S., and Letko, C. (1977). Battered women: a social psychological perspective, in *Battered Women* (Ed. M. Roy). New York: Van Nostrand Reinhold, pp. 72–96.
Price, J., and Armstrong, J. (1978). Battered wives. *Australian and New Zealand Journal of Psychiatry*, **12**, 43–47.
Renvoize, J. (1978). *Web of Violence*. Harmonsworth: Penguin Books.
Ridington, J. (1977). The transition process: a feminist environment as reconstitutive milieu. *Victimology*, **2**, 563–575.
Rounsaville, B. J. (1978*a*). Battered wives: barriers to identification and treatment. *American Journal of Orthopsychiatry*, **48**, 487–494.
Rounsaville, B. J. (1978*b*). Theories in marital violence. *Victimology*, **3**, 11–31.
Roy, M. (Ed.) (1979). *Battered Women*. New York: Van Nostrand Reinhold.
Scott, F. D. (1974). Battered wives. *British Journal of Psychiatry*, **125**, 433–441.
Select Committee on Violence in Marriage (1975). *Report HC 553-i*, London: HMSO.
Shainess, N. (1977). Psychological aspects of wife battering, in *Battered Women* (Ed. M. Roy). New York: Van Nostrand Reinhold, pp. 311–313.
Shainess, N. (1979). Vulnerability to violence. *American Journal of Psychotherapy*, **33**, 174–189.
Stahley, G. B. (1977). A review of selected literature on spousal abuse. *Victimology*, **2**, 591–607.
Star, B. (1978). Comparing battered and non-battered women. *Victimology*, **3**, 32–44.
Steinmetz, S. K. (1977*a*). Violence between spouses to resolve marital fights, in *Battered Women* (Ed. M. Roy). New York: Van Nostrand Reinhold, pp. 63–72.
Steinmetz, S. K. (1977*b*). The battered husband syndrome. *Victimology*, **2**, 499–509.
Steinmetz, S. K. (1977*c*). *The Cycle of Violence*. New York: Praeger.

Stephens, D. W. (1977). Domestic assault: the police response, in *Battered women* (Ed. M. Roy). New York: Van Nostrand Reinhold.

Straus, M. A. (1973). A general systems theory approach to a theory of violence between spouses. *Social Science Information*, **12**, 105–125.

Straus, M. A. (1977*a*). A sociological perspective on the prevention and treatment of wife beating, in *Battered Women* (Ed. M. Roy). New York: Van Nostrand reinhold, pp. 194–239.

Straus, M. A. (1977*b*). Wife beating: how common and why? *Victimology*, **2**, 443–458.

Sutton, J. (1977). The growth of the British Movement for Battered Women. *Victimology*, **2**, 576–584.

Symonds, A. (1979). Violence against women. *American Journal of Psychotherapy*, **33**, 161–173.

Symonds, M. (1978). The psychodynamics of violence-prone marriages. *The American Journal of Psychoanalysis*, **38**, 213–222.

Taylor, S. P., and Gammon, C. B. (1975). Effects of type and dose of alcohol on human physical aggression. *Journal of Personality and Social Psychology*, **32**, 161–175.

Waites, E. A. (1977). Female masochism and enforced restriction of choice. *Victimology*, **2**, 535–544.

Walker, L. (1977). Battered women and learned helplessness. *Victimology*, **2**, 525–533.

Walster, E., Walster, G. W., and Berscheid, E. (1978). *Equity Theory and Research*. Boston: Allyn and Bacon.

Wolfgang, M. E. (1958). *Patterns in Criminal Homicide*. Philadelphia: University of Pennsylvania Press.

Developments in the Study of Criminal Behaviour, Volume 2: Violence
Edited by Philip Feldman

3

Sexual Violence

KATE OSBORNE

Introduction

The ultimate and most extreme form of sexual violence is rape. Recent evidence from both victim and attacker has shown the extent to which rape and attempted rape reflect the ambiguous nature of prevailing social constructions of the expression of male and female sexuality. Because of this it is important to consider the extent to which rape represents an exaggeration of the threat that women in particular commonly experience. This threat is of many forms of sexual harassment and abuse, expressed both verbally and physically, in the course of their interactions with men. The legal definition of rape is restricted, omitting violence within marriage (although the Criminal Law Revision Committee is proposing to change this) and sexual abuse that does not actually involve labial penetration by the penis, which are considered to be less serious criminal events and thus frequently remain unreported. Even rape attacks themselves are infrequently reported to the police, and of those that are the majority do not result in prosecution. In 1973 51 000 rapes were reported in the USA and the FBI estimated that 10 times that many actually occurred (Tavris and Offir, 1977). In 1974 the number of reported rapes was almost two and a half times what it had been in 1960 (Shorter, 1977). By 1975 nationwide interview samples indicated that 151 000 rapes or attempted rapes had occurred, i.e. one out of every 600 women had been so abused (Bard and Sangrey, 1979). Of the 1170 rapes reported to the police in England and Wales in 1979, less than 500 went to the Crown Courts (for trial before a jury). Anywhere from between one and one and a half to 100 times more rapes are estimated actually to occur, compared to those that are reported (Katz and Mazur, 1979). Until recently, women's experiences of being sexually assaulted have remained undocumented in the scientific literature and were frequently considered by clinicians to be fantasy rather than fact. Now, the emergence of many crisis-intervention groups of women offering practical help and counselling services to those who have experienced sexually violent attacks has provided more detailed evidence concerning the nature of the events themselves, and of their physical and psychological after-effects.

The crime of rape is one that is known to be increasing in incidence, (Bard and Sangrey, 1979). It is a violent and humiliating crime against women, often carrying with it a real threat of murder and potentially bringing in its wake emotional disturbance, fear, self-blame, feelings of unreality and difficulties in sustaining and making relationships (Hall, 1977). Yet the extensive literature on sexual offences has until recently overlooked the problems of the victim. In the following sections the experiences of being raped and the characteristics of rape attacks will be examined, along with the ways in which rape crisis intervention has been used to reduce the long term psychological disruption of the victim of sexual violence.

Rape attacks: myths and facts

Most of the information concerning rapists and their victims comes from the USA and Australia, but will have implications for the study of sexual violence in the advanced industrial countries in general. The earliest comprehensive sociological account of the incidence of rape was made by Amir (1971) in his study of all cases of forcible rape listed by the Philadelphia police during the years 1958 and 1960. These statistics generated 646 victims and 1292 offenders, the numbers in themselves illustrating that in nearly two-thirds of these cases the rape attack was conducted by a pair or group of offenders. Some of Amir's findings have challenged existing myths about the nature of rape. For example, rapes were seldom 'explosive' events, as expected from the prevailing ethos of uncontrollable male sexual urges, in that three-quarters of the rapes were planned, especially group rapes. Similarly, rape is not always a crime conducted in a dark alley by a complete stranger. In almost of the cases (47%) the victim and offender were acquaintances, neighbours or members of the same family and the rape was often (56% of the time) in the home of the victim or her attacker. Only 18% of the rapes were committed outdoors and 15% in cars. In addition, Amir found that rape was predominantly an intraracial rather than an interracial event, with both black victims and offenders being more prevalent than their proportion in the Philadelphia population. However, since all of these findings are based on data from police records of convictions, they may reflect the nature of crimes committed from populations of men who are more likely to be traced and prosecuted, e.g. men whose identity can be established and who do not have access to expensive defence counsel. Despite this reservation, many other myths concerning the nature of rape and attempted rape were challenged by the evidence. For example, alcohol was used by only one-third of the attackers, although when it was used the offender was more violent and there was more sexual humiliation of the victim. This was also the case where men raped in groups, when there was increased use of forced oral and anal sex, use of bottles and other instruments for penetration and spitting and urinating on the victim. In Amir's sample force was used in 85% of the rapes, often involving weapons such as knives and 60% involving beating in varing degrees of brutality. When physical force was used, 31% of the victims were documented as displaying resistence and a further 30% had physically fought back. Amir noted that higher degrees of resistance provoked higher degrees of violence and he suggested that his findings put paid to the myth that it is impossible to rape a struggling woman. Amongst the victims, Amir found a significant association between age and rape, with the age range of 15–19 years having the highest frequency amongst both victims and offenders.

In an analysis of crime in the City of Denver, USA, MacDonald (1971) considered other aspects of the act of rape. There was evidence that demands for co-operation and affection were often made by rapists when their victims, as was usually the case, refused to participate actively. Also, attempts to take some care of their victims was noted, for example occasionally rapists used contraceptives or instructed their victims to do so, although in only 4% of Amir's cases had the offenders used contraceptives. This apparent contradiction in the behaviour of rapists will be examined later in documenting different styles of rape attack.

From a different continent, an Australian study (New South Wales Bureau of Crime Statistics and Research, 1974) examined the total number of reported rapes investigated and accepted as genuine by the police in 1973. Of these 169 rapes, 69% involved a single offender, and one in six rapes were pair rapes. One-third of the victims was threatened with a weapon, principally a knife or a gun. This study showed, as did Amir's, that the location of half of the rapes studied was a house or flat, usually the house of the victim. A third of the victims raped in a house or flat were initially voluntarily in the company of their attackers. In the remaining cases, the rapist broke into the victim's house. Half of the rapes studied took place between 11 p.m. and 3 a.m. and 59% occurred at the weekend.

Therefore the prevailing image of the rapist as an unknown assailant overtaken by sudden sexual impulses is mistaken. The rapist is just as likely to know his victim already; he may have been drinking with her and they are likely to be at one or other of their places of living. He is likely to be violent with her and she is more likely to be seriously hurt if she resists.

From the results of his survey, Amir (1971) developed an explanation of rape attack based on prevailing assumptions of the victim precipitating the crime. He based this on the evidence that 50% of the victims failed to resist their attackers in any way, particularly if they were younger women, and that 19% of the victims had a previous police record. Amir claimed that when a victim enters what he described as a 'vulnerable' situation charged with sexuality, or makes what would be interpreted as an 'invitation' to sexual relations, she precipitates the rape. Victim behaviour, he argues, can be identified either through acts of commission (such as agreeing to a drink or a lift from a stranger) or acts of omission (such as failing to react strongly enough to sexual suggestions or overtones). Hence, he says, through 'stereotypes of low moral worthiness, females become legitimate objects of probable victimization' (Amir, 1971, p. 261).

The implications of such assumptions reinforce lay and professional legal and medical attitudes towards victims of rape and all sexual violence, reducing the culpability of the offender and making prosecution less likely. To take first the issue of resistance, or acts of omission, advice given to women by a leading organization for civil liberties (Coote and Gill, 1975) recommends that the victim should struggle as little as possible, particularly if the attacker has a weapon. This does make prosecution more difficult, as a lack of evidence of her struggle can be used for the offender's defence, but potentially lessens the extent of the physical injury. Nevertheless, Coote and Gill (1975) show that standard texts on forensic medicine state that unless it can be proved that the woman resisted her alleged assailant with all the force of which she was capable at the time, it is unlikely that the accused will be found guilty of rape. Secondly, there is the issue of whether the woman 'asked for it'. Amir's notion of acts of commission implies that women should act and dress in a careful manner, not easily make acquaintances with men and travel and live in their environment in a cautious, respectable way. Any free behaviour on the part of the woman is therefore seen as being provocative to the rapist (Reynolds, 1978).

The theory of victim precipitation influences assumptions made by judge and jury in rape trials where evidence concerning the woman's previous sexual history is used as a defence for the rapist. Hence a woman who lives alone, is sexually experienced, uses the contraceptive pill or has had an abortion or an illegitimate child is less likely to prove a rape charge successfully. Research which focuses on the victim's experience of sexual violence (e.g. Burgess and Holmstrom, 1974) and criticism of theories based on assumptions concerning the social role of women (e.g. Brownmiller, 1975) argue strongly against Amir's interpretations of his data. The balance is now shifting from blaming the victim to understanding how to protect women from the vulnerability imposed on them from the ever-present threat of sexual violence.

Victims: research findings

An examination of the demographic features of victims of reported rapes makes it possible to determine whether or not they are a random sample from the population, or whether certain groups are at risk, for example in terms of their sex or age. Most definitions of rape include only female victims, although males are victims of sexual violence such as forced anal intercourse, particularly in prison populations (Schultz, 1973). In the general population, only a small percentage of male rapes are reported; approximately 4% of the victims reported in the literature are male (e.g. Hayman *et al.*, 1972; Hursch and Selkin, 1974).

Woman of every age are vulnerable to rape, with ages reported varying from 5 months old (Massey *et al.*, 1971) to 91 years (Hayman, 1970). Children are particularly vulnerable to all forms of sexual assault; Hursch and Selkin (1974) found that one-quarter of all sexual offences were against children, while only 13% of the forcible rapes in their sample of 535 were committed on children. Katz and Mazur (1979) argue that the evidence shows that child sexual victimization may occur far more frequently than child physical abuse, forcible rape or assault.

Adolescents accounted for the largest category of rape victims reported to the police, although the age range has been defined differently by different investigators. There is much support for Amir's finding that the 15–19 year old age group do appear to be particularly vulnerable. Young adults constituted from one-fifth to one-third of rape victims reported to the police and are an increasing category, possibly partly because more young women are now reporting rapes than previously. In adulthood, the rate of reported rapes appears to decline with age, although it could be that mature women conceal their victimization. Compared with other crimes, however, the high risk age for rape victims is the same as that for all serious crimes reported to the police, hence the age factor does not appear to be a special characteristic of rape (Katz and Mazur, 1979).

In the USA, demographic statistics have focused also on the race of the victim, showing that black women of every age have been far more vulnerable than white women, but which is again similar for all crimes of violence. Most specifically for adolescents, the risk for young black women is 20 times greater than that for white adolescents (Hayman *et al.*, 1968).

The single woman is most vulnerable to rape, partly due to the high rate of rape among young people. Schiff (1969) calculated that women who had never been married (52% of his sample) and those who were divorced or separated (28% of his sample) were five times more susceptible to rape than the married woman. But yet again, the high risk single status of the rape victim is not a specific feature of rape, but part of the general crime rate. Similarly, although women from all social classes are vulnerable to rape, most reported rape occurs to victims of lower socioeconomic status, who are at higher risk for all serious crimes. In terms of occupations, students (presumably because of their age) are particularly vulnerable. A further group at risk are women in the helping professions. Selkin (1975) found that many of the rape victims in his study were attacked by strangers who had requested help from them.

Therefore, apart from the fact that most victims of sexual violence are women, a rape attack may be as random as any other serious crime. Particular populations of women are more vulnerable in terms of their age and social class, but there is no evidence demographically that they precipitated a rape attack any more than they precipitated being violently robbed.

Victims: reactions to sexual violence

Until recently, most of the literature on sexual offences focused on the offender. With the formation of rape crisis centres in the USA and lately in the UK information has been made available on the reactions of victims of sexual violence. Since most sexual attacks are unexpected by the victim, the element of surprise often induces immediate shock (Storaska, 1975). During a rape, the primary emotional reaction for almost all victims is fear (Burgess and Holmstrom, 1974). Peters (1975) documented the 'fear of dying' among rape victims and found this greater in adults than in adolescents and children. Coping strategies used varied from verbal tactics of trying to talk themselves out of the situation to fighting, attempting to get away and dissociating themselves from the actions in order to get through it (Burgess and Holmstrom, 1976; Russell, 1975). Patterns of resistance tended to depend on the woman's previous experiences of physical violence and varied with age and socioeconomic status (Symonds, 1975). Older and middle-class women tended to be more passive and use verbal strategies to resist the rape.

The reactions of victims after sexual assault have been closely studied, particularly in order to provide more effective crisis support. The earliest work was by Sutherland and Scherl (1970), who studied a group of 13 victims of rape, each of whom was young, middle class and white, with a history of good prior emotional adjustment. They described a three-phase response pattern, the first of which is an acute reaction, occurring in the first few hours to days after the assault. It is characterized by shock, succeeded by gross anxiety and fearfulness. Many expressed concern about how others would respond to them, and women with a higher degree of self-blame, who felt that they should have protected themselves more adequately against the attack, tended to delay in reporting the rape to police or medical authorities. At this stage the women were found to be receptive to intervention and wanted to talk to someone about the experience. The second phase was one of outward adjustment, where over the next few weeks to months non-specific anxiety decreased. There was a resumption of normal activities, although these were reduced, and a reduction of willingness to talk about the experience. The timing of the third phase varied, but was characterized by the onset of depressive responses, obsessive thoughts about the rape, self-blame, feelings of being damaged and anger towards the attacker. Sutherland and Scherl (1970) called this stage one of 'integration and resolution', since there was a marked increase in the desire to talk about the experiences, again giving rise to a greater likelihood that the emotional problems associated with the rape could be re-examined and reduced. They argue that the depressive reaction is psychologically 'normal', in that it happened to the majority of these women in their sample, and should not be taken as a sign of illness.

Since these 13 women constitute a small, homogeneous group, the authors are cautious about generalizing their findings to other populations. Burgess and Holmstrom (1974) studied a larger, more heterogeneous sample in terms of racial and socioeconomic dimensions which was composed of 92 adult women who came into the emergency room of a Boston hospital as victims of rape or attempted rape. In their findings they reduced Sutherland and Scherl's last two phases into one period of reorganization. During the initial period of disorganization they observed a wide spread of emotions, including embarrassment, humiliation, anger and most frequently fear and self-blame. Repetitive thoughts of the attack tend to occur which the victim attempts to black out. Somatic reactions such as sleep disturbances, loss of appetite, headaches, startle reactions and gastro-intestinal complaints were common. They described two general styles of coping: (1) the 'expressed' style in which affect was demonstrated in verbal and non-verbal behaviour and (2) the 'controlled' style in which affect was not observable and outward behaviour was calm, composed and contained. About half of the women they saw in the emergency room were expressive and talkative, the other half were quiet and guarded.

The second period of reorganization often involved making changes in the victim's life-style as a coping strategy for dealing with the disruption caused by the rape attack. Many victims were able to resume only a minimal level of functioning even after the acute phase ends. Some women could go back to work or school but were unable to be involved in more than limited activities. Others responded by staying at home, or only going out when accompanied by a friend. A common response was to turn for support to family members who had previously not been seen on a frequent basis. Thus visiting family, taking holidays and sometimes moving place of residence were all attempts by victims to restructure their life-styles. There were frequent occurrences of dreams and nightmares associated with the attack. Two types of nightmare appeared to predominate, one in which the victim dreams of being in a similar situation and is attempting to escape but fails, and a second type, which occurred more frequently as time progressed, in which the dream changes and the victim will report mastery over the attacker. However, the dreams are usually still violent, with the victims seeing themselves killing and stabbing people (Burgess and Holmstrom, 1974).

Fears and phobias also develop that are specific to the circumstances of the rape. Some victims become fearful of being with large groups of people; others are afraid of being alone. The woman may develop specific fears related to characteristics noted in the attacker, such as the smell of alcohol or the features of a moustache. Feelings of paranoia may prevail, particularly that everyone knows about the rape and therefore thinks badly of her. Many women expressed worries about future sexual adjustment and relationships with men. The normal sexual style of the victim became disrupted following a rape. The experience was particularly alarming for the victim who had never had any sexual experience before the rape, in that she had no comparison experience to know whether sex is always like that. For victims who had already been sexually active, the fear increased when their sexual partner wanted to resume that sexual relationship. Women who were not currently involved with a man at the time of the rape frequently expressed a fear that they would never be able to be sexually active with men again.

Burgess and Holmestrom (1974) call these patterns of reaction the 'rape trauma syndrome', which they claim are normal psychological responses and attempts to cope with a fearful life-threatening crisis. However, they also distinguish two variants which, they claim, involve pathological reactions. First, the 'compounded reactions' refer to those women who developed severe depression, psychosomatic disturbances and psychotic reactions or who attempted suicide. This reaction was seen in victims with a past or current history of physical or psychological problems, or whose behaviour patterns created social difficulties for them. These victims were frequently known to other therapists, doctors or agencies, and were already experiencing life problems. Burgess and Holmstrom (1974) argue that under the stress of the rape, the victim will deteriorate according to her existing vulnerability. Hence women with a history that involves, for example, previous psychiatric symptoms, social and family problems or drug and alcohol addiction may be more vulnerable to a compounded reaction to rape.

Secondly, a 'silent reaction' was noted, when women would show increasing signs of anxiety as the post-rape interview progressed, long periods of silence, stuttering and physical distress. This was most frequently found to occur in those women who had a history including a previous rape and who often had not revealed it before. A number of the victims seen by Burgess and Holmstrom stated when giving life history information that they had been previously raped or sexually molested as children or adolescents. The current rape then reactivates their emotional responses to the earlier experience. Such women became increasingly anxious during interviews and reported histories of sudden onset of avoidance of sex, a history of acute phobic reactions to being alone or going outside and chronic loss of self-confidence. In counselling women with silent reactions to sexual attack, Burgess and Holmstrom highlight the importance of being aware of the possibility of a history of similar experiences.

The rape trauma syndrome therefore described both the acute or immediate phase of disorganization and the long term process of reorganization that occurs as a result of attempted or actual rape. The acute phase includes an immediate impact reaction which is exhibited by either an expressed or a controlled style of response, physical and emotional reactions to a life-threatening situation. The long term process includes changes in life-style, dreams and nightmares of the attack and phobic reactions. More complex and less frequent responses showed either compounded or silent reactions. Psychiatrists who examined rape victims 1–2 weeks after an attack have found one or more post-rape changes in almost three-quarters of their victims (Peters *et al.*, 1976). When compared with other crisis stresses that are unexpected and life-threatening, such as fire or floods, response patterns in these situations show a similar pattern of being either apparently calm and controlled, or more commonly expressed with crying or screaming (Notman and Nadelson, 1976).

Reactions of family and professionals to the sexual attack

The emotional distress experienced by family members as a result of the sexual assault may be equally as disruptive as for the victim. Burgess and Holmstrom

(1974) again report both acute and long term reactions on the part of parents. A common response is to blame someone for the event: the attacker or the victim or themselves. The parents of a rape victim are just as likely to reflect a victim precipitation view of rape, and wonder why their daughter did not scream louder or fight harder, as is the rest of society. If they have not previously talked to their child about sexual matters, the rape attack will mean that somehow as a family they have to deal with the issue of the child's developing sexuality.

Where the victim is older, and is either married or has a close relationship with a man, her rape by another man frequently will provoke many problems for the relationship. As Brownmiller (1975) points out, the property relationship between a woman and her spouse may have a profound effect on his reaction. He may, like other people, blame the victim herself (Weis and Borges, 1973) and, even when there was no indication that she precipitated the event, view the sexual intercourse as a marital infidelity. It is therefore not uncommon for a marriage to end in divorce after a rape attack on the wife (Weis and Borges, 1973; Brodyaga *et al.*, 1975), and relationships between unmarried couples have been permanently ended. Thus as well as experiencing a rape attack, the victim may also lose a significant relationship.

The reactions of legal and medical professionals have also been shown to be dominated by assumptions of victim precipitation. Most rape victims do not automatically call the police (Katz and Mazur, 1979) and those who do have generally been raped in very dramatic situations. Many women are later persuaded by friends or relatives to lodge a complaint, but some wait days or weeks before doing so, long after evidence has been destroyed, and it is likely that the vast majority of rapes are never reported (Toner, 1977). On average, only one-third of rapes recorded lead to rape convictions; many of those originally reported are not proceeded with either because the victim withdraws her allegation or because the police are unable to find enough evidence to support it.

When police are called to a rape victim, their two primary concerns are to obtain information about the assault and to detain the alleged offender. Thus the victim is informed not to destroy any evidence (Brodyaga *et al.*, 1975). She is told not to take a bath, so that evidence can be collected for signs of sexual intercourse. Her fingernails may be clipped to examine traces of hair, skin and other fragments of torn clothing. She is also asked to retain any soiled clothes for forensic examination and if the rape occurred in her own home she is required not to touch anything so that fingerprints can be collected. If necessary the police will take the victim to a hospital; if not they will interview her to obtain a statement. For the rape victim, the initial interview has often been a harrowing experience (Toner, 1977). Police attitudes have been a source of great complaint by rape victims, with some police officers being criticized for implying that the woman was lying or that she really enjoyed the experience (Weis and Borges, 1973). Russell (1975) found that it was not unusual for policemen to use sexual overtones in their interrogation of the victim. However, many of the victims in

Burgess and Holmstrom's (1975) sample spoke either favourably about police treatment of them (31.5%) or were neutral (52.1%). The remaining 10.3% felt negatively toward the police. Of the 30% of women in Medea and Thompson's (1974) study of 60 raped women who reported the rape to the authorities, nearly half (44%) said that the police were unsympathetic and 38% said they were sympathetic, the remaining 18% being undetermined.

Where a victim reports or is taken to a hospital, she may have a long wait before a medical examination (Brodyaga *et al.*, 1975). She is then treated for any physical injury and given a gynaecological examination. Any evidence of sperm in the vagina is taken, and gynaecological trauma, bruises and other injuries are noted and treated. Victims may also be given prophylactic treatment for the prevention of pregnancy and venereal disease. It has frequently been reported that doctors, nurses and other medical staff have the same moralistic and judgemental attitudes as the police (Katz and Mazur, 1979). Indeed, Burgess and Holmstrom (1975) found that their victims felt more negatively towards the medical staff who treated them than towards the police who interviewed them. They have produced guidelines for the use of legal and medical personnel to improve the quality of the care given to victims (Burgess and Holmstrom, 1974).

Despite the fact that along with low reporting of rape attacks, the low incidence of identifying the attacker and the frequency with which allegations are later withdrawn, some rape victims do continue to proceed through the legal system in their attempt to convict the rapist. In Britain, most rape cases are decided at a Crown Court, where the jury hears evidence from both accused and complainant. Rape victims who take their cases to court are therefore required to withstand lengthy cross-examinations. They will have to report their evidence and defend their character against a defence lawyer who will be attempting to discredit the victim and show that she 'invited' the attack (Peters, 1973). Coote and Gill (1975) have provided a legal rights handbook which details some of the common practices in such situations and gives advice to rape victims about how to deal with cross-examination situations. Brodyaga *et al.* (1975) have followed victims through this process and documented the high levels of psychological stress involved. The low conviction rate in rape cases (Brodyaga *et al.*, 1975; Katz and Mazur, 1979) means that the experience will frequently be very disappointing for the victim. Brownmiller (1975) has shown that only 3% of arrest cases have been convicted. This gap between the victim's expectations and the outcome of the court proceedings has frequently made later adjustment more difficult (Peters *et al.*, 1976). Particularly when the verdict is 'not guilty', Burgess and Holmstrom (1974) found the effect on the victim to be very marked.

Hence for family members and significant others, as well as for members of the medical and legal professions dealing with the rape crisis, there is a marked tendency to respond in an unhelpful way. This may involve either not believing the victim, or blaming her for the situation. The rape victim's participation in her plight is even more starkly highlighted by the difficulties which surround attempted prosecution. All of these attitudes reflect general public assumptions about the nature of rape which become embedded in the attitudes of both lay and professional opinion.

Men who rape: research findings

The finding that rape is not an expression of sudden sexual desire and that the rapist, rather than being oversexed, generally is married or has other opportunities for sexual gratification has led to detailed studies of the developmental history and current emotional state of men who rape. Groth (1979), following clinical experience with more than 500 sexual offenders, describes the psychological factors that predispose a person to react to life events with sexual violence. In a detailed description of life histories of men who commit many types of forcible rape, three psychological components have been identified; namely power, anger and sexuality (Groth *et al.*, 1977). The interrelationship between these factors and the relative intensity with which they are expressed vary, Groth (1979) argues, from one offender to another. However, the clustering of these dimensions led him to conclude that three basic patterns of rape can be distinguished: (1) the anger rape, in which sexuality becomes a hostile act; (2) the power rape, in which sexuality becomes an expression of conquest; (3) the sadistic rape, in which anger and power become eroticized. Groth *et al.* (1977) claim that whatever other factors are operating during a rape offence, the components of anger, power and sexuality are always present and prominent. More specifically they have found either anger or power to be the dominant component and that rape is the use of sexuality to express these issues of power and anger. Groth describes rape as a 'pseudosexual' act, a pattern of sexual behaviour in the primary service of non-sexual expressions of hostility, control, status and dominance.

In order to examine the psychological complexities of men as they rape, these three types of rape show the different factors involved. In the anger rape, the sexual assault is characterized by physical brutality. Much greater force is used in carrying out the assualt than would be necessary if the intention was simply to overpower and sexually penetrate the victim. Here, the offender physically attacks the victim, knocking her to the ground, striking and beating her, tearing her clothes and raping her. The assault may be a 'blitz' rape (Burgess and Holmstrom, 1974), in which the offensive is a violent surprise with the unassuming victim caught off her guard, or the attacker may use a 'confidence' rape approach (Burgess and Holmstrom, 1974) to gain access to the victim and then launch a sudden overpowering attack. For example he may pretend to be reading the gas meter, then without warning he suddenly becomes angry, in sharp contrast to a quite pleasant initial encounter. During such an aggressive attack the offender may express his rage both physically and verbally, forcing the victim to submit to or perform additional sexual acts that he may regard as particularly degrading such as sodomy or fellatio. He may express contempt for the victim by urinating or ejaculating on to her, and by using abusive language.

Groth (1979) reports that typically such an offender does not describe being in a state of sexual arousal during the attack. He may be initially impotent and only be able to achieve an erection by masturbating or having the victim perform oral sex on him. The anger rapist generally appears to find little or no sexual gratification in the rape and may react with revulsion and disgust to the sexual act, which he generally considers to be a 'dirty' offensive experience. These sudden assaults appear to be impulsive rather than premeditated, and are often experienced with a sense of unreality by the offender. In describing the build-up to the attack he frequently reports being in an upset and distressed state of mind, with angry and depressed mood states. The offence itself is typically preceded by some upsetting event, often involving a significant woman in the attacker's life. Thus such an assault appears to be in response to an identifying precipitating stress, such as marital conflict, arguments with or rejections by girlfriends and conflict with parents. Others in Groth's study reported distressed feelings following some life disappointment, such as being given the sack from work or being financially burdened. The common theme was one of the offender feeling that he had been wronged, hurt, or treated unjustly and that the rape was an attempt to revenge himself for the perceived wrongs done to him by others, especially women. The 'anger rapist's' relationships to significant others are frequently found to be characterized by conflict and aggravation. In some instances the victim of the rapist's anger is the actual person who is the focus of his anger, but generally she is simply a substitute person, an available target at whom he can vent his fury.

In the second pattern of rape distinguished by Groth *et al.* (1977), power was the dominant factor. Here, sexuality served to express the offender's mastery, strength, control and authority over the victim. Since the goal is the demonstration of sexual conquest, the offender uses the minimum amount of force necessary to achieve the capture and control of his victim. This may be done through verbal threat, intimidation with a weapon and physical force to overpower and subdue her. In many cases, the victim is kidnapped or held captive and subjected to repeated assaults over a period of time. Men who demonstrated this type of sexual assault typically reported thoughts and masturbatory fantasies about sexual conquest and rape. Again, however, in reality the offender appears to find little sexual satisfaction in the rape, since it never lives up to his fantasy. Since he does not gain the reassurance of his own performance and his victim's response to the assault, the offensive becomes repetitive and compulsive, with frequently a series of rapes being committed over a short period of time, in order to try once again to be as good as the fantasy. There may therefore be an increase in aggression over time as the offender attempts to achieve his goal.

The offences themselves are either premeditated or opportunistic, with the victim frequently being obviously less powerful than the offender, i.e. younger and smaller. Such a rape appeared to be a means of asserting the individual's manhood and demonstrating his heterosexuality. Such an offender tends to interact in conversations of a sexual nature with his victim that are both assertive, such as giving commands as to her actions, or inquisitive, particularly about her sexual interests and her evaluation of his sexual prowess. The issue of power and control appears to be central to such an attacker's life situation, as he frequently perceives himself to be powerless in relation to the people around him. Therefore, conquering a less powerful person than himself represents an important counterbalance to his normal existence. Because of his wishes to be sexually competent in the encounter, he frequently denies that it was forced, claiming that the victim wanted him. Following the assault he may attempt to be friendly to her, buying her a drink or asking to see her again. Clinical case histories of such men show them to have a history of failure, at school, at work and in relationships. In this one area of sexual conquest they appear to attempt to achieve some competence, as has been seen without the experience of success. For the victim of a 'power rape' the attack is usually psychologically rather than physically traumatic, and as will be seen in the next section this may have long term implications as regards the extent to which her story is believed.

The third category of patterns of rape described is the sadistic rape, where both sexuality and aggression are fused. Here the anger and power of the offender become eroticized and the offender finds the intentional abuse of the victim gratifying in itself. Such an assault may involve bondage and torture and often has a ritualistic nature. The offender may force the victim to dress or behave in some specific way and involve her in abusive acts such as burning with cigarettes or biting, specifically focused on the sexual areas of her body. Prostitutes or woman whom the offender considers to be promiscuous may be particularly vulnerable to sadistic attacks. Generally the assault is deliberately considered and planned, with the offender using disguises or blindfolding his victim, who is stalked, abused and sometimes murdered.

In contrast to the anger rapist, who explodes in range, the offences of the sadist are fully premeditated. The infliction of pain may provide sexual gratification for the attacker, or lead to other forms of sexual activity. Increasing aggression leads to feelings of power, which in turn become arousing. Here, the more a victim struggles the more aggressive the rapist becomes. The sadistic rapist reports having masturbatory fantasies that are sadistic in nature, and although he may be leading an apparently normal life between assaults, his sadistic impulses are frequently observable in his consenting sexual encounters, especially in the marital relationships of such offenders. The victim of the sadistic rapist may not survive the attack and if she does will require, as will be described in the following section, sensitive aftercare.

Despite their range and obvious idiosyncratic differences, sexual assaults can be categorized in these three ways. In examining the incidence of these patterns,

Groth *et al.* (1977) found that power rapes were the most common, with more than half (55%) of their cases of this type. Approximately 40% were anger rapes and about 5% were sadistic rapes. Because they were collecting information primarily from convicted rapists, anger rapes may be over-represented since they involved more physical abuse and are therefore more likely to lead to a conviction. In a UK sample of men convicted of rape, Gibbens *et al.* (1977) found that 20% of a sample of 207 men convicted in 1961 were 'aggressive' rapists. They defined such rapists as having had at least one, and usually more, aggressive, non-sexual convictions, either before or after the rape conviction. Gibbens *et al.*'s other categories, however, do not allow for direct comparisons with the data of Groth *et al.*, (1977) since they involve a combination of the type of victim (30% were paedophiliac rapes) and style of rape (50% showed physically non-violent but threatening behaviour). These appear to be more like Groth's 'power' rape category, since they involve attempts to rape by domination, fraud and threat.

Sexuality can therefore be seen to be not the main motive for rape. It is, however, always in combination with degrees of anger and power that the hostile expression of sexuality is the way in which the offender attempts to deal with a current life experience. The trigger may or may not be an acute life event: the chronic build-up of experiences of failure, incompetence or rejection may well culminate in the acting out of aggression or dominance which are expressed through the sexual humiliation and control of a victim. It is not yet clear why it is that some men with such developmental histories react in this way to women who may be complete strangers to them but become targets of their lived fantasy. The extent to which this reflects the nature of the expression of potential aggression and control of women will be considered later.

Rape-crisis intervention

The psychological and physical after-effects of rape have been shown to be distinctive and often disrupt the victim's functioning. Because of the inadequacy of the statutory provision for rape victims, voluntary self-help groups have developed to provide the support, information and counselling that they might require at this time. Centres have been recently established in the USA and Europe specifically oriented towards crisis intervention work with women who have been raped. When a victim of sexual violence contacts police or medical authorities, there is no formal attempt to provide her with any help with her psychological reactions to the assault. Research shows that many women turn to their peers for support, but are reluctant to confide immediately in their families in any detail (Hall, 1977). If they report the event to the police, many women undergo experiences especially in the questioning and medical examination which, as has been previously noted, can be experienced as worse than the rape itself (Coote and Gill, 1975).

The victim's recovery from the rape experience is in part dependent on the reactions of those who come into contact with her after the event. Where these are supportive and non-judgemental, her chances for recovery have been shown to be good; however, if these are insensitive and accusing the victim's emotional stress can be exacerbated (Brodyaga *et al.*, 1975). Any suggestion of force may be perceived by the victim as another form of aggression not unlike the rape. Sensitive enquiries are more likely to enable the victim to provide details necessary for the capture and prosecution of the offender (Abarbanel, 1976). Similarly, medical personnel are in a position to aid or delay the victim's recovery. Mental health professionals such as psychiatrists and psychologists have counselled very few rape victims because the victims have rarely sought psychiatric help immediately after the attack. In Medea and Thompson's (1974) study of 60 adolescents and young adults who were victims of rape or attempted rape, 70% did not report the attack, only 8% sought and received professional counselling and a further 2% were helped by hospital staff. Few college women who were sexually attacked sought the help of their university counselling service (Kirkpatrick and Kanin, 1957) and college sex counsellors Bauer and Stein (1973) reported that they only treated about 12 rape victims each year. Hence there is much need in the professions for training and information about the nature of reactions to rape.

However, many women have argued that the rape victim does not need professional therapy, since it might further 'victimize' the victim. It has been argued that most victims need only a supportive person who can listen sympathetically and help the victim face the many medical and legal aspects that result from the rape (Katz and Mazur, 1979). Most rape victim counselling has taken place through rape crisis centres which have used trained volunteers who have provided the necessary support services.

The model for crisis intervention centres, developed by Burgess and Holmstrom (1974), is to provide training for volunteers who can respond to the individual requests of the rape victim, whether these be for legal or medical advice, for support during the reporting of the attack and the giving of evidence, for counselling during the phases of emotional reaction to the rape, or for ongoing help through any legal proceedings that may occur. In the USA, the earliest interventions of this type were based around casualty departments of large city hospitals, where women volunteer counsellors could be called out by medical duty staff at the time that the victim presented herself at the hospital. Yet a vast number of rape victims do not contact professional services, and consequently a number of rape crisis telephone 'hot-lines' were introduced, where emergency calls could be taken which were serviced by a rota of volunteers. Guidelines for training rape victim counsellors are now readily available (Fox and Scherl, 1972; Burgess and Holmstrom, 1974; Bassuk *et al.*, 1975; McCombie *et al.*, 1976). These stress the need to prepare the counsellor for a wide range of emotional reactions from the victim. Burgess and Holmstrom (1974) found that many interviews began with considerable stress and difficulty. They emphasize the importance of the establishment of a good early alliance with the client to develop a calm and warm rapport. In particular, the counsellor will require considerable training and on-going support to control her own identifications with a female victim experiencing terror, violence and sexual assault. Most rape victims who seek therapeutic help have preferred to talk to a woman (Silverman, 1977), since, as with other interactions with helping personnel, the victim's increased feelings of vulnerability precipitated by the rape may cause her to fear any further confrontations with men.

The experience of rape crisis centres in the USA and the UK is that many of their clients do not make contact at the time of the attack, but at some later stage after the shock reaction has subsided. Burgess and Holmstrom (1974) therefore distinguish between the clinical implications of crisis intervention work with recently raped women, and with those who have experienced rape in their past history. In the management of the rape trauma responses they argue that crisis intervention is the treatment method of choice, in order to return the woman to her previous level of functioning as quickly as possible. Hence any counselling is issue-oriented, with previous problems not being a priority for discussion. This model is based on the two assumptions that the rape represents a crisis in that the woman's life-style is disrupted, but that she is regarded as having functioned adequately before the rape. Where other problems emerged during intervention, the woman may then, they argue, require referral for more detailed psychological help. Compared with other forms of intervention, the original crisis cousellors took an active role in initiating therapeutic contact by visiting the victim in hospital and establishing regular telephone contact with her during the recovery period.

Women who developed what Burgess and Holmstrom called a 'compounded reaction', that is who had either a past or current history of physical psychiatric or social difficulties as well as the rape trauma, generally required more than crisis counselling. For these women the rape crisis counsellors in their project assumed a secondary role, and provided information on reactions to rape for therapists or professionals from other agencies. Their observations also showed the different impact of the varying types of rape experiences. Victims of anger rapes reported experiencing the rape as a life-threatening situation. Therefore although the anger rape is physically brutal and violent, the victim may have less long-lasting traumatic effects precisely because there is more concrete evidence in terms of her injuries to support her claims to have been raped. Thus there is less suspicion of false accusation or victim precipitation, and she may therefore receive much more support from those who come into contact with her. She has survived the attack and therefore her primary aim is to devise strategies that will make her less accessible and vulnerable in future. Her sense of intimidation can be reduced through realizing that since her attacker acted out of rage directed at her as a random target, he is not likely to single her out again. Many blitz-style rapists have said that when they saw the victim again in court they were unable to recognize her (Groth, 1979).

However, the victim of the power rape may not have obvious physical injuries to lend credibility to her story. Police, hospital staff and family may feel that she deliberately or inadvertently invited or encouraged the assault. To maximize his sense of power over her the offender may have found out where she lives or works and may have threatened to repeat the attack, which increases the victim's sense of powerlessness. She may therefore fear that he will return, although statistically this is unlikely (Groth, 1979). Hence one of the main counselling themes for victims of power rapes is to examine their sense of self-blame and the guilt that they could have prevented or avoided the assault. Such victims tend to have an exacerbated sense of helplessness following the rape and require assistance in regaining their independence.

The victim of the sadistic rape may not survive the attack, and when she does she may frequently need extended therapeutic help to recover from the horror of the assault. Many such victims express the feat that they will never fully recover from the impact and will suffer long term psychological damage (Groth *et al.*, 1977). There is a greater risk of severe depression and of suicide for the victims of sadistic rapes.

The establishment of rape crisis centres in the USA, and particularly the pioneering work of Burgess and Holmstrom, has provided a wealth of information concerning the nature of rape, its after-effects and the provision of volunteer help for victims. At the time of writing there are 12 established centres in the UK developed along the lines suggested by Burgess and Holmstrom, and based in large cities such as London, Birmingham, Newcastle and Edinburgh. The first rape crisis centre in the UK was started in London in 1976, funded by donations, loans and charitable trusts (London Rape Crisis Centre, 1977, 1978). A 24 hour telephone crisis line was operated by two full-time staff and 16 volunteers who cover night and weekend calls on a rota basis. Their experiences of the reactions of women who contacted them closely parallel the American projects. During the first 6 months of operation they were contacted by 84 women, 64.3% of whom had been raped by one man and 20.2% who were the victims of group rape. The remainder had been victims of indecent assault (14.3%) or there was insufficient information obtained (1.2%). In 46% of the cases the attacker was a stranger to the victim, and 29% of the times he was an acquaintance. Ten per cent of the attacks were by friends or relatives. These proportions appear to be confirmed by statistics from other UK centres in other parts of the country.

In terms of the time lapse between rape and telephone call to the rape crisis centre, only 6% called within 8 hours. Twenty-seven women (32.1%) called between 1 and 7 days after the attack and a further 27 called between 1 week and 3 months after the occurrence. As was found in the American centres, many women (in London it was 20.2%) made contact 1 year or more after the event had occurred. Only one-third (37.5%) of the rapes took place outside in a street or park; they just as frequently occurred in the home of the attacker (34.7%) or in the victim's house (22.2%). Thus the pattern of rapes is shown to be similar to the American data outlined earlier.

Over the period that the London Rape Crisis Centre has been in operation the number of contacts has risen sharply, from 118 in 1976 to 673 in 1978, with at least a 6% increase during 1980, giving an average of at least 13 new callers per week. Approximately half of the women contacting the centre had already reported to the police, although a few more did so after talking with a counsellor and with her support. Where women chose not to report their stated reasons were concern about concealing the fact from those closest to them and in wanting to forget the whole experience. Some women expressed a fear of retribution, whether they told anyone or not, and others found the idea of a medical internal examination too traumatic so soon after the rape. Other centres in the UK are also showing these trends although, as many have been in operation for under a year at the time of writing, they have not yet produced sufficient information.

Prevention of sexually violent attacks

Preventative measures against the possibility of being the victim of a sexually violent attack involve changes in the way women think and act, changes in men's socialization and assumptions about the behaviour of women—and inevitably changes in men's expression of sexual aggression.

As a result of their work with rape victims and the analyses made of their vulnerability, Burgess and Holmstrom (1974) provide a lengthy check-list of preventative measures that women can take in order to increase their personal safety. These include actions to protect their living environment, such as keeping entrances lit, asking visitors to identify themselves before opening the door and if living alone arranging a signalling system with reliable neighbours. A woman's physical protection can be increased by making sure that the clothing she wears is unrestrictive enough to run in (especially that her shoes are suitable for this) and to carry warning devices such as a whistle or buzzer. Any weapons carried, unless competently handled, can easily be removed and used by the attacker against her, and recent prosecutions have been made against women carrying deterrent sprays. More importantly, Burgess and Holmstrom (1974) argue for adequate psychological protection, so that women act and think of themselves less as victims. They advise women to walk positively rather than hesistantly, keep a vigilant lookout for any men following, and to be alert enough to escape if caught. They also recommend the use of self-defence training for women so that they are practised at escaping or defending themselves. Looking at the methods of 165 successful resisters of attempted rape, Hursch and Selkin (1974) found that 130 victims (79%) escaped by means of active resistance such as screaming, fighting and running. Sixteen women succeeded by talking their way out of the attack, and in 13 cases the act was interrupted. Selkin (1975) suggests that active resistance may be effective, although Burgess and Holmstrom (1974) warn that fighting with the attacker may exacerbate his assault. A particular common misconception by many people is that an effective defence is to kick the man in the groin, which Medea and Thompson (1974) argue is difficult to execute and can result in unbalancing the woman, therefore making her more vulnerable. Storaska (1975) argues against immediate resistance, basing his prevention strategies on conversation with dozens of rapists and observations of hundreds of victims (most of whom knew the rapist beforehand). By utilizing the knowledge that many rapists are aiming to control and dominate their victims, Storaska argues that the best defence is to feign submission, using communication with the rapist to increase his sense of power and well-being, and then try to turn him off sexually, by the victim making herself unattractive or unfeminine (e.g. urinating or belching). Only in extreme cases of severe threat to life does Storaska recommend physical defensive strategies, such as squeezing the testicles of the attacker, or poking his eyes. However, such a form of resistance is difficult for many women to contemplate, as they are usually not culturally trained to be physically aggressive. Katz and Mazur (1979) point out that since Storaska's strategies were based on evidence from women who knew their attackers, and Selkin's study was of referred cases of victims and convicted rapists, where there was more likelihood that the attacker was a stranger, women should use different defence strategies in these two different situations.

However, even if individual women act to prevent themselves from being raped, the intending attacker need only find another victim. Wider societal changes are required in order to reduce the currently increasing incidence of sexual violence. Although many people argue far harsher penalties (Schiff, 1973), it can be argued that severe penalties reduce the likelihood of conviction (Peters, 1975). Peters suggests that if the law carried realistic penalties, it would be more likely to be enforced. The Center for Women Policy Studies (Brodyaga *et al.*, 1975) recommends classifying assaults according to severity, giving a range of penalties so that juries might be more inclined to make a conviction. Legal reforms also should change the difficulty of prosecution, for example by omitting the victim's testimony of her previous sexual history and clarifying the degree of resistance required to overcome the defence of victim consent.

Such changes depend on the alteration of popular assumptions concerning the nature of victim precipitation. Such a concept, which underlies the thinking of both lay and professional people, has a vital impact on the way rape victims are selected and treated. A more serious view of the nature of the crime of rape may increase the likelihood of detection, which may in turn reduce its incidence.

Finally, the education of young people about the sexual natures of the male and the female, dispelling myths concerning biological functioning and teaching self-help concerning relationship interactions, may enable future generations to take more adequate care of themselves and enable young men and women to develop more appropriate and mutual relationships. As Jackson (1978) clearly argues, rape is an extreme manifestation of culturally accepted patterns of male–female relationships. As long as the predominant view of women is that they are legitimate sexual targets, which permeates advertising, press, television, theatre and all popular beliefs concerning the nature of communications between the sexes, sexual violence will continue.

Conclusion

The provision of crisis counselling for victims of sexual violence has provided information concerning the nature of victimization, the style and method of the attack, and the physical and psychological effects on the victim. The violence and sexual humiliation experienced by women is shown to have far reaching implications and may temporarily or permanently alter her life-style. Research has shown that prevailing beliefs about when and how rapes occur have to be altered, since far from being the uncontrollable sexual urges of a crazed stranger, they may as frequently result from the expression of anger and dominance of men who are already acquaintances. Although counselling support for victims is becoming more available, vital steps to protect women are being taken by women themselves. However, until the fundamental expression of relationships between the men and women change, sexual violence will not easily be prevented.

References

Abarbanel, G. (1976). Helping victims of rape. *Social Work*, **21**, 478–482.

Amir, M. (1971). *Patterns in Forcible Rape*. Chicago: University of Chicago Press.

Bard, M., and Sangrey, D. (1979). *The Crime Victim's Book*. New York: Basic Books.

Bassuk, E., Savitz, R., McCombie, S., and Pell, S. (1975). Organizing a rape crisis program in a general hospital. *Journal of the American Medical Women's Association*, **30**, 486–490.

Bauer, R., and Stein, J. (1973). Sex counseling on campus: short term treatment techniques. *American Journal of Orthopsychiatry*, **43**, 74–79.

Brodyaga, L., Gates, M., Singer, S., Tucker, M., and White, R. (1975). *Rape and Its Victims: A Report for Citizens, Health Facilities and Criminal Justice Agencies*. Washington, DC.: US Government Printing Office.

Brownmiller, S. (1975). *Against Our Will: Men, Women and Rape*. New York: Secker and Warburg.

Burgess, A. W., and Holmstrom, L. L. (1974). *Rape : Victims of Crisis*. Bowrie, Md: Brady.

Burgess, A. W., and Holmstrom, L. L. (1975). Accountability: a right of the rape victim. *Journal of Psychiatric Nursing*, **13**, 11–16.

Burgess, A. W., and Holmstrom, L. L. (1976). Coping behavior of the rape victim. *American Journal of Psychiatry*, **113**, 413–418.

Coote, A., and Gill, T. (1975). *The Rape Controversy*. London: Russell Press.

Fox, S. S., and Scherl, D. J. (1972). Crisis intervention with victims of rape, in *Rape Victimology* (Ed. L. G. Schulz). Springfield; Ill.: Charles C. Thomas, pp. 131–162.

Gibbens, T. C. N., Way, C., and Soothill, K. L. (1977). Behavioural types of rape. *British Journal of Psychiatry*, **130**, 32–42.

Groth, A. N. (1979). *Men Who Rape*. New York: Plenum Press.

Groth, A. N., Burgess, A. W., and Holmstrom, L. L. (1977). Rape, power, anger and sexuality. *American Journal of Psychiatry*, **134**, 1239–1243.
Hall, J. (1977). Rape and some of its effects. *Midwife, Health Visitor and Community Nurse*, **13**, 96–100.
Hayman, C. R. (1970). Sexual assaults on women and girls. *Annals of Internal Medicine*, **72**. 277–278.
Hayman, C. R., Lanza, C., Fuentes, R., and Algor, K. (1972). Rape in the District of Colombia. *American Journal of Obstetrics and Gynecology*, **113**, 91–97.
Hayman, C. R., Stewart, W. F., Lewis, F. R., and Grant, M. (1968). Sexual assault on women and children in the District of Columbia. *Public Health Reports*, **83**, 1021–1028.
Hursch, C. J., and Selkin, J. (1974). *Rape Prevention Research Project*. Annual report of the Violence Research Unit, Division of Psychiatric Service, Department of Health and Hospitals, Denver.
Jackson, S. (1978). The social context of rape: sexual scripts and motivation. *Women's Studies International Quarterly*, **1**, 27–38.
Katz, S., and Mazur, M. A. (1979). *Understanding the Rape Victim*. New York: John Wiley.
Kirkpatrick, C., and Kanin, E. (1957). Male sex aggression on a university campus. *American Sociological Review*, **22**, 52–58.
London Rape Crisis Centre (1977). *Rape Counselling and Research Project First Annual Report*.
London Rape Crisis Centre (1978). *Rape Counselling and Research Project Second Annual Report*.
McCombie, S. L., Bassuk, E., Savitz, R., and Pell, S. (1976). Development of a medical centre rape crisis intervention program. *American Journal of Psychiatry*, **133**, 418–421.
MacDonald, J. H. (1971). *Rape Offenders and Their Victims*. Springfield, Ill.: Charles C. Thomas.
Massey, J. B., Garcia, C. R., and Emich, J. P. (1971). Management of sexually assaulted females. *Obstetrics and Gynecology*, **38**, 29–36.
Medea, A., and Thompson, K. (1974). *Against Rape: A Survival Manual for Women*. New York: Farrar, Straus and Giraux.
New South Wales Bureau of Crime Statistics and Research (1971) *Rape Offences*, reported in Toner (1977), *q. v.*
Notman, M. T. and Nadelson, C. C. (1976). The rape victim: psychodynamic considerations. *American Journal of Psychiatry*, **133**, 408–413.
Peters, J. J. (1973). Child rape: defusing a psychological time bomb. *Hospital Physician*, **1973**, 46–49.
Peters, J. J. (1975). Social, legal and psychological effects of rape on the victim. *Pennsylvania Medicine*, **78**, 34–36.
Peters, J. J., Meyer, L. C., and Carroll, N. E. (1976). *The Philadelphia Assault Victim Study*. Final report from the National Institute of Mental Health, ROIMH 21304.
Reynolds, J. M. (1978). Rape as social control. *Telos*, **18**, 62–67.
Russell, D. E. H. (1975). *The Politics of Rape*, New York: Stein and Day.
Schiff, A. F. (1969). Statistical features of rape. *Journal of Forensic Sciences*, **14**, 102–111.
Schiff, A. F. (1973). A statistical evaluation of rape. *Forensic Science*, **2**, 339–349.
Schultz, L. G. (1973). The child sex victim: social, psychological and legal perspectives. *Child Welfare*, **52**, 147–157.
Selkin, T. (1975). Rape: when to fight back. *Psychology Today*, **1975**, 71–76.
Shorter, E. (1977). On writing the history of rape. *Signs*, **3**, 471–482.
Silvermann, D. (1977). First do no more harm: female rape victims and the male counselor. *American Journal of Orthophychiatry*, **47**, 91–96.

Storaska, F. (1975). *How to Say No to a Rapist . . . and Survive*. New York: Random House.

Sutherland, S., and Scherl, D. T. (1970). Patterns of response among victims of rape. *American Journal of Orthopsychiatry*, **40**, 503–511.

Symonds, M. (1975). The psychological patterns of response of victims to rape. Paper presented to John Jay College of Criminal Justice and American Academy for Professional Law Enforcement, reported in Katz and Mazur (1979), *q.v.*

Travis, C., and Offir, C. (1977). *The Longest War: Sex Differences in Perspective*. New York: Harcourt Brace Jovanovich.

Toner, B. (1977). *The Facts of Rape*. London: Hutchinson.

Weis, K., and Borges, S. S. (1973). Victimology and rape: the case of the legitimate victim. *Issues in Criminology*, **8**, 71–115.

Developments in the Study of Criminal Behaviour. Volume 2: Violence
Edited by Philip Feldman

4

Vandalism and its Prevention

PAT MAYHEW and RON CLARKE

Introduction

For the critic of contemporary society, vandalism is a particularly potent symbol of a supposed breakdown in social order. The media reinforce this view, but just how seriously most people take the problem of deliberate damage to property is difficult to say. One-third of the adults interviewed in a recent survey felt that vandalism was over-sensationalized by the newspapers and those living in the most deprived areas saw such damage as one of their lesser problems (Research Bureau Limited, 1977*a*). Some scepticism about the social significance of vandalism is therefore needed; nevertheless, local authorities and others are faced with a considerable problem of the accumulation of countless rather petty incidents of damage which impoverish the environment and cost large sums of public money in repairs, even if they rarely cause danger or hardship.

The term 'vandalism' is retained in this chapter because it is used by criminologists in this country (the UK) and elsewhere as a convenient way of referring to deliberate damage to property. As such it is roughly equivalent to the legal category of criminal damage, but it is sometimes used in other ways. For example, it can encompass hooliganism or rowdy behaviour—in the aforementioned survey (Research Bureau Limited, 1977*a*) nearly a quarter of those interviewed defined the dangers of being intimidated, attacked, or even robbed in the street as vandalism. Environmental campaigners occasionally use the term in referring to industrial pollution or to what they see as desecration of the national heritage by planners and architects. It may also be extended to cover much of the careless and indifferent treatment of the environment which is less intentionally harmful than vandalism but which is just as unsightly in its results. In fact, it was not always possible in the research reported in this chapter to exclude from analysis damage that may have been the result of less deliberate action.

It is impossible to gauge the 'true' extent of deliberate damage to public and private property. Some local authorities and public bodies such as the Post Office keep records of repairs for vandalism, but these are not always centrally collated and, again, it can be difficult to exclude normal wear and tear. Because of low levels of reporting, police statistics on criminal damage are also far from satisfactory. Local authorities and other public bodies seem to inform the police only when substantial damage has been committed, or when there seems a real chance of catching the culprit; businesses appear not to report unless an insurance claim is made; and members of the public, who rarely witness damage actually being done, seem not to report vandalism because it may appear trivial or because there seems little chance of anything useful being done.

It is also impossible to put a reliable figure on the costs of damage. Cross (1979) has argued that it is the most economically harmful crime involving absolute losses to the community, rather than the redistribution of resources which results from, say, theft. Most estimates are put in the region of hundreds of millions of pounds, which allows for a conveniently large margin of error while still indicating the rough scale of the problem. Some figures are available. In America, it is claimed that more is spent in schools on repairing vandalism damage than on textbooks, a calculation that has not been attempted in this country. British Rail spent between £3 million and £5 million in repairs resulting from vandalism in the financial year 1977/78 (Central Policy Review Staff, 1978), while the Post Office's bill for deliberate damage to public call-boxes amounted to £1.3 million in the following financial year. A recent Home Office (1980) report calculated that fires caused by vandalism might cost in the region of £80 million to £100 million a year.

Financial costs are only part of the picture. There are cases of vandalism involving fire or tampering with traffic signals which can lead to accident or even death. Such incidents inevitably attract considerable publicity, but this can deflect attention from what may be a more insidious problem: individually less serious but much more commonplace incidents of damage (broken saplings, defaced road signs, torn bus seats, broken lifts in high-rise blocks of flats) contribute to a general process of environmental decay in which age, poor maintenance and litter also play a part. The sense of hopelessness induced by the blighted appearance of so many urban localities is an unquantifiable but still real cost of vandalism which should not be forgotten when weighing the costs of remedial action.

Explanations of vandalism

Definitional problems, the inadequacies of the statistics, and the relative anonymity of the vandal all help to explain the fact that rather little research has been conducted on vandalism as a specific form of antisocial behaviour. It was formerly treated only as one aspect of juvenile crime in general, featuring sometimes as the archetypal 'negativistic' act of juvenile subcultures. In so far as vandalism has been singled out in 'psychological' theories of deviant behaviour, the conclusion has been drawn—usually on the basis of studies of small samples of apprehended offenders—that the offender has been 'disposed' to commit damage because of some kind of emotional maladjustment or defect of character (e.g. Lippman, 1954; West, 1967). Typically, the apparent purposelessness of damage has been emphasized (e.g. Shalloo, 1954), this being seen as an expression of unhealthy levels of aggression and frustration born of innate personality deficiencies, faulty socialization or the particular stresses of adolescence. West (1967), for instance, concludes that 'acts of malicious damage may provide one substitute for aggression against people'. Arson in particular has lent itself to being explained in terms of maladjustment: attention has been paid to clinically bizarre and apparently sexual components of offences, to different types of arsonists (e.g. Hurley and Monahan, 1969; Prins, 1978), and to the compulsive element of the behaviour and risks of recidivism (e.g. Soothill and Pope, 1973). For these reasons, arson has been treated as a separate phenomenon in more recent research, although some fires which have been deliberately set by children may be included under the heading of vandalism.

As with explanations of other forms of antisocial behaviour, psychological theories of vandalism stressing personality deficiencies have been largely displaced by 'sociological' explanations encompassing a wide range of social disadvantage. Here again, however, particularly where vandalism has been treated as phenomenologically indistinct from other forms of criminal deviance, a 'dispositional' slant is evident (cf Clarke, 1980). The fact that vandalism, even more than other offences, is a predominantly male activity (Mannheim, 1954; Martin, 1961) has featured quite largely in explanation. Cohen (1955) has implicated 'role' frustration among boys which he sees as operating differently in different classes: among middle-class youths vandalism is an assertion of masculinity in the face of oppressive maternal influences, while among lower-class boys, it is an attack on the symbols of middle-class respectability and a protest against being made to feel inferior by higher status groups.

These kinds of explanation still inform a great deal of public rhetoric about the inherent difficulties of modern life which are seen as predisposing certain groups to destructive behaviour. Sentiments expressed in the early 1970s by the Director of the National Children's Bureau, for instance, strike a typical chord when (covering a host of possibilities), blame is put on high density living, job mobility and unemployment, impersonal neighbourhoods, overcrowding, the influence of television, and inadequate leisure provision (Kellmer Pringle, 1973).

Dividing dominant explanations of vandalism under simple psychological and sociological headings is inevitably crude, particularly in that it glosses over combined accounts which have emphasized the social context in which damage occurs as well as individual reactions. The fact remains, however, that most traditional explanations have focused upon predisposing personal and social factors although these accounts are now beginning to be displaced by a more situationally informed view of property damage. This is most evident in writings which have treated vandalism as a specific type of deviant behaviour rather than as one aspect of crime in general, and though largely of recent origin, a situational element is not entirely absent from earlier theories. Essays on vandalism by Clinard and Wade (1958) and Wade (1967), for instance, stress that vandalism is often 'behaviour of the moment', arising in response to certain situations which provide easy opportunities for damage and various personal and social rewards. It has frequently been noted also that vandalism is not a solitary activity but more the result of group dynamics (e.g. Clinard and Wade, 1958; Martin, 1961; Sveri, 1965; Wade, 1967; Erikson, 1971; Hindelang, 1976). Leaning heavily on subcultural theory, vandalism is seen as emanating from group norms emphasizing strength, fighting prowess, toughness and willingness to take risks—the need to demonstrate these qualities being put forward as a more important factor in explaining vandalism (and indeed violence) than impulsive, uncontrolled aggression. In this country, Downes' (1966) position is not untypical: working-class boys become delinquent (and commit damage) because they disassociate themselves from work and school, adopting manufactured excitement as a solution to the restrictions under which they live.

The shift towards a situational interpretation of vandalism became particularly noticeable with the publication of a collection of essays edited by Ward (1973). While these essays also reflect the influence of social interactionist theory (a good deal being made of the point that different types of damage provoke different degrees of social tolerance), their situational emphasis is evident in three ways. First, effort is directed towards subdividing vandalism into discrete types of behaviour. Cohen's (1973*a*) introductory essay, for instance, proposes five categories of 'acquisitive', 'vindictive', 'malicious', 'tactical' and 'play' vandalism—this a development on Martin's (1961) previous division of damage into 'predatory', 'vindictive' and 'wanton' forms. Secondly, the essays reflect a growing tendency to put paid to the image of vandalism as the purposeless manifestation of diffuse aggression: evidence is adduced that most vandalism is instrumental behaviour, committed in furtherance of explicable aims. For example, windows may be broken in the furtherance of theft, by teenagers acting out a dare, as a gesture of ideological discontent, or to get the apochryphal prison roof over one's head (Prewer, 1959). Thirdly, simultaneous with Newman's then new theory of 'defensible space' (Newman, 1972), the book provides evidence of an emerging interest in the relationship between crime and the built environment: architects and planners are exhorted to design in ways which will minimize the consequences of vandalism and reduce opportunities for it to occur.

Home Office research and its implications for theory

The more situationally oriented view of vandalism evident in Ward's book (Ward, 1973) has been developed further by a programme of research conducted within the Home Office Research Unit. This research, which aimed to provide information about vandalism which would inform thinking about prevention, concerned itself explicitly with situational aspects of particular forms of vandalism. It consisted of the following discrete studies:

(1) A study of the extent of different kinds of vandalism on a public housing estate consisting of some 5000 households in Manchester. Police and local

authority records were studied and 'victim' surveys were conducted of residents, shopkeepers and head teachers in the area to see if they had suffered from vandalism (see Sturman, 1978).

(2) A self-report study in which 584 boys aged between 11 and 15 in a northern city were asked about vandalism and other offences they had committed in a 6 month period. They were also questioned about their leisure pursuits, the extent of supervision by their parents and their attitudes to school and to work (see Gladstone, 1978).

(3) A study of vandalism on 38 London housing estates designed to test Newman's (1972) ideas about the relationship between architectural design ('defensible space') and crime. Data concerning vandalism in 285 separate housing blocks of five basic design types were collected, as well as that on other features of the estates, such as the numbers of children resident (see Wilson, 1978).

(4) A study of vandalism on 99 double-deck buses of varying design to see if the amount of supervision that could be given to passengers by the driver or conductor affected the commission of vandalism (see Mayhew *et al.*, 1976).

(5) A study of vandalism to over 200 telephone kiosks in a representative London borough. Damage was studied in relation to such variables as the physical location of the kiosks and the characteristics of the population living in the surrounding areas (see Mayhew *et al.*, 1979).

(6) A study of a television anti-vandalism publicity campaign conducted in the north of England in 1978. The incidence of vandalism before, during and after the campaign was measured in the 'test' and a 'control' region using local authority vandalism repair records, Post Office records of telephone kiosk damage, and police statistics of criminal damage offences (see Riley and Mayhew, 1980).

(7) An account of an 'action' project conducted by the Home Office Crime Policy Planning Unit which sought to identify effective preventive measures for 11 'target' schools on the basis of close analysis of the nature of the vandalism problem being faced (see Gladstone, 1980).

The evidence from this research highlights a number of points about vandalism which are somewhat inconsistent with earlier academic thinking. In the first place—and this is something mentioned above—it underlines the fact that most incidents of vandalism are individually petty rather than the serious acts of destruction which traditional perspectives would see as reflecting psychologically or socially determined aggression. While such acts are not unknown, their contribution to the general problem of vandalism has been greatly exaggerated, not least because of the attention hitherto paid to officially defined vandals who are likely to have caused unusually substantial damage or to have increased their chances of detection by committing offences while excessively drunk. Typical incidents of vandalism are rather different. In the study of London housing

Table 1 Location of damage on 38 London housing estates for a 15-month period

	Lifts	Private dwellings	Stairs, corridors, walkways	Communal facilities*	Entrances	Outside areas	Underground garages†	Roofs	Total
Number of items of damage	1643	1475	1416	776	361	289	176	89	6225
Percentage(%)	26	24	23	12	6	5	3	1	100

*'Communal facilities' covers tenants' store-sheds, cupboards for fittings, caretakers' rooms, laundries, etc.

†Several underground garages had, because of vandalism, ceased to be used and had been left unrepaired, so the figure given is likely to be an underestimate.

estates, for instance, just over half the incidents of damage involved broken glass. In the study of the 5000 households on the Manchester estate, the greater proportion of the 940 incidents occurring in the 6-month period involved small sums of money, which helps to explain the fact that only some 7% of incidents were reported to the police.

A second general conclusion of the research somewhat at variance with traditional explanations is that damage seems to be committed predominantly against public rather than people's personal and private property (i.e. their homes, gardens, and cars). Evidence submitted to a Home Office Working Party (Home Office, 1975) indicated that most vandalism is directed at local authority property. This picture is confirmed by the results of the Manchester estate study where the rate of damage to dwellings or to residents' property was found to be appreciably less than the corresponding rate of damage to other targets. (On the basis of a crude rate of damage per 10 properties, houses experienced 0.4 instances of damage, shops 34.0, telephone kiosks 78.1 and schools 191.8.) In the study of the 38 London housing estates, individual dwellings were the target of only a quarter of the 6225 incidents of vandalism recorded by the local authority (Table 1), for the most part involving broken windows in ground floor dwellings, many of which were unoccupied.

These findings fit rather uneasily with the implicit contention of traditional explanations that the vandal will be so internally charged as to commit damage randomly, or so socially frustrated as to choose targets which stand as symbols of the 'better life' from which he is being excluded. There may be an element of such selectivity in some cases of vandalism, for instance where a number of cars are damaged in the same street, but most targets seem to be chosen because they present easy and perhaps morally unproblematic opportunities for committing damage undetected. The vandal, that is, may direct himself towards public property because it is less likely to be guarded (as a private house is) by someone with a strong sense of ownership or because it is seem as not belonging to anyone who might have to pay for repairs out of their own pocket.

Thirdly, recent evidence suggests that most vandalism is committed either by younger children in the course of unsupervised play or by older adolescents in groups for whom damage is 'an outgrowth of restless and exuberant youth' (Clinard and Wade, 1958). A study in Blackburn (Marshall, 1976) found that the peak age of male vandals coming to the notice of the police was less than 10. (Current official statistics on those cautioned and convicted for offences of criminal damage signify a disproportionate involvement of children given the numbers in the population, though in the light of Marshall's findings these seem to underestimate the involvement of the very youngest age-groups who may be dealt with informally by the police—if they come to police notice at all. Moreover, as mentioned earlier, adult vandals often seem to be excessively drunk, thereby increasing their chances of being arrested and therefore of appearing in the statistics.) The trivial nature of much damage (torn telephone directories, broken street lamps, etc.) also suggests it is childish in origin, as well as the fact that damage to schools, for which children of school age are usually seen as responsible, accounts for as much as 40% of local authority spending on vandalism (Home Office, 1975). In the Home Office study of London housing estates, the single variable most highly correlated with damage was a measure of the densities at which children were accommodated; damage seemed inevitable on housing blocks of all types of design after a certain level of child density had been reached (see Table 2). In the Home Office telephone kiosk study the number of children resident in the localities immediately surrounding each kiosk was an especially important determinant of the level of damage it sustained, particularly in 'council' housing areas.

The fact that so much vandalism is committed by young people was not entirely neglected by earlier explanations (e.g. Martin, 1961) and it is less this fact which creates difficulties for dispositional theories than the fact that such large proportions of children and adolescents are involved in vandalism. This widespread involvement is documented in the Home Office self-report study of

Table 2 Vandalism and child densities on London housing estates

Children per 10 dwellings	Number of housing blocks	Percentage of blocks with 'fair amount' or 'extensive' vandalism (%)
Less than 1	41	7
1–2	74	31
3–5	106	40
6–8	40	55
9 or more	24	62
Total	285	37

Table 3 The prevalence of vandalism among 584 boys in a northern city

Act of vandalism	Percentage of boys who had carried out such an act (%)
1. Scratched desk at school	85
2. Broken a bottle in the street	79
3. Broken a window in an empty house	68
4. Written on walls in the street	65
5. Broken trees or flowers in a park	58
6. Written on the seats or walls of buses	55
7. Broken the glass in a street lamp	48
8. Scratched a car or lorry	42
9. Smashed things on a building site	40
10. Broken a window in an occupied house	32
11. Broken the glass in a bus shelter	32
12. Damaged park buildings	31
13. Broken furniture at school	29
14. Broken a window in a public toilet	29
15. Broken the glass of a telephone kiosk	28
16. Broken a car radio aerial	28
17. Damaged the tyres of a car	28
18. Broken a window at school	27
19. Slashed bus seats	22
20. Broken a seat in a public toilet	20
21. Damaged telephone in a kiosk	20
22. Put large objects on a railway line	19
23. Broken a window in a club	16
24. Slashed train seats	12

11–15 year old boys. For example, 68% of the boys questioned had broken a window in an empty house within the previous 6 months, while 48% had broken the glass in a street lamp (see Table 3); and boys from all backgrounds admitted to vandalism, even though a 'hard core' of vandals was identifiable in other respects. Other studies undertaken in this country tell the same tale. Eighty-two per cent of West and Farrington's (1973) sample of boys had broken a window in an empty house, while a quarter of the boys admitted to more serious offences of vandalism. Corrigan's (1979) study of 15-year old working-class boys in Sunderland shows that 75 out of 93 had smashed a street lamp or done some other equivalent damage in the preceding 2 years. And comparable levels of involvement are evident from the responses of 10–11 year old schoolboys in Birmingham studied by Wilson (1980)—the degree of social handicap of the boys' families not being a distinguishing factor.

Vandalism in social learning terms

Without neglecting predisposing psychological and social factors, a more complete explanation of vandalism can be achieved by incorporating 'situational' factors more directly into criminological explanation in the manner proposed by Clarke (1980). His suggestions boil down to seeing crime not in dispositional terms, but as being the outcome of the offender's choices and decisions. These will be influenced not simply be the individual's make-up and past experiences but also by the circumstances of his present life and features of the immediate behavioural setting for crime.

To the extent that it emphasizes subjective choice, this formulation of criminal behaviour has affinities with 'control theory' (Hirschi, 1970) and with the 'new criminology' (Taylor *et al.*, 1973) though these can still be regarded as 'dispositional' theories seeking to account for the involvement of certain individuals in crime rather than, as in Clarke's formulation, the occurrence of particular criminal events. In fact, the emphasis on learning and the immediate social and physical setting suggests a rather closer debt to social learning theory. This should be clear from the discussion below of the factors affecting the decision to commit vandalism, even though these have not been arranged under the conventional social learning heads (cf. Feldman, 1977), of acquisition of response, the evoking situation, and maintenance by outcome:

(1) *Motives.* The primary motivation underlying much of the vandalism taking place in adolescent groups or gangs would seem to be the need to prove masculine 'toughness' in a competitive situation. This is supported by the Home Office self-report study in which it was found that the boys most heavily involved in vandalism were likely to belong to a 'tough' group (Table 4). As often stressed, group dynamics can also prompt acts of damage because of the excitement induced by the situation and the knowledge that everyone will be taking a risk. No doubt some acts of vandalism, in a particular teacher's classroom or against a neighbour's car, will be committed for revenge. The variety of other possible motives for vandalism is implicit in the typologies of the behaviour developed by Cohen (1973*a*) and Martin (1961) which were mentioned above.

Table 4 Involvement in vandalism by group membership for 584 boys in a northern city

Reported involvement in vandalism	Boys seldom or never in a group (%)	Boys in groups		All boys
		Toughness not important (%)	Toughness important (%)	
Low	50	46	12	34
Medium	31	34	36	34
High	19	21	51	33
Total number of boys, n (=100%)	238	101	245	584

$\chi^2 = 103.1$; 4 degrees of freedom; $P < 0.001$.

(2) *Mood.* Not altogether distinct from motivational pressures, a transitory subjective mood may well play a part in prompting an individual to commit damage. Though mood may be influenced by inherited temperament, much more salient are likely to be the individual's hopes and current prospects, and the effects of recent crises or events. Boredom is often cited as an explanation for teenage vandalism, and 'having nothing else to do' was a frequently quoted reason for vandalism by the children surveyed by Research Bureau Limited (1977*b*). Boredom apart, it is difficult to know how much vandalism is the result of some temporary unhappiness and it may also be difficult to draw a line between tensions of a random nature (e.g. a tiff with a girlfriend, or Arsenal losing to Spurs) and the supposed 'structural' tensions of vandals' lives (e.g. restricted living conditions or unstimulating schooling). As far as schooling is concerned, the evidence of the Home Office self-report study indicates that the most committed vandals are those who do poorly at school, do not like it (Table 5), and usually leave early. This may be of relevance in building up general antisocial attitudes, though it is equally likely that particular instances of damage, perhaps committed by a pupil against the school itself, will result from some upsetting incident such as being bullied by other children.

(3) *Moral evaluation.* Although many people will be deterred from committing damage because of moral constraints, feelings of moral impropriety may not operate strongly among those most involved in vandalism; this is likely particularly to the extent that the targets of damage are publicly owned. Vandals may employ a wide range of 'techniques of neutralization' (Matza, 1964) to justify their actions or, in the language of psychology, to reduce the 'cognitive dissonance' (cf. Feldman, 1977, pp. 80–81) between their actions and previously

Table 5 Involvement in vandalism of 584 boys in a northern city by attitude to school and achievement

	Self-perceived school achievement				
	Successful*		Unsuccessful†		
Reported involvement in vandalism	Likes school (%)	Dislikes school (%)	Likes school (%)	Dislikes school (%)	All boys (%)
Low	55	24	40	23	34
Medium	30	44	34	30	34
High	15	32	26	48	33
Total number of boys, n (= 100%)	142	113	102	227	584

*$\chi^2 = 26.3$; 2 degrees of freedom; $P < 0.001$.
†$\chi^2 = 16.8$; 2 degrees of freedom; $P < 0.001$.

held, but incompatible, attitudes. Thus boys damaging an empty building may see it as belonging to no one in particular or as likely to be demolished anyway. It is also questionable how far they consider themselves to be breaking strong social norms. Clinard and Wade (1958) contend that the teenage vandal may view himself as a 'prankster' (particularly where nothing is stolen), while Corrigan (1979), on the basis of his research in Sunderland, goes further in concluding that working-class adolescents feel little guilt at all about damaging property. This may hold only for certain boys committing less serious damage in the worst environmental areas, although the fact remains that many people currently treat property in a casual manner and in adolescent circles at least certain types of damage are, as Corrigan puts it, 'culturally unremarkable'. In relation to younger children engaging in 'play' vandalism, the 'moral' significance of damage (if it is not actually accidental) may rarely be appreciated: it is fairly common to hear children excused by the fact that they have not yet matured to a responsible evaluation of property rights and values.

(4) *Criminal knowledge and opportunities.* Whereas some offences may require detailed knowledge and considerable organizational ability (fraud and bank robbery, for instance, or even stealing cars and burglary), committing damage poses few such problems: little technical competence is required, instruments of destruction are easy to obtain, and there is usually no property to dispose of. Moreover, there is a very wide range of potential targets for damage; this is true even if public property alone is considered, given Wilson's (1979) point that the increase of vandalism in the post-war period runs concurrent with a considerable expansion of property in municipal ownership. Many of these potential targets will have characteristics facilitating if not actually encouraging vandalism—in particular, a lack of supervision. This lesson has emerged from the House Office study of bus vandalism where the extent and location of damage on 99 double-deck buses was much influenced by whether there was one or two crew members, and hence by the degree of supervision exercised over passengers (Table 6). The point is also evident in relation to the test of Newman's 'defensible space' hypothesis on London housing estates in that the results confirmed Newman's claim that vandalism is most prevalent in public areas to which residents' feelings of territorial responsibility are unlikely to extend. As well as the widespread

Table 6 Mean seat damage score by deck and type of bus

	One-man operated ($N = 48$)	Dual purpose ($N = 22$)	Conductor-operated with front entrances ($N = 12$)	Conductor-operated with rear entrances ($N = 17$)
Lower deck	0.22	0.12	0.23	0.37
Upper deck	5.12	2.47	2.70	1.97

availability of targets, the considerable freedom of movement allowed to children also plays a part. Whatever the wider social desirability of this freedom, the fact remains, as the Home Office study shows, that involvement in vandalism is greatest among boys who spend long hours out of the house with a group of 'tough' friends (Gladstone, 1978).

(5) *Assessment of risk*. In deciding whether to commit a particular offence, except perhaps when under the influence of drink or strong emotions, the offender will weigh the *chances* of being caught as well as the formal and informal *consequences* likely to ensue. While this assessment of risk will vary considerably according to the offence involved and the individual's previous experience of offending, the widespread nature of vandalism may have much to do with the fact that it is one of the safest and most anonymous of offences (cf. Griffiths and Shapland, 1979). The vandal can easily choose his moment and, as there is seldom an immediate victim to complain or to retaliate, the chances of being held to account are remote. That the youngster learns this soon enough from his own experience or from that of his peers is confirmed by the Research Bureau Limited (1977*b*) study in which about 50 boys aged between 8 and 16 were interviewed about their involvement in vandalism. All showed themselves aware of the low risks involved: they claimed that the police were unlikely to witness their misbehaviour and that passers-by would be fearful to apprehend them; even if a 'chase' did occur, they thought they would easily be able to escape. No doubt vandalism will less readily become habitual where action is taken against a culprit or where he comes to know about punishments meted out to others. Even here, however, fear of repercussions may be lessened by the fact that detection often results in minor sanctions. Most boys in the survey conducted by Research Bureau Limited, while worried about their parents learning about their misdeeds, were cavalier about police action—not perhaps without reason: *Criminal Statistics, 1978* (Home Office, 1979) indicates that of those dealt with formally by the police (and there are not doubt many who are informally warned) four out of five were cautioned (15%) fined (53%) or discharged by the court (14%).

A first act of vandalism committed by a youngster may be the result of a chance motivational state combined with an easy opportunity and, depending on reinforcements (whether he gets away with the act or finds it rewarding), the response may take up a permanent place in the individual's behavioural repertoire. In this way it becomes part of that past experience which he brings to any new situation, and it thus has some affinities with traditional concepts about predispositions. The important differences are that the response is a specific behaviour (not 'delinquency' nor even vandalism committed to all and every possible target but to ones possessing specific characteristics), and that repetitions will depend on reinforcements and on whether the individual finds himself again in a similar situation. Positive reinforcement may indeed encourage him actively to seek out appropriate settings to perform further acts of vandalism, regardless of the reasons which led him to do so in the first place.

The fact that low risks of detection may combine with positive rewards helps to explain the widespread nature of vandalism. Nevertheless, most habitual delinquents grow up into reasonably mature and law-abiding adults for reasons that are not difficult to understand: in the case of the adolescent vandal his dependence on a 'tough' group of friends may evaporate when he acquires a steady girl-friend, his need for excitement may be satisfied by a car or motor bike, and his hours may be more completely filled by a job than by school (cf. Trasler, 1979). The interplay of changing circumstances, growing maturity, and experiences at the hands of the law which led to the declining involvement of a group of Liverpool boys in car thefts has been graphically described in a case study by Parker (1974).

Inevitably, a 'choice' model of vandalism has its limitations. In particular, it seems less applicable to vandalism committed by the youngest age-groups for which, indeed, no very elaborate explanation might be needed. Vandalism may be no more than part of the natural development of young children which leads them to explore and manipulate their environment in ways which involve throwing stones, breaking bottles, scratching, scribbling or playing with matches. When this activity is unsupervised, damage will inevitably result. Again, some impulsive acts of vandalism, or those committed under the influence of alcohol or strong emotion, may not easily be seen as the result of choices or decisions, although it is doubtful that these constitute a significant proportion of all vandal acts.

Reducing vandalism

Individualized treatment

The dispositional slant of traditional psychological and sociological explanations of vandalism implies intervention to bring about change in the individual's personality or attitudes so as to make him less likely to commit damage. As Wilson (1975) has argued, such interventions, especially those premised on the psychological model, are rarely practicable: there appear to be no acceptable ways of modifying temperament or other biological variables, while there are obvious problems of making parents provide a home environment less conducive to involvement in vandalism. Many forms of therapy have been suggested, such as community service or placement within residential therapeutic communities, but these treatments could only be available for those most at risk of recidivism. Even supposing this group could be identified, there is little reason to think that available 'treatments' manage to rectify behavioural problems at all (see, for instance, Brody, 1976). Behaviour modification or reality therapy might seem more appropriate alternatives consistent with social learning principles, but it is not clear how far these techniques—which are drawn from the mental health field—are applicable in the area of criminal deviance and in particular to vandalism. In any case, because of costs they too could only be selectively applied.

Publicity

Attempts to strengthen moral inhibitions about committing damage seem no more promising. The chief way this is done at present is through publicity directed at children themselves, or their parents, to increase awareness of the seriousness of vandalism—its financial costs to the community, the potential dangers involved and its threat to social values. Parents seem little moved by such campaigns, perhaps because they find it difficult to believe that their children are at fault. They may also be reluctant to report more incidents to the police (should they witness them) when, as the survey by Research Bureau Limited (1977*a*) shows, they fear reprisals or hesitate to get culprits into too much trouble. Evaluations of an anti-vandalism publicity campaign televised in the north of England in 1978 found only very little effect on what parents believed about vandalism or how they supervised their children's activities (Research Bureau Limited, 1978), and no evidence of an effect on levels of damage to schools, housing estates or telephone kiosks (Riley and Mayhew, 1980).

As far as children are concerned, a recognized danger is that publicity campaigns about vandalism run the risk of 'putting ideas into their heads' (Cohen, 1973*b*; Home Office, 1975). Moreover, a Home Office review of recent evidence (Riley and Mayhew, 1980) suggests that such publicity has been of benefit only where it manages to convince children (which it by no means always does) that risks of detection have been significantly increased; general exhortation seems of little value because it competes poorly with the more powerful group pressures operating at the time damage occurs and with other situational inducements to vandalism. As something of an exception, 'vandalism' to railway lines is believed to have been reduced by educational compaigns, but this type of damage may be more often exploratory and non-malicious in character than most urban damage and children may not have been sufficiently aware of the real dangers to life.

Social provision

Tackling the disadvantages indicted by sociological theory might appear more promising than 'psychological' interventions, but blaming vandalism on unemployment, for instance, is one thing—'stemming the tide' is another. Nor is it known which social ills need most attention: vandalism, like many other offences, has increased in the face of general improvements in socioeconomic conditions since the war, and it is not confined simply to those most socially deprived.

The provision of better schooling is a particularly popular 'social' approach to vandalism prevention. Some empirical support for it can be found in the results of the Home Office self-report study that vandals are poor achievers who dislike school, and Goldman's (1961) evidence that the characteristics of schools themselves seem important in determining levels of damage—heavily vandalized schools were those in which morale was low, the equipment poor and staff turnover high. There is not much immediate prospect of lessening academic failure, but there may be ways of tackling dislike of school. Sometimes what may be needed is to relax an overly coercive approach to discipline; in other cases it may be more a matter of shifting the emphasis in the curriculum towards studies for which the low achiever can muster more enthusiasm. Other approaches will be more directly related to vandalism (for a comprehensive review see Hope, 1980): involving pupils in improving the appearance of a school and its grounds had been advocated (e.g. Moncure, 1978), while in the United States success has been claimed for schemes in which funds normally devoted to the repair of damage have been set aside for special activities or equipment on the condition that no vandalism occurs (Olson and Carpenter, 1971; Cross, 1979).

While there will always be a case on intrinsic grounds for improving leisure provision (youth clubs, adventure playgrounds, city farms, playing fields, etc.), it is far from clear to what extent this might combat the boredom that is seen as the motivation for much vandalism, or channel behaviour into supposedly safe or constructive alternatives. Bagley's (1965) study showed a correlation between local authority spending on youth services and the incidence of delinquency, though any causal relationship between these has been challenged by more recent work (see Baldwin and Bottoms, 1976). For younger children, providing play-space to divert them away from the temptations of derelict houses or lifts in high rise flats is no easy matter; as Ward (1973) puts it: 'No self-respecting child will confine his activities to a recognized playground and the whole housing environment should be designed to cope with the activities of children'. It has also been claimed that new play facilities merely attract additional numbers of children from less well endowed areas. To have a real impact on the life-style of those older children involved in vandalism, any increase in leisure provision would again have to be substantial. Facilities would need to be open for much longer than is common at present, and to employ additional youth workers on this scale might well cost as much as the vandalism it would prevent. Vandalism is also not particularly time-consuming and there will always be plenty of available targets *en route* between home and club. It is even possible that better facilities would attract boys to the streets and into 'bad' company who might otherwise remain at home. (The Home Office self-report study found that boys were more likely to attend clubs if they were 'highly involved' in vandalism—a finding which runs counter to the prevalent notion of 'unclubbable' youths.) A further difficulty is that new club premises or playground equipment, which may often be left unsupervised, would provide easy targets for vandalism.

Prevention and the 'choice' model

To the extent that a 'choice' model of vandalism lends as much weight to the more immediate circumstances and conditions of offending as to the more distant causal factors identified in traditional psychological and sociological theories, it implies a rather broader range of preventive options. Even so the preventive pay-off should not be exaggerated. There may be little that can be done, for instance, to undermine some of the immediate motivational pressures towards vandalism: where destructive behaviour is prompted by misfortune or temporary unhappiness or where boredom alone provokes vandalism it is difficult to see how the necessary changes in the lives of many boys and girls could be achieved.

The more practicable preventive options arising from a 'choice' model stem from manipulation of the immediate settings in which vandalism takes place so as to (1) increase the risks of being caught, and (2) reduce the physical opportunities for vandalism. Discussion of these measures below has to be rather general and the point needs to be made here that preventive action cannot properly be considered in isolation from the administrative and wider social contexts in which it must be developed. In every case action taken 'on the ground' will depend on who has the responsibility to take action, and the pressures and constraints under which he operates. In most cases action will have to be taken by some such person as a local housing manager or telephone manager who will have a limited number of measures at his disposal. Ideally, each of these should be assessed in terms of the effort needed to implement it, the costs, and the effects upon things other than vandalism.

Not only do solutions have to be found separately for vandalism of different kinds, but the feasibility of particular measures will also vary from place to place. These points have been clarified by the Home Office action project in Manchester (Gladstone, 1980), where assistance was offered to the local education department in tackling vandalism in 11 separate schools. The measures recommended varied between the schools according to their different circumstances as well as the differing manifestations of the problem; and, although the final evaluation of the project is still under way, the degree to which recommended measures were in fact implemented appears also to have varied between schools.

Increasing the risks

A distinction was drawn above between the assessments made by an offender of the chances as well as of the consequences of being caught. In general, there seems to be greater scope for influencing the offender's assessment of his chances of being caught than for actually apprehending and punishing him. There is little evidence that harsher deterrent penalties deter crime (e.g. Zimring and Hawkins, 1973) and many vandals are too young to bear the full weight of the law—especially if their offences are of a minor nature. Punishment might be meted out indirectly by penalizing parents, but this option poses legal difficulties and is generally opposed by the social services and even magistrates. The application of sanctions depends in any case on catching the vandal—in itself no easy matter.

A higher level of 'formal' surveillance provided by the police or security guards might in theory increase risks of detection, but there seems little way of providing an adequate deterrent to vandals who can commit damage when nobody—police or anyone else—is in sight. Various experimental studies have found little effect on the crime rate as a result of increases in the general level of police present (see Clarke and Hough, 1980, for a review) and there is no reason to think the position would be different for vandalism. Some success has been claimed for specially mounted anti-vandal patrols in local areas such as parks or housing estates (e.g. Cohen, 1973*b*), or police escorts on trains carrying football supporters (Central Policy Review Staff, 1978), but given the comparatively minor nature of most vandalism these initiatives are difficult to sustain for any length of time. Surveillance aids such as closed circuit television or entry phones in high-rise flats, whether put into operation by the police or by others, have some potential value, though the installation and maintenance costs are high, and the equipment itself may be susceptible to vandalism (Musheno *et al.*, 1978). London Transport's now extensive use of closed circuit television on the underground railway system is believed to have reduced vandalism, but in that case it was possible to offset the considerable costs of the system against other gains such as the prevention of 'mugging' and, of greater importance, the facilitation of crowd control (Mayhew *et al.*, 1979).

Of greater potential value in altering the vandal's assessment of the risks of apprehension is the surveillance adventitiously provided by employees such as caretakers on housing estates or conductors on buses. Such employees already have broad responsibility for maintaining social order in the places they work and may be expected to take effective action in the event of trouble arising. In the Home Office study of bus vandalism it was found that damage was at a much lower level on buses which carry a conductor as well as a driver, while a Department of the Environment (1977) study concluded that estates with resident caretakers have fewer problems of vandalism. Merely the presence of such employees in increased numbers, or for greater parts of the day, may be enough to prevent much vandalism, though the costs of this may be only rarely justified by the savings in repairs; in other cases, it may be necessary to train employees for a greater security role and to provide them with the necessary facilities and support to enable them to carry it out.

A great deal has been made since the publication of Newman's (1972) *Defensible Space* of the possibility of using architectural design to improve security and surveillance opportunities by heightening people's feelings of responsibility towards their immediate living environment. The results of a number of empirical tests of the 'defensible space' hypothesis (see Mayhew, 1979, for a review) suggests that the approach is more limited than Newman contended (not least because of the difficulties of affecting sufficient defensible space changes in existing urban localities) but that design has still some part to play. In the study of vandalism on London housing estates (all of which had resident caretakers), it was found that rates of vandalism were particularly high in housing blocks which lacked defensible space characteristics. For example, blocks with few children and with entrances intended only for use by residents suffered less damage to lifts than those with entrances acting as a through-way to other parts of the estate—see Table 7. Similarly, in the study of telephone kiosk vandalism, it was found that kiosks which were afforded some degree of natural surveillance by being overlooked from dwellings had slightly lower rates of damage (Table 8). Here again, however, the effect of design was much less strong than that of the number of potential offenders (i.e. children, and particularly boys) housed in the locality.

Table 7 Damage to lifts in blocks with a low child density, by type of entrance, in a sample of London housing estates

Type of entrance	Number of blocks	Lift call-outs: Percentage of blocks with 0–4 call-outs (%)	Lift call-outs: Percentage of blocks with 5 or more call-outs (%)
Discrete entrance	30	70	30
Entrance acting as a throughway	21	24	76
Total	51	51	49

$\chi^2 = 10.5$; 1 degree of freedom; $P < 0.01$.

Reducing opportunities for vandalism

The most obvious way of restricting physical opportunities for deliberate damage is through 'target hardening'—i.e. the use of more appropriate finishes or materials, placing objects (e.g. lights in underpasses) out of reach or behind grilles, putting alarms in bus shelters, etc. These 'defensive' measures now have a good deal of support from those involved in dealing with vandalism 'on the ground'. A recent Design Council (1979) publication, for instance, has publicized the approach in rather more detail than Ward's (1973) book. More might also be achieved through a rather broader approach to design and management. Large areas of unsupervised semi-public spaces on housing estates and elsewhere should be reduced, for example, and buildings should not be left unoccupied for long periods. And given that damaged objects seem to invite further attack

Table 8 Kiosk vandalism and the effect of overlooking windows in 'council' and other areas in one London borough

	Average number of vandal incidents per kiosk	
	Non-council areas	Council areas
Less than median number of windows	4.3 ($n=76$)	7.1 ($n=36$)
More than median number of windows	3.5 ($n=72$)	5.6 ($n=33$)
All kiosks	3.9 ($n=148$)	6.4 ($n=69$)

NB: Kiosks in each of the two sectors are divided into two similarly-sized groups according to the number of windows which overlooked them. The split was made at the median number of windows: 19 in the case of kiosks in non-council areas, 28 in the case of the more overlooked kiosks in council areas.

(Zimbardo, 1973), there are good grounds for encouraging efficient maintenance and repair.

There may also be scope for trying to restrict access to the sorts of places where vandalism is most likely to occur. Children might be kept off building sites by higher fences, or it might be made easier through design for mothers to watch children playing on the environs of public housing estates. The findings concerning the importance of numbers of children resident on estates might suggest a policy of dispersing families with young children, but there may be few families willing to be uprooted unless provided with much better accommodation. Dispersal may therefore be more viable at the allocation stage, particularly as in some areas there is now a surplus of public housing.

Opportunity-reducing measures of the sort discussed above have had little appeal in many criminological circles. Apart from the fact that they tend to be seen merely as cosmetic palliatives leaving the root causes of the problem untouched, they provoke criticism on the grounds that the costs involved may outstrip the costs of damage itself. They are also seen to threaten a fortress society in which everyone is surrounded by guard dogs, barbed wire and television cameras—or at least by cheap and robust materials lending an embattled appearance to the environment as objectionable as vandalism itself. These fears are exaggerated. In developing preventive measures, care can be taken that the benefits do not exceed costs and there is no reason, for example, why a robust housing estate should not be attractively designed: defensible space designs are preferred by residents and, at a more mundane level, polycarbonate is indistinguishable from glass, while stippled paint surfaces, less inviting to the graffiti artist, can be as pleasing as plain ones.

A stronger objection to opportunity-reducing measures is that they merely result in a displacement of vandalism to less well protected targets or—indeed—to other forms of antisocial behaviour. To a certain extent this argument derives its force from a 'dispositional' view of crime—'bad will out'—and it receives less support from a 'choice' model in which vandalism is seen to be heavily influenced by particular situational inducements and the balance of risks and rewards involved. Thus, in the case of young children playing unsupervised, much damage may be the simple result of the vulnerability of targets, for which better protection might suffice. As far as the adolescent is concerned, however, the fact that he may use vandalism as a source of excitement and prestige may mean that greater impediments would often constitute a greater challenge or, given his greater mobility, he may attack less well-protected targets. Whether frustrated from vandalism he would turn instead to altogether more harmful crime such as robbery or assault is much more questionable. The Home Office self-report study did show that many vandals are also thieves, but as social learning theory would imply, theft and vandalism are not necessarily functional alternatives. Although committed by the same boys, they may satisfy different motives, they occur under different conditions, and they bring different rewards. Stopping one will not therefore inevitably lead to an increase in the other; the boys involved may even adopt some more positive responses if they do not naturally mature out of the crime-inducing circumstances of their youth.

Acknowledgement

This chapter is Crown copyright.

References

Bagley, C. (1965). Juvenile delinquency in Exeter. *Urban Studies*, **2**, 35–39.

Baldwin, J., and Bottoms, A. E. (1976). *The Urban Criminal*. London: Tavistock.

Brody, S. R. (1976). *The Effectiveness of Sentencing*. Home Office Research Study No. 35. London: HMSO.

Central Policy Review Staff (1978). *Vandalism*. London: HMSO.

Clarke, R. V. G. (1980). Situational crime prevention: theory and practice. *British Journal of Criminology*, **20**, 136–147.

Clarke, R. V. G., and Hough, J. M. (Eds) (1980). *The Effectiveness of Policing*. Farnborough, Hants: Gower.

Clinard, M. B., and Wade, A. L. (1958). Towards the delineation of vandalism as a sub-type in juvenile delinquency. *Journal of Criminal Law and Criminology*, **48**, 493–499.

Cohen, A. K. (1955). *Delinquent Boys: the Culture of the Gang*. Glencoe, Ill.: The Free Press.

Cohen, S. (1973*a*). Property destruction: motives and meanings, in *Vandalism* (Ed. C. Ward). London: Architectural Press, pp. 23–53.

Cohen, S. (1973*b*). Campaigning against vandalism, in *Vandalism* (Ed. C. Ward). London: Architectural Press, pp. 215–258.

Corrigan, P. (1979). *Schooling the Smash Street Kids*. London: Macmillan.

Cross, A. (1979). Vandalism: an Anglo-American perspective. *Police Studies*, **2**, 31–38.
Department of the Environment (1977). *Housing Management and Design*. Lambeth Inner Area Study IAS/IA/18. London: Department of the Environment.
Design Council (1979). *Designing against Vandalism*. London: The Design Council.
Downes, D. (1966). *The Delinquent Solution*. London: Routledge and Kegan Paul.
Erikson, M. L. (1971). The group context of delinquent behaviour. *Social Problems*, **19**, 114–129.
Feldman, M. P. (1977). *Criminal Behaviour*. Chichester: John Wiley.
Gladstone, F. J. (1978). Vandalism amongst adolescent schoolboys, in *Tackling Vandalism* (Ed. R. V. G. Clarke). Home Office Research Study No. 47. London: HMSO, pp. 19–39.
Gladstone, F. J. (1980). *Co-ordinating Crime Prevention Efforts*. Home Office Research Study No. 62. London: HMSO.
Goldman, N. (1961). A socio-psychological study of school vandalism. *Crime and Delinquency*, **7**, 221–230.
Griffiths, R., and Shapland, J. M. (1979). The vandal's perspective: meanings and motives, in *Designing Against Vandalism*. London: The Design Council, pp. 11–18.
Hindelang, M. J. (1976). With a little help from their friends: group participation in reported delinquent behaviour. *British Journal of Criminology*, **16**, 109–125.
Hirschi, T. (1970). *The Causes of Delinquency*. Berkeley, Calif.: University of California Press.
Home Office (1975). *Protection against Vandalism*. Report of the Home Office Standing Committee on Crime Prevention. London: Home Office.
Home Office (1979). *Criminal Statistics England and Wales, 1978*. Cmnd 7670. London: HMSO.
Home Office (1980). *Fires Caused by Vandalism*. Report of a Home Office Working Party. London: Home Office.
Hope, T. J. (1980). Four approaches to the prevention of property crime in schools. *Oxford Review of Education*, **6**, 231–240.
Hurley, W., and Monahon, T. M. (1969). Arson: the criminal and the crime. *British Journal of Criminology*, **9**, 4–21.
Kellmer Pringle, M. (1973). *The Roots of Violence and Vandalism*. London: National Children's Bureau.
Lippman, H. S. (1954). Vandalism as an outlet for aggression. *Federal Probation*, **18**, 5–6.
Mannheim, H. (1954). The problem of vandalism in Great Britain. *Federal Probation*, **18**, 5.
Marshall, T. (1976). Vandalism: the seeds of destruction, *New Society*, **36**, No. 715, 17 June, 625–627.
Martin, J. M. (1961). *Juvenile Vandalism*. Springfield Ill.: Charles C. Thomas.
Matza, D. (1964). *Delinquency and Drift*. New York: John Wiley.
Mayhew, P. (1979). Defensible space: the current status of a crime prevention theory. *The Howard Journal of Penology and Crime Prevention*, **18**, 150–159.
Mayhew, P., Clarke, R. V. G., Sturman, A., and Hough, J. M. (1976). *Crime as Opportunity*. Home Office Research Study No. 34. London: HMSO.
Mayhew, P., Clarke, R. V. G., Burrows, J. M., Hough, J. M., and Winchester, S. W. C. (1979). *Crime in Public View*. Home Office Research Study No. 49. London: HMSO.
Moncure, L. B. (1978). *Crime Prevention through Environmental Design*. Program Manual, Vol. II. Arlington, Va: Westinghouse Electric Corporation.
Musheno, M. G., Levine, T. P., and Palumbo, D. J. (1978). Television surveillance and crime prevention: evaluating an attempt to create defensible space in public housing. *Social Science Quarterly*, **58**, 647–656.

Newman, O. (1972). *Defensible Space: Crime Prevention Through Urban Design.* New York: Macmillan. (Published by Architectural Press, London in 1973.)

Olson, H. C., and Carpenter, J. B. (1971). *A Survey of Techniques Used to Reduce Vandalism and Delinquency in Schools.* Virginia: Research Analysis Corporation.

Parker, H. (1974). *View from the Boys.* Newton Abbott, England: David and Charles.

Prewer, R. (1959). Some observations on window smashing. *British Journal of Delinquency,* **10**, 104–113.

Prins, H. (1978). "Their candles are all out" (Macbeth) . . . or are they? *Royal Society of Health Journal,* **98**, 4, 191.

Research Bureau Limited (1977*a*). *Vandalism Research: a Survey of the General Public.* Job No. 11381. London.

Research Bureau Limited (1977*b*). *A Qualitative Study of Vandals and their Peers.* Job No. 69153. London.

Research Bureau Limited (1978). *Evaluation of an Anti-Vandalism Advertising Campaign.* Job No. 11500. London.

Riley, D., and Mayhew, P. (1980). *Crime Prevention Publicity: an Assessment.* Home Office Research Study No. 63. London: HMSO.

Shalloo, J. P. (1954). Vandalism: whose responsibility? *Federal Probation,* **18**, 6–8.

Soothill, K. L., and Pope, P. J. (1973). Arson: a twenty-year cohort study. *Medicine, Science and the Law,* **13**, 127.

Sturman, A. (1978). Measuring vandalism in a city suburb, in *Tackling Vandalism* (Ed. R. V. G. Clarke). Home Office Research Study No. 47. London: HMSO, pp. 9–18.

Sveri, K. (1965). Group activity, in *Scandinavian Studies in Criminology.* Vol. I (Ed. K. O. Christiansen). London: Tavistock, pp. 173–187.

Taylor, I., Walton, P., and Young, J. (1973). *The New Criminology.* London: Routledge and Kegan Paul.

Trasler, G. B. (1979). Note on 'vandalism'. *British Journal of Criminology,* **19**, 168–170.

Wade, A. L. (1967). Social process in the act of juvenile vandalism, in *Criminal Behaviour Systems* (Eds M. B. Clinard and R. Quinney). New York: Holt, Rinehart and Winston, pp. 94–109.

Ward, C. (Ed.) (1973). *Vandalism.* London: Architectural Press.

West, D. J. (1967). *The Young Offender.* Harmondsworth, Penguin Books.

West, D. J., and Farrington, D. P. (1973). *Who Becomes Delinquent?* London: Heinemann.

Wilson, H. (1980). Parental supervision: a neglected aspect of delinquency. *British Journal of Criminology,* **20**, 203–235.

Wilson, J. Q. (1975). *Thinking about Crime.* New York: Basic Books.

Wilson, S. (1978). Vandalism and 'defensible space' on London housing estates, in *Tackling Vandalism* (Ed. R. V. G. Clarke). Home Office Research Study No. 47. London: HMSO, pp. 41–65.

Wilson, S. (1979). 'Observations on the nature of vandalism, in *Designing against Vandalism.* London: The Design Council, pp. 19–29.

Zimbardo, P. G. (1973). A field experiment in auto-shaping, in *Vandalism* (Ed. C. Ward). London: Architectural Press, pp. 85–90.

Zimring, F. E., and Hawkins, G. J. (1973). *Deterrence.* Chicago: University of Chicago Press.

Developments in the Study of Criminal Behaviour. Volume 2: Violence
Edited by Philip Feldman

5

Violence in Psychiatric Hospitals

JONQUIL DRINKWATER

Introduction

The management of violence has always been a problem in psychiatric hospitals, but it has been assumed by many that the problem diminished greatly after the development of psychoactive drugs and the changes in the philosophy of care in the 1960s. At the International Nursing Congress 'Psychiatric Nursing Towards the Eighties', in September 1980, it was reported that in fact the frequency of violent incidents in 1980 was expected to be the highest since records were first kept.

Violence in psychiatric hospitals is of vital concern, and this review will begin with an outline of the historical and political background to research in this area. This will be followed by a discussion of issues that have been selected to indicate the current state of research and future directions. First of all the few studies which have focused on the extent and types of violence will be outlined. The next issue to be examined is common methods of managing violent behaviour. Two of the most frequently used techniques are seclusion and mechanical or physical restraint, and available research will be discussed. The published guidelines for the management of violent behaviour will be reviewed, as well as research on staff–patient interactions as an example of one important aspect of ward management. Finally, future research directions will be described.

One major problem in this field is the definition of, and distinction between, violence and aggression. A survey of the literature reveals a wide range of different definitions with very little consensus between them. Researchers using a range of global definitions have had difficulty in categorizing behaviours as violent, leading to inconsistent and unreliable results. There is a need for established criteria, the implications of which would be the facilitation of recording and monitoring violent behaviours, and their subsequent management.

Historical and political background

The move away from custodial care towards rehabilitation has resulted in unlocked wards and mobile patients, which create difficulties for managing violence. Currently it is often the case that the only secure facilities available to nursing staff are lockable side-rooms.

Unfortunately, methods of controlling and managing such newly mobile patients, already labelled as violent, have not kept pace with these rehabilitative developments. Traditional methods of controlling the problem continue to be used, as highlighted in a number of recent enquiries into British psychiatric hospitals (DHSS, 1972, 1973; South East Thames Regional Health Authority, 1976; Surrery Area Health Authority, 1980; Northern Regional Health Authority, 1976), mental subnormality hospitals (DHSS, 1969, 1971, 1974, 1978; Mersey Regional Health Authority, 1977) and a special hospital (DHSS, 1980*b*). The enquiries led to the formation of two committees. The first, the Butler committee (DHSS and Home Office, 1975), looked specifically at the issue of providing facilities for patients described as aggressive or assaultive. The second committee, the Nodder committee (DHSS, 1980*a*), investigated the general organization and management of psychiatric hospitals. The report of the Butler committee is of particular interest in this review. Its major recommendation was to establish medium secure facilities, initially as interim units attached to psychiatric hospitals, to be followed later by regional secure units. Although a few interim units have since been established, implementation of the recommendations of the Butler committee has been delayed. Reasons for this include the following: difficulty in obtaining the agreement of nursing staff and local residents; ambiguity over the categories of patients to be housed in the units; difficulty in directing finances towards the venture; and the problem of providing new forensic staff for this service (Bluglass, 1980). Bluglass also drew attention to the difficulty of transferring patients from special hospitals, such as Rampton, to local psychiatric hospitals where the interim secure units recommended by the Butler committee are still lacking. In such local hospitals the problem of managing violent patients persists.

The involvement of two major British nursing unions (Confederation of Health Service Employees and National Union of Public Employees) is an important factor in any negotiations. They continue to express great concern about the number of violent incidents in psychiatric hospitals, and several strikes and workings to rule have taken place in efforts to change conditions and staffing levels. Nursing staff have protested that they have neither the training nor facilities to manage violent patients.

Other groups interested in resolving violence in hospitals include doctors, physiotherapists, occupational therapists and of course the patients themselves. General public interest has also been aroused by media reports of enquiries into alleged nursing abuses in psychiatric hospitals. Violence in British psychiatric hospitals has become a sensitive issue with considerable political overtones.

Violent incident studies

Before discussing some of the major issues in this field it is necessary to focus first on what is known about the extent of violence in psychiatric hospitals. Relatively few studies have been published on the frequency and nature of violent outbursts. Smith and McKay (1965) based their reported findings on hospital injury forms, from which they concluded that more women than men are involved in incidents, that schizophrenics are the leading diagnostic group involved, and that patients aged between 11 and 30 years of age are more often involved in incidents than those in higher age groups.

Subsequent studies have given mixed support to these findings. Garai (1970) and Evenson *et al.*, (1974) found higher frequencies of violent incidents amongst male patients than females, while Fottrell (1980) found the reverse. Evenson *et al.* (1974) supported the finding that younger patients were more often involved in incidents, but Depp (1976) found that while patients initiating violent incidents tended to be younger, their victims were typically in older age groups.

Fottrell (1980) supported the finding that schizophrenics are more frequently involved in violence than other diagnostic groups, but did not take into account the relatively higher number of schizophrenics found in psychiatric hospitals. Evenson *et al.* (1974) studied risk rates rather than absolute frequencies, and found that, compared with other diagnostic groups, schizophrenics had the lowest risk rate.

Other findings from incidence studies are that blacks are more frequently involved in incidents than whites (Fisher, 1970; Evenson *et al.*, 1974), that in two of three hospitals studied nearly all incidents occurred during the day shifts (Fottrell, 1980), and that a small number of repeatedly violent patients are responsible for the majority of incidents (Madden, 1977).

All of these studies have suffered significantly from less than reliable methodology. First, data were based on routine incident forms which were only completed when an incident had resulted in an injury needing medical attention. Secondly, the reliability of nursing staff in completing written reports was not checked, although many forms were completed some time after the event, often by charge nurses not involved in the particular incident. Thirdly, the type of violence which occurred was not categorized; for example, no information was available as to whether or not it involved assault on another patient or on a staff member, whether it was a suicide attempt, and whether a weapon was used. Incidents involving damage to property usually went unrecorded.

Fottrell *et al.* (1978) reported one study which broke down incidents into assault on others, self-assault and assault on property. However, information was not recorded about the types of violent behaviour involved, nor about the victims. Depp (1976) reviewed 238 incidents in which one patient struck another patient who did not retaliate but needed medical attention. He found interesting differences between the aggressors and their victims: aggressors on average had more physical handicaps than their victims; men tended to assault men and women assaulted women; blacks were more aggressive towards whites than whites towards blacks. He also found that patients involved in more than one incident tended to persist in the same role of either aggressor or victim. Finally, he found that some victims were repeatedly involved in violent incidents but with a variety of aggressors.

Drinkwater and Feldman (1982) made a preliminary study in which incidents were classified into assaults on another person with or without a weapon, assaults on property, and self-assaults. They found that while the frequency of incidents in three wards studied remained constant, interesting patterns emerged when assaults were broken down by type. The most frequent type was assault on another person without a weapon, followed by assault on property, self-assault and finally assault with a weapon. Furthermore, each ward had a significantly higher frequency of one type of assault than the other two. The recorded first assault by each patient did not reveal this pattern by ward. This adds support to Madden's (1977) finding that a small number of patients were committing a series of repeat assaults of the same type, or perhaps to the possibility that patients on a particular ward learn one type of assault through the modelling of other violent patients.

The assaults studied were further categorized by type of violent behaviour, type of property assaulted and the suicide method selected. The type of violent behaviour most frequently manifested in assaults on another person without a weapon were as follows, with the percentage of incidents in which they occurred shown in parentheses: punching (63%), pushing (47%), kicking (33%), scratching (27%) and slapping (26%). The most frequently assaulted types of property were windows (41%) and crockery (35%). The most frequently attempted suicide methods were slashing of arms or legs (48%) and overdosing (14%).

Other investigated aspects included the time of day, location, the sex of the instigator of the incident, and the consequences of the incident. It was found that incidents occurred more frequently during the day-time, with a greater number in the afternoon than in the evening. When examined in detail it emerged that incidents occurred most often when the majority of staff were temporarily occupied off the ward, when there were no planned ward activities, or during meals when all of the patients were in a communal canteen. Eighty per cent of all incidents occurred on the ward, and most commonly in the dormitory. In considering the types of assault it was found that weaponless assaults on another and suicide attempts were more likely to occur on the ward, assaults on property were equally likely to occur on or off the ward. The likelihood of each type of assault was independent of the sex of the instigator. The most frequent consequences of violent incidents were as follows: seclusion (39%), discussion of the incident between the patient and one staff member (30%), sedation (25%), calling the duty doctor (19%) and putting the patient to bed (11%).

From the foregoing it is clear that some information about violent incidents in psychiatric hospitals is available. However, more detailed assessments of such variables as the nature, frequency, types of violence, location, duration, and aggressor and victim variables are clearly required. Furthermore, all of the research so far has been based on routine record sheets, whereas studies involving participant observation by researchers would be preferable. A detailed assessment study using participant observation is currently under way at the University of Birmingham.

Two current management techniques: seclusion and restraint

Seclusion

Seclusion, i.e. enforced isolation of the patient, is frequently used in psychiatric hospitals, but few studies have been made of the method employed or of the rationale for its use. Aspects which have been investigated to a limited extent include the reasons for seclusion, its duration, the distinguishing characteristics of secluded patients, if any, and staff and patient attitudes to seclusion.

Plutchik *et al.* (1978) studied reasons for employing seclusion and found the following frequencies: agitated and uncontrolled behaviour (21%), physical aggression towards another patient (15%), loud and noisy behaviour (10%), physical aggression towards staff (8%) and prevention of patients leaving the ward (7%). Other reasons, with relative frequencies less than 5%, included: engaging in inappropriate sexual behaviour, damaging property, deliberately disrupting the activities of others, verbal abuse, waking other patients at night, refusal to participate in a ward activity, refusing medication, seclusion requested by the patient, and self-mutilation.

Drinkwater and Feldman (1982) found that the use of seclusion varied following different types of violent behaviour. Weaponless assaults on another person and damage to property led to seclusion in only half the cases. Self-mutilation was unlikely to result in seclusion. Furthermore, as Plutchik *et al.* (1978) found, seclusion was also used after incidents not involving violent behaviour, such as on attempting to abscond, on admission to hospital, on attempting to avoid electro-convulsive therapy and on running shoeless around the hospital grounds. Hence, it appears that seclusion is not systematically applied following violent behaviour, and that there are no established criteria for its application.

When investigating the duration of seclusion, Plutchik *et al.* (1978) reported that in short term psychiatric wards the average length of seclusion was 4 hours. Drinkwater and Feldman (1982) found that the duration of seclusion in fact ranged from 5 minutes to over 4 months. Patients admitted to hospital following violent behaviour stayed in seclusion longer than those admitted for other reasons, and spent a significantly longer time in seclusion for a second assault than for their first assault. No established criteria were found for the duration of seclusion nor for releasing patients from seclusion.

Wells (1972) and Plutchik *et al.* (1978) attempted to identify demographic and diagnostic factors distinguishing secluded from non-secluded patients. Plutchik *et al.* (1978) found no significant sex or race differences between them, but both studies revealed that secluded patients were significantly more frequently diagnosed as schizophrenic rather than other diagnostic categories. Unfortunately the higher proportion of schizophrenics usually found in psychiatric hospitals was again not taken into account. Plutchik *et al.* (1978) investigated hospital staff attitudes to the use of seclusion, and discovered that 67% of aides and 57% of nurses felt that the wards could not operate effectively without seclusion rooms.

These findings raise questions about the theoretical basis for seclusion. There is considerable confusion about whether seclusion is a punishment technique or not. It would seem that for seclusion to be an effective punishment procedure it would have to involve isolation in a non-reinforcing environment, and the exclusion from normal ward activities would need to be aversive. However, neither of these preconditions are necessarily found in practice. Plutchik *et al.* (1978) asked hospital staff to suggest possible changes in the use of seclusion, and discovered that the majority agreed that the seclusion room should be a comfortable, unlocked side-room available to patients who would like to be alone for a while. When they asked patients for their ideas about how to change usage, 70% were of the opinion that patients should be free to spend time in the seclusion room whenever they desired. Wells (1972) found that patients were in fact receiving special attention from members of staff while in seclusion, including regular visits and conversation. Boynton noted in the Rampton Hospital report (DHSS, 1980*b*) that some of the traditional punishment techniques used did not appear to decrease violent behaviour, and rather appeared to maintain it, at least. Hence the apparently paradoxical finding that a supposed punisher can operate on a negative reinforcement basis.

Seclusion is superficially similar to another punishment technique, time out (TO). However, there is also debate about whether or not TO is consistently punishing (Leitenberg, 1965). It involves the contingent or non-contingent withdrawal of access to positive reinforcement, and is usually achieved by isolation in a non-reinforcing environment. Many studies have shown TO to be effective in decreasing aggressive and violent behaviour in children (e.g. Alevizos and Alevizos, 1975; Caraffa *et al.*, 1976), the mentally handicapped (e.g. Husted *et al.*, 1971; Clark *et al.*, 1973) and adult psychiatric patients (Cayner and Kiland, 1974).

However, there are several major differences between TO and seclusion. MacDonough and Forehand (1973) and Hobbs and Forehand (1977) have identified eight parameters of response-contingent TO. These parameters are as follows: duration; type of release from TO; location of TO; the use of an explanation in conjunction with TO; presence or absence of a stimulus to indicate the onset and offset of TO; use of instructional versus physical administration; schedule of administration of TO (continuous versus intermittent); and use of a warning prior to TO. Several of these factors have been investigated in relation to TO (e.g. Bostow and Bailey, 1969; Pendergrass, 1971;

Burchard and Barrera, 1972; White *et al.*, 1972; Sachs, 1973; Kendall *et al.*, 1975; Scarboro and Forehand, 1975). By contrast few of them have been considered regarding seclusion, much less applied or systematically studied. Furthermore, as mentioned, seclusion is not invariably used after incidents of previously specified unacceptable behaviour.

It could be argued that if the seclusion procedure more closely approximated TO it would be more effective and easier to evaluate. However, it is becoming apparent that TO itself is effective in decreasing violent behaviour only when more acceptable alternative behaviours are positively reinforced at the same time (known as differential reinforcement of other behaviour—DRO). Several studies have shown that individual treatment programmes involving combined TO and DRO can be successful in reducing aggressive and violent behaviour (Burchard, 1967; Bostow and Bailey, 1969; Vukelich and Hake, 1971; Repp and Dietz, 1974). Unfortunately, behaviour changes when produced are often not maintained when the individual programme ends. Hence for seclusion to be an effective punishment technique, based on the TO model, it would appear to be necessary to combine it with permanently altered staff management of appropriate patient behaviour on the ward. As Solnick *et al.* (1977) concluded, the nature of the 'time-in' environment is a very important determinant of the effect of TO.

It may well be that seclusion has uses other than as a punishment technique. From a social learning theory perspective, aggressive behaviour is similar to all other types of behaviour, and is therefore explicable by the same learning principles and subject to the same environmental influences (Bandura and Walter, 1965; Bandura, 1973, 1977). One important implication of this theory is that it should be possible to prevent patients from learning violent behaviour through modelling by other patients. Seclusion of patients exhibiting violent behaviour may be one means of preventing learning occurring. A second implication of the theory is that even when a patient has learned violent behaviour the occurrence of this behaviour is probably under environmental control. It is likely that the violent behaviour of one patient can initiate violence in others, resulting in chains of violent incidents. Drinkwater and Feldman (1982) found that violent incidents were not temporally independent. Instead, they occurred simultaneously or in quick succession in the three wards studied, and were followed by incident-free periods. Seclusion may be an effective means of breaking chains of violent incidents. The use of seclusion both for preventing modelling and for breaking chains of violence would seem to warrant further investigation.

In brief, there are unresolved methodological and theoretical problems with the current practices of seclusion. Moreover, even if future research improved the effectiveness of seclusion there are ethical and moral issues bearing on its use at all (Harris and Ersner-Hershfield, 1978; Gutheil, 1978; Strutt *et al.*, 1980). It is also open to question whether individual programmes of any kind provide more than a partial solution to the problem in adult psychiatric wards. Other approaches using individually based programmes for managing violent behaviour in adults and children have been tried. They include over-correction procedures (e.g. Foxx and Azrin, 1972; Epstein *et al.*, 1974; Foxx, 1978), self-control programmes (McCullough *et al.*, 1977); and social skills training (Matson and Stephens, 1977; Panepinto, 1977). All of these approaches aim to eliminate violent behaviour in the individual, and rarely take into consideration the fact that physical and social environments can greatly influence the development, performance and maintenance of violent behaviour. It is suggested that significant and lasting decreases in violent behaviour may only be achievable by improving the violence management strategies of ward staff.

Physical and mechanical restraint

Physical restraint is used routinely in British psychiatric hospitals, and in the United States both physical and mechanical restraint are used. Despite its extensive use very little research has been done on restraint, in particular of its effectiveness, criteria for use, and rationale. Neither ethical considerations nor the possible negative consequences for both the patients and staff of its use have been investigated in depth, and while the use of physical restraint in the United Kingdom has become a sensitive topic attracting media attention (e.g. Yorkshire Television, 1979) little has been done to investigate the facts of its usage.

Rosen and DiGiacomo (1978) set out guidelines for the use of mechanical restraint in American hospitals. In their view, mechanical restraint is a specific therapeutic technique with definable indications, dosages, contraindications and side effects. They suggested that mechanical restraint should be used only for 'florid psychotics', antisocial behaviour and when requested by the patient. The means of restraint should be leather bracelets attached by a belt to the bed frame, with bracelets being normally attached to all four limbs. The length of time for which mechanical restraint is applied may vary and in most cases the release from restraint should be in stages, with the patient allowed out of restraint for progressively longer periods of time. It is not clearly stated how long this process takes, but the implication is that it is a period of days.

Lion *et al.* (1972) also produced a set of guidelines. They suggested that mechanical restraint should be used only after failure to calm the patient by discussion and after attempted physical restraint and injection of medication have also failed. Once a decision has been made to use mechanical restraint, the authors recommended that four nurses, each taking a limb, should secure the patient in a sheet or by using leather bracelets.

Physical restraint was the subject of a paper by the staff of St Thomas's Hospital, Ontario, Canada (St Thomas's Psychiatric Hospital, 1976) giving a description of a programme to teach staff karate as a form of physical restraint. It was stated that in the subsequent year violent incidents decreased, but no figures were given.

These reports are representative of the published studies of physical and mechanical restraint, an evaluation of the effectiveness of which still remains to be made.

A study by Soloff (1979) determined the antecedents of restraint. He noted that although it is largely assumed that restraint is used for controlling violent behaviour unresponsive to drugs, results showed that only 45 out of 111 episodes of restraint followed violent behaviour. The most frequent antecedents for restraint in the other 66 episodes were violations of community rules (e.g. absconding, or screaming in the night), and refusing medication.

Considering the frequent use of physical restraint, and the lack of real knowledge about it, its importance as an issue in the study of violence in psychiatric hospitals can be clearly seen. The current study at the University of Birmingham includes the following: investigation of various aspects of the use of restraint, including types of incidents which result in its use; whether or not other patients are involved with staff in applying restraint; the number of individuals used in applying restraint; who decides that restraint is necessary; leadership of staff during the application of restraint; follow-up action taken in the short term and in the long term after restraining (e.g. use of medication); and whether or not alternatives to restraint had been tried before it was applied.

Published guidelines for the management of violent incidents

Many documents, but far fewer studies, have been published which give guidelines for nursing staff about managing violent incidents. The potentially excellent suggestions often included have rarely been evaluated or incorporated into staff training programmes. Many appear to end up filed away and not acted upon.

Among the papers which have been published, Rusk (1970) suggested that one method of managing a violent incident is to confront the patient with 'overwhelming force', meaning several nurses. The effectiveness of this method has been disputed (e.g. Lion, 1975). Levy and Hartocollis (1976) attempted to determine whether or not using female nurses only would decrease the likelihood of violent incidents. They compared a ward staffed with female nurses with a ward with both male and female staff, and claimed that using female staff only effectively decreased the frequency of incidents. Unfortunately, the study failed to take account of the fact that previously violent patients had been eliminated from the all-female staff ward, and also that one was a rehabilitation ward while the other was a chronic, long stay ward.

Penningroth (1975) reported developing and implementing a training programme for staff which included a definition of violence for management purposes, organizational policies and a discussion of the staff obligation to control violence. Evaluation of the effectiveness of this training programme is lacking. The need for a clear ward policy for violence management appears to be a most important element in such programmes. Guirguis (1978) suggested other improvements to ward management, including routine reviews of the management of incidents occurring; records of the nature of each incident; records of action taken after incidents; and routine preparative discussion of the ward policy to be adopted for managing individual patients.

Among documents produced by the health services and labour unions in Britain appear guidelines published by the Department of Health and Social Security (DHSS, 1976). These take a medical view of violent behaviour that violence is a manifestation of individual mental disorder. The document notes that 'environmental factors may foster its expression' but nowhere considers what these might be, nor their role in preventing or maintaining violent behaviour. The guidelines for dealing with an incident are loose and far from clear—leaving it up to individual nurses to decide appropriate action, and thus placing them in a difficult position because whatever action they take can be criticized adversely. For example, the guidelines state, 'The degree of force should be the minimum required to control the violence, and it should be applied in a manner that attempts to reduce rather than provoke a further aggressive reaction.' This guidance is difficult for nurses to follow, as most have no training in how to restrain physically, and therefore lack experience by which to judge the minimum force required. Nor do they know which methods of applying force reduce aggression rather than provoke it. Furthermore, their legal position is not spelt out at all.

The guidance provided in the document about reporting is that only serious violent incidents should be reported. It places responsibility for the report on the nursing officer—who would normally be unlikely to have observed the incident and needs to rely on information provided by the charge nurse, who in many cases is informed by another nurse. The filtering and distortion possible within this system is unacceptable. The guidelines are clear that all nurses have a duty to intervene in a violent incident, but the responsibility for reporting their actions then rests with others.

The Confederation of Health Service Employees (COHSE), a large British nursing union, published a report criticizing the DHSS guidelines and providing guidelines of its own (Confederation of Health Service Employees, 1977). This report stated that nurses reading the DHSS guidelines are left uncertain about how to deal with violent patients. (COHSE's National Executive Committee instructed union members to ignore the DHSS circular, and set up a working party of its own to provide the guidelines.)

Unfortunately those sections in the COHSE report dealing with preventing and managing a violent incident were, in fact, very similar to those in the DHSS guidelines. However, the report gave much more information about the legal position of nurses, such as the Mental Health Act of 1959. It also included suggestions about improving training, forming multidisciplinary teams, increasing planned ward activities, establishing behavioural standards and ward rules, and setting up an emergency warning system.

A consultative document published by the National Association for Mental Health (1979) suggested discussion points for staff involved in the management of violence. The suggestions made were as follows: seclusion should never be for a predetermined period, as it may be seen as a sentence; it is not the purpose of electro-convulsive therapy (ECT) to subdue outbursts of excitement or aggression; drugs should be used sparingly; there should be a clearly stated policy for the use of restraint and each incident in which it has been used should be reviewed; clear medical and nursing policy should be developed for each patient; each member of staff has a duty to report cruelty or any situation in which a nurse is seen to be unprepared to cope with the needs of a patient. It is apparent that these suggestions were mainly concerned with safeguarding the rights of patients, and are notable for including reference to the unpublished practice in some hospitals of using ECT for patients after violent incidents. A searching investigation of such use of ECT seems to be imperative, notwithstanding the difficulties.

Many other sets of guidelines have been produced by area health authorities and individual hospitals. Some of these are clear and helpful, e.g. those of the Bethlem Royal Hospital and the Maudsley Hospital (1976), but others are incomplete or suffer from ambiguities. An overview of those available shows that, while policy guidelines can be helpful, they have not been adequately evaluated, have rather rarely been incorporated into ward management practices in hospitals, are often not available to student nurses at the time when they start to encounter violent incidents, and are largely discretionary. From this it appears that guidelines are currently an ineffective means of changing the ward management of violence.

Violence and staff–patient interaction

Research into staff–patient interactions can provide good leads towards improving ward management of violent behaviour. It is also a field in which relatively few studies have been done so far. Attention has concentrated on the observation of child–adult interaction (e.g. Patterson *et al.* 1969; Patterson and Reid, 1970; Tars and Appleby, 1973). Sociometric surveys have attempted to discover the characteristics determining 'interpersonal attractiveness' among psychiatric patients. The most consistent finding has been that the more acutely disturbed the patient the less he is seen as socially 'attractive' by other patients, and the lower his rates of interaction with other patients become (Gilliland and Sommer, 1961; Doherty, 1971; Brown *et al.* 1973). Experiential articles about staff–patient relationships have appeared frequently, mainly in nursing journals (Hays, 1966; Jacobson, 1975; Cherkofsky, 1978; Goodykoontz and Stone, 1978).

It is rather difficult to draw clear conclusions from the few research studies of staff–patient interaction. Reasons for this are that, first, studies were done in widely varying settings including chronic long stay wards, acute admission wards in psychiatric or general hospitals and research wards in mental health centres or institutes. Because the frequency and content of interactions between staff and patients may vary with the type of ward and patient population involved, generalization of the results obtained poses problems. As yet no studies have compared staff–patient interactions in differing settings. Secondly, available studies also differed in that some were of wards segregated by sex while others were not, as regards both patients and staff. Thirdly, the definitions of participant observation and non-participant observation varied, and similar techniques were categorized differently. Fourthly, most studies considered frequency of interaction only, while a few considered both frequency and content. Where the content of interactions was investigated very different categorizations of interactions resulted.

Bearing in mind that this lack of comparability may make generalization of results unwise, the research on staff–patient interaction has been focused on two aspects: the assessment of current ward management, and the evaluation of changes in ward management. In an assessment study, Hargreaves (1969) stated that he considers that the study of interaction rates can provide practical measuring tools useful in ward management. He assembled two sets of time-sampled observations of interactions between nursing staff and patients in a ward. Staff observations were coded by job assignment and patient contact, while patient observations were coded by ward assignment and interaction categories. Hargreaves found that when staff were free of assignments on the ward the time they spent in contact with patients varied with whether or not they had supervisory duties. Nurses with supervisory duties had a low patient contact time (7–16%) and a high unavailability time (59–73%). Other members of staff showed large individual differences, with increased interaction rates during evenings and weekends.

Observations of patients showed that they spent more time alone and in conversation with other patients than in talking with staff, and that individual differences were just as pronounced as amongst the staff. The data assembled about staff work assignments appeared to show that they were not a major determinant of patient contact, and that individual differences were more important.

Hargreaves (1969) found that the overall ward rate of staff–patient interaction bore a fairly linear relationship to the total number of nursing staff available for interaction. He also found that staff tended to interact more with patients of their own sex.

Kandler *et al.* (1952) made a time-sampling observational study of staff–patient interaction in a Boston psychiatric hospital. They found, like Hargreaves (1969), that there was a clear relationship between status level in the nursing hierarchy and the amount of nurse interaction with patients. Ward attendants (equivalent to British auxiliary nurses) interacted most with the patients, followed in decreasing order by student nurses, graduate nurses (charge nurses), and supervisors (nursing officers). The rate of interaction between patients was significantly lower than the rate of interaction between staff members.

Kandler *et al.* (1952) measured the affective content of staff–patient interactions (on a scale of positive, negative or neutral affect) and found that student nurses expressed fewer positive and negative feelings towards patients than attendants or graduate nurses. They report that patient interaction with staff increased directly with an increase in the number of staff, but detected a cut-off at five staff. When more than five staff were present they interacted more with each other and less with the patients.

Cohler and Shapiro (1964) studied the frequency and the content of staff–patient interactions. They paid particular attention to the frequency of staff-initiated interactions with other staff or with patients, and whether or not the content of staff interactions with patients was either 'instrumental' (commands or information) or 'socioemotional' (support, agreement, display of tension or tension reduction). Their results agreed with Hargreave's (1969) finding that staff talk significantly more to each other than to patients. Staff interactions with patients were significantly more instrumental than socio-emotional, while staff interactions with staff were significantly more socio-emotional. They also found that staff interacting with others in a mainly socio-emotional way interacted significantly more with patients than did staff who mainly interacted in an instrumental way. This would support large individual differences between staff members in interaction rates. It should be noted, however, that their results were obtained from a ward of chronic schizophrenics, and their finding of higher 'instrumental' staff–patient interactions may owe something to that fact. As has been mentioned, there is evidence that the degree of disturbance and diagnostic group affects interaction rates. Moreover, Cohler and Shapiro did not investigate differences in the content of interactions at different levels of the nursing hierarchy, and the study by Kandler *et al.* suggests that this is an important factor.

Sanson-Fisher *et al.* (1979) made an interesting assessment study of a psychiatric unit in a general hospital. They used staff–patient interaction as a means of assessment prior to an intervention. Unlike Hargreaves (1969), Sanson-Fisher *et al.* found that most interactions, especially between staff and patients, occurred between 9.00 a.m. and 5.00 p.m. on weekdays rather than during evenings and weekends. They found that patients spent about half their time in non-interactive behaviour, and recognized that altering the amount of structured contact between staff may increase the amount of staff–patient interaction.

They also found that staff spent more time interacting with each other, and in administrative work, than in interacting with patients. Hence a suggested interaction 'hierarchy' on the ward would be, first, staff–staff interactions; second, patient–patient interactions; and third, staff–patient interactions.

Unlike previous authors Sanson-Fisher *et al.* (1979) speculated on why this might be, and suggested that either staff find interacting with each other very reinforcing, or interacting with patients less reinforcing than talking to other staff or completing returns. They considered that if interacting with patients provides a negative experience then the most disturbed patient group would receive the least attention, a finding which was previously noted. These findings also suggest that if staff reinforced each other for interacting with patients then the overall rate of staff–patient interactions should increase.

McGuire *et al.* (1977) reported an interesting study to identify those features of psychiatric ward behaviour and social organization which are either stable, or sensitive over time, to changes in ward policy, in ward nursing staff, in patients and in the physical environment. They observed staff–patient interactions, staff and patient spatial segregation, and patterns of staff and patient behaviour on the ward. Their investigation covered two Veterans Administration hospital wards and two university hospital wards before and after changes in one or more of the factors previously mentioned. They found that the frequency of staff–patient interaction was very resistant to such changes. This is revealing in the light of their finding that the frequency of staff–patient interactions is controlled largely by the staff, as demonstrated by the observation that although the number of patients increased on three of the four wards the staff still continued to spend the same amount of time interacting with them. This was despite ward directives that staff–patient interactions be increased via policy, personal or architectural changes.

Other notable findings included a tendency for both patients and staff to congregate with other members of their own group. There were no significant effects on staff spatial relationships of changes in administrative policy, personnel or physical environment. The customary pattern revealed by two observation periods on four wards was for staff to spend from 17 to 24% of their time whilst being observed near patients, 39–48% near other staff, and 29–38% isolated from others by at least 3 metres.

Some patient and staff behaviours were found to be sensitive to changes in the physical environment. When the arrangement of furniture was changed to serve a social function the patients responded by using the area more. Simply removing the glass between the nurses' station and the hall in one ward led to an increase in the amount of staff observations of the adjacent hallway intersection (from 14.5 to 24.9% of the observations) but did not, however, lead to increased staff–patient interaction. In general, staff behaviour patterns were found to be unaffected by changes in ward policy.

The finding from this study which has perhaps most bearing on the relationship between staff–patient interactions and the incidence of violence was that the behaviour of patients was very responsive to changes in staff–patient interaction rates. It was found that in two wards an increase in the number of patients decreased the staff–patient interaction rate while patient–patient interaction rates remained unchanged. When total patient interactions decreased it was found to be followed by an increase in patient non-involvement, a decrease in patient mobility, and an increase in 'deviance'. It is interesting to speculate that if staff interact less with more severely disturbed patients, as has been found in sociometric surveys, then extreme behaviour such as violence may be the most effective way for these patients of gaining staff attention. This hypothesis would be strengthened if it could be shown that patients behaving appropriately on the ward are largely ignored, and that few ward activities take place which provide for structured staff interaction with patients. In that case it would be clear that staff are in effect reinforcing violent behaviour.

From the foregoing it can be seen that staff–patient interactions can be used both to assess the effectiveness of existing ward management and to evaluate changes in ward management. Attention has been drawn to the high probability that the number and content of staff–patient interactions plays an important part in developing and maintaining violent behaviour on psychiatric wards. It follows that a role may be found for staff–patient interaction features as a means of intervention at ward management level if further studies confirm a correspondence between the frequency and quality of interactions between individual staff members and patients and the observed frequency of violent behaviour. As has been mentioned, however, staff–patient interaction rates in general, and probably of specific patients as well, are resistant to new directives in ward policy towards an increase in staff–patient interactions. Hence a shift towards differential reinforcement of other behaviour (DRO) at ward level would not be easy to achieve. It is suggested that factors to facilitate this could include the following: improving staff training in the management of appropriate and inappropriate behaviour; providing contingent reinforcement by senior staff for achieving increased interactions with patients; increasing structured ward activities which involve staff–patient interaction and improving and structuring staff communications about violent behaviour on the ward.

Attention thus far has been focused on the part staff–patient interactions play in the development of violent behaviour. It now seems necessary to investigate also the frequency, quality and content of staff–staff interactions, and the flow of reliable information about patient behaviour and violence on the ward which should be forthcoming. Incomplete, distorted, misdirected or blocked communication within the nursing hierarchy can only maintain violent behaviour on the ward.

Future directions

The social learning theory of aggression suggests that aggressive behaviour is similar to all other types of behaviour, and therefore can be environmentally controlled. It is suggested here that while individually based treatment programmes may be effective in the short term, the maintenance of appropriate behaviour on wards depends greatly on the effectiveness of ward management strategies. It is further suggested that the majority of cases of violence in an adult psychiatric setting do not require individual intervention. Both the learning and later production of violent behaviour can be prevented by effective ward management, and it follows that intervention to decrease violence on psychiatric wards is most appropriately made at ward management level.

The University of Birmingham study in progress is a detailed assessment of current ward management. We believe that the future directions of research into violence must include identifying the most crucial aspects of psychiatric ward management. Only then can effective interventions at ward management level be planned, with all their implications for changes in nursing training.

Although one study cannot hope to investigate all aspects of ward management, several important areas are included. A brief outline will be given of these areas, and the methods developed to assess them. First, participant observations are made to assess staff–patient interaction, the participation of both staff and patients in planned ward activities, and patient behaviour in three ward settings: acute admission, disturbed and long stay.

Four questionnaires are used to investigate staff and patient opinions on various topics. Staff attitudes towards violence, and possible differences in attitudes at each level of the nursing hierarchy, are investigated by a questionnaire seeking opinions about the management of violent incidents, seclusion, security and physical restraint. A further questionnaire looks at ward organization, with emphasis on evaluating communications between staff, the leadership style of senior nurses, the co-ordination of staff between shifts, and the opportunities for staff to influence policies and decisions which concern patients. A questionnaire on ward climate is completed by staff, while in the fourth questionnaire staff are asked to rate the appropriateness of all the observed behaviours of patients on their wards.

Thirdly, a detailed and comprehensive violent incident report sheet is completed by staff for each incident which they are involved in or observe. Further record sheets provide background information on all staff and patients on the wards involved in the study. Finally, levels of medication are being investigated for patients most frequently involved in violent incidents. Blood samples are taken to establish the actual blood levels of all drugs which have been prescribed and should have been administered.

This study examines some of the important aspects of ward management of violence—many others remain to be investigated. If the levels of violence occurring on psychiatric wards are to be decreased, it is important that future studies continue to provide the information necessary for implementing and evaluating changes in management strategies. It is to be hoped that the political sensitivity and hidden nature of this problem area will not be allowed to prevent this work being done.

References

Alevizos, K. J., and Alevizos, P. N. (1975). The effects of verbalizing contingencies in time-out procedures. *Journal of Behavioral Therapy and Experimental Psychiatry*, **6**, 253–355.

Bandura, A. (1973). *Aggression: A Social Learning Analysis*. Englewood Cliffs, N. J.. Prentice-Hall.

Bandura, A. (1977). *Social Learning Theory*. Englewood Cliffs, N. J.: Prentice-Hall.

Bandura, A., and Walter, M. (1965). Modifications of self-imposed delay of reward through exposure to live and symbolic models. *Journal of Personality and Social Psychology*, **2**, 698–705.

Bethlem Royal Hospital and Maudsley Hospital (1976). *Guidelines for the Nursing Management of Violence*. London: Bethlem Royal Hospital and Maudsley Hospital.

Bluglass, R. (1980). *Secure Units for Violent Psychiatric Patients*. BBC Radio, 26 November.

Bostow, D. E., and Bailey, J. B. (1969). Modification of severe disruptive and aggressive behavior using brief timeout and reinforcement procedures. *Journal of Applied Behavior Analysis*, **2**, 31–37.

Brown, J. S., Woodridge, P. J., and Van Brugen, Y. (1973). Interpersonal relations among psychiatric patients: the determinants of social attractiveness. *Journal of Health and Social Behavior*, **14**, 51–60.

Burchard, J. D. (1967). Systematic socialization: a programmed environment for the rehabilitation of antisocial retardates. *The Psychological Record*, **17**, 461–476.

Burchard, J. D., and Barrera, F. (1972). An analysis of timeout and response cost in a programmed environment. *Journal of Applied Behavior Analysis*, **5**, 271–282.

Caraffa, R. J., Truckey, E. M., and Golden, F. (1976). A comparison of the effects of timeout with no stimulation vs. timeout with stimulation. *Corrective and Social Psychiatry and Journal of Behavior, Technology, Methods and Therapy*, **22**, 40–45.

Cayner, J. J., and Kiland, J. R. (1974). Use of brief time out with three schizophrenic patients. *American Journal of Behavior Therapy and Experimental Psychiatry*, **5**, 141–145.

Cherkofsky, N. (1978). Communicating with a difficult patient. *Journal of Practical Nursing*, **28**, 26–35.

Clark, H. B., Rowbury, T., Baer, A. M., and Baer, D. M. (1973). Timeout as a punishing stimulus in continuous and intermittent schedules. *American Journal of Applied Behavior Analysis*, **6**, 443–455.

Cohler, J., and Shapiro, L. (1964). Avoidance patterns in staff-patient interaction on a chronic schizophrenic treatment ward. *Psychiatry*, **27**, 377–388.

Confederation of Health Service Employees (1977). *The Management of Violent or Potentially Violent Patients*. London: COHSE.

Depp, F. C. (1976). Violent behavior patterns on psychiatric wards. *Aggressive Behavior*, **2**, 259–306.

DHSS (1969). *Report of Committee of Inquiry into Allegations of Ill-treatment of Patients and Other Irregularities at the Ely Hospital, Cardiff. Cmnd 3975*. London: HMSO.

DHSS (1971). *Committee of Enquiry, Report of the Farleigh Hospital. Cmnd 4557*. London: HMSO.

DHSS (1972). *Report of the Committee of Inquiry into Whittingham Hospital. Cmnd 4861*. London: HMSO.

DHSS (1973). *Report of the Professional Investigation into Medical and Nursing Practices on Certain Wards at Napsbury Hospital, nr St Albans*. HC (124). London: HMSO.

DHSS (1974). *Report of the Committee of Inquiry into South Ockendon Hospital*. London: HMSO.

DHSS (1976). *The Management of Violent or Potentially Violent Hospital Patients.* HC (76) 11. London: HMSO.

DHSS (1978). *Report of the Committee of Inquiry into Normansfield Hospital. Cmnd 7357.* London: HMSO.

DHSS (1980*a*). *Organisational and Management Problems of Mental Illness Hospitals. Report of a Working Group* (Chairman: Mr T. E. Nodder). London: HMSO.

DHSS (1980*b*). *Report of the Review of Rampton Hospital. Cmnd 8073.* London: HMSO.

DHSS and Home Office (1975). *Report of the Committee on Mentally Abnormal Offenders* (Chairman: Lord Butler). *Cmnd 6244.* London: HMSO.

Doherty, E. G. (1971). Social attraction and choice among psychiatric patients and staff: a review. *Journal of Health and Social Behavior*, **12**, 279–290.

Drinkwater, J. M., and Feldman, M. P. (1982). Violent incidents in a British psychiatric hospital: a preliminary study. Unpublished manuscript. Department of Psychology, University of Birmingham.

Epstein, L. H., Doke, L. A., Sajwaj, T. E., Sorrell, S., and Rimmer, B. (1974). Generality and side effects of overcorrection. *Journal of Applied Behavior Analysis*, **7**, 385–390.

Evenson, R. C., Sletten, I. W., Altman, H., and Brown, M. L. (1974). Disturbing behavior: a study of incident reports. *Psychiatric Quarterly*, **48**, 266–275.

Fisher, G. (1970). Discriminating violence emanating from over-controlled versus under-controlled aggressivity. *British Journal of Social and Clinical Psychology*, **9**, 54–59.

Fottrell, E. (1980). A study of violent behavior among patients in psychiatric hospitals. *British Journal of Psychiatry*, **136**, 216–221.

Fottrell, E., Bewley, T., and Squizzoni, M. (1978). A study of aggressive and violent behavior among a group of psychiatric in-patients. *Medicine, Science and the Law*, **18**, 66–69.

Foxx, R. M. (1978). An overview of overcorrection. *Journal of Pediatric Psychology*, **3**, 97–101.

Foxx, R. M., and Azrin, N. H. (1972). Restitution: A method of eliminating aggressive-disruptive behavior of retarded and brain damaged patients. *Behavioral Research and Therapy*, **10**, 15–27.

Garai, J. E. (1970). Sex differences in mental health. *Genetic Psychological Monograms*, **81**, 123–142.

Gilliland, G. W. and Sommer, R. A. (1961). A sociometric study of admission wards. *Psychiatry*, **24**, 367–372.

Goodykoontz, L., and Stone, E. L. (1978). Your assertive behaviour benefits patients. *Journal of Nursing Care*, **11**, 22–24.

Guirguis, E. F. (1978). Management of disturbed patients. An alternative to the use of mechanical restraints. *Journal of Clinical Psychiatry*, **39**, 295–303.

Gutheil, T. G. (1978). Observations on the theoretical bases for the seclusion of the psychiatric inpatient. *American Journal of Psychiatry*, **135**, 325–328.

Hargreaves, W. A. (1969). Rate of interaction between nursing staff and psychiatric patients. *Nursing Research*, **18**, 418–425.

Harris, S. L., and Ersner-Hershfield, R. (1978). Behavioral suppression of seriously disruptive behavior in psychotic and retarded patients: a review of punishment and its alternatives. *Psychological Bulletin*, **85**, 1352–1375.

Hays, J. S. (1966). Analysis of nurse–patient communications. *Nursing Outlook*, **14**, 32–35.

Hobbs, S. A., and Forehand, R. (1977). Important parameters in the use of time out with children: a re-examination. *Journal of Behaviour Therapy and Experimental Psychiatry*, **8**, 365–370.

Husted, J. R., Hall, P., and Agin, B. (1971). The effectiveness of timeout in reducing maladaptive behaviour of autistic and retarded children. *Journal of Psychology*, **79**, 189–196.

Jacobson, Z. A. (1975). Counter-aggression toward patients: the hidden enemy. *Supervisory Nurse*, **6**, 36–38.

Kandler, H., Behymer, A. F., Kegeles, S. S., and Boyd, R. W. (1952). A study of nurse–patient interaction in a mental hospital. *American Journal of Nursing*, **52**, 1100–1103.

Kendall, P. C., Nay, W. R., and Jeffers, J. (1975). Timeout duration and contrast effects: a systematic evaluation of a successive treatments design. *American Journal of Behavior Therapy*, **6**, 609–615.

Leitenberg, H. (1965). Is time-out from positive reinforcement an aversive event? *American Psychologist Bulletin*, **64**, 428–441.

Levy, P., and Hartocollis, P. (1976). Nursing aids and patient violence. *American Journal of Psychiatry*, **133**, 429–431.

Lion, J. R. (1975). Conceptual issues in the use of drugs for the treatment of aggression in man. *The Journal of Nervous and Mental Disease*, **160**, 77–82.

Lion, J. R., Levenberg, L. B., and Strange, R. E. (1972). Restraining the violent patient. *Journal of Psychiatric Nursing and Mental Health Sciences*, **10**, 9–11.

McCullough, J. P., Huntsinger, G. M., and Nay, W. R. (1977). Self-control treatment of aggression in a 16-year old male (case study). *Journal of Consulting and Clinical Psychology*, **45**, 322–331.

MacDonough, T. S., and Forehand, R. (1973). Response-contingent time out: important parameters in behaviour modification with children. *Journal of Behaviour Therapy and Experimental Psychiatry*, **4**, 231–236.

McGuire, M. T., Fairbanks, L. A., Cole, S. R., Sbordone, R., Silvers, F. M., Richards, M., and Akers, J. (1977). The ethological study of four psychiatric wards: behavior changes associated with new staff and new patients. *Journal of Psychiatric Research*, **13**, 211–224.

Madden, D. J. (1977). Voluntary and involuntary treatment of aggressive patients. *American Journal of Psychiatry*, **134**, 553–555.

Matson, J. L., and Stephens, R. M. (1977). Overcorrection of aggressive behavior in a chronic psychiatric patient. *Behavior Modification*, **1**, 559–564.

Mersey Regional Health Authority (1977). *Report of the Committee of Inquiry into Mary Denby Hospital.* Liverpool: Mersey Regional Health Authority.

National Association for Mental Health (1979). *MIND's Views for the Rampton Review Team.* London: MIND.

Northern Regional Health Authority (1976). *Report of the Committee of Enquiry held at Memorial Hospital Darlington.*

Panepinto, R. A. (1977). Social skills training for verbally aggressive children. *Dissertation Abstracts International*, **38**, 1897.

Patterson, G. R., and Reid, J. B. (1970). Reciprocity and coercion: two facets of social systems, in *Behaviour Modification in Clinical Psychology* (Eds C. Neuringer and J. L. Michael). New York: Appleton-Century-Crofts, pp. 133–177.

Patterson, G. R. Ray, R. S., Shaw, D. A., and Cobb, J. A. (1969). *Manual Coding of Family Interactions*, 6th revision. Portland, Ore: Oregon Research Institute and University of Oregon.

Pendergrass, V. E. (1971). Effects of length of time-out from positive reinforcement and schedule of application in suppression of aggressive behaviour. *The Psychological Record*, **21**, 75–80.

Penningroth, P. E. (1975). Control of violence in a mental health setting. *American Journal of Nursing*, **75**, 606–609.

Plutchik, R., Karasu, T. B., Conte, H. R., Siegel, B., and Jerrett, I. (1978). Toward a rationale for the seclusion process. *Journal of Nervous and Mental Disease*, **166**, 571–579.

Repp, A. C., and Dietz, S. M. (1974). Reducing aggressive and self-injurious behavior of institutionalised retarded children through reinforcement of other behaviors. *Journal of Applied Behavior Analysis*, **7**, 313–325.

Rosen, H., and DiGiacomo, J. N. (1978). The role of physical restraint in the treatment of psychiatric illness. *Journal of Clinical Psychiatry*, **39**, 228–232.

Rusk, T. N. (1970). Psychiatric emergencies in medical practice. Survey of the literature and some proposals. *Journal of Oklahoma State Medical Association*, **63**, 483–494.

Sachs, D. A. (1973). The efficacy of time-out procedures in variety of behavior problems. *Journal of Behavior Therapy and Experimental Psychiatry*, **4**, 237–242.

St Thomas's Psychiatric Hospital (1976). A program for the prevention and management of disturbed behavior. Hospital and Community Psychiatry, **27**, 724–727.

Sanson-Fisher, R., Poole, A. D., Small, G. A., and Fleming, I. R. (1979). Data acquisition in real time—an improved system for naturalistic observations. *Behavior Therapy*, **10**, 543–554.

Scarboro, M. E., and Forehand, R. (1975). Effects of two types of response-contingent time-out on compliance and oppositional behavior of children. *American Journal of Experimental Child Psychology*, **19**, 252–264.

Smith, C. M., and McKay, L. (1965). The open psychiatric ward and its vicissitudes. *American Journal of Psychiatry*, **121**, 763–767.

Solnick, J. V., Rincover, A., and Peterson, C. R. (1977). Some determinants of the reinforcing and punishing effects of timeout. *American Journal of Applied Behavior Analysis*, **10**, 415–424.

Soloff, P. H. (1979). Physical restraint and the non-psychotic patient: clinical and legal perspectives. *Journal of Clinical Psychiatry*, **40**, 302–305.

South East Thames Regional Health Authority (1976). *Report of the Committee of Inquiry, St Augustine's Hospital, Chartham, Canterbury*. London: South East Thames Regional Health Authority.

Strutt, R., Bailey, C., Peermohamed, R., Forrest, A. J., and Corton, B. (1980). Seclusion: can it be justified? *Nursing Times*, **76**, 1629–1633.

Surrey Area Health Authority (1980). *Report of the Committee of Inquiry into Standards of Patient Care at Brookwood Hospital.* Kingston: Surrey Area Health Authority.

Tars, S. E., and Appleby, L. (1973). The same child in home and institution—an observational study. *Environment and Behaviour*, **5**, 3–28.

Vukelich, R., and Hake, D. F. (1971). Reduction of dangerously aggressive behavior in a severely retarded resident through a combination of positive reinforcement procedures. *American Journal of Applied Behavior Analysis*, **4**, 215–225.

Wells, D. A. (1972). The use of seclusion on a university hospital psychiatric floor. *Archives of General Psychiatry*, **26**, 410–413.

White, G. D., Nielsen, G., and Johnson, S. M. (1972). Timeout duration and the suppression of deviant behaviour in children. *Journal of Applied Behavior Analysis*, **5**, 111–120.

Yorkshire Television (1979). Rampton: a secret hospital—The Big House 22 May; Rampton: a secret hospital—East Dale—The way out, 23 May; The secret hospital—A discussion, 24 May. Producer: John Willis.

Developments in the Study of Criminal Behaviour. Volume 2: Violence
Edited by Philip Feldman

6

Violence in Prisons

WILLIAM DAVIES

Introduction

Violence in prison is always a major concern for a variety of reasons, not least of which is that many prison inmates have the capacity to be very destructive to property or individuals if they so decide; in addition, prisons in England and Wales have a staff to inmate ratio that heavily favours the inmates, so that the smooth running of the prison implicitly relies on the co-operation of its inhabitants.

This chapter deals mainly with interpersonal violence in prisons in England and Wales (those in Scotland are administered separately) but American and other international material is also drawn upon. It is divided into three sections: hostage-taking, riots, and what has been termed 'endemic' violence, so called because of its constant and repetitive nature.

In recent years prisons in England and Wales have been fortunate in escaping physical injuries on the scale that might be feared, although the horror of what can happen has been demonstrated time and again in prisons elsewhere, with hostages mutilated and killed. For example, the riot at Attica Prison in the USA resulted in many deaths. 'Endemic' violence, although less newsworthy than either riots or hostage-takings, is probably more feared by inmates. Although an individual is relatively unlikely to be involved in either a riot or a hostage-taking, there is the constant threat of assault from another inmate, and for this reason there is a facility for inmates to serve their sentences isolated from most of their fellow prisoners if they wish. Indeed there are prisons in which there are units especially for the purpose of segregating inmates from their fellows because they feel they are at risk.

Throughout this chapter, emphasis is placed on what might be accomplished to reduce the incidence of violence and for this reason the literature reviewed is highly selected.

The views expressed in this chapter are the author's and do not necessarily represent those of the Home Office Prison Department.

The author would like to thank Mr K. Baxter and Mr B. Conlin, Senior Psychologists in the Home Office Prison Department, for their help in writing the section on hostage-taking.

Hostage-taking

Historical perspective

The modern spate of hostage-taking began in the 1960s, and has been a recurring theme since then. At the early stages it was felt that a hostage-taking presented the authorities with two stark alternatives: either to capitulate to the perpetrators' demands in order to save lives (the 'soft' approach), or to mount an assault on the siege area in order to apprehend the perpetrator at the possible cost of the hostages' lives (the 'hard' approach).

One of the earliest examples of the 'hard' line paying off was in 1961 when an American convict, Leon Bearden, tried to hijack a Continental 707 at Phoenix Airport, demanding that he and his son be flown to Cuba. During refuelling at El Paso, FBI agents shot at the tyres of the plane, and during the heated exchanges that followed one of the agents slipped on board, grabbed Bearden in an armlock, and the incident was over.

In a further incident at Lod Airport, Tel Aviv, on 9 May 1972, four Palestinian terrorists were overpowered by Israeli security forces before the explosives they carried could be detonated, and 86 passengers were freed unharmed.

But the hard line has had its failures too, and they have been costly. In September 1972 eight members of the Black September organization kidnapped 11 Israeli athletes by storming their quarters at the Munich Olympic Games. Encouraged by the Israeli government, the Bavarian police moved in while the hostages were being transferred to an aircraft at Munich airport. All 11 hostages were killed, as well as five of the terrorists. The other three terrorists were arrested.

The essential problems for the hard line approach are (1) its failures are immediately obvious and the consequences are borne by those immediately involved; (2) the costs are high, particularly in terms of public opinion. The effects and power of this opinion cannot be dismissed lightly, nor should the appeal of the hostage be underestimated. Moreover, the determined and ruthless politically motivated hostage-taker may be regarded by some as a terrorist but by many others as a freedom fighter.

The 1976 Entebbe incident illustrates these points. Palestinians hijacked a plane with a large number of Israeli passengers on board and flew it to Entebbe Airport in Uganda, where the hijackers were well regarded and given at least tacit assistance. The hijackers threatened to massacre the Israeli passengers unless their demands for the release of a large number of pro-Palestinian terrorists were met. Even the Israeli government in Tel Aviv was forced by a mounting clamour from relatives to consider a deal with the terrorists to save the hostages.

Whether a deal could have been worked out we shall never know, because the Israelis mounted the highly successful raid of the night of 3 July. Indeed the whole show of negotiation may have been a device to gain time until a raid could be organized. This may be so with many other incidents as well; negotiations have a twofold effect, whereby they may lead in themselves to the safe release of the hostages, but also allow time for other plans to be developed.

The chief attraction of the 'soft' approach lies in the fact that, in the short term at least, the lives of innocent people will be saved. However, the long term and political costs of capitulation may be very high indeed.

An important example of the 'soft' approach came about in 1970, during the British premiership of Edward Heath. It was important because it crystallized the policy of the British government, the Home Office and the Prison Service. Palestinian terrorist Leila Khaled and a male associate called Patrick Arguello tried to hijack an El Al 707 but Israeli sky marshalls rushed them. Although Arguello pulled the pin on his grenade it did not explode and he was killed. Leila Khaled was overpowered and eventually held by the British police.

But this was only part of the picture. On the same day two other planes were hijacked to Dawson's Field near Amman, which was where Khaled and Arguello's 707 was also planned to be, the plan being to have three planes and passengers to bargain with. The Popular Front for the Liberation of Palestine (PFLP) decided they still needed a third plane and so hijacked a British VC 10 and had it put down in the desert with the other two planes. This was a powerful emotional weapon as the VC 10 contained 21 unaccompanied school children returning from holiday, an immediate source of appeal to public opinion.

The situation was complicated as five governments were now involved in the incident; the American, British and Swiss governments had planes in the desert and many had nationals on board, as did the Germans and Israelis. Of these five governments, only the Americans did not hold PFLP prisoners. The attitudes of the governments varied: The British Prime Minister, Edward Heath, argued that Leila Khaled and the other six terrorists in Germany and Switzerland should be released, but only after all the hostages were freed. After a long process all the passengers were freed and the three European governments released the seven terrorists and returned them to Cairo as promised.

Such was the international reaction, and the reaction of British public opinion, that the Heath administration resolved that from then on, whatever the circumstances, Britain would never again grant safe passage to terrorists, regardless of the risk to hostages. If such a firm line can be held then there is no doubt that this is the right policy as perpetrators have shown a close knowledge not only of the methods used in previous incidents, but also of the results of previous sieges. There is little doubt that a successful model will very quickly be copied time and again. In September 1969 the US Ambassador to Brazil was kidnapped and freed after the demand for the release of 15 terrorists was met. In June 1970 the German Ambassador to Brazil was kidnapped but this time the price that had to be paid was the release of 40 terrorists. In December 1970 it cost the Brazilian government the release of 70 terrorists to secure the release of the Swiss Ambassador.

There follows the question as to what happens to terrorists who are sent on operations. The report by the Rand Corporation (Jenkins and Johnson, 1975) shows that the chances of a terrorist being killed or given a substantial prison term were very low. In the period March 1968 to July 1974 terrorists had a 79% chance of evading death or punishment, whether or not they successfully seized the intended hostages. Even if captured, the terrorists would be in jail only a short while before the government concerned released them out of fear, or as a result of their comrades using further terrorism to force the authorities to let them go.

In this connection, the Prison Service is particularly at risk, since it faces an accumulating number of terrorists serving very long sentences, dangerous not only because of their own training and natures, but also because of the existence of groups interested in their release. However, recent hostage-taking in the English Prison Service has tended not to be by or for terrorists, although the most common demand is for release (Davies, 1981*a*).

Their reaction to the evidence was slow, but increasingly governments toughened their stance and started to formulate agreements roughly in line with the decision by the Heath administration. The results were both encouraging and obvious, and by 1976 a healthy change in hijackings could be demonstrated. The figures in Table 1 are an abridged set from a US report published in 1977. They cover all international hijackings, and show a dramatic drop in the rate as their success fell. (Successful here is used to mean that the perpetrators either had some of their demands met, or that they were allowed to escape.) These results demonstrate that an approach which prevents perpetrators from achieving their ends is likely to be effective in quickly reducing the number of hostage incidents. One might therefore have expected governments to favour the tough approach of physical intervention as one which would fulfil the twin aims of releasing the hostages and of deterring future incidents. However, two major incidents in 1972 provided the impetus for an examination of the handling of hostage incidents. The first was the massacre of the Israeli athletes at the Munich Olympic Games, and the second was the take-over of Attica Prison in the USA by the inmates.

A series of seminars and conferences organized by Scotland Yard, with police and consultants from around the world, produced some simple but clear conclusions. The general lesson was that the choice between the 'hard' and the 'soft' approaches is a false one, and there is a middle road. A 'no concessions' approach is perfectly compatible, both morally and in practice, with the energetic pursuit of skilled negotiations to secure the release of the hostages. Quite simply,

Table 1 Total international hijacks

	Year		
	1968–70	1971–73	1974–76
Number of attempted hijackings	190	147	71
'Successful' attempts	149	53	22

the crucial feature of most hostage situations was found to be time. The longer a siege could be maintained without the authorities doing anything precipitous, the better the chances of getting everybody out alive. The longer that the authorities could keep a dialogue with the perpetrators going, the better the chances of avoiding both casualties and concessions.

The Rand Corporation document on hostage-takings (Jenkins and Johnson, 1975) illustrates this point. In only nine of the 66 incidents discussed were hostages deliberately killed, with or without the provocation of an assault. Of these only 3% were 'executed in cold blood', while 11% died during assaults by the authorities. A further Rand study (Jenkins, 1976) concluded that most hostages were killed in the very early stages of a siege, largely due to panic. Even if one or more hostages had already been killed, the chances of a killing without the threat of intervention were very low indeed, once the first few hours have elapsed.

This newly developing tactic became known as the 'softly softly' approach, but it was the New York Police Department's dealings with criminal hostage-takings which successfully developed it. Their tactics were to stand firm, whilst stressing their lack of intention to assault the area, and by use of trained negotiators to establish a dialogue with the perpetrators and then to exert their control over the situation, wearing down the morale and the will of the perpetrators to the point where they surrendered. The success rate was extremely high, and by late 1975 a number of Western governments were adapting their plans accordingly.

Although this approach was developed with criminal, rather than political, hostage-taking, the technique was put to the test in Eire during the 18 day siege of the kidnappers of Dr Tiede Herrema in late 1975, when two Provisional IRA members promised his release in return for the release of three IRA prisoners held by the Dublin government. The Irish government firmly but gently said, 'No', and soon the demands fell to the release of one IRA man. The negotiations continued and the price came down to £3 million. This too was refused and after a further period of talking Dr Herrema was freed unharmed.

After this successful use of the strategy, the techniques became British police policy, and they showed themselves to be successful at the Spaghetti House and Balcombe Street sieges.

Given these successes, it is interesting to see how the British police tackled the Prince's Gate siege of the Iranian Embassy in London in 1980, inevitably an extremely difficult situation to resolve because there were a large number of hostages, it was politically motivated, and there were language barriers.

Notwithstanding the complicated situation, the police embarked upon what were to be protracted negotiations in an attempt to secure the release of the hostages. In the event, the negotiations proved not to be successful, and when the hostages were in danger of the extensive use of violence against them, it was decided that the Special Air Service should attempt a rescue by force. This was a qualified success, in that although the hostages were released unharmed some of the perpetrators were killed and injured. This siege pointed up several important considerations. First, it confirmed an important by-product of the 'softly softly' policy, namely that it gives time to organize an effective assault if the situation is not resolved by negotiation alone. Secondly, it appeared to be a major surprise to the public that there existed in Britain a force capable of dealing with such incidents in the way that it had. The reaction to this news was in many ways little short of euphoria, which is worrying if it should ever result in the commander of a hostage incident being tempted to use physical intervention before all possibilities of a negotiated release have been exhausted.

In summary, the hostage-takings through the 1960s and early 1970s generally found governments unprepared. Although public opinion and international reaction meant that it became necessary to resist the demands of hijackers, there seemed to be no effective means of doing this; where the tough approach of physical intervention was used it sometimes had disastrous consequences—as at Attica and Munich. More recently progress has been made in developing a negotiating strategy which has proved effective time and again regardless of whether the hostage-takings have been criminally or politically inspired.

Notable successes have been the release of Dr Herrema in Eire, and the resolution of the Spaghetti House siege in London. In parallel with this has been the development of equipment and strategy for a physical intervention if this is necessary. This has been demonstrated by the Israelis at Entebbe and the Special Air Service at Prince's Gate in London.

Hostage taking in English prisons

The English Prison Service, possibly in common with most others, has long suffered the phenomenon of inmates barricading the doors of their cells to prevent staff from entering. Sometimes this would be done with only the inmates themselves in the cell; sometimes there would be an inmate or member of staff held there under threat. Although this was by no means an everyday occurrence, it was sufficiently common that the situation was usually resolved without drama by a diplomatic member of staff.

In more recent years 'hostage incidents' outside the Prison Department have become either more common or more widely recognized, and the prisons have kept abreast of developments in the strategies for hostage release. In 1972 a central file was established, on which all Prison Department hostage incidents should be recorded. Up to, but not including, 1981, 20 incidents were on this file (Davies, 1981). This figure should not be taken as definitive as there is probably still a tendency on the part of some prison staff not to conceptualize all relevant incidents as 'hostage-takings', and some may therefore go unreported as such.

Looking at the 20 hostage incidents that have been recorded since 1972, there are several points that can be made about them (Davies, 1981*a*):

(1) Seventy per cent of them have occurred in dispersal prisons (a small

number of prisons which accommodate inmates in conditions of maximum security).

(2) their duration ranged from virtually instantaneous resolution to something over 16 hours.

(3) Only one of the 20 incidents involved an inmate convicted of a politically motivated offence, and the hostage-taking itself was not politically motivated.

(4) The most common demands of hostage takers were release (six), to see a loved one (five), and transfer (three).

(5) Fifteen of the 20 incidents took place in a cell or an office.

(6) In 16 out of the 20 cases the perpetrator's sentence length was recorded. All but two were serving 5 years or more, including six who were serving life sentences.

(7) In nine out of the 11 cases in which the perpetrator's offence was recorded, it involved violence.

(8) Staff were considered much more valuable hostages than inmates. Of the 20 hostages 17 were staff and three were inmates. Indeed in one case the perpetrator had power over both a member of staff and an inmate but did not regard the inmate as a hostage.

(9) The most commonly used weapons were knives or scissors. Sometimes the knives were fashioned from available materials.

(10) In only one incident was the hostage harmed during resolution. His injuries were minor ones. In two cases the perpetrator was injured, and four people involved in a physical intervention were injured. One perpetrator hanged himself the day after the incident.

(11) In no case was there evidence of 'transference' (the hostage eventually showing support, sympathy or liking for the perpetrator). However, because accounts of hostage incidents are written almost immediately after their resolution, there is generally little information about the reactions of the hostage, particularly in the long term.

(12) Ten of the 20 incidents were resolved by physical intervention, six by negotiation along, three by negotiation with limited concessions, and one by conceding what was demanded.

The most noticeable difference between these incidents and those outside is their relatively short duration. This may be due to the special circumstances that exist inside prison, where the perpetrator may quickly realize that he is in a dire situation, being still within the prison walls and heavily outnumbered by staff, even though he has a hostage. Alternatively it may be due to the skill of those resolving the incident, or it may be a combination of the two. Another interesting point is that although the English Prison Department's guidelines make no distinction between a staff hostage or an inmate hostage (both are regarded as equally valuable), this view is not shared by hostage-takers, who evidently feel that a member of staff will provide them with greater bargaining power. Finally the figures confirm those of the Rand survey (Jenkins and Johnson, 1975), suggesting that however precarious the situation may feel to the hostage, he is much less likely to be harmed than at first sight seems to be the case.

Training for hostage incidents

The Prison Department's aims when obtaining the release of a hostage are similar to those of outside agencies: first, there should be no injury or loss of life; secondly, there should be no intolerable concessions to the hostage-taker; thirdly, the outcome of this incident should not make future incidents more likely. The Prison Department is well aware of the danger that the details of any successful hostage-taking will spread rapidly throughout the Prison Service and may very quickly be copied. Similarly, if the taking of hostages leads to no advantage for the prisoner, this too will be known quickly and should lead to a reduced risk of such incidents. Therefore, for the safety of both staff and prisoners, the Prison Department is most concerned that incidents are handled as well as they possibly can be. The most likely way of achieving all the stated aims is seen as negotiation rather than physical intervention, although the latter is always held as a possibility, paralleling outside experience. The exact arrangements for a physical intervention are left to the individual prisons, as there is no Prison Service equivalent of the Special Air Service, which contains a group specially trained to resolve these kinds of situations by physical force. A prison governor would normally notify the local police immediately an incident starts. The police would then offer assistance, which may or may not be accepted, or authority may transfer from the prison authorities to the police while the incident is dealt with. This would inevitably happen if the perpetrator managed to gain his illegal release from the prison and the hostage incident continued outside the prison walls. If the police are handling the incident, whether inside or outside the prison, they may in turn ask for assistance from another group, such as the military.

In order to train prison staff to achieve these aims by negotiation, the Prison Service College has, since 1979, run 1 week courses in an attempt to teach the most successful strategies. Each course is staffed by two tutors, one of governor grade and the other a prison psychologist with the assistance of staff who are familiar enough with previous incidents to role-play them realistically. Generally there will be four teams of three people, each team from a different establishment. Of the team of three, one is to be trained as the commander in charge of the incident, and the other two are trained as negotiators. The format of the course is to role-play incidents similar to those that have happened in the prison service and give participants the opportunity to practise the use of strategies that have been taught.

The commander of a hostage incident is likely to be the governor in charge of the prison at the time, who will delegate the responsibility of running the rest of the prison to another member of staff while he concentrates on resolving the hostage situation. The negotiator is responsible only for negotiating, and is supposed to refer all decisions on, for example, whether specific concessions can be made, to the commander. Indeed the commander will make all the tactical management decisions, but he in turn is governed by guidelines laid down by headquarters. The commander would be supported by a headquarters representative who would be at the scene as quickly as practicable, and prior to his arrival the commander would be in touch with the operations room at headquarters. Headquarters staff would be able to advise on, for example, a planned physical intervention, although if this became necessary through an immediate threat to the hostage's well-being then a decision would be taken by the most appropriate person 'on the spot'.

As a matter of policy the Prison Department does not train staff in how to behave if they are taken hostage. This is partly because of the danger that one will expend a lot of resources training staff who will probably not be taken hostage, but may still not train those who are unfortunate enough to be 'selected' by inmates. However, written guidelines on the best tactics for survival if one is taken hostage have been issued to staff. One of the advantages of giving all staff some information might be that it would immunize staff against the after-effects of being taken hostage. (Although there are no detailed records of the effect on staff of having been taken hostage, it is known that of the 20 recorded incidents, at least two of them resulted in the hostage being discharged from the Prison Service.)

The job of the negotiators is firstly to calm the perpetrator, who will often be in an excited and abusive mood, then to establish rapport with him or her, and finally to exercise powers of persuasion to bring the incident to a satisfactory conclusion from all points of view. Generally the negotiator will attempt to be not too yielding yet not too provocative, although in practice it has been found that the negotiator can be surprisingly assertive without any undesired consequences. He will attempt to alter the perpetrator's perception of the situation from one where the perpetrator has all the power, because he holds one or more hostages, to a more realistic appraisal whereby it is recognized that the perpetrator has some power by virtue of his actions, but that it is severely limited in that he is typically barricaded in a small room within an institution containing several hundred staff. It is of course a very tense situation for the negotiator as well as for the others involved, and in at least one incident there was an episode where the perpetrator felt moved to reassure the negotiator that all would end well! (It did, with the safe, negotiated release of the inmate/hostage; this is spite of the perpetrator having taken and killed a hostage previously—not in a prison.)

In calming the perpetrator the negotiator will show understanding of his feelings in whatever way he finds easiest, possibly be 'reflecting' what the perpetrator says. He will attempt to display calmness by his tone of voice, ideally keeping out of sight of the perpetrator to avoid non-verbal 'leakage' of anxiety.

He will reassure and avoid provocation and encourage the perpetrator to talk. At this stage it will not be considered too important what the topic of conversation is.

This leads into the next stage of establishing rapport, or a relationship. To some extent this will develop with the passage of time, particularly if the negotiator and perpetrator see themselves as involved in a joint venture, that of resolving the difficult situation that has arisen. Once the perpetrator begins to see that he is not in the powerful situation that he at first thought, this feeling of mutual problem-solving is much more likely to develop. The negotiator will try to establish recognizable routines, to increase the predictability and calmness of the situation, and may feel inclined to disclose information about himself to further the developing rapport. Ideally he will have been chosen as a person who finds it easy to display genuine empathy and warmth. From the point of view of his own survival the hostage should develop a relationship with the perpetrator; this will lessen the likelihood of him being harmed subsequently. However, the prison authorities do not rely on this happening, and indeed rule out any course of action that relies upon the participation of the hostage.

In the 20 recently recorded incidents in the Prison Service the hostage has generally been very shaken and upset (in at least one instance needing injection of a tranquillizer during the incident) and has not felt able to develop a realistic relationship. There has been no evidence of the 'Stockholm syndrome' whereby the hostage identifies with the aims of the perpetrator. (The best known recent example of this was where newspaper heiress Patty Hearst was kidnapped by the 'Symbionese Liberation Army', and after a time became so persuaded by their aims that she turned against her family and willingly took part in SLA activities, spurning the opportunity to 'escape'. This resulted in her eventual arrest and criminal conviction.)

The third stage is to persuade the perpetrator to bring the situation to an end. The negotiator will probably deal with smaller issues first to establish that successful negotiations can be achieved. He will recognize the perpetrator's argument but counter it with some of his own. He will try to consider the perpetrator's motives and attempt to satisfy them without yielding any substantial concessions. He will persuade gradually, always giving the perpetrator the opportunity to save face, and by not allowing an audience present will by-pass the pressures that this might create. Allied to the gradual persuasion he will probably request delayed compliance on difficult issues by pointing out what is required but asking the perpetrator not to make up his mind immediately—rather he will give the perpetrator time for consideration and decision at a later time.

Sometimes there will be little persuasion involved, as the perpetrator himself will have realized that he wants to bring the situation to a close and resume normal prison life. In this case the role of the negotiator is to enable him to do this as smoothly and easily as possible.

What has been described is a counsel of perfection, and in many instances it has not been possible to adhere to it strictly. It will be noted that in the English Prison Service it is intended that the roles of 'commander' and 'negotiator' are filled by separate individuals, on the basis that the negotiator then always has a higher authority to refer to, and for that reason cannot be directly pressurized by the hostage-taker; additionally the commander, and particularly headquarters, may be able to take a more dispassionate view of the situation, taking into account not only the immediate hostage situation but also the long term interests of the prison and the Prison Department. However, what has frequently happened in the 20 recorded incidents is that the governor in charge of the prison has negotiated directly with the perpetrator, and this has met with considerable success in terms of the speed and safety in resolving the incident. Although this follows the tactics effectively pioneered by the New York Police Department, it has the inherent risk that the negotiator/commander will be over-generous in the concessions he gives to the perpetrator in order to resolve the immediate situation as quickly as possible. This danger, of being over-generous with concessions, is much more evident in prisons, as the governor can affect an inmate's life much more than a police officer can affect that of a member of the public. For example, a governor could in theory grant an extra visit from an inmate's wife, whereas a police officer would not be able, say, to change the level of rates that a member of the public is charged.

Another aspect that diverges from the ideal is that half the recorded incidents have been resolved by physical intervention. However, this is not generally against policy, as in all but three of the cases intervention was a forced decision in order to stop the perpetrator from harming the hostage. So far this has been an effective way of releasing the hostage safely, and only a few injuries have been sustained by the perpetrator or the intervention force; however, the inherent dangers are obvious.

Concluding comments on hostage-taking in English prisons

It appears that although hostage-takings in English prisons are much more common occurrences than in the outside world, they have not had such serious consequences in terms of loss of life, and have been resolved relatively quickly. The constructive action one might take to cope with hostage taking falls into three areas: (1) prevention; (2) resolving those incidents that are not prevented; (3) minimizing the damage to individuals after the incident has been resolved.

As far as prevention is concerned there is a wide range of possibilities; the following is a selection:

(1) Never let a hostage-taking succeed. It is likely that a hostage-taking which is successful in achieving the aims of the perpetrator will very quickly be copied time and again. The English Prison Service is well aware of this danger and so far

has had remarkable success in bringing incidents to a safe conclusion without granting major concessions.

(2) Limit the availability of weapons. Of the 22 weapons used in the 20 recorded incidents, 14 were ready-made weapons such as knives and scissors (eight), razors (three), chisels (two), and a pencil. Four further ones were improvised daggers or knives, and three utilized broken glass. In English prisons some inmates have access to razors, scissors and knives, particularly, for example, if they work in the prison kitchens. Again various implements are necessary to work in the workshops or to repair buildings. It would be possible, though not necessarily desirable, to make these weapons much more difficult to come by. One would need to weigh the potential dangers from them against the limitations caused by their removal. In any case, inmates have shown considerable ingenuity in the past in fashioning weapons from whatever materials are available.

(3) Making staff conscious of the risk of being taken hostage may enable them to avoid some potential incidents.

(4) Physical design. Of the 20 recorded incidents 75% took place in an office or a cell. These were generally made secure by the hostage-taker barricading the door which in all cases opened *into* the room. This deters any physical intervention because even with the hydraulic jacks available it takes several minutes to enter a barricaded cell, by which time the hostage could have been severely harmed. It may be feasible to fit doors which open both ways, inwards or *outwards*, which deter any logically thinking inmate from barricading them. Although it may be prohibitively expensive to replace all the existing doors, new buildings could, as a matter of policy, be fitted with inward/outward opening doors at little additional expense.

(5) Provide better inmate support. Of the 15 incidents in which the perpetrators' demands were recorded six asked for release, five asked to see or talk to a loved one, three for a transfer and one for a cat and a record-player in his cell. Most of these suggest a degree of despair or isolation, which might have been avoided by effective support. However, English prisons already have extensive welfare, psychological and medical services available, so to what extent any increase in these services would be cost effective is debatable.

As far as the resolution of incidents is concerned it seems that, to date, the English prisons have a good record. However, areas which might warrant further examination are as follows:

(1) The separation of the roles of commander and negotiator. At present these roles are intended to be filled by different individuals, as distinct from the practice in the New York Police Department. It is unclear which of these two strategies is the more appropriate for the prison setting.

(2) Physical intervention. Although half the recorded incidents have been

resolved by physical intervention, English prisons do not have available to them a specialized unit of men trained for this task. This is in spite of the fact that experience from hostage incidents outside of prison has shown that the effective training of intervention personnel can make the difference between success and failure. It may be, however, that it is considered sufficient to be able to call on outside resources if necessary. The Prison Department does have a unit which specializes in the 'hardware' which might be useful in hostage-takings, such as facilities for obtaining sound and vision of the siege area.

There is some suggestion that all those involved in a hostage incident is English prisons are likely to be affected by it for some time afterwards. In this connection one thinks naturally of the hostage, although it has already been mentioned that one perpetrator hanged himself immediately after the incident was resolved, and simply from talking to negotiators it seems that they too are deeply affected. Evidence on this is necessarily anecdotal as no rigorous studies have been completed in the prison system. Possible actions that might be taken are (1) to issue all staff with information designed to 'immunize' them against the after-effects of having been taken hostage if they are unfortunate enough ever to find themselves in this situation; (2) to provide psychological support for hostages once released. It may be that the latter would be appropriate for perpetrators and negotiators as well, but it is at present impossible to be certain of this.

In summary, the Prison Service's tactics and record for dealing with hostage-takings in the 1970s reflect realization in the outside world that the options open to those negotiating on behalf of the victim are not as limited as they once seemed. This has meant that nearly all the incidents have been resolved whilst still maintaining the three criteria laid down for success, namely that none of the personnel involved should be injured, no major concessions should be granted, and further incidents should not be encouraged. Nevertheless, this is clearly a developing area, and there may yet be several substantial refinements which can be made to existing procedures.

Endemic violent incidents

The term 'endemic' is used to indicate that these incidents are part of institutional life, and to differentiate them from hostage-takings and riots, which are relatively rare occurrences. There has been very little research into the day to day violence that occurs in English prisons, and this section concentrates on one study which looked at the violence shown by inmates in Birmingham Prison in the 2 year period from July 1977 to June 1979 (Davies, 1980).

Background

Birmingham Prison is a local prison of the type found in most large towns in England, designed to hold any man arrested in the Birmingham area for at least a limited time. Those inmates with short sentences will probably complete them in Birmingham Prison, while long term men and serious offenders are generally transferred to training prisons which have better facilities and higher staff to inmate ratios. Birmingham Prison therefore contains all ages of men, charged with anything from being drunk and disorderly to murder or various terrorist offences. It is a Victorian structure built in the middle of the nineteenth century, designed to house 600 men; although the cell accommodation has not been expanded or modified to any large extent since the prison was built, it now houses approximately 1000 inmates with consequent overcrowding and severe strain on facilities. This is not unusual for local prisons in England. Although this study was conducted in a local prison, this is not meant to imply that such prisons are more prone to unrest than training prisons; there is no evidence to suggest that this is the case.

The study examined violent incidents in two ways: (1) by examining incidents that were reported as being against the prison rules and were therefore recorded in the disciplinary reports; (2) by examining the nature of the injuries that occurred in the prison, whether or not they were attributed to assaults—these are recorded in the injury reports.

Incidents from disciplinary reports

Data from officially reported and recorded incidents (Table 2) suggest that assaults by inmates on other inmates are held at a relatively low level in spite of the need for inmates to mix with each other at work and in educational and social activities in the prison. The major danger times for this type of incident corresponded with 'slopping out' and using the overcrowded toilet facilities. (All cells contain a pot for the use of the one, two or three inmates in that cell and 'slopping out' refers to the time when inmates are unlocked to empty their pots.) A landing (housing perhaps 50 inmates) uses one toilet 'recess' which contains perhaps two sit-down lavatories with low barn doors to enable supervision, and one or two open urinals and basic washing facilities. These have long been recognized as inadequate, particularly as access even to these facilities is limited. Many inmates are reluctant to use their pots and this leads to some of them wrapping their excrement in underclothes or socks and disposing of it through the cell windows. As well as being a distasteful state of affairs, this is also held by many to be a major source of waste as far as prison clothes are concerned. Given this background, it is not really surprising that some friction occurs during the 'slopping out' period.

While the 'slopping out' period corresponds with the peak for inmates assaulting each other, the quietest time is during the night when inmates are locked in their cells. In the 2 year period under study there were only 12 reported incidents between the hours of 8 p.m. and 7 a.m. This is a somewhat surprising finding as during the day-time the cells are one of the most common places for

Table 2 The number and causes of violent incidents recorded on disciplinary reports at Birmingham Prison, July 1977 to June 1979 (holding approximately 1000 inmates)

Number of fights involving inmates only	141
Number of assaults on prison officers	70
Causes of inmates being put on violence report	
1. Tension between cell mates	31
2. 'Odd' behaviour (odd enough to result in an observation period in the prison hospital)	30
3. Arguments over stealing, borrowing or scrounging	25
4. 'Cracking up'	11
5. Subsequent to an order	8
6. Tension between racial groups	8
7. Pushing past on stairs or doorway	5
8. Argument at foot servery	5
9. Other	34
10. Cause not identifiable	116

assaults to occur. In local prisons inmates spend a substantial amount of time locked in their cells, often with one or two cellmates, during the day as well as the night. At Birmingham, it is generally only those prisoners who are serving long term sentences who leave their cells to go to the workshops for 4–5 hours per day. Other inmates will leave their cells for an hour's exercise, to collect their meals, for 'slopping out', and possibly for periods of association with other inmates. Therefore the fact that assaults tail off so dramatically during the night hours is a little surprising and may be attributed to the fact that there is enforced darkness, or a basic need for sleep, or to the fact that in the quiet of the night scuffles or fights would be much more easily heard and detected.

Interestingly there are also fewer assaults between inmates on Sundays. This is difficult to explain, as although the Sunday routine is different from that of weekdays, it is very similar to the procedure on Saturdays, which do not show the same drop. Some possibilities are as follows:

(1) Visits, which happen every day except Sunday, may make prisoners less tolerant of others. This is unlikely, however, as visits normally take place in the afternoon and most inmate assaults take place in the morning.

(2) The religious nature of Sunday, perhaps demonstrated by the popular church service, may inhibit prisoners from assaulting each other.

(3) The fact that there are fewer staff on Sundays may make the prison atmosphere less oppressive. This is an appealing possibility, particularly when linked with the finding that short-staffed local prisons suffer fewer major disturbances than relatively better staffed dispersal prisons. A related possibility is that staff, aware that there are fewer of them in the prison on Sundays, behave differently from during the week.

The two most common causes of fights between inmates were 'odd' behaviour on the part of an inmate and friction between cellmates. These two causes accounted for approximately 38% of the incidents in which it was possible to determine a cause. 'Odd' behaviour was defined as behaviour which warranted an observation period in the prison hospital but did not lead to a transfer to a psychiatric hospital. The odd behaviour might be on the part of the offender or the victim. In both cases the incident frequently happens between two inmates who share a cell. Where the odd behaviour is on the part of the offender, the nature of the incident usually seems to be that the victim displays no provocation and may indeed be asleep, and the offender has no rational grudge against the victim. Nevertheless, the victim is subjected to some sort of attack, usually minor in nature. Where the odd behaviour is displayed by the victim, the offence usually seems to occur as a result of exasperation felt by the aggressor. For example, the victim may be walking around a cell in the middle of the night talking, muttering or shouting to himself for no apparent reason, and after a number of unsuccessful attempts to control this behaviour by reasoning and threats his cellmate feels that there is no alternative left but to resort to physical means in a usually vain attempt to obtain some peace and quiet. A related but different cause, accounting for 7% of attributable incidents, is 'cracking up'. This is different from 'odd' behaviour in that the person concerned has no history of behaviour noted as strange, and there is usually an identifiable stimulus such as a 'Dear John' letter (a letter from the man's wife telling him that she is leaving him) that provokes the incident.

Tension between cellmates is one of the most frequent causes of incidents in Birmingham Prison. At first sight this is not surprising as it holds a population which is heterogeneous in terms of age, offence and race and, as has been mentioned earlier, is heavily overcrowded. However, as will be explained later, even the overcrowding and shared cell accommodation does not appear to raise the overall rate of violent incidents.

Only 5% of attributed incidents were noted as being caused by racial friction, although an inmate's race is not recorded on the report form and therefore this may be an under-estimate. It is interesting, however, that the showing of the film *The Clansman* which, amonst other things, depicts the rape of a white woman by a gang of black men, was a major cause of racial incident. It so incensed some of the audience that they felt it necessary to seek vengeance on some of the coloured inmates. In a sense this provides support for the findings of Leyens *et al.* (1975), who showed films of a violent nature to one section of a home for boys in Belgium, and found that this group responded with more immediate violence after the film than did those who were shown neutral films. However, it is not an exact parallel as *The Clansman* did not tutor the audience how to aggress, it merely provided a good justification for displaying aggression that already existed in their behavioural repertoire. Bandura (1973, p. 27) says that 'television... teaches how to aggress, by the way it portrays the functional value of aggressive behaviour'; in the particular instance of *The Clansman* prisoners had no need to be taught how to aggress, rather they anticipated that the 'functional value' of aggression would be to deter coloured men from attacking white women. Perhaps more directly, the aggression served to alleviate their sense of indignation.

A more major cause of incidents were arguments over stealing, borrowing and 'scrounging' (hinting or asking for others' possessions, or borrowing without repaying), accounting for a further 16% of attributable incidents. These arguments usually occur between cellmates, but have been listed separately because the cause of the disagreement was discernible and therefore, superficially at least, different from 'diffuse tension between cellmates'. However, if these two causes of argument were classified together, they would represent the single major cause of incidents between inmates. It is therefore understandable that some importance is attached to the person with whom one shares a cell.

So far we have been talking only about assaults between inmates. Prison officers too are the victims of assaults, although not as commonly as are the prisoners themselves. Officers are most usually assaulted when there is a small number of them trying to control a large number of prisoners required to do a tedious or irritating task. An example of this is where they queue for meals, when inmates have the additional worry about whether their fellow prisoners who serve the food will give them a sufficiently large helping. This, allied with the importance attached to food in prisons mentioned earlier, makes meal-times a sensitive period. Another example is where officers are required to escort a body of inmates from the wing containing the cells to the workshops. One of the more common causes of incidents in a situation such as this is when an inmate is reluctant to lose face, having been ordered by an officer to do something he is unwilling to do. On occasions this leads to arguments and an assault. There was little evidence in this study of planned assaults against officers.

Violence occurs in a variety of different settings in prisons: the exercise yard and the workshops have their fair share, and two inmates simultaneously trying to get through a doorway from opposite directions is another common setting event; however, the vast majority occur in or near a cell in one of the four wings. Two of the four wings have more reported incidents *pro rata* than the other two. The two apparently more troublesome wings house mainly remanded prisoners (awaiting trial) and short term convicted prisoners, whereas the two apparently less troublesome wings hold long term inmates and a number of young inmates (under 21 years). However, it should be borne in mind at this stage that we are dealing with figures representing only those incidents that are *reported*, and it is indicated below that these do not represent the true picture.

Violent incidents evident from injury reports

Another part of this study examined the injury reports that were filed during this period. This was an attempt to establish the size of the 'dark figure' (Walker, 1971)—the number of violent incidents that go unreported. In fact the picture that emerged from the injury reports suggests that it is not feasible to think in terms of any absolute figure for fights and assaults.

Injury reports are made out by a hospital officer or a doctor following an injury or a suspected injury. Such injuries may be accidental, for example slipping downstairs, falling out of bed, walking into a door, or scalding accidents, or they may have been sustained deliberately, either self-inflicted or inflicted by a second party. It was decided to examine these reports because of the suspicion that many assaults by inmates may go unreported, as the victim may fear reprisals and therefore report them as accidents or as assaults by an unnamed person (therefore resulting in no disciplinary report).

The injury reports were examined to determine how many injuries were deliberately inflicted. As it is not always possible to tell from the report whether or not an injury was deliberate, a conservative judgement was made when a case was in doubt. Bearing this in mind, the reports yielded the following figures over the 2 year period in Birmingham Prison (Davies, 1980):

(1) The total number of injury reports over the period was 500; 213 of the men featuring in these probably sustained their injuries in a fight or assault.

(2) Sixty of the subjects of the injury reports were suffering from self-inflicted injuries.

(3) Treatment in an outside hospital was necessary in 21 cases.

The picture of violent incidents yielded by the injury reports differs in several respects from that suggested by the disciplinary reports. The first of these is that injury reports show that fights or assaults carry on much later into the evening than would have been suggested by discipline reports. This means that there are an appreciable number of fights or assaults taking place in prisoners' cells which do not lead to a disciplinary report. However, both sets of reports agree that fights tail off at 10.30 p.m. until 7.00 a.m. These times coincide with the lights-out period, and one might speculate that it is too difficult to fight in the dark, or that the quiet that prevails in a prison wing at night discourages inmates from scuffling for fear of detection, or simply that most men need their sleep.

Another main difference between the two sets of reports is that the two wings that had fewer discipline reports recorded per head had more deliberate injury reports recorded. In other words, it appears that the two wings that were having most fights were actually recording the least disciplinary reports. One can understand this in terms of reporting, as the two wings where offences are under-reported are those with the young prisoners and the long term prisoners respectively. Long term prisoners are traditionally allowed a little more lee way than other prisoners, because of the supposed strain they are under, and young prisoners are expected to be high-spirited and troublesome, and therefore staff perhaps set a higher threshold before putting them on report. Conversely, one of the wings where offences are apparently reported meticulously is that which holds remanded prisoners, and one can see the wisdom, from the staff's point of view, of careful reporting of all incidents, as remanded prisoners are constantly in touch with visitors and the outside world and can therefore make complaints more easily. In such cases it is plainly necessary to have a written record of the occurrence.

Two of the four wings are large (270 inmates each), and the other two are smaller (175 inmates each). Interestingly, the two relatively more troublesome wings are one small wing and one largewing, and of course the relatively less troublesome wings are also one small and one large. This suggests that varying the size of a wing between 175 and 270 inmates would not be a powerful factor influencing the number of assaults.

Areas in which the injury reports confirm the findings on disciplinary reports are that there are many more fights amongst inmates in the morning, gradually tailing off as the day progresses, and that Sunday is indeed a much quieter day than the rest of the week.

As far as the nature of the injuries is concerned, the majority are cuts, scratches, grazes, black eyes and a small number of bites. Also there was a surprisingly high incidence of burns and scalds; for example, in the second year under study there were a total of 20 such injuries, mostly scalds.

Sometimes the injured party volunteered how he had sustained his injury. Out of the 365 injury reports in the second year, 16 men said that they had slipped, 14 had sustained their injury in the process of assaulting or trying to assault an officer, 11 said they had fallen downstairs, and seven that they had fallen out of bed. Although these are the most common reasons given, not too much reliance should be put on their frequency, as in the majority of cases there is simply no information of how the injury was sustained, and there is no guarantee that the inmate's account represents the true picture.

'The dark figure'

Initially it seemed logical to estimate the total number of violent incidents by adding together the number of reported incidents and the number of unreported incidents that become apparent from the injury reports. There is of course some overlap between the figures on the disciplinary reports and those on the injury reports, because some inmates booked for fighting will have been injured during the fight. But the real argument against adding together the figures from the respective sets of reports is that one would not be adding like to like. This needs some clarification, and can best be illustrated by a comparison with another area of crime, car theft. If one considers car theft, there is one unique figure which represents the number of cars stolen per year, as a car is either stolen or not stolen. One might obtain an estimate of this figure by finding out how many cars are reported stolen and adding an estimate of the number of stolen cars that are not reported for various reasons.

The same is not the case with violent incidents, because of the difficulty of defining what is or is not a violent incident. It is not true to say that an inmate is either assaulted or not assaulted in the same way as a car is either stolen or not stolen. There are degrees of aggression and violence which lie on a continuum, for example: shouting 'squaring up', pushing or shoving, slapping, scratching, butting, punching, biting, elbowing, kneeing, kicking, knifing, shooting, exploding.

In prison an inmate might find himself on a violence disciplinary report for virtually any of these activities from pushing to knifing inclusive. Many of the minor incidents may go unreported, but this depends more on the reporting officer than the incident. An officer is liable to use his discretion, particularly with the minor incidents, and what may be a breach of rules to one officer may be part of prison life to another. The same is not true of an injury report, the criterion for medical attention being the severity of the injury. Thus by adding the two figures together one would produce a confused statistic representing a *melée* of different activities but which might be interpreted as the incidence of some kind of stereotype of 'violent behaviour'. Additionally, of course, there will be some incidents which appear on neither set of reports, as the incident may not have been observed by an officer and the inmate may successfully hide any injuries sustained.

Action which might reduce the occurrence of 'endemic' violence

The Davies (1980) study suggests that in a 2 year period in Birmingham Prison at least 213 men featured on injury reports as a result of being involved in a fight or an assault. This is probably an under-estimate of the true figure. One might regard this level of violence as reasonably low for a prison containing approximately 1000 men housed in very poor conditions. Nevertheless, it is not a level to be complacent about and various possibilities present themselves for lessening the number of incidents that occur.

The study suggests that the vast majority of incidents take place in or around inmates' cells, and that the three most common causes are diffuse tension between cellmates, arguments over stealing and borrowing, and 'odd' behaviour, with 'cracking up' being the next most common cause. These suggest some possibilities for improving matters:

(1) Prison rebuilding. Ideally the tension between cellmates and arguments over stealing, etc., should be resolved by eliminating the system whereby two or three men have to share a very small cell in poor conditions. (However, in some cases there seems to be an advantage to men sharing a cell; see concluding comment.) This would mean an extensive nationwide prison rebuilding programme which, however overdue, is unlikely to take place in the near future.

(2) Cell change on demand. Plainly if you are in constant close proximity with

one or two other men, it is important that you get on as well as possible with them. Although it would not be feasible to have an allocation system of any sophistication for cells in a local prison, it may well be possible to allow men to change their cell whenever they wish. This would mean that although they would not have the power to choose, they would at least have the power of veto, and this fairly simple strategy would attack two out of the three main causes of incidents.

(3) More readily available medical and psychological attention. The two other major causes were 'odd' behaviour and 'cracking up'. In the case of the former the person concerned always was sent to the prison hospital, and this occurred with the latter too in some cases. One might speculate that had this occurred at an earlier stage of the proceedings the incident might have been prevented.

Concluding comment

An examination of disciplinary and injury reports reveals that there is an appreciable number of violent incidents occurring in a local prison such as Birmingham, and one of the principal reasons for this is tension between cellmates. This implies that the very act of sharing a cell will necessarily cause tension, but this appears not to be the case.

In a supplementary study (Davies, 1981*b*) undertaken during a period when the population of Birmingham Prison fell from around 1000 to approximately 600 as a result of industrial action, it was shown that there was no *prorata* reduction in measures of unrest such as discipline reports and sick reporting. This adds support to the suggestion by G. Lakes (personal communication that cell sharing has a twofold effect: in some instances it may cause friction and even violence; in others the presence of another may work against the likelihood of violence. Any study of the cases of violent incidents would pick up only the former effect, for obvious reasons. On an anecdotal level, there seem to be inmates who prefer to share a cell. The crucial variable may be with whom the cell is shared rather than the simple fact of sharing.

Riots

Overview

Riots in English prisons have attracted increasing attention since the late 1960s because they have appeared to be more frequent and destructive since that time. During this period the major disturbances have tended to occur in a handful of dispersal prisons, notably Hull, Gartree and Parkhurst. At first sight this might be what one would expect, in that dispersal prisons are so named because of the policy of dispersing the longer-term security risk prisoners amongst these prisons following the recommendations of the report of the Advisory Council on the Penal System (1968). However, one might be reluctant to accept that these prisons will necessarily suffer disturbances, for three reasons: first, dispersal prisons have a significantly higher staffing ratio than others; secondly, the facilities available for prisoners are superior to those in other prisons; thirdly, any man in a dispersal prison will have spent some time in the allocation centre of a local prison, and these prisons do not seem to suffer the same disturbances. Any attempt to understand riots in English prisons should explain why they happen in those prisons where they do occur, as well as taking account of at least these three points.

A great deal of research was stimulated by the period of unrest in American prisons and reformatories from 1950 to 1955, during which time major riots and disturbances were occurring at the rate of approximately two per month. Many of the findings from the study of these disturbances seem to be applicable to recent events in English prisons. For example, Schrag (1960) makes the point that most of the American riots had certain features in common: (1) initial unrestrained violence and destruction; (2) the emergence of inmate leaders who had control over inmates and any staff who were held as hostages; (3) a presentation of inmate grievances to the authorities, together with an attempt to win public support and sympathy; (4) a gradual resumption of legal responsibilities by prison officials.

A riot began with a sudden flare-up of violence. Schrag (1960) states that there was no perceptible forewarning, although a state of heightened tension and anxiety was widely recognized. Certainly this was the case in the Hull (England) riot of 1976 (Forde, 1976), the tension being so marked that the institution's psychologist was asked to identify its causes a little while before the riot occurred. Fox (1971) describes this slightly differently, differentiating between predisposing causes and precipitating causes, where the former set the scene for heightened tension and help to increase the likelihood of disturbance and the latter are the 'sparks' that set it off. This trigger might be negligence or poor judgement on the part of an officer, which allows prisoners to stumble into rebellion without any definite plan, or it may be the result of luring an officer into a trap where his authority can be negated.

Whatever the immediate cause, this first stage is characterized by wanton damage and violence, with no particular purpose behind it. Again, this was observed in the British prisons, Hull and Gartree. The former was stripped of its roof slates twice within the space of 3 years, and in the latter inmates found themselves able to break down the walls between each others' cells. Schrag (1960) and Fox (1971) agree that it is at this stage that the use of force by the prison authorities would be most likely to pay off. They say that in American prisons there are several reasons why such a course of action is not taken, not least of which are the pragmatic ones such as the lack of any definite plan of how to deal with a sudden inmate rebellion, a dearth of well trained personnel in the prison, or a lack of appropriate weapons. Other reasons might be termed policy decisions; for example, if hostages are held, the hasty use of force might be considered too great a risk to their safety; similarly it might be thought that public opinion would be against the use of overwhelming force, whether or not the lives of the hostages were at stake. It is also perhaps worth contrasting the policy of immediate forceful retaliation suggested here with the 'softly softly' approach appropriate for hostage situations. While a forceful reaction might be appropriate if there were no hostages, it probably would not be if there were.

Certain inmates take advantage of this chaotic and destructive situation to establish themselves as leaders. Schrag (1960) maintains that with a few exceptions these leaders are the 'outlaws' or the 'gorillas' of the institution, whose aggressive tendencies had been restrained previously only by the vigilance of staff and inmates alike. It appears, however, that the opportunity to subjugate official authority outweighs the more immediate pleasures of unrestrained violence. These men have a complex task to achieve: on the one hand they must avoid alienating the bulk of the prison population, most of whom are keen to maintain a passive role, and they must not provoke retaliation from the prison authorities; at the same time they must ensure the continuance of all essential services, so that life can continue as comfortably and as normally as possible for the duration of the insurrection.

The most widely used strategy in American prisons is to take hostages; in English prison riots this has been done more rarely. Hostages were usually told that no harm would come to them if they offered no resistance, but force was willingly used if resistance was offered, and the fear of retaliation against these officials generally discouraged any use of force by the authorities. Hostages were uniformly impressed by the sincerity of their captors' threats against them. Additionally the inmate leaders attempted to monopolize the communications system between the authorities and the main inmate body so that they could, if necessary, censor any messages in either direction. Finally, the less enthusiastic inmates were encouraged to continue supporting the riot by threats of violence if their enthusiasm showed further signs of waning.

Threats of violence were only effective for a limited period of time. Once the exhilaration from having overthrown authority began to wear off, it became apparent to the inmate leaders and to the main body that the situation they had produced was an unstable one and that demands needed to be drawn up and presented to the authorities so that normal life could resume, although it was hoped that some concessions could be wrung from the authorities before that happened. In the meantime, the physical side of life had probably taken a turn for the worse since the riot began. Although there were attempts to maintain essentials such as power, food and medical aid, the ransacking of parts of the prison and general vandalism continued, and certain inmates became the victims of assaults now that they no longer had official protection.

Skelton (1969), in his study of the inmates involved in a major riot at El Reno Reformatory, identified two groups of inmates whom he termed 'assaulters' and 'defenders'. As the titles suggest, the former group had an inclination to assault officials who were held as hostages and were differentiated from defenders by having a younger than average age and more frequently having a record of violent behaviour in their past. This variation in prisoner reaction to a riot was again demonstrated in the Gartree riot of the late 1970s where members of staff trapped during the insurrection were only saved from physical harm by the very assertive intervention of a rescue force of prisoners.

During this middle stage of the riot it becomes clear to inmate leaders that in order for them to retain control they have to make clear to the rest of the population what their aims are and how they intend to achieve them. This generally poses problems, as little thought has been given by them to any purpose for the riot beyond wresting control away from the authorities. Furthermore, the courses of action open to them promise little hope of improving their lot. Escape is generally out of the question as perimeters are strongly guarded and there is little support for such a move from the mass of the prison population. Release of the hostages would make them vulnerable to the use of force by the prison authorities, as would the liquidation of the hostages. Even further destruction would only serve to make their own situation more uncomfortable.

One might speculate that the use of force at this stage might put a rapid end to a riot. In the American situation it was generally decided not to take this action for two reasons: the first was that the hostages were generally held in such inaccessible parts of the prison that it was unlikely that they would be reached before serious harm had been done to them; the second was that the study of the records of prisoners involved in the riot revealed that there were usually at least a small number who had already shown themselves willing to use extreme force. This, combined with the fact that prisoners were now finding that, after their initial elation, they were far from being in a strong position, led officials to the conclusion that there was a distinct possibility of acts of murder-suicide on the part of several prisoners, with the hostages as the murder victims. An additional consideration might be the lack of suitably trained personnel for a physical intervention. The potentially disastrous results of such an intervention have since been demonstrated at Attica Prison and the Munich Olympic Games.

In the El Reno riot it was at this difficult stage the emergence of 'cool-heads' became apparent. These men were against the use of violence and tried to convince the bulk of the prison that if the advantage they had gained was handled correctly, they could win some substantial concessions. Such sentiments tended to be welcomed by the rank and file and by the 'gorillas', both of whom feared that the situation had reached an impasse and that the most likely outcome was their surrender. This meant that the men who had formerly been at the front of the riot and had caused much of the destruction now fulfilled a dual role of communicating with the authorities and keeping the rest of the prisoners in line. The difference in the situation was that the communications were now from the 'cool-heads' via the 'gorillas', whereas previously what was spoken by the 'gorillas' had also been generated by them.

because the same men were still fulfilling the role of speaking to the authorities, the underlying change in authority was difficult to discern from the outside. However, the inmates were now able to draw up a plan to resolve the situation to their advantage. This generally involved informing the public of the conditions inside the prison, gaining their sympathy and support and using this to produce changes in the prison regime. On their side they promised to release the hostages unharmed if these demands were met. This won for the inmates a considerable degree of publicity and a wider recognition of their grievances. Generally public reaction was on the side of the inmates and critical of the administration and this led the authorities to give in to some of the demands made by the prisoners. Sometimes these concessions were conciliatory rather than substantial, but nevertheless led to the control of the prison being handed back to the lawful authorities and expedited the safe release of the bostages.

During the months following the resumption of normality there was a certain amount of tension and unrest on the part of both the prisoners and the staff and several minor incidents occurred. In view of the recent riot and the part played by the media, these incidents were given ample publicity and public opinion quickly swung away from the prisoners and towards those who called for stricter control and greater vigilance over those in prison. Both staff and inmates perceived that this was happening, and most of the alterations in prison policy were usually abandoned so that no longterm benefits accrued from the riot. Perhaps because they realized that they no longer had public support or perhaps because they could not face more unrest so recently after a riot, prisoners did not react against the removal of these privileges and the whole prison was 'back to square one'.

Reference has been made at several points to the prison authorities being reluctant to use force for fear of harm coming to the hostages. By no means all riots involve hostage-taking, particularly in English prisons, and this is bound to be so by their spontaneous unplanned nature; if no potential hostages are easily available at the time of the riot, then it has to go ahead without hostages whether or not this would be what the inmates would choose. It is interesting in these cases that the authorities both in England and the United States have generally rejected the use of force, although there are a few notable exceptions. One assumes that this is because of anticipated public reaction or the shortage of trained personnel to put such a plan into practice. Therefore the presence or absence of hostages does not make a significant difference to the description of the events in the riot, although it may feature largely in the deliberations of the protagonists. However, this may become increasingly less the case as the authorities become aware that it is possible to have teams of men trained to intervene swiftly and efficiently, as has been demonstrated by the Israelis at Entebbe and the special Air Service in the seige of the London Iranian Embassy. The English Prison Service has been aware that successful resolution of incidents may depend upon having suitably trained personnel available, and to this end introduced MUFTI training (MUFTI being an acronym standing for 'minimum use of force tactical intervention'). this training is designed to enable squads of suitably trained prison officers to restore order following a disturbance. To do this they are equipped with protective clothing such as helmets and shields and given staves which they are trained to use effectively but with minimum risk to the inmate. Thus equipped they might be used to break up a demonstration or riot in an open area, or, with more extensively trained officers, to re-occupy a wing or cell taken over by inmates who may have utilized barricades. Although this training was introduced approximately 6 years ago (1976), MUFTI squads have only rarely been used and it is probably fair to say that prison authorities have mixed feelings about their use, perhaps because of awareness of public opinion.

Causes

The spate of prison riots in the United States between 1950 and 1955 led to many attempts to explain their causes. Some explanations dealt largely with external factors such as the nature of the governors of particular states, while others dealt with internal matters such as the food and hygiene in the prisons concerned. It is worth looking at this second class of explanations. According to Fox (1956) the riot in Michigan Prison was claimed by many people to be the result of a rift between the divisions of custody and individual treatment. Those who worked in these two divisions were surprised to hear of this rift (Fox, 1956), for although there were disagreements about various points they had never thought this could be perceived as a 'rift', let alone be the cause of a prison riot. However, such a rift was a convenient discovery at the time and was widely promoted, to the extent that not only was this new-found rift definitely thought to exist but it was also labelled as a major cause of the riot. This in turn produced a rift between the two divisions, both reasoning that if the blame was inevitably going to land near them, then the least that they could do was to push it as far away as possible, namely on the other division. There were numerous other explanations for this particular riot, although the motivation of many of the writers may have been to escape blame themselves rather than uncover the true situation. After a succession of blaming and counter-blaming the opinion was that the riot was due to a number of factors: (1) the excessive size of the prison; (2) the heterogeneous population; (3) the overcrowding and consequent lack of segregation; (4) understaffing; (5) inadequate training programmes for guards. These are interesting, in that virtually all of them conflict with what was the case at Gartree Prison in England. Gartree is a small prison, and, because it is a dispersal prison, has a relatively homogeneous population which is not overcrowded by the standards of the English Prison Service. It also has a relatively high staff to inmate ratio and a slow turnover of staff compared with many prisons. These later four factors apply to all dispersal prisons, which are the ones which have tended to have riots in England.

Fox (1956) makes the point that 'causes' of riots are largely determined by

(1) what is convenient and expedient and (2) the weight of writing rather than its accuracy. One should therefore consider writings about the causes of riots with some suspicion, but, having said this, the American Prison Association Committee on Riots (1953) differentiated 'basic' riot causes from 'immediate' causes (analogous to Fox's predisposing and precipitating causes (Fox, 1971)). They describe basic causes as follows: (1) inadequate financial support; (2) official and public interference; (3) substandard personnel; (4) enforced prisoner idleness; (5) lack of professional programmes; (6) excessive size of prisons; (7) overcrowding; (8) political domination and motivation of management; (9) unwise sentencing and parole practices. Again these are interesting, in that although many of them are criticisms which would apply to many prisons in England, they apply much less so to dispersal prisons than to others. (One must bear in mind all the time that it is dispersal prisons that have been prone to riots in the English system and one might therefore suspect that this list of 'causes' represents what is plausible rather than what is accurate.) Indeed Fox (1956) says that if these are the causes of riots then he wonders why riots have not been reported from a host of other prisons where the same descriptions would apply.

Several writers, including Schrag (1960), Hartnung and Floch (1954) and Fox (1971), have emphasized the importance of good food, making the point that food becomes a key source of pleasure in a community deprived of the usual pleasures of life. It is also a tangible item on which many other discontents can be focused. Therefore administrations should not consider solely nutritional factors when considering the provision of food, as it may be an important predisposing and even precipitating cause of riots. Certainly at least one of the recent British riots was preceded by occasional complaints and demonstrations about the quality of the food for a period of around 6 weeks.

A concept advocated particularly by Hartnung and Floch (1954) is that of inmates' self-government, which can be used to the advantage of the authorities in maintaining the *status quo*. Conversely, the failure of the authorities to make use of this strategy can be considered as contributing to unrest. Ironically it is likely to be the least well staffed prisons that will make use of inmate labour in positions of influence. Hartnung and Floch (1954) emphasize that inmates in positions of responsibility will seek to maintain the stability of the prison, and this will be a powerful force for tranquillity in the prison if the responsible inmates are influential people in their own right. Conversely, if these positions are allocated to men who are generally unpopular, the remainder of the inmates have an added incentive to cause disruption. Consequently these positions should be allocated with great care, and it is interesting that in the English Prison Service there is no policy on how prison orderlies should be selected. (Prison orderlies are trusted prisoners who are allowed free access to specified areas of the prison, and can come and go as they please within that area in order to achieve their tasks. They wear a red cloth band on their arm, together with a small photograph of themselves. To be a 'redband' carries a certain amount of status.)

Schrag (1960), in his description of the process of a riot, points out that there comes a stage when the aim of the rioters is to gain publicity for their plight, the assumption being that the general public is not already aware. It would seem that this assumption is a valid one, as an outcry usually follows the publication of details about conditions and regimes that exist in the prisons, with the result that reforms are made. These reforms persist until the general public's attitude to prisoners hardens again following the continuation of minor disturbances even when the concessions have been granted. Interestingly, withdrawal of these hard-won concessions a few months after the riot is accepted with relative equanimity by the prisoners. Presumably one factor that causes this is the knowledge that they would get little or no further support from the general public, who are by now well aware of the conditions that prisoners are held in and believe that they are by no means too harsh in view of their now seemingly unreasonable behaviour. On the basis of this, one could describe another cause of unrest as either (1) a prison not being run along the lines that are imagined by the outside community, or (2) the outside community not being informed of the way in which the prison is being run. Either of these situations would put prisoners in a position of having something to gain from the publicity following their riot. In this respect it is interesting to speculate what might be the effect of English television programmes such as *Porridge* and *Strangeways*. They inform the public of the conditions under which prisoners are kept and it will have been noted by prisoners that this information has not produced widespread or concerted unrest or sympathy for them. The implications of this are that disturbance would not produce public support simply by showing that conditions are poor; there would have to be a particular local reason that applied only to the prison in which unrest occurred.

Related to this is the ability to communicate inside the prison. Hartnung and Floch (1954) and Fox (1956) maintain that unrest will be generated unless there is a mechanism for protests to be made. Both agree that the means of expression need not be a sophisticated one. Informal group meetings would be sufficient to allow some king of protest; simple association between inmates allows for some expression of aggression through sarcasm or verbal abuse. If competitive games such as table tennis can be arranged then this is thought to be better still. Fox (1956) suggests that if such provisions for aggression release are not built into the prison rules then aggression must be expressed outside those rules, and a riot is more likely to result. The exception to this, he maintains, is where prisoners are so heavily guarded that their moral sinks to such a low level that they cannot contemplate revolt. Generally such a situation is prevented by financial constraints limiting the number of staff that can be employed in a prison.

A general point made by Fox (1956) is that riots are a protest *against* something rather than a struggle *for* something. To this extent one might predict that an effective complaints procedure would be an essential element in any riot prevention strategy. Therefore the English prison system, whereby any inmate may first complain to his wing principal officer or assistant governor in charge of the wing, and then to the prison governor, and later still make a petition to the Home Office, is likely to have prevented many relatively minor grievances being magnified into disturbances. Nevertheless, one can envisage at least two categories of complaint that will not be satisfied by this procedure: (1) long-standing grievances affecting a large number of inmates, such as poor food, and (2) acute short-lived grievances which provoke a reaction from inmates before the grievance can be investigated. An example of the later would be inmates' belief that one of their number had been assaulted by officers.

A further factor which has become apparent in English riots, but has not been commented on directly in American writings, is the physical layout of the prison. In the Gartree riot, for example, it became apparent that it was relatively easy for inmates to take control of a complete wing and therefore be quite impregnable. In all English prisons inmates heavily outnumber staff and therefore if it is easy to barricade the entrance to a wing this is a possible source of temptation to the inmates whenever grievances arise. Having done this they have effectively usurped authority and are then in a position to make demands. Wings in the older Victorian prisons, which still play a large part in the English prison system, are by their design much more difficult to isolate because of the many corridors and exits that lead off each wing and the open landings which mean that it is not sufficient to isolate a single floor. Although these have worked well, they disguise the fundamental conflict of interests in designing a prison, namely that one is seeking a structure that is easy for staff to defend against prisoners, but difficult for inmates to defend against staff. So the problem is straightforward, but the solution is a little more obscure.

Prevention

The following measures would help to minimize the likelihood of a riot in any prison:

(1) There should be an efficient and rapid procedure for dealing with grievances, and possibly a facility for inmates to air their feelings without making an official complaint.

(2) The importance of good food should be recognized by making it as attractive as possible within financial constraints. Letters, visits and medical services appear to be an equally important source of grievance in some English riots (G. Lakes, personal communication).

(3) Care should be exercised to ensure that the desirable positions given to inmates should be allocated to those who have an influence on and are respected by other inmates.

(4) The public should be made as aware as possible about the conditions inside prisons.

(5) The design of buildings plays an important part, but it is difficult to specify what would be the formula for a prison to be as secure as possible.

The work of prison psychologists in England has centred more around the prediction of riots than their prevention. They have used the mathematical concept of catastrophe theory (Zeeman *et al.*, 1976), and by tying this in with measurable phenomena from the life of the prison (e.g. frequency of sick reporting and number of disciplinary reports) have attempted to predict when disturbances might occur. This has had two major drawbacks: (1) the unreliability of predictions; (2) predicting a riot, however accurately, does not necessarily prescribe how to prevent it.

The first of these objections is perhaps the more minor of the two as the catastrophe theory model is a relatively recent one and with more development may improve the power of its predictions. The second objection is the more serious, and forces one to ask whether one is interested more in predicting or in preventing riots. The dilemma is illustrated very clearly by the Hull riot of 1976 where unrest was clearly recognized, and because a riot had occurred 2–3 years previously another riot was expected. Data such as sick reporting and disciplinary reports confirmed the high level of unrest. However, this only led to confirmation of the anxiety of the authorities without informing them what action should be taken, and in due course the riot took place, with resulting extensive and expensive damage. Ideally one should minimize the possibility of riots or disturbance in any institution, and if this were done the necessity of prediction would be obviated, for even if there were a positive prediction of a riot no more could be done to prevent it. This would mean that the only other reason for predicting riots would be to control or quell those which were unavoidable.

Concluding comment

In summary, riots serve no useful purpose and regimes can be designed to minimize their likelihood. The technology of predicting them is at present unreliable. Riots tend to take a predictable pattern, and at certain times are amenable to being resolved by force, although whether this is desirable is another question. Otherwise the negotiation of return to normal routine would depend partly on whether hostages are held, and should take a form similar to the strategy developed for dealing with hostage-taking situations. Much of the quoted literature is anecdotal, and for this reason any conclusions drawn from it should be viewed as tentative; certainly there is ample scope for more rigorous research, particularly on how riots may be prevented.

Conclusion

Although each section, on hostage-taking, 'endemic' violence and riots, has been dealt with as an entity in itself, there is one general conclusion: although prisons in England and Wales have escaped *large scale* injuries and deaths from violence in the last 20 years, the constant occurrence of incidents gives no room for complacency. This is so not only in the areas of riots and hostage-takings, where one poorly handled situation may have disastrous consequences, but also with 'routine' situations which serve to put some prisoners in fear of their safety. The same general conclusions are likely to apply equally throughout the prisons of the Western world.

References

American Prison Association Committee on Riots (1953) *Prison Disturbances and Riots*. Cited in Fox (1956, p. 305).

Advisory Council on the Penal System (1968). *The Regime of Long Term Prisoners in Conditions of Maximum Security*. London: HMSO.

Bandura, A. (1973). *Aggression: A Social Learning Analysis*. Englewood Cliffs, N. J. Prentice-Hall.

Davies, W. (1980). Assaults by prisoners in Winson Green Prison, July 1977 to June 1979. Internal Home Office Prison Department document.

Davies, W. (1981*a*). A brief analysis of hostage incidents in the prison service, 1972 to 1980. Internal Home Office Prison Department document.

Davies, W. (1981*b*). An analysis of disturbance at Birmingham Prison during the period before during and after the Prison Officers' industrial dispute 1980/1981. Internal Home Office Prison Department Document.

Forde, R. (1976). Disciplinary reporting at Hull Prison. Internal Home Office Prison Department document.

Fox, V. (1956). *Violence behind Bars*. New York: Vantage Press.

Fox, V. (1971). Why prisoners riot. *Federal Probation*, **1971**, March, 9–14.

Hartnung, F. E., and Floch, M. (1954). A social-psychological analysis of prison riots: an hypothesis. Paper presented to a meeting of the section on criminology of the American Sociological Society, University of Illinois, September 1954.

Jenkins, B., and Johnson, J. (1975). *International Terrorism: A Chronology, 1968–1974*. Santa Monica: Rand Corporation.

Jenkins, B. (1976). *Hostage Survival: Some Preliminary Observations*. Santa Monica: Rand Corporation.

Leyens, J. P., Camino, L., Parke, R. D., and Berkowitz, L. (1975). Effects of movie violence on aggression in a field setting as a function of group dominance and cohesion. *Journal of Personality and Social Psychology*, **32**, 346–360.

Schrag, C. (1960). The sociology of prison riots. *Proceedings of the American Correctional Association*, **1960**, 136–146.

Skelton, W. D. (1969). Prison riot: assaulters vs. defenders. *Archives of General Psychiatry*, **21**, 350–362.

Walker, N. (1971). *Crimes, Court and Figures. An Introduction to Criminal Statistics*. Harmonsworth: Penguin Books.

Zeeman, E. C., Hall, C. S., Harrison, P. J., Marriage, G. H., and Shapland, P. H. (1976). A model for institutional disturbances. British *Journal of Mathematical and Statistical Psychology*, **29**, 66–80.

Developments in the Study of Criminal Behaviour. Volume 2: Violence
Edited by Philip Feldman

7

Mental Disorder and Violent behaviour

KEVIN HOWELLS

Introduction

The aim of this chapter is to review some studies relevant to understanding the relationship between mental disorder and violent behaviour, and, more generally, to review psychological studies of violent behaviour in abnormal groups which have attempted to explain violence in terms of variables other than mental disorder as such. Before commencing this discussion it is necessary to emphasize that the vast majority of the studies which will be reviewed have been concerned with criminal offenders, a group which is clearly unrepresentative of the total population of people who perform violent acts. It is very likely that most violent behaviour is not reported to the police and that persons actually brought to court form a highly selected group, the survivors of a series of filters which will have biased the characteristics of the group in ways that are largely unknown. (For a discussion of the biases involved in, for example, sexual offending, the reader is referred to papers by McClintock (1980) and Howells (1981*a*).) It follows, therefore, that caution is necessary in interpreting, and generalizing from, such studies.

The terms 'mental disorder', 'mental abnormality' and 'mental illness' will be used synonymously to cover the whole range of psychiatric abnormalities covered by the 1959 Mental Health Act in England and Wales, including mental illness, mental subnormality, psychopathic disorder and other 'disabilities of mind'.

Conceptual problems

This chapter will focus on mentally abnormal offenders and on the relationship between mental abnormality and violent offending. For the purposes of the chapter, I will assume the logical and scientific validity of the concept of mental abnormality (except for psychopathy), though it is necessary to point out that the medical model, which terms such as 'disorder' and 'abnormality' imply, has been (Szasz, 1968) and continues to be (Sarbin and Mancuso, 1980) the source of considerable controversy. The very distinction between abnormal and normal offenders may, in fact, be very difficult to maintain. The label 'abnormal' is often applied to behaviours that are *statistically* unusual (most people do not do them) and behaviours which are *normatively* unacceptable (it is wrong to act like that). The inference that such behaviours are the product of a mental illness or disease is not logical. Two criminological examples of such inferences would be, for example, the assumption that a person who horribly mutilates a victim in the course of a murder or a person who habitually sexually assaults children must be 'sick' or 'mentally ill'. Both these forms of behaviour are clearly statistically unusual and normatively unacceptable (for most people) but they are not necessarily the result of a physical, organic dysfunction. It is equally unacceptable to state that the behaviours are a product of a 'mental' (functional) illness. It has been pointed out elsewhere (British Psychological Society, 1973) that to talk about *mental* illness is to talk *analogically* (with physical functioning) in that 'mind' is an abstraction and has no physical location. The dangers and difficulties in drawing analogies between physical and mental illness have been lucidly described by Wootton (1980), who points out that the definition of physical disorder, and physical health, involves *functional failure* and *functional inadequacy* (the eye, for example, is disordered when it cannot serve the function of seeing) but that mental processes have no *natural* function. As a consequence, judgements of mental abnormality tend to depend on subjective moral criteria rather than on medical criteria. These conceptual difficulties with the medical model of disorder, although it will be accepted here, are more than academic, in that they may produce, for example, spurious correlations between disorder and crime. If the same social criteria are important as to who is defined as mentally abnormal and who is defined as deviant and criminal, then the two categories will appear, falsely, to be highly correlated.

The relationship between mental disorder and violent behaviour

There is no doubt that mentally disordered people do sometimes behave in a violent manner and that convicted offenders can sometimes be shown to be schizophrenic, depressed or suffering from some other psychiatric condition. When these two conditions are seen to exist in the same person it is not uncommon for observers to conclude that the psychiatric disorder is a *cause* of the deviant behaviour, that the person was aggressive *because* he was schizophrenic or depressed. If there were such a relationship it would be expected that people who had a history of violent behaviour would show a level of psychiatric disturbance higher than that found in the general population, and also that mentally disordered people would have a higher prevalence of violent behaviour than is found in the general population. The demonstration that such predictions were supported by the evidence would, of course, prove only that the two classes of behaviour were *correlated*, not that the causal relationship was in the direction suggested.

Psychiatric disturbance in violent and criminal groups

In that we are interested in violent behaviour rather than criminality, the ideal study would investigate mental disorder in people who could be demonstrated to have acted in a violent or deviant way. Unfortunately, virtually all of the studies have been conducted with those who have acted in this way and *also* have been caught, convicted and sent to prison. The confounding of violent behaviour with these other factors makes interpretation of such studies difficult.

Prins (1980) has summarized the findings of 20 studies which have investigated the prevalence of psychiatric disorders in penal populations. These studies show substantial disparities. The percentage of prisoners found to be suffering from psychosis (schizophrenia, affective disorders) ranged from 0.5% to 26%, from mental subnormality from 2.4% to 28%, from psychopathy from 5.6% to 70%, from neurosis from 2% to 7.9% and from alcoholism/excessive drinking from 11% to 80%. Such variation is likely to be in part a function of the different definitions of disorder used and of the different populations surveyed. In Gillies' study (1965) of homicides, for example, psychosis was relatively common, while it was infrequent in Scott's (1964) very different sample of Approved School boys. In spite of these disparities, these studies do suggest a high level of mental disturbance in criminal groups. Those who believe that psychiatric morbidity is high is penal populations also point to the phenomenon of suicide in English prisons which is roughly three times more frequent than in the general population (Topp, 1979).

Two relatively recent, large scale surveys of penal populations have also concluded that psychiatric problems are common. Guze (1976) studied a sample of several hundred criminals convicted of more serious offences (felonies) recruited from Missouri courts, reformatories and prisons. Standardized and reliable psychiatric interviews were performed and the prevalence of a wide range of disorders recorded. The most significant findings were the low frequencies of schizophrenic states (1%), affective disorders, organic syndromes and mental deficiency and the high frequencies of sociopathic disorder (78%), alcoholism (43%) and anxiety neurosis (12%). The fact that 90% of the sample were diagnosed as suffering from a psychiatric disorder would suggest an extremely liberal definition of 'disorder' in this study. Two other difficulties arise with this study: first, that violent offenders (homicides, rapists, etc.) formed only a minority of the sample, so that generalization of the findings to groups of homicides and seriously violent assaulters is dubious; secondly, that any offenders sent directly by the courts to the state hospital, or kept at the state hospital for observation, were omitted. This latter fact would clearly lower the incidence of psychotic and other extreme disturbed states in the main sample.

Gunn *et al.*, (1978) surveyed psychiatric morbidity and perceived need for treatment in two English prisons. Approximately half of the prisoners in the two samples had been convicted of violent offences. A variety of questionnaires were administered (validated by a structured psychiatric interview) which indicated that approximately 20–30% were suffering a marked or severe psychiatric disturbance. Almost a half showed significant symptoms of depression and a third of marked anxiety states. Drug abuse and alcoholism were found to be frequent, but schizophrenic states were rare. Almost a half in the Wormwood Scrubs sample had histories of mental hospital admissions and of suicidal behaviour.

Both these studies (Guze, 1976; Gunn *et al.*, 1978) were conducted firmly within the medical model and tell us something about the prevalence of mental disorder, as perceived by psychiatrists, in prison populations. Both used standardized and relatively objective measures and concur that levels of disturbance are high. These studies do not demonstrate, of course, that the disturbance noted *caused* the deviant behaviour. The psychiatrically disturbed offenders in both the societies studied are likely to gravitate towards institutions such as prisons whereas the stable offenders will not. In addition, neither study used a control group to study the level of disturbance in non-criminals. Gunn (1979) suggests that the level of disturbance would be higher than that typically recorded in the general population, though, clearly, the relevant comparison would be with non-criminals matched for sociodemographic and other variables. Finally, the conclusions of both studies are open to the interpretation that the conditions of prison life may have caused the high level of disturbance shown. Gunn and his colleagues acknowledge this, pointing to the deprivation of family, friends, comforts and self-determination that prison life entails and to the 'considerable periods of cellular confinement' (Gunn *et al.*, 1978, p. 133). The marked differences in the frequency of aggressive behaviour in the two prisons in this latter study, even though the two groups had similar histories of aggression prior to their imprisonment, points to the powerful effect of institutions in producing disturbed behaviours. West (1980), similarly, notes how the extreme violence and disturbed behaviour of a group of prisoners in Scotland was considerably reduced when they were admitted to a unit in which they received individual attention and 'psychologically insightful management'.

Violent and criminal behaviour in mental patients

A large number of studies has attempted to assess whether people who are diagnosed as mentally ill have higher rates of violent behaviour than members of the general population. Some of these studies have been reviewed by Rappeport *et al.* (1967), Eynon (1970), Mesnikoff and Lauterbach (1976), Greenland (1978), Rabkin (1979), Prins (1980) and Fottrell (1981). This question has been of considerable interest to those concerned with the community placement of the mentally ill, who have been generally concerned to reassure members of the public that mental patients pose no significant threat. Resistance to community treatment has often come from those convinced that patients from hospitals are more likely to act dangerously than other members of society. The assumption that mentally disorderd patients are more likely to be violent is probably widespread amongst members of the public (Steadman and Cocozza, 1978) and may exist even amongst mental health professionals (Quinsey, 1975).

If the studies are looked at *in toto*, with no regard to *when* they were conducted, conflicting and inconsistent findings emerge. It is becoming apparent, however (Mesnikoff and Lauterbach, 1976; Rabkin, 1979), that there are consistent discrepancies between earlier and more recent investigations. The former tended to conclude that hospital patients had an incidence of violent and criminal behaviour in prospective studies similar to, or less than, that found in the general population (Cohen and Freeman, 1945; Brennan, 1964). Later studies have suggested that patients are *more* likely to commit offences, and it is to these later studies that we now turn.

One of the most influential and widely quoted studies in the 1960s was that of Brill and Malzberg (1962), carried out, like many of the studies in this field, in New York. These authors studied the subsequent arrest records of 10 247 male patients released from mental hospitals and compared them with the rates for males in the general population. The general findings were complex. The overall arrest rate for the patients was no higher than in the comparison group. However, two sub-groups were apparent. Patients with no prior history of arrests had *lower* subsequent arrest rates than the controls. Patients with prior histories of arrests had markedly higher arrest rates in the follow-up period. In addition the experience of illness and hospitalization did not elevate the level of criminal activity above the level preceding the illness. The important conclusion of this study, and one which has been confirmed by subsequent work, was that where higher arrest rates are found in mental patients they are likely to be a product of the fact that people with arrest records constitute a larger proportion of patient populations than of the general population (Rabkin, 1979).

Rappeport and Lassen (1965, 1966, 1967) used an essentially similar design to that of Brill and Malzberg in a study of patients discharged from Maryland psychiatric hospitals. This study is of particular interest, in the context of this chapter, in that it focused specifically on violent crimes. In general, arrest rates were as high or higher in the patients than in the controls. Rappeport and Lassen (1967, p.104) concluded,

> 'We certainly do not find any clear-cut indications that the mentally ill are to any great extent less involved in criminal behavior than those in the general community. Instead, we find that for some offences our population was as involved as the general community, while for other offences such as robbery and also probably rape, our patients were more frequently arrested than the general population. This suggests that we as psychiatrists may be biased when we malign others for suggesting that some of our patients may represent a threat to the community'.

Giovannoni and Gurel (1967) studied a large sample of male veteran chronic schizophrenics. The general incidence of violent crimes was higher than had been reported in previous studies, and rates for particular categories of violence were higher than in controls (including homicide and aggravated assault). Rates for non-violent crimes (larceny, burglary, etc.) were lower than in controls. Since this study was completed, a number of other studies have confirmed that violent and other forms of crime may be more common in patient groups (Zitrin *et al.*, 1976; Lagos *et al.*, 1977). Rabkin (1979, p. 71) summarizes a series of studies by Sosowsky as providing 'powerful support for the proposition that both outpatients and hospital patients in state-supported facilities have higher arrest and conviction rates for violent crimes than do non-treated California residents, and presumably, the general public'. Rabkin (1979) has also reviewed some recent work by Steadman and his colleagues confirming these overall trends.

One study which is inconsistent to some extent with these studies is that of Häfner and Böker (1973), conducted in the Federal Republic of Germany. In this study the proportional frequency of crimes of violence committed by the mentally ill and the mentally retarded was compared with that of the general population. The general conclusion of this study was that the mentally abnormal groups accounted for no more of the violent crimes that occurred than would be expected from the general population rates. Particular diagnostic categories, however, appeared to be more at risk. Schizophrenics had a higher risk than other disordered groups and than the general population, and depression had some association with violence involving extended suicides. More significantly, perhaps, the absolute rates for violence in patient groups were tiny. Even amongst schizophrenics, Häfner and Böker estimate that the expected frequency of violent offending would be five violent offenders among 10 000 schizophrenics. The differences between this study and some of the American studies suggest that the relationship between abnormality and violence may be culturally relative.

The overall conclusion from such studies would seem to be that the studies have not been entirely consistent in showing a higher rate of violent offending in patients but that, *in toto*, they suggest an elevated risk. This elevated risk, however, is a function of prior criminality in a small proportion of mental patients rather than of mental illness in itself (Rabkin, 1979). The upward trend in the crime rates of American mental patients, for example, is a product of the increased use of hospital facilities to deal with persons who show socially deviant and criminal behaviour. I would agree with the conclusions of Rabkin, in her critical review of studies in this area, that

> 'patients discharged from mental hospitals are not, by virtue of their psychiatric disorders or hospitalization experience, more prone to engage in criminal activity than are people demographically similar to them who do not have a history of mental illness. Although patients considered in groups do have higher arrest rates than non-patients considered as a group, it is largely because the patients include in their midst a disproportionate share of people with prior police records' (Rabkin, 1979, p. 26).

This conclusion is of considerable significance for those who attempt to predict dangerous behaviour in the mentally ill, in that it suggests that the presence of violent behaviour in the patients' prior history will be the best predictor of future violent crime.

Before leaving this topic, some of the considerable and serious methodological problems, which produce difficulties of interpretation, must be reiterated. Even if a clear statistical link could be demonstrated betwen mental illness and violent behaviour, independent of prior criminality (and it has not been), such an association would still be difficult to interpret as evidence of a causal relationship. It may be that mental patients are more inept in their crimes, more visible and more liable to police surveillance (Rabkin, 1979). In addition, most of the studies conducted have looked at hospitalized groups. It is clear that whether or not a disturbed patient is hospitalized depends on factors additional to his illness (Levine, 1970). The nuisance and threat value of the mental patient's behaviour may determine whether or not he is admitted to hospital. Hospitalized groups, as a result, are probably a biased sample of the mentally ill, with a higher proportion of patients prone to deviant (socially unacceptable) behaviour than non-hospitalized groups, even though this deviance may not (as yet) have shown itself in criminal behaviours. The comparisons with the general population, therefore, confound mental illness and hospitalization. A very different, and very difficult, research strategy would be required to show that illness as such was the critical variable, namely, a study of violent behaviour in patients who had not been hospitalized. It must be concluded, therefore, that it has yet to be demonstrated that mental illness *per se* is significantly causally related to violent behaviour.

Specific diagnoses

Virtually every category of mental illness has, at some time, been seen as causing violent behaviour. Gunn's (1973) review of 'violence in disease', for example, covers brain damage, epilepsy, depression, schizophrenia, morbid jealousy, psychopathy, chromosome abnormalities, drug addiction and alcoholism. Prins (1980) has also thoroughly reviewed the whole range of psychiatric syndromes which might contribute to a propensity for violence and the reader is referred to his book for a comprehensive account. I will restrict the discussion to a few of the major categories of disorder and to studies focusing on violent (as opposed to generally criminal) behaviour.

Schizophrenia

Schizophrenia is unlikely to be a homogeneous category, and, indeed, some have questioned whether it is an acceptable category at all (e.g. Sarbin, and Mancuso, 1980). The failure of most studies to make discriminations within the group may account in part for the failure to find strong associations with violent behaviour. Schizophrenics are frequent in populations of mentally abnormal offenders (Black, 1973; Walker and McCabe, 1973; Tennent *et al.*, 1980) and have committed a large proportion of violent acts occurring in mental hospitals (Fottrell, 1980), but it cannot be inferred that schizophrenia is causal in these cases as schizophrenia is a common diagnosis in *any* (non-violent) group of psychiatric patients. There appears to be some, though not entirely consistent, evidence that schizophrenics are marginally more at risk for violent offences than are other patients or the general population (Rappeport and Lassen, 1965, 1966; Ekblom, 1970; Häfner and Böker, 1973; Zitrin *et al.*, 1976; Sosowsky, 1978; Rabkin, 1979) but the overwhelming majority of schizophrenics are never arrested for violent assaults (Häfner and Böker, 1973). It is also possible that schizophrenics are over-represented amongst very serious assaults, such as homicide, where, at least in England and Wales, a sizeable proportion of offenders are deemed to be mentally abnormal (West, 1968; Home Office, 1961, 1975).

Where there is a link between schizophrenia and violence it would clearly be important to know which psychological features of the schizophrenic state determine the violent behaviour. Prins (1980) has drawn attention to the affective poverty of some schizophrenics and suggests that this may be important in bizarre violent offences where the patient shows none of the strong inhibiting emotions that such acts would elicit in most people. The most plausible relevant process, however, is the presence of delusional, and particularly paranoid, beliefs. McKnight *et al.* (1966), West (1968), Walker and McCabe, (1973) and Planansky and Johnston (1977) have all provided evidence of an association between paranoid ideas and violent behaviour. Häfner and Böker (1973) concluded that, 'in schizophrenia, certain disturbances which can be found in chronic systematized paranoid syndromes seem to co-determine the motive of the offence, and are likely to favour its manifestation'. The same authors also noted that such delusions often centred on spouses and significant others who were the victims of the violent assaults. Mowat (1966), similarly, has described unrealistic beliefs about the unfaithfulness of spouses ('morbid jealousy') which were found in 12% of a sample of mentally disordered murderers. These suggestions that violent behaviour may be under the control of paranoid, and related, beliefs are consistent with findings in experimental psychology (see below) that beliefs and attributions concerning the social environment may be important determinants of aggressive behaviour. It must be borne in mind, however, that a variety of other processes, apart from beliefs, may be relevant. Planansky and Johnston (1977), for example, noted hallucinatory instructions and subjective compulsions as common precursors of violence.

Taylor (1982), in an excellent review of this area, suggests that there are two highly plausible alternatives to the assumption that the link between schizophrenia and violence is mediated by some aspect of the phenomenology of schizophrenia. The first alternative would be that social factors, perhaps independent of the illness itself, cause the violent behaviour (the same factors that cause normals to be violent); and the second would be that schizophrenia *and* violence are both caused by some third social or organic variable. Taylor reviews work which would support both of these hypotheses.

The general conclusion that can be made about the relationship between schizophrenia and violence would seem to be that, although there is some elevated risk of violence in this group, the overall association is weak, with the consequence that in most cases the violent behaviour of schizophrenics cannot be explained in terms of the schizophrenic state itself. In the small number of cases where there *is* a casual relationship, paranoid and other delusional beliefs may be important. For the majority of schizophrenic aggressors, however, it is likely that causes must be sought in the same social and psychological variables that have been shown to determine aggressive behaviour in non-schizophrenic persons.

Depression

One of the most widely accepted links between mental abnormality and violence, in clinical practice, is that between depression and serious violence, such as homicide. The very high proportion (one-third) of suicides following murders (West, 1965) is usually taken as an indication of an underlying depression which caused the offence. The assumption is, typically, that the murder was part of an extended suicide in which the offender wanted to put his (or her) family, including himself, out of their misery. West (1965) estimated that 28 out of his sample of 78 murder/suicides were suffering from depression. Depression is also commonly observed in surviving murderers. The difficulty, in these cases, lies in disentangling what is an intropunitive *reaction* to the offence (guilt over what happened) from a depressed mood *preceding* the offence.

The evidence that depression is significantly related to lesser forms of violent behaviour is harder to find. Walker and McCabe (1973), however, did find a moderately strong association between violence and depression. In this study depressives were the only group of abnormal offenders in which violent offences outnumbered acquisitive offences. The authors point also to the way in which depressive states can lead to violence 'out of the blue' in persons with no previous history of violent behaviour, the assault often being directed towards another family member. Häfner and Böker (1973) confirm this latter finding. In their sample 95% of the crimes of patients with 'affective psychoses' (primarily depression) had assaulted family members or other closely related people. These authors also concur that offences in depressives are of an extended suicide kind and that 'other motives' practically do not occur.

Fottrell's finding that depressives showed little propensity for violence in hospital settings (Fottrell, 1980) may indicate that the violence of depressed people is engendered only in intimate relationships over a prolonged period of time. Such relationships are less likely to occur in hospital environments. The pattern of violence in depression appears to be consistent with the notion of 'over-control' which is discussed later in this chapter. Again, it is important to remember that only a tiny proportion of depressed people are violent and that the alternative hypotheses (to the causal hypothesis) discussed for schizophrenia could equally well be applied to depression.

Organic syndromes

A very wide range of organic variables has been correlated with violent behaviour in an attempt to demonstrate that biological dysfunctions are of aetiological significance (Hinton, 1981). Several studies, for example, have attempted to relate electroencephalogram (EEG) abnormality to violent behaviour. Blackburn (1975*a*) has reviewed such studies and concluded that in most studies both aggression and EEG abnormality had been too poorly defined to establish any convincing findings.

One of the more interesting hypotheses has been that antisocial aggression is particularly associated with a predominance of diffuse slow wave activity in the theta band (Hill, 1944). Williams (1969) compared 206 habitually aggressive criminals with 127 isolated aggressors and found a 65% rate of abnormality in the former and a 25% rate in the latter group. The abnormality consisted of bilateral slow wave activity in the theta range and/or focal abnormality in the temporal lobe. However, Fenton *et al.* (1974) compared two groups, one with posterior temporal slow wave foci and one with normal EEG records, but found no differences between the groups on a range of developmental, forensic, psychiatric, behavioural and psychometric variables. Blackburn's data (1975*a*) also failed to support the view that a high prevalence of theta activity characterizes more aggressive abnormal patients.

As Gunn (1979) has suggested, there is a long mythology associating crime with a phenomenon related to EEG abnormality—epilepsy. This mythology is founded perhaps on the disturbing nature of epileptic automatism. Although epilepsy is more common in prisons than in the general population (Gunn, 1977), it is rarely an explanation of violent crime. Gunn and Fenton (1971) could find only two cases in which epilepsy appeared to have some causal relationship to an actual aggressive offence. When matched epileptic and non-epileptic prisoners are compared, few differences in criminal behaviour are observed (Gunn, 1979). The common belief that temporal lobe epilepsy (TLE) and violence are causally related is, similarly, not supported by the finding that TLE prisoners do not have a larger number of violent offences in their histories than non-TLE prisoners, though Gunn points out that many TLE cases, and presumably those in which TLE *does* appear to cause aggression, are sent to hospitals rather than prisons. The same author (Gunn, 1979) lends support to Kligman and Goldberg's (1975) conclusion that 'TLE is too heterogeneous and ill defined and human aggression is too complex to allow definite interpretations of correlations between them at present'. Both Kligman and Goldberg (1975) and Gunn (1979) point to the various different interpretations that are possible when epilepsy and aggression appear to be related: (1) brain malfunction may cause both the violence and the fits; (2) fits may lead to social stigmatization and subsequent reactive aggression; (3) environmental factors could produce both fits and aggression (e.g. being battered as a child); (4) 'criminal' impulsive life-styles may produce brain damage (head injuries through accidents). In this respect the role of epilepsy in violence would appear to be as problematic as the role of the other disorders discussed above.

The relevance of a range of other chromosomal, hormonal and psychophysiological variables for crime, and the difficulties of methodology and interpretation that exist in this area, have been reviewed by Hinton (1981) and this large body of studies will not be discussed in further detail in this chapter, except to point to some of the findings of Hinton and his colleagues (Woodman and Hinton, 1978; Woodman *et al.*, 1978; Hinton, 1981). This group of workers investigated the relationship between stress hormones and violence by assessing urinary noradrenaline to adrenaline ratios and urinary and plasma cortisol in mentally abnormal offenders. Offenders with serious violent offences in their histories had higher levels of noradrenaline relative to adrenaline and smaller rises in cortisol under stress conditions than did less violent controls. It is, of course, always unclear in these and other physiological/biochemical studies whether observed differences are simply *reactive* to environmental and behavioural differences rather than being causes of behaviour. There is also, clearly, a need to relate differences of the sort detected by Hinton to a *model* of aggressive behaviour and to determine the psychological processes (cognitive, affective or behavioural) which might be correlates of the biochemical variables—this will be returned to later in the chapter.

This review of the relationship between specific psychiatric/physical conditions and violence is obviously not exhaustive. The role of mental retardation, drugs and, particularly, alcohol could be discussed profitably and at length (see Prins, 1980). The intention has been to draw attention, through examples, to the very tentative nature of the conclusions that can be drawn about the causal significance of mental disorder for violent behaviour, and to suggest the necessity for including non-pathological processes in any explanation of why a disordered person has acted violently. Any review of this area, however, would be incomplete without a thorough discussion of the importance of psychopathic disorder.

Psychopathic disorder

It might have been expected that research and theory in the area of 'psychopathy' (synonymous in this chapter with 'psychopathic disorder', 'psychopathic personality', etc.) would be very relevant to understanding violent behaviour in mentally abnormal offenders. Psychopathy is, after all, a frequent diagnosis amongst mentally abnormal offenders (Walker and McCabe, 1973) and a sizeable proportion of patients admitted to the Special Hospitals are classified as suffering from a psychopathic disorder under the 1959 Mental Health Act (Black, 1973; Tennent *et al.*, 1980). It will be argued here that psychopathy, although it has been the focus of a considerable amount of experimental research (Hare, 1970; Hare and Schalling, 1978; Smith, 1978; Reid, 1978), is of limited usefulness in this context.

From its very beginnings in concepts of 'mania without delusions' (Pinel, 1806), 'monomania' (Esquirol, quoted in Pichot, 1978) and 'moral insanity' (Prichard, 1835), the notion of psychopathy has engendered confusion and controversy of a philosophical, moral and clinical nature. Most descriptions of the syndrome have some resemblance to Prichard's early account:

> 'the moral and active principles of the mind are strongly perverted or depraved; the power of self-government is lost or greatly impaired, and the individual is found to be incapable not of talking or reasoning upon any subject proposed to him, for this he will often do with great shrewdness and volubility, but of conducting himself with decency and propriety in the business of life' (quoted by Treves-Brown, 1977).

In recent years definitions, as far as psychological research is concerned, have been dominated by Cleckley (1964). Spielberger (1978) comments, for example: 'the clarity and comprehensiveness of Cleckley's formulations have resulted in widespread acceptance of his definition of the psychopath as a personality type'. Most experimental work in the field has been informed by Cleckley's book (Hare, 1970; Hare and Schalling, 1978). Cleckley listed 16 characteristics as defining the psychopathic personality, which he sees as a disjunctive syndrome, rather than as the end point of a continuous dimension. These characteristics include (1) superficial charm and good intelligence; (2) absence of delusions; (3) absence of neurotic features; (4) unreliability; (5) untruthfulness and insincerity; (6) lack of remorse; (7) poor judgement and failure to learn by experience; (8) pathological egocentricity and incapacity for love; (9) poverty of affective reactions and a number of similar traits.

The usefulness of a particular diagnostic category can be evaluated in a number of ways. Walker and McCabe (1973) have suggested that a good psychiatric category would have four functions: it would be descriptive, explanatory, prognostic and therapeutic.

Descriptive usefulness of psychopathy

For the diagnosis of psychopathy to be descriptively useful it would need to be demonstrated that the application of the label to a person would convey information about the way he or she is likely to act. There are several reasons why the diagnosis of psychopathy often fails to convey such information. A major difficulty is that the reliability of the diagnosis is apparently low, though there have been few attempts to study reliability empirically. Different researchers and clinicians describe the condition in very different terms and would be unlikely to agree on whether the label could be applied to a particular individual. The Cleckley–Hare description (above), for example, stresses internal states such as lack of affect and guiltlessness and sees psychopathic characteristics as non-equivalent to criminality. In fact it is an important feature of many of the psychopaths described by Cleckley that they do *not* get into serious trouble with the law. Eysenck and Eysenck (1978), on the other hand, state that 'the majority of prison inmates are criminal in the sense intended here . . . and many of them (probably a majority) are psychopathic on any reasonable definition of that term'. Hare (1981) has noted the tendency of the draft version of the American Psychiatric Association's new *Diagnostic and Statistical Manual of Mental Disorders* (Williams, 1980) to define psychopathic-type conditions too liberally, with the result that he defined less than half of a sample of prison inmates diagnosed as 'antisocial personality disorder' as psychopaths in the strict sense of the term.

The definition of psychopathic disorder in the 1959 Mental Health Act for England and Wales is equally broad: 'a persistent disorder or disability of mind . . . which results in abnormally aggressive or seriously irresponsible conduct on the part of the patient, and requires, or is susceptible to medical treatment'. A study by Blackburn (1974, 1975*b*) of psychopaths admitted to a hospital under this definition demonstrated that fewer than one-quarter showed personality traits similar to those described by Cleckley (1964). When the term is used in such broad and diverse ways I would support Walker and McCabe (1973) in their conclusion that the term 'obliterates' more than it conveys, and that when terms such as 'sexual psychopath' or 'aggressive psychopath' are used it is the words 'sexual' and 'aggressive' that are the informative half of the label. Relatively few researchers and clinicians have heeded Walker and McCabe's other conclusion that, 'it would be of more use to psychiatrists to tell them that this or that person is easily provoked to violence, is prone to sexual sadism, exploits women, commits impulsive thefts or whatever it is about his conduct that arouses disapproval, than to call him a psychopath' (Walker and McCabe, 1973, p. 234).

Cleckley's delineation of the syndrome is more specific than most but suffers from the fact that many of the defining features are highly inferential and apparently subjective ('superficial charm', 'lack of remorse', 'incapacity for love', 'emotionally shallow'). Many of Cleckley's conclusions about psychopaths (Cleckley, 1964) are based on the observation of 'normal' behaviour in his subjects and a secondary inference that this normality is no more than a 'mask of psychobiologic health', hiding a cold and affectless inner life, devoid of compassion. In effect Cleckley puts himself in the position of being an attributor of the *real* meaning of the person's behaviour, which although apparently normal is fake and unreal. As instances of psychopaths in everyday life he quotes (Cleckley, 1964, p. 199), for example, 'the fake poet who really feels little; the painter who, despite his loftiness, has his eye chiefly on the lucrative fad of the day; the fashionable clergyman, who despite his burning eloquence, is primarily concerned with his advancement'. Inferences of inner motives in this fashion are clearly susceptible to idiosyncratic biases. Hare (Hare and Cox, 1978; Hare, 1981) has claimed that rating scales based on Cleckley's criteria produce inter-rater correlations of 0.85 when experienced raters base their judgements on behavioural histories. A principal components analysis in the latter study revealed five factors to be involved in Cleckley's criteria, suggesting that the syndrome is not unidimensional. The major factor was one of lack of empathy and concern for others and it was this factor which contributed most strongly to overall ratings of psychopathy. The check-list subsequently derived from Cleckley's criteria by Hare (1981) may give a rigour and robustness to these criteria which they have lacked to date.

Taxonomic and multivariate studies

Many workers have acknowledged the heterogeneity existing in groups of patients and offenders labelled as psychopathic and have attempted to define discrete sub-groups using statistical techniques. Hewitt and Jenkins (1946) carried out a cluster analysis of trait variables as recorded from the case notes of 500 problem children referred to a child guidance clinic. The three most important clusters derived were identified as (1) unsocialized aggressive behaviour; (2) socialized delinquency, and (3) over-inhibited behaviour. The unsocialized aggressive group is frequently taken as equivalent to a psychopathic type and many of the defining behaviours resemble psychopathic traits, e.g. assaultive tendencies, cruelty, defiance of authority and lack of guilt. Ten per cent of the total sample showed three or more of these characteristics, though other studies have found these characteristics to be more rare (Field, 1967).

Blackburn (1974, 1975*b*) has reported a study of 79 male abnormal aggressive offenders admitted to a Specal Hospital suffering from a psychopathic disorder. Twelve personality scales were used to form the elements of a personality profile. A cluster analysis procedure was used to sort profiles into mutually exclusive types. Four types emerged which accounted for 80% of the population and resembled those found in a previous study of homicides (Blackburn, 1971). As mentioned above, less than one-quarter of the sample showed the pattern typically described as defining Cleckley psychopaths. A large 'secondary psychopathic' and a large 'defensive/denying' group were also found. The primary psychopathic group (Cleckley) was found to have more aggressive and destructive behaviour in their histories and to show a greater variety of types of antisocial behaviour. This study, then, confirms the existence of Cleckley primary psychopaths but suggests that it is a minority type. There is a striking similarity between these results and those of Schalling (1975), who used latent profile analysis to generate types in a sample of 67 hospitalized criminal psychopaths and 70 prison recidivists. Twenty-three scales were used, including measures of anxiety, extraversion, psychoticism, socialization, aggression and social desirability. In the prison sample three profiles were generated. Profile 1 was characterized by low anxiety and high extraversion and was identified as 'psychopathic'. Profile 2 was characterized by high scores of anxiety associated with low conformity and high impulsiveness and aggression; this was identified as a 'secondary psychopathic' or 'neurotic criminal' profile. Profile 3 accounted for only a few individuals and was characterized by low impulsiveness and high conformity scores. Essentially similar profiles were found in the hospitalized group, with a higher proportion of the conforming profiles. A study by Widom (1978) demonstrated that similar profiles are found in female samples. The heterogeneity of psychopathic states is also confirmed by Holland *et al.* (1980), who also found some differences between hospitalized and incarcerated psychopathic groups.

The high frequency of secondary psychpathic types is noteworthy in these studies and confirms the relevance of the distinction (Karpman, 1947) between primary psychopaths, who show low anxiety, guilt and empathy, and secondary psychopaths, whose antisocial behaviour is secondary to subjective disturbance and emotional problems. It appears that this distinction is also important for aggressive behaviour. Fagan and Lira (1980) found that psychometrically defined primary and secondary psychopaths differed in the frequency and severity of aggressive antisocial behaviours in an institutional setting. Secondary psychopaths were found to engage in significantly fewer and less severe aggressive behaviours. Blackburn (1980*b*, *c*) has argued that primary and secondary psychopaths (and other types) are formed from combinations of two higher-order personality dimensions—psychopathy/conformity and withdrawal/sociability, primary psychopaths being high on psychopathy and low on withdrawal, and secondary psychopaths being high on psychopathy and on withdrawal. Blackburn suggests that the withdrawal dimension functions as a moderator variable in determining the behavioural correlates of the psychopathy dimension—abnormal offenders with high psychopathy and low withdrawal are most likely to have habitually violent histories (53%), while those with high psychopathy and high withdrawal are least likely to be habitually violent (20%), though this relationship failed to hold up for rated aggression in institutional settings (Blackburn, 1980*b*). Blackburn makes the interesting speculation that aggression in primary psychopaths is 'incentive-motivated' and that in secondary psychopaths is 'annoyance-motivated'. Blackburn suggests the secondary psychopath is hypervigilant for danger and threats to self-esteem in social situations. The relevance of cognitions for aggression will be discussed in more detail below.

Explanatory usefulness of psychopathy

The concept of a psychopathic disorder represents to some the most extreme, and perhaps the most absurd, of attempts to medicalize problems that are social-psychological or sociological in origin, an attempt to be particularly resisted because of the harmful effects of such a diagnosis on a person's legal rights and status (see, for example, Szasz, 1968). There are logical problems in inferring any mental illness from deviant behaviour. Earlier in this chapter, for example, it was pointed out that mental abnormality cannot be logically inferred from unusual or extreme acts of violence. Such difficulties are even more marked with some definitions of psychopathy in that the imputation of psychopathy often cannot be validated by reference to symptoms *independent* of the objectionable behaviour (e.g. violence). Wootton (1959) was the first to draw attention to the circular process by which 'mental abnormality is inferred from anti-social behaviour while anti-social behaviour is explained by mental abnormality'. The idea that psychopathic behaviour is *caused* by an inner entity is clearly stated in the 1959 Mental Health Act, where psychopathic disorder is defined as a disorder 'which *results* in abnormally aggressive or seriously irresponsible conduct' (italics added). As Blackburn (1969) indicates, the effect of this attribution of the deviant behaviour to some inner entity is often to obviate the necessity for further explanation—the person is habitually violent or sexually aggressive because 'he is a psychopath'!

The medical reification of deviant behaviour in the form of psychopathic disorder often produces a second logical error—the tendency to treat psychopathy as a *disjunctive* clinical type (Blackburn, 1969). In clinical contexts psychiatrists and psychologists might often ask, 'Is this person a psychopath or is he suffering from some other disorder (schizophrenia, neurosis)?' This question can only be properly asked if the two states are mutually exclusive. In fact psychopathic behaviour may co-exist with a variety of different clinical states, without, as Blackburn suggests, there being any necessity to use a different order of explanation for each state. The violent and antisocial behaviour of the psychopathic patient may be explained in the same terms as the violent behaviour of someone diagnosed as schizophrenic.

Prognostic usefulness of psychopathy

Long term follow-ups of individuals who show psychopathic traits indicate that psychopathy is of some use in predicting future offending and social difficulty. Two bodies of work are particularly relevant—the Cambridge study of delinquency (West and Farrington, 1973, 1977) and Robins' studies of the precursors of psychopathic behaviour (Robins, 1966, 1978). The Cambridge study demonstrated that children who were at high risk for delinquency had shown 'psychopathic' type behaviour and attitudes many years before becoming 'officially' delinquent. Criminal behaviour, for this group, was the end point of a long-standing syndrome of deviance in many spheres. At 8 years of age subsequent delinquents were rated as more delinquent by teachers on variables not directly associated with crime, including truancy, troublesome behaviour and aggressiveness. West and Farrington (1973, p. 199) comment:

'Altogether the findings of the present study strongly support the concept of a typical delinquent, in the sense that most delinquents display a behavioural syndrome which encompasses far more in the way of deviant conduct than the limited range of illegal acts for which they are apt to be convicted. Moreover, this general syndrome of deviancy was apparent from an early age.'

It must be remembered of course that not all children showing early 'psychopathic' signs in this study subsequently became delinquent.

Robins' conclusions (1966, 1978) are essentially similar to those of West and Farrington—psychopathic personality begins early in childhood and does not suddenly emerge in a previously conforming person. Most boys in Robins' sample began having difficulties as soon as they attended school, in the form of truancy, failure to perform well academically despite adequate IQs, stealing and disciplinary problems in the classroom. Robins found that certain recorded childhood behaviours were good predictors of subsequent psychopathy, though no childhood symptom occurred in *every* child who was later diagnosed psychopathic. The high level of school retardation found is consistent with findings in England by Rutter *et al.* (1970) that antisocial behaviour in school correlates with reading difficulties. The most powerful prognostic factor proved to be the total number of antisocial behaviours shown. The larger the number, the more likely a child was to be diagnosed as a psychopath as an adult. It is important to stress again, however, that many children showing a large number of antisocial behaviours did not grow up to be psychopaths. Robins' studies, of course, are not strictly studies of the prognostic utility of psychopathy in that psychopathy was the independent variable in a retrospective rather than a prospective study, nevertheless the temporal consistencies demonstrated would suggest, indirectly, that psychopathic traits would predict subsequent adjustment problems.

Studies attempting to predict future behaviour from a current diagnosis of psychopathy in adults have fared less well. Gibbens *et al.* (1959) followed up a group of imprisoned psychopaths over 8 years and compared them with a control group of prisoners. Little difference was found between the two groups, as assessed by subsequent reconvictions. Walker and McCabe (1973) compared groups of offender patients in a 2 year follow-up on frequency of reconviction and hospitalization and on employment and found only weak differences between patients diagnosed as psychopaths and those with other diagnoses. Finally, Black (1977) followed up a sample of patients released from Broadmoor Hospital and found some tendency for psychopathic offenders to have more reconvictions than schizophrenic and other groups. The actual number of previous offences, however, was the best predictor of re-offending, and the differences found between the psychopathic and other groups was probably a function of the greater number of previous offences in patients classified as psychopathic.

These various studies have used different measures and definitions of psychopathy or have not used the term at all (West and Farrington, 1973, 1977). There are indications, nevertheless, of a stability of psychopathic-type traits from childhood to adulthood. There is a clear need, however, for further prognostic studies to determine whether carefully defined psychopaths differ prognostically from controls matched for previous violent or criminal behaviour.

Therapeutic usefulness of psychopathy

A diagnostic classification, such as psychopathy, might be expected to be therapeutically useful in two senses. First, a diagnosis might suggest an appropriate treatment, and secondly a diagnosis might encourage therapeutic attitudes on the part of professionals and others involved with the person who has been diagnosed. It is rare, in the literature, for some clear treatment approach to follow from a diagnosis of psychopathy. Feldman (1977) points out the circular nature of much thinking in this area: 'If a person is changed by a treatment, then he could not have been a "true" psychopath, as psychopaths are, by definition, untreatable.' As Feldman suggests, the fault may often lie with the inappropriateness of the treatment rather than with some permanent and unchangeable deficit in the person concerned. Therapeutic pessimism may be unwarranted in that the problem behaviours of psychopaths (aggression, sexual deviance, impulsiveness) are behaviours considered treatable when they occur in people with no, or a different, diagnosis (see below).

Treves-Brown (1977) has explored the intriguing paradox that psychopathy is often considered, by definition, to be untreatable, yet professional staff often continue to treat psychopaths. He suggests, rather provocatively, that it follows that either those with experience of the condition do *not* regard it as untreatable, or 'that the professional staff are displaying psychopathic characteristics themselves by giving treatment, knowing it to be ineffective' (Treves-Brown, 1977, p. 56).

There is a sense in which the diagnosis of psychopathy renders treatment ineffective. The application of the label to persons with a wide range of heterogeneous problems (above) promotes a global treatment approach which will be inappropriate for many. Additionally, relatively intangible psychopathic traits become the focus for treatment rather than specific problems of aggression, sexual acting-out, alcoholism or work difficulty. Programmes aimed at changing general psychopathic traits have produced few encouraging results (Suedfeld and Landon, 1978; Lion, 1978; Carney, 1978; Kellner, 1978; Sutker *et al.*, 1981). Sutker *et al.*'s very thorough review concludes:

'In terms of individual treatment, it is important to reiterate that sociopathy is obviously inclusive of a heterogeneous group with respect to numerous salient characteristics, and that individuals so labelled should not be expected to respond similarly across a set of environmental conditions . . . any treatment programme must be prepared by functional analysis, specification of *individualized targeted behaviours for change*, flexibility for a multifaceted treatment plan, and appropriate behaviour monitoring and following-up' (Sutker *et al.*, 1981, p. 697; italics added).

The diagnosis of psychopathy could also be said to be anti-therapeutic in the second sense of the term therapeutic mentioned above. The pejorative and hostile use of the term by some workers reinforces negative social evaluations of patients so labelled. Psychopathy appears to be one of the most negatively perceived psychiatric labels and, in my experience, encourages rejection of the person as 'bad', 'untrustworthy' and 'manipulative'. Rejection is clearly an inadequate basis for treatment. Treves-Brown (1977, p. 62) suggests:

'One might assume that so long as any doctor believes that psychopaths are mostly "bad", his successful treatment rate will be dismal. Since it takes two to form a relationship, an outside observer could be forgiven for suspecting that a doctor who describes a patient as unable to form a relationship is simply justifying his own hostility to this patient.'

Possible hidden functions of the diagnosis

Given some of the difficulties with the concept of psychopathy sketched above, it is not unreasonable to consider why it has been so entrenched in psychiatric and legal thinking. It is possible that psychopathy is functional in ways that are unlikely to be stated explicitly. Rotenberg (1978) has suggested that conceptions of psychopathy are traceable to a Christian 'predestinal-dualistic doctrine', which divides people into treatable successful 'elects' and the hopeless 'damned'. The idea of the untreatable psychopath may serve the function of justifying failure and reluctance to treat patients who may be unco-operative and hostile. The vehemence of the dislike of psychopaths expressed by some writers and the general mystification of the condition suggest that it may be reassuring in some way for society to localize the world's wickedness in a fantasized 'sick' abnormal group of deviants. Similar tendencies have been noted in the evaluation of war criminals as 'monsters'.

Finally, the diagnosis may sometimes be functional in a very pragmatic way. Szasz (1968) refers to the process of 'semantic conversion' whereby the renaming of a behaviour is a *device* for changing the social status of the person labelled. Although Szasz has used the renaming of malingering as hysteria as his main example, the same argument could be applied to the labelling of 'bad' behaviour as psychopathic. The label may serve to move the person into a 'therapeutic' context in which attempts to control and modify his behaviour medically are legitimized.

The widespread criticisms of the concept of psychopathic disorder have been reflected in two British government reports—the Butler committee's report on mentally abnormal offenders (Home Office and DHSS, 1975) and the DHSS review of the Mental Health Act (DHSS *et al.*, 1976). The writers of the former report, in particular, were clearly tempted to eliminate the term altogether as a legal category:

'Psychopathic disorder is no longer a useful or meaningful concept; it is not associated with any of the sub-categories or mental disorder contained in the International Statistical Classification of Diseases . . . the class of persons to whom the term 'psychopathic disorder' relates are not a single category identifiable by any medical, biological or psychological criteria' (Home Office and DHSS, 1975, p. 86).

As Wootton (1980) suggests, the committee's recommendation that dangerous psychopaths be 'treated' in prison amounts to an at least partial obliteration of the distinction between the sick and the wicked.

Alternatives to medical models

It has been argued so far in this chapter that when mental disorder and violent behaviour co-exist, the mental disorder may be of limited value in explaining the violent behaviour and in indicating appropriate treatment strategies. In fact the presence of schizophrenic or psychopathic symptoms are often of less concern in clinical situations than are the 'offending' or 'deviant' behaviours themselves. Similarly, although a diagnosis of schizophrenia or psychopathic disorder may be a necessary condition for admission to a treatment, rather than a penal, facility, it is generally not a sufficient condition. The schizophrenic's delusions and thought disorder and the psychopath's lack of love and empathy are often less important than the fact that the particular person has acted 'dangerously'. The predominant reason for admission to a Special Hospital in England and Wales, for example, is that the patient has 'dangerous, violent or criminal propensities'. It may be more appropriate to direct explanatory and therapeutic efforts towards the specific dangerous behaviour itself rather than towards the symptoms of the mental disorder. This is often acknowledged, in practice, and this acknowledgement is reflected in the fact that release from such institutions is often dependent on a decreased probability of dangerous behaviour occuring rather than on having produced a 'cure' for the disorder. Dangerous behaviour, in these contexts, comprises mainly interpersonal aggression, such as homicide, and sexual assault, including rape and offences against children, though some mentally abnormal offenders may have been admitted to a hospital following self-mutilation, arson or other forms of deviant or criminal activity. The alternative to the medical model is clearly to apply psychological models of how aggressive and sexually deviant behaviour are determined and modified. Such models would stress the continuity between normal and abnormal groups in the nature of the psychological processes involved. The application of such models is greatly facilitated by the fact that both aggression and sexual learning have been the focus of considerable attention from psychologists and medical researchers and practitioners (Bandura, 1971*a*, *b*; Bancroft, 1974; Geen and O'Neil, 1976; Zillman, 1979; Feldman and MacCulloch, 1980).

Deviant sexual behaviour in mentally abnormal offenders

A significant proportion of mentally abnormal offenders will have been convicted of sexual assaults (Walker and McCabe, 1973; Black, 1973; Tennent *et al.*, 1980). When unselected cases are considered, many of the offences will be of a relatively trivial nature, including exhibitionism and incidents often considered to be unlikely to have a traumatic effect on the victim (Walker and McCabe, 1973). For both minor and more serious offences children form a large proportion of victims. Sexual offenders confined to security institutions for mentally abnormal offenders, on the other hand, will tend to have been convicted for more serious assaults, with paedophilic offenders and rapists (of adult women) forming the two largest sub-groups (Crawford, 1980*b*).

Research into sexual assault has been reviewed elsewhere in this volume (see Chapter 3) and in a variety of recent texts (Walker and Brodsky, 1976; Rada, 1978; West *et al.*, 1978; Burgess *et al.*, 1978; Cook and Howells, 1981). There is little reason to expect that the conclusions of such workers, based mainly on studies of normal offenders, should not be applicable to abnormal offenders also. It is proposed here to draw attention to some work conducted with institutionalized mentally abnormal sexual offenders and to some important issues that arise in working with such groups.

An important conclusion of many workers in this field is that abnormal sexual behaviour is as complex in its nature and aetiology as is normal sexual behaviour, and that, as a consequence of this fact, assessments and treatment interventions need to be correspondingly complex and broadly based (Barlow, 1974; Crawford, 1979; Howells, 1981*a*). As Barlow (1974) suggests, deviant sexual behaviour is more than simply a problem of deviant sexual arousal. Sex offenders (and particularly abnormal offenders) tend to have difficulties and problems in many non-sexual areas of their lives (Gebhard *et al.*, 1965) as well as in the sexual area. Paedophilic offenders, in particular, tend to have problems in dealing with relationships with adults which contribute to their choice of an atypical sexual partner (Howells, 1979, 1981*a*). Although not all sex offenders have sexual problems and inadequacies in normal relationships, it is clear that a significant minority do (Gebhard *et al.*, 1965). Howells and Wright (1978) investigated this question by comparing a group of abnormal aggressive sexual offenders (mainly rapists) in an English Special Hospital with non-sexual aggressors on tests of sexual attitudes, interests and of personality and found that the sexual offenders reported more sexual difficulties and problems than did the controls. Sexual difficulties, in this study, tended to be correlated with social anxiety and social avoidance. It may well be the case, however, that the level of sexual difficulty will be found to be higher in hospitalized groups than in prison groups because the former are likely to have been selected on the basis of 'having problems'.

It is likely that sex offenders, like other groups of offenders, are a heterogeneous group and that real progress in explaining and treating such forms of deviance can be made only when this has been recognized and appropriate typological systems devised. A number of dimensions for subdividing sex offenders have been suggested in the literature. Two potentially useful dimensions will be discussed here. One distinction that is particularly important for mentally abnormal offenders (for whom questions as to 'dangerousness' and 'fitness for release' arise more frequently than for normal offenders) concerns the role of aggression in the sexual offence. There is some evidence that it is mistaken to view all acts of rape as precipitated by sexual needs (Howells, 1980). Similarities exist between some rapes and acts which are aggressively motivated. Howells and Steadman-Allen (1977), for example, demonstrated that some (though not all) rapists perceive their affective response preceding the offence as one of 'angry' rather than sexual arousal. Thus, although violence is common in most rape offences (Wright, 1980), a distinction needs to be made between instrumental and angry aggression in the incident, i.e. whether the violence is merely a means of securing the sexual contact or whether the violence is, in itself, the desired activity. The latter form of motivation clearly has some relationship to sadistic interest. Aggressive motivation and aggressive behaviour are less common in sexual assaults on children (Howells, 1981*a*), though instrumentally aggressive and sadistic paedophiles may form a sizeable proportion of the highly selected populations of abnormal offenders confined to security institutions.

The second dimension is more relevant to the assessment and treatment of paedophilic offenders rather than to rapists. A distinction can be made between sexual preference-mediated assaults on children and assaults which are situationally induced (Swanson, 1968; Howells, 1981*a*). Offenders in the former category have a sexual preference for children as opposed to adults; those in the latter category have a normal preference structure but are induced to engage in deviant behaviour by situational influences, including domestic upsets, separations and the consumption of alcohol. Some implications of this dimension for assessment and treatment have been discussed more fully in a recent paper (Howells, 1981*a*).

The assessment and treatment of sexual offenders has been discussed in detail elsewhere (Abel *et al.*, 1978; Crawford, 1981) as have the considerable problems met (Crawford, 1980*b*). Mentally abnormal offenders are frequently confined to institutions far removed from the contexts in which sexual assaults occur, with the result that assessment of what the patient's problems are and of how well he has learned to cope with them may be almost impossible. Techniques, however, do exist for assessing some relevant aspects of the patient's behaviour, even in institutional environments, and for promoting generalization of treatment effects from the treatment situation to real life environments. Crawford's treatment programme for abnormal offenders (Crawford, 1979, 1981) is comprehensive and includes anxiety reduction techniques, social skills training, sex education (Crawford and Howells, 1978) and covert sensitization. Although assessment and evaluation of such programmes is difficult and at a preliminary stage, they would seem to represent a promising start at intervention in this area. What is most striking, perhaps, about such projects is that they are the product of normal, non-pathological models of how deviant and non-deviant sexual behaviours are acquired, applied to offenders defined as a abnormal.

Studies of aggressive behaviour relevant to mentally abnormal offenders

There is no *a priori* reason why most studies of 'normal' aggression should not be equally relevant to abnormal aggression. It is proposed here to outline some features of normal aggressive behaviour which might also be true for abnormal groups. Some of this material is reviewed in more detail in Howells (1981*b*). First, however, it needs to be emphasized that aggression in abnormal persons, like aggression in normals, is likely to occur predominantly in domestic contexts between individuals who are often intimately related (Home Office, 1961, 1975; McClintock, 1963; West, 1965; Mulvihill *et al.*, 1969). Typically, much serious violence arises out of angry disputes and disagreements in such relationships. West (1965) comments on murder/suicides that 'the predominant pattern ... was a history of personal friction between victim and offender, culminating in a final outburst of violence'. It should also be borne in mind that a sizeable proportion of homicidal offenders have no officially recorded history of criminality. West (1965), for example, found that only 13% of murder/suicides had previous convictions, and that many offenders were of a 'normal' personality structure as far as criminal traits were concerned.

Over-control in abnormal offenders

Megargee (1966, 1971) has put forward a theory to explain why well socialized, relatively controlled, habitually non-aggressive and even meek individuals sometimes perform extreme acts of violence such as homicide. The interest of Megargee's theory, as far as this chapter is concerned, lies in the fact that some of the predictions of the theory have been supported by empirical studies of both normal and abnormal groups, thus confirming the hypothesis (above) that similar psychological processes of a non-pathological kind may underlie aggression in both groups.

Megargee proposes that people vary in their degree of inhibition of violent behaviour and that the threshold point at which inhibitions are exceeded by environmental frustrations also varies. Individuals with very high levels of inhibition will be induced to behave aggressively only by extremely high levels of provocation—such individuals are labelled as 'over-controlled'. Individuals with low levels of inhibition will be induced to behave aggressively relatively easily by low levels of provocation, and are labelled 'under-controlled'. Megargee predicts that when over-controlled offenders do offend they will show excessive violence, as the degree of violence is proportional to the level of provocation, and that temporal summation of frustration is required to produce a sufficiently high level of provocation for aggression to be induced. Thus the over-controlled person's frustration is seen as accumulating over time in, for example, a difficult and abrasive relationship with a wife until an explosive and uncharacteristic assault occurs.

The specific testable prediction from Megargee's theory is that over-controlled persons will be found more frequently among offenders who have committed extreme assaults (EAs) than among offenders who have committed moderate assaults (MAs).

Evidence for the theory Megargee (1966) compared EA and MA delinquent subjects, and found that the EAs obtained lower scores on measures of hostility and aggression. Evidence that serious assaulters are more socialized was also provided by Molof (1967). Both of these studies involved mentally normal offenders. Of more interest for understanding abnormal offenders are the studies of Blackburn (1968, 1971), both of which used abnormal violent offenders admitted to a security hospital. In his first study, Blackburn compared EA and MA subjects on psychometric scales derived from the MMPI and demonstrated that the EAs obtained higher scores on scales measuring denial, low hostility and control. Whereas 82% of the EA group had attacked known victims (family, close acquaintances), this applied to only 36% of the MA group, confirming Megargee's prediction that the EA aggressor is violent only in social contexts involving sustained frustration. In his second study, Blackburn (1971) used a clustering technique to identify types amongst abnormal homicides, and identified two of the four profiles found as over-controlled. Similar results have been found in a number of studies of normal offenders (McGurk, 1978; Widom, 1978), and of abnormal offenders (Arnold and Quinsey, 1977). Several studies have, however, failed to confirm predictions (Crawford, 1977; Hoppe and Singer, 1977). The study of McGurk and McGurk (1979) suggests that some caution is required before interpreting classic over-control profiles as demonstrating over-controlled behaviour, in that such profiles are common in normal, non-violent control groups. More research is needed to demonstrate conclusively that the level of control found in extreme assaulters is indeed greater than that found in normals, and not simply greater than that found in moderately assaultive groups.

Megargee has usefully drawn attention to the fact that extreme violence sometimes occurs in characteristically controlled people. The theory itself however, can be criticized on a number of counts (see Howells, 1981*b*). The concept of summation of frustration and of the over-controlled person's failure to discharge aggression, is hydraulic and based on a model which receives relatively little support (Quanty, 1976). I have suggested elsewhere (Howells, 1981*b*, *c*) that Megargee's theory might be buttressed by incorporating behavioural and cognitive variables. The excessively controlled person may be finally induced to behave aggressively because his deficient assertiveness skills make him unable to stop provocation from his potential victim (Howells, 1976). In this sense, over-controlled people may expose themselves to more provoking environments than do normals. Alternatively, the over-controlled person's violent outburst may be mediated by changed cognitive evaluations of other people, circumstances, self, and the victim. I studied cognitive evaluations of self and others (including victims), in over-controlled, abnormal, violent offenders, using repertory grid technique (Fransella and Bannister, 1977). The results (Howells, 1982) were interpreted as suggesting that over-controlled offenders may be prone to biased cognitive evaluations of other prople, in which hostile evaluations are 'submerged' (Kelly, 1955). Such construct systems may be inherently unstable and prone to sudden dramatic change under stress, producing uncharacteristically hostile evaluations, which induce intense anger and subsequent aggression against the victim (Howells, 1982).

Cognitive control of aggression

Cognitive variables are clearly relevant to the understanding of aggressive behaviour, as they are to a number of other forms of social difficulty. Particular ways of interpreting and attributing social events seem to engender aggressive responses. Bandura (1971*a*, *b*) has described two pathways for the learning of aggressive responses. Aggression may be learned 'instrumentally' through reinforcement and imitation, or it may be learned as an 'angry' response to negative arousal states, engendered by frustrating or aversive environmental events. A number of responses may be learned to cope with negative states of affective arousal, including withdrawal, aggression and intropunitive behaviour. How aversive environmental events are interpreted and attributed will determine how the affective response is labelled and also the nature of the ensuing behaviour. The attribution of malevolent intent may be particularly likely to evoke an aggressive response (Epstein and Taylor, 1967; Greenwell and Dengerink, 1973; Nickel, 1974; Dyck and Rule, 1978; Nasby *et al.*, 1980; Howells, 1981*b*). Biases towards attributing hostile intention as an explanation of social events may *mediate* aggressive behaviour, but it is also possible that attributional biases are a *product* of aggressive behaviour, i.e. that attributions and behaviour have reciprocal causal relationships. A person who is aggressive to others because he perceives them as hostile to him may cause them to become hostile, thus confirming his predictions.

It is possible, though this has yet to be demonstrated empirically, that particular categories of abnormal offender show cognitive and attributional biases which induce them to behave violently. A number of studies (see above) have pointed to the high frequency of paranoid states amongst abnormal offenders. People with paranoid delusions are, by definition, biased in their interpretive schema and they are likely to explain their social world in terms of hostile conspiracies and plans on the part of others. In my clinical experience, there would seem to be many examples of mentally abnormal offenders whose violent behaviour was clearly controlled by such biased cognitions. A typical example would be the person who has no history of either violent behaviour or mental disorder who suddenly becomes acutely deluded. The content of such delusions may involve beliefs that, for example, his neighbours are performing black magic in order to harm or even kill him. Violence frequently occurs in such circumstances as an attempt to defend oneself against the perceived danger, and is perceived subjectively as necessary and even legitimate. Such delusions may sometimes disappear as quickly as they appeared, and the instigation to defensive aggression is totally removed.

Little is known as yet about cognitive biases in other forms of disorder which might contribute to aggression. It is feasible that the link between depression and violence (see above) is mediated by depressive cognitions. It is clear that depression involves cognitive distortions, though not typically of the sort that might increase hostility to others (Beck, 1979). West (1965) has suggested that the violent behaviour of some murder/suicides is determined by depressive world views which lead to a form of extended suicide. Similarly, it is not uncommon clinically to see women who have been violent to their young children in an attempt to remove the child—for the child's sake—from a world too bleak to live in. It is important, of course, to realize that the vast majority of people with paranoid or depressive cognitions are not led to act violently. Research clearly needs to be directed towards finding out whether, for example, the *content* of paranoid delusions is subtly different in those who are violent compared to those who do not behave violently.

Novaco's contribution

Novaco (1975, 1976*a*, *b*, 1977*a*, *b*, 1978) has drawn attention to the importance of cognition for aggression, and also to the intimate links between the affective state of anger and cognitions. In Novaco's model, anger is viewed as having a bi-directional causal relationship with three classes of phenomena: external events (aversive events, frustrations, annoyances), internal cognitive processes (appraisal, attribution, self-talk) and behavioural reactions (aggressive behaviour itself). Aversive events are subject to cognitive structuring, which determines whether or not anger is induced; the cognitive structuring includes processes of attribution, subjective expectation, internal dialogue and mental rehearsal. Anger in itself can reciprocally influence such cognitions. Mutually facilitating relationships also exist between anger and aggressive behaviour (anger induces roponent of the view that 'nothing works' as far as treatments for rime are concerned has been Martinson (1974), who reviewed the ss of several hundred prison treatment programmes. Martinson's e been widely quoted both by those who would wish to expose as likely to have adverse consequences for prisoners and by those with ce for a more punitive penal ideology. There are now many indications nson's conclusions were over-generalized and premature. The fact that s *have* been ineffective clearly does not show that they will or must be . Blackburn (1980*a*) recently reviewed 40 treatment studies completed tinson's paper and demonstrated that, of those studies which looked at rates, half reported positive results, and that the most methodologically dies all showed positive outcomes. Given the severe difficulties in mplementing genuinely therapeutic programmes in the penal system 80), it is, perhaps, not surprising that results have been disappointing, nnot be assumed that treatment efforts in hospital or other health will be equally bleak. West (1980) suggests that 'a rethinking of strategy, rather than an abandonment of hope' is the appropriate Undue pessimism concerning the possibility of intervening effectively inal or deviant behaviour is illogical in some respects. Crawford (1980*b*) the important point that we do not need a psychology of deviance *and* a gy of normality; the fact that society has conferred the label 'criminal' nt' on certain sorts of behaviour does not imply that psychological s known to be valid and effective for non-criminal behaviours cease to and effective. A guarded optimism about the future of psychological ions with mentally disordered offenders may not be entirely riate.

k reviewed in this chapter is interpreted as indicating that although gical disturbance is high amongst offenders, and although some studies icated a slightly higher rate of violent crime in patients leaving hospitals, little firm evidence as yet that mental illness is of major significance in ng the occurrence of violent behaviour. Some specific psychiatric s have been discussed and psychopathy, in particular, has been evaluated . It follows that treatments which are intended to reduce the level of ous' behaviour in mentally abnormal offenders (though this is not the rapeutic goal) should also focus on the non-pathological psychological ial processes which have contributed to the emergence of the problem urs. Much of the work developed in the areas of sexual deviance and on in normal persons will be of clear relevance for abnormal offenders. mental disorder *is* seen as causally significant, there is a need for future n to specify the psychological processes which link the disorder and the

aggression, aggression induces anger), and aggressive behaviour may, in turn, increase the level of aversive stimulation (by provoking retaliatory aggression). Novaco has developed a 'stress inoculation model' to modify these cognitive, affective and behavioural components of aggression (Novaco, 1978).

Figure 1 is a modified version of a diagram presented by Novaco (1978). This diagram shows some of the components of aggressive behaviour and has been modified to suggest some of the possible influences of some of the mental disorders and processes discussed so far in this chapter. The evidence for the possible links is as yet speculative. The purpose of the diagram is to suggest that those who are attempting to describe connections between aggressive behaviour and disorder (and personality traits) need to specify the common psychological processes involved in the disorder and in aggression. It is plausible that most forms of mental disorder change the external events (box 1) that the person will encounter. People diagnosed as schizophrenic, depressive or neurotic would be expected to have more difficulties in living and to meet more frustrations and annoyances than other people.

The mentally disordered are also more likely to live in more aversive environments, particularly if they are institutionalized. Cognitive processes (box 2) may be affected by some of the cognitive changes which accompany states of disorder, such as schizophrenic states and depression. Whether organic states produce related cognitive changes is unclear. We also know little about what contributes to individual variation in anger arousal (box 3). Given the relationship between anger and physiological arousal, it may be that biological processes (Hinton, 1981) are most relevant at this point in the chain. It is not clear from the work on psychopathy whether psychopaths would be expected to differ from normals in their anger responses. It may be that secondary psychopaths are

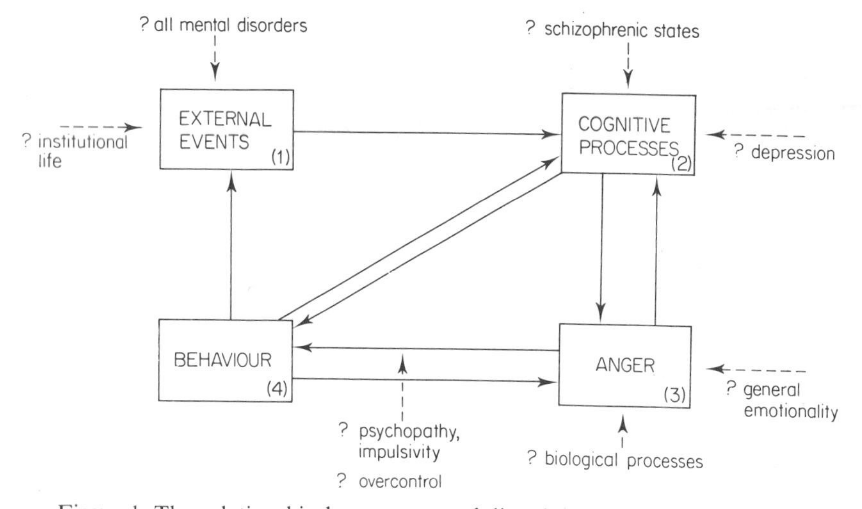

Figure 1. The relationship between mental disorder and aggressive behavior

more prone to excessive anger (Blackburn, 1980*b*) but that primary psychopaths are not. Psychopathic traits (Hare, 1970; Hare and Schalling, 1978) are perhaps more relevant to whether or not a behavioural response occurs following anger arousal. Primary psychopaths might be presumed to be impulsive and have difficulty in restraining behavioural responses. The over-controlled person, on the other hand, may be excessively inhibited about behavioural expression. Both an over-readiness and an over-inhibitedness about behavioural expression (box 4) might be expected in turn to affect the subsequent external events which the person will meet. The under-controlled aggressor will be exposed to negative feedback from others and to informal and judicial sanctions which will raise the level of frustration to which he is exposed, whilst the over-controlled aggressor provokes further victimization. The complexities of the psychological processes involved in aggression, in abnormal offenders, will clearly require complex and multifaceted assessments and treatment interventions. Novaco's model does not extend to instrumental (non-angry) aggression. This form of aggression clearly occurs in abnormal offenders (sadistic aggression, instrumental aggression, to produce compliance in rape and assaults on children) but would need a separate analysis. The important point being emphasized here is that the effects of mental disorder on the propensity for aggressive behaviour need to be located within some sort of model of the processes involved in normal aggression.

Some general issues relevant to treatment

The evidence discussed so far in this chapter, that mental disorder itself is of limited value in explaining violent behaviour in mentally abnormal offenders, would seem to have many important consequences for both assessment and treatment. First, however, it is necessary to emphasize that there are two relatively, but not entirely, separate treatment goals with differing assessment requirements. Mentally disordered offenders are like other psychiatric patients with regard to their high levels of subjective distress and unhappiness. To this extent they will require the same treatments and diagnostic assessment procedures as do other patients. It is clearly a humane and desirable goal that symptoms of depression or disturbing hallucinatory experiences should receive therapeutic attention. As has been described above, in most contexts in which abnormal offenders are found this goal co-exists with the goal of reducing the level of the 'dangerous' behaviour which has led to admission to the particular psychiatric or penal facility. These two goals are not entirely independent in that the propensity for the offending behaviour itself may be one of the factors that contributes to the sense of subjective distress, as in the paedophilic offender who is disturbed by his socially deviant sexual preference and the effect it has had on his life.

The implication of the studies reviewed above is that the offending behaviour requires a different, non-medical, model which stresses the continuity between

abnormal and normal offending. It is, howev
these two models simultaneously and there
settings, attention will be predominantly fo
diagnosis ('Is this person schizophrenic?') and
attention being paid to psychological and s
significant. The goal of changing dangerou
fundamentally different, non-medical orientati
planning in which medical symptoms are
consequence.

There are difficulties in achieving both t
dangerous behaviour reduction goals. It is
offenders are one of the groups most badly se
services. Local psychiatric hospitals are often
offenders. This latter fact is widely attributed t
policy of community treatment and to the ina
institutions (Crawford, 1980*a*). The effect of this
are forced to stay in security institutions for long
warrants (Dell, 1980), or are subjected to the rigo
(1980) suggests, security and discipline rather tha
mainstream tradition. A large number of ment
prisons even though, as Orr (1978), the Direct
comments, 'the mentally disordered cannot co
prison discipline'. (From a Szaszian point of view
appropriate a place for abnormal offenders as the
the appropriate remedial course of action w
institutions for *all* offenders rather than to re
treatment facilities.)

A number of difficulties also exist in achiev
treatment goal. A large number of mentally ab
within security institutions far removed from
Whereas this fact would not necessarily impede a
programme (e.g. drugs), this is a marked problem
psychological and social model, which often requi
vivo with everyday problems and stresses. Hend
treatment facility for abnormal offenders in Hollan
can be overcome. One item in the 'credo' of this
'society is a prerequisite for any programme of reso
which aims to bring its patients back into society
situated within this society'.

A second fundamental difficulty, it might be ar
behaviour through psychosocial methods is that th
social interventions being advocated have been
reducing criminal behaviour in normal criminal

fluential p
reducing
effectiven
views hav
treatment
a preferen
that Mart
treatment
ineffective
since Mar
recidivist
sound st
properly
(West, 19
and it ca
contexts
treatmen
attitude.
with crim
has made
psycholo
or 'devia
principle
be valid
interven
inappro

Summar

The wo
psycholo
have ind
there is
explaini
disorder
in detai
'danger
only th
and so
behavio
aggress
Where
researc

fluential proponent of the view that 'nothing works' as far as treatments for reducing crime are concerned has been Martinson (1974), who reviewed the effectiveness of several hundred prison treatment programmes. Martinson's views have been widely quoted both by those who would wish to expose treatment as likely to have adverse consequences for prisoners and by those with a preference for a more punitive penal ideology. There are now many indications that Martinson's conclusions were over-generalized and premature. The fact that treatments *have* been ineffective clearly does not show that they will or must be ineffective. Blackburn (1980*a*) recently reviewed 40 treatment studies completed since Martinson's paper and demonstrated that, of those studies which looked at recidivist rates, half reported positive results, and that the most methodologically sound studies all showed positive outcomes. Given the severe difficulties in properly implementing genuinely therapeutic programmes in the penal system (West, 1980), it is, perhaps, not surprising that results have been disappointing, and it cannot be assumed that treatment efforts in hospital or other health contexts will be equally bleak. West (1980) suggests that 'a rethinking of treatment strategy, rather than an abandonment of hope' is the appropriate attitude. Undue pessimism concerning the possibility of intervening effectively with criminal or deviant behaviour is illogical in some respects. Crawford (1980*b*) has made the important point that we do not need a psychology of deviance *and* a psychology of normality; the fact that society has conferred the label 'criminal' or 'deviant' on certain sorts of behaviour does not imply that psychological principles known to be valid and effective for non-criminal behaviours cease to be valid and effective. A guarded optimism about the future of psychological interventions with mentally disordered offenders may not be entirely inappropriate.

Summary

The work reviewed in this chapter is interpreted as indicating that although psychological disturbance is high amongst offenders, and although some studies have indicated a slightly higher rate of violent crime in patients leaving hospitals, there is little firm evidence as yet that mental illness is of major significance in *explaining* the occurrence of violent behaviour. Some specific psychiatric disorders have been discussed and psychopathy, in particular, has been evaluated in detail. It follows that treatments which are intended to reduce the level of 'dangerous' behaviour in mentally abnormal offenders (though this is not the only therapeutic goal) should also focus on the non-pathological psychological and social processes which have contributed to the emergence of the problem behaviours. Much of the work developed in the areas of sexual deviance and aggression in normal persons will be of clear relevance for abnormal offenders. Where mental disorder *is* seen as causally significant, there is a need for future research to specify the psychological processes which link the disorder and the abnormal and normal offending. It is, however, probably difficult to maintain these two models simultaneously and there is a danger that, in psychiatric settings, attention will be predominantly focused on questions of medical diagnosis ('Is this person schizophrenic?') and of medical 'cure', with insufficient attention being paid to psychological and social factors which are causally significant. The goal of changing dangerous behaviour clearly requires a fundamentally different, non-medical orientation to assessment and to treatment planning in which medical symptoms are of small, though not negligible consequence.

There are difficulties in achieving both the distress alleviation and the dangerous behaviour reduction goals. It is clear that mentally disordered offenders are one of the groups most badly served by health and other social services. Local psychiatric hospitals are often reluctant to care for abnormal offenders. This latter fact is widely attributed to the advent of the 'open-door' policy of community treatment and to the inadequate funding and staffing of institutions (Crawford, 1980*a*). The effect of this reluctance is often that patients are forced to stay in security institutions for longer periods than their behaviour warrants (Dell, 1980), or are subjected to the rigours of prison life where, as West (1980) suggests, security and discipline rather than therapeutic endeavour are the mainstream tradition. A large number of mentally disordered offenders are in prisons even though, as Orr (1978), the Director of Prison Medical Services, comments, 'the mentally disordered cannot cope with [the] routine and with prison discipline'. (From a Szaszian point of view, of course, prisons would be as appropriate a place for abnormal offenders as they are for normal offenders and the appropriate remedial course of action would be to humanize penal institutions for *all* offenders rather than to remove disordered offenders to treatment facilities.)

A number of difficulties also exist in achieving the second (behavioural) treatment goal. A large number of mentally abnormal offenders are located within security institutions far removed from community and family life. Whereas this fact would not necessarily impede a medically oriented treatment programme (e.g. drugs), this is a marked problem for a programme based on a psychological and social model, which often requires teaching patients to cope *in vivo* with everyday problems and stresses. Hendriks' (1976) description of a treatment facility for abnormal offenders in Holland suggests that such problems can be overcome. One item in the 'credo' of this clinic, for example, was that, 'society is a prerequisite for any programme of resocialization . . ., an institution which aims to bring its patients back into society in the proper way should be situated within this society'.

A second fundamental difficulty, it might be argued, in reducing dangerous behaviour through psychosocial methods is that the sorts of psychological and social interventions being advocated have been shown to be ineffective in reducing criminal behaviour in normal criminal populations. The most in-more prone to excessive anger (Blackburn, 1980*b*) but that primary psychopaths are not. Psychopathic traits (Hare, 1970; Hare and Schalling, 1978) are perhaps more relevant to whether or not a behavioural response occurs following anger arousal. Primary psychopaths might be presumed to be impulsive and have difficulty in restraining behavioural responses. The over-controlled person, on the other hand, may be excessively inhibited about behavioural expression. Both an over-readiness and an over-inhibitedness about behavioural expression (box 4) might be expected in turn to affect the subsequent external events which the person will meet. The under-controlled aggressor will be exposed to negative feedback from others and to informal and judicial sanctions which will raise the level of frustration to which he is exposed, whilst the over-controlled aggressor provokes further victimization. The complexities of the psychological processes involved in aggression, in abnormal offenders, will clearly require complex and multifaceted assessments and treatment interventions. Novaco's model does not extend to instrumental (non-angry) aggression. This form of aggression clearly occurs in abnormal offenders (sadistic aggression, instrumental aggression, to produce compliance in rape and assaults on children) but would need a separate analysis. The important point being emphasized here is that the effects of mental disorder on the propensity for aggressive behaviour need to be located within some sort of model of the processes involved in normal aggression.

Some general issues relevant to treatment

The evidence discussed so far in this chapter, that mental disorder itself is of limited value in explaining violent behaviour in mentally abnormal offenders, would seem to have many important consequences for both assessment and treatment. First, however, it is necessary to emphasize that there are two relatively, but not entirely, separate treatment goals with differing assessment requirements. Mentally disordered offenders are like other psychiatric patients with regard to their high levels of subjective distress and unhappiness. To this extent they will require the same treatments and diagnostic assessment procedures as do other patients. It is clearly a humane and desirable goal that symptoms of depression or disturbing hallucinatory experiences should receive therapeutic attention. As has been described above, in most contexts in which abnormal offenders are found this goal co-exists with the goal of reducing the level of the 'dangerous' behaviour which has led to admission to the particular psychiatric or penal facility. These two goals are not entirely independent in that the propensity for the offending behaviour itself may be one of the factors that contributes to the sense of subjective distress, as in the paedophilic offender who is disturbed by his socially deviant sexual preference and the effect it has had on his life.

The implication of the studies reviewed above is that the offending behaviour requires a different, non-medical, model which stresses the continuity between aggression, aggression induces anger), and aggressive behaviour may, in turn, increase the level of aversive stimulation (by provoking retaliatory aggression). Novaco has developed a 'stress inoculation model' to modify these cognitive, affective and behavioural components of aggression (Novaco, 1978).

Figure 1 is a modified version of a diagram presented by Novaco (1978). This diagram shows some of the components of aggressive behaviour and has been modified to suggest some of the possible influences of some of the mental disorders and processes discussed so far in this chapter. The evidence for the possible links is as yet speculative. The purpose of the diagram is to suggest that those who are attempting to describe connections between aggressive behaviour and disorder (and personality traits) need to specify the common psychological processes involved in the disorder and in aggression. It is plausible that most forms of mental disorder change the external events (box 1) that the person will encounter. People diagnosed as schizophrenic, depressive or neurotic would be expected to have more difficulties in living and to meet more frustrations and annoyances than other people.

The mentally disordered are also more likely to live in more aversive environments, particularly if they are institutionalized. Cognitive processes (box 2) may be affected by some of the cognitive changes which accompany states of disorder, such as schizophrenic states and depression. Whether organic states produce related cognitive changes is unclear. We also know little about what contributes to individual variation in anger arousal (box 3). Given the relationship between anger and physiological arousal, it may be that biological processes (Hinton, 1981) are most relevant at this point in the chain. It is not clear from the work on psychopathy whether psychopaths would be expected to differ from normals in their anger responses. It may be that secondary psychopaths are

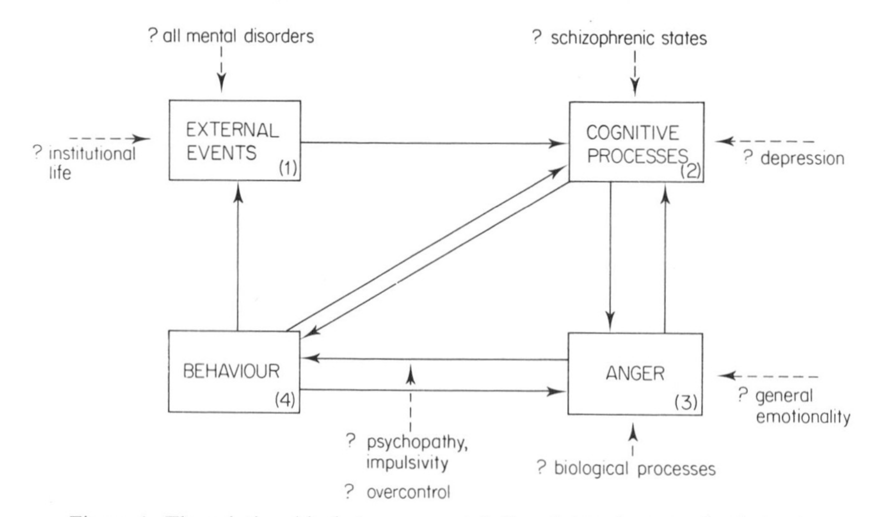

Figure 1. The relationship between mental disorder and aggressive behavior

offending behaviour. Finally, although research into the effects of psychosocial treatments has sometimes produced disappointing results, outright pessimism is not in order.

References

Abel, G. G., Blanchard, E. B., and Becker, R. L. (1978). An integrated treatment programme for rapists, in *Clinical Aspects of the Rapist* (Ed. R. T. Rada). New York: Grune and Stratton, pp. 161–214.

Arnold, L. S., and Quinsey, V. L. (1977). Overcontrolled hostility among men found not guilty by reason of insanity. *Canadian Journal of Behavioural Science*, **9**, 330–340.

Bancroft, J. (1974). *Deviant Sexual Behaviour*. Oxford: Clarendon Press.

Bandura, A. (1971*a*). Social learning theory of aggression, in *Control of Aggression: Implications from Basic Research* (Ed. J. F. Knutson). Chicago: Aldine-Atherton, pp. 201–252.

Bandura, A. (1971*b*). *Aggression: A Social Learning Analysis*, New York: Prentice-Hall.

Barlow, D. H. (1974). The treatment of sexual deviation: toward a comprehensive behavioural approach, in *Innovative Methods in Psychopathology* (Eds K. S. Calhoun, H. E. Adams and K. M. Mitchell). New York: John Wiley, pp. 121–148.

Beck, A. T. (1979). *Cognitive Therapy of Depression*, New York: Guilford.

Black, D. A. (1973). A decade of psychological investigation of the male patient population of Broadmoor. *Special Hospitals Research Reports*, No. 8.

Black, D. A. (1977). A 5-year follow-up study of male patients discharged from Broadmoor. Paper presented to the Annual Conference of the British Psychological Society, Exeter, April 1977.

Blackburn, R. (1968). Personality in relation to extreme aggression in psychiatric offenders. *British Journal of Psychiatry*, **114**, 821–828.

Blackburn, R. (1969). Some logical problems in the use of the term psychopath. Unpublished manuscript, Broadmoor Hospital.

Blackburn, R. (1971). Personality types among abnormal homicides. *British Journal of Criminology*, **11**, 14–31.

Blackburn, R. (1974). Personality and the classification of psychopathic disorders. *Special Hospitals Research Reports*, No. 10.

Blackburn, R. (1975*a*). Aggression and the EEG: a qualitative analysis. *Journal of Abnormal Psychology*, **84**, 358–365.

Blackburn, R. (1975*b*). An empirical classification of psychopathic personality. *British Journal of Psychiatry*, **127**, 456–460.

Blackburn, R. (1980*a*). Still not working? A look at recent outcomes in offender rehabilitation. Paper presented to the Scottish Branch of the British Psychological Society Conference on 'Deviance', Stirling, February 1980.

Blackburn, R. (1980*b*). On the relevance of the concept of the psychopath. Paper presented to the London conference of the British Psychological Society, London, December 1980.

Blackburn, R. (1980*c*). Personality and the criminal psychopath, in *Lo Psicopatico Delinquente*. Facolta di Giurizprudenza, Universita di Messina, Milan: Giuffre, pp. 37–68.

Brennan, J. J. (1964). Mentally ill aggressiveness, popular delusion or reality? *American Journal of Psychiatry*, **120**, 181–184.

Brill, H., and Malzberg, B. (1962). Statistical report on the arrest record of male ex-patients released from New York State mental hospitals during the period 1946–8, in *Criminal Acts of Ex-mental Hospital Patients* (Supplement No. 153). Washington D.C.: American Psychiatric Association Mental Hospital Service.

British Psychological Society (1973). Memorandum of evidence to the Butler Committee on the law relating to the mentally abnormal offender. *Bulletin of the British Psychological Society*, **26**, 331–342.

Burgess, A. W., Groth, A. N., Holmstrom, L. L., and Sgroi, S. M. (Eds), *Sexual Assault on Children and Adolescents*. Lexington, Mass.: D.C. Heath.

Carney, F. L. (1978). Inpatient treatment programmes, in *The Psychopath: A Comprehensive Study of Anti-social Disorders and Behaviors* (Ed. W. H. Reid). New York: Brunner/Mazel, pp. 261–285.

Cleckley, H. (1964). *The Mask of Sanity*. St Louis, Mo.: C. V. Mosby.

Cohen, L. H., and Freeman, H. (1945). How dangerous to the community are State Hospital patients? *Connecticut State Medical Journal*, **9**, 697–700.

Cook, M., and Howells, K. (Eds)(1981). *Adult Sexual Interest in Children*. London: Academic Press.

Crawford, D. A. (1977). The HDHQ results of long-term prisoners: relationships with criminal and institutional behaviour. *British Journal of Social and Clinical Psychology*, **16**, 391–394.

Crawford, D. A. (1979). Modification of deviant sexual behaviour: the need for a comprehensive approach. *British Journal of Medical Psychology*, **52**, 151–156.

Crawford, D. A. (1980*a*). Deviant behaviour: problems and issues. Paper presented to the annual conference of the British Association of Behavioural Psychotherapy, Sheffield, July 1980.

Crawford, D. A. (1980*b*). Problems for the assessment and treatment of sexual offenders in closed institutions: and some solutions. Paper presented to the London conference of the British Psychological Society, London, December 1980.

Crawford, D. A. (1981). Treatment approaches with pedophiles, in *Adult Sexual Interest in Children* (Eds M. Cook and K. Howells). London: Academic Press, pp. 181–217.

Crawford, D. A., and Howells, K. (1978). The effects of sex education on mentally abnormal violent offenders. Unpublished manuscript.

Dell, S. (1980). Transfer of Special Hospital patients to the NHS. *British Journal of Psychiatry*, **136**, 222–234.

DHSS, Home Office, Welsh Office and Lord Chancellor's Department (1976). *A Review of the Mental Health Act, 1959*, London: HMSO.

Dyck, R. J., and Rule, B. G. (1978). Effect on retaliation of causal attributions concerning attack. *Journal of Personality and Social Psychology*, **36**, 521–529.

Ekblom, B. (1970). *Acts of Violence by Patients in Mental Hospitals*. Uppsala: Scandinavian University Books, Almquist and Wiksells Boktycheri AB.

Epstein, S., and Taylor, S. P. (1967). Instigation to aggression as a function of defeat and perceived aggressive intent of the opponent. *Journal of Personality*, **35**, 265–289.

Eynon, T. G. (1970). The mentally disordered offender, in *Law, Psychiatry and the Mentally Disordered Offender* (Eds L. M. Irvine and T. R. Brejle). Springfield, Ill.: Charles C. Thomas, pp. 3–17.

Eysenck, H. J., and Eysenck, S. B. G. (1978). Psychopathy, personality and genetics, in *Psychopathic Behavior: Approaches to Research* (Eds R. D. Hare and D. Schalling). Chichester: John Wiley, pp. 197–224.

Fagan, T. J., and Lira, F. T. (1980). The primary and secondary sociopathic personality: differences in frequency and severity of antisocial behaviours. *Journal of Abnormal Psychology*, **89**, 493–496.

Feldman, M. P. (1977). *Criminal Behaviour: A Psychological Analysis*. Chichester: John Wiley.

Feldman, M. P., and MacCulloch, M. (1980). *Human Sexual Behaviour*. Chichester: John Wiley.

Fenton, G. W., Tennent, T. G., Fenwick, P. B. C., and Rateray, N. (1974). The EEG in antisocial behaviour: a study of posterior temporal slow activity in Special Hospital patients. *Psychological Medicine*, **4**, 181–186.

Field, E. (1967). *A Validation of Hewitt and Jenkins' Hypothesis* (*Home Office Research Unit Report*). London: HMSO.

Fottrell, E. (1980). A study of violent behaviour among patients in psychiatric hospitals. *British Journal of Psychiatry*, **136**, 216–221.

Fottrell, E. (1981). Violent behaviour by psychiatric patients. *British Journal of Hospital Medicine*, **25**, 28–38.

Fransella, F., and Bannister, D. (1977). *A Manual of Repertory Grid Technique*, London: Academic Press.

Gebhard, P. H., Gagnon, J. H., Pomeroy, W. B., and Christenson, C. V. (1965). *Sex Offenders: An Analysis of Types*. New York: Harper and Row.

Geen, R. G., and O'Neal, E. C. (Eds) (1976). *Perspectives on Aggression*, London: Academic Press.

Gibbens, T. C. N., Pond, D. A., and Stafford-Clark, D. (1959). Follow-up study of criminal psychopaths. *Journal of Mental Science*, **105**, 108.

Gillies, H. (1965). Murder in the west of Scotland. *British Journal of Psychiatry*, **111**, 1087–1094.

Giovannoni, J. M., and Gurel, L. (1967). Socially disruptive behaviour of ex-mental patients. *Archives of General Psychiatry*, **17**, 146–153.

Greenland, C. (1978). The prediction and management of dangerous behavior: social policy issues. *International Journal of Law and Psychiatry*, **1**, 205–222.

Greenwell, J., and Dengerink, H. (1973). The role of perceived versus actual attack in human physical aggression. *Journal of Personality and Social Psychology*, **26**, 66–74.

Gunn, J. (1973). *Violence in Human Society*. Newton Abbot, Devon: David and Charles.

Gunn, J. (1977). *Epileptics in Prison*. London: Academic Press.

Gunn, J. (1979). Forensic psychiatry, in *Recent Advances in Clinical Psychiatry* (Ed. K. Granville-Grossman). Edinburgh: Churchill Livingstone, pp. 271–295.

Gunn, J., and Fenton, G. (1971). Epilepsy, automatism and crime. *The Lancet*, *i*, 1173–1176.

Gunn, J., Robertson, G., Dell, S., and Way, C. (1978). *Psychiatric Aspects of Imprisonment*, London: Academic Press.

Guze, S. B. (1976). *Criminality and Psychiatric Disorders*. Oxford: Oxford University Press.

Häfner, H. and Böker, W. (1973). Mentally disordered violent offenders. *Social Psychiatry*, **8**, 220–229.

Hare, R. D. (1970). *Psychopathy: Theory and Research*, New York: John Wiley, 1970.

Hare, R. D. (1981). A research scale for the assessment of psychopathy in criminal populations. *Personality and Individual Differences*, in press.

Hare, R. D., and Cox, D. N. (1978). Clinical and empirical conceptions of psychopathy, and the selection of subjects for research, in *Psychopathic Behavior: Approaches to Research* (Eds R. D. Hare and D. Schalling). Chichester: John Wiley, pp. 1–22.

Hare, R. D., and Schalling, D. (Eds) (1978). *Psychopathic Behavior: Approaches to Research*, Chichester: John Wiley.

Hendriks, P. A. M. (1976). The treatment of the mentally abnormal offender at the Van der Hoeven Klinik in Holland. *International Journal of Offender Therapy and Comparative Criminology*, **20**, 255–267.

Hewitt, L., and Jenkins, R. L. (1946). *Fundamental Patterns of Maladjustment*, Illinois: State of Illinois.

Hill, D. (1944). Cerebral dysrhythmia: its significance in aggressive behaviour. *Proceedings of the Royal Society of Medicine*, **37**, 317–328.

Hinton, J. W. (1981). Biological approaches to criminality, in *Multidisciplinary Approaches to Aggression Research* (Eds P. Brain and D. Benton). Amsterdam: Elsevier/North Holland Biomedical Press, pp. 447–462.

Holland, T. R., Levi, M., and Watson, C. G. (1980). Personality patterns among hospitalized vs incarcerated psychopaths. *Journal of Clinical Psychology*, **36**, 826–832.

Home Office (1961). *Murder*. London: HMSO.

Home Office (1975). *Homicide in England and Wales, 1967–1971*. London: HMSO.

Home Office and DHSS (1975). *Report of the Committee on Mentally Abnormal Offenders. Cmnd 6244*. London: HMSO.

Hoppe, C. M., and Singer, R. D. (1977). Interpersonal violence and its relationship to some personality measures. *Aggressive Behavior*, **3**, 261–270.

Howells, K. (1976). Interpersonal aggression. *International Journal of Criminology and Penology*, **4**, 319–330.

Howells, K. (1979). Some meanings of children for pedophiles, in *Love and Attraction* (Eds M. Cook and G. Wilson). Oxford: Pergamon, pp. 519–526.

Howells, K. (1980). Social reactions to sexual deviance, in *Sex Offenders in the Criminal Justice System* (Ed. D. J. West). Cambridge: Institute of Criminology (Cropwood Publications), pp. 20–33.

Howells, K. (1981*a*). Adult sexual interest in children: considerations relevant to theories of aetiology, in *Adult Sexual Interest in Children* (Eds M. Cook and K. Howells). London: Academic Press, pp. 55–94.

Howells, K. (1981*b*). Social relationships in violent offenders, in *Personal Relationships, 3: Personal Relationships in Disorder* (Eds S. Duck and R. Gilmour). London: Academic Press, pp. 215–234.

Howells, K. (1982). Social construing and violent behaviour in mentally abnormal offenders, in *Dangerousness: Problems of Assessment and Prediction* (Ed. J. Hinton). London: Allen and Unwin, (in press).

Howells, K., and Steadman-Allen, R. (1977). The emotional mediation of sexual offences. Paper presented to the annual conference of the British Psychological Society, Exeter, April 1977.

Howells, K., and Wright, E. (1978). The sexual attitudes of aggressive sexual offenders. *British Journal of Criminology*, **18**, 170–174.

Karpman, B. (1947). Passive parasitic psychopathy: toward the personality structure and psychogenesis of idiopathic psychopathy (anethopathy). *Psychoanalysis Review*, **34**, 102–118, 198–222.

Kellner, R. (1978). Drug treatment of personality disorders and delinquents, in *The Psychopath: A Comprehensive Study of Antisocial Disorders and Behaviours* (Ed. W. H. Reid). New York: Brunner/Mazel, pp. 301–330.

Kelly, G. (1955). *The Psychology of Personal Constructs*, Vols 1 and 2. New York: W. W. Norton.

Kligman, D., and Goldberg, D. A. (1975). Temporal lobe epilepsy and aggression. *Journal of Nervous and Mental Disease*, **160**, 324–341.

Lagos, J. M., Perlmutter, K., and Saexinger, H. (1977). Fear of the mentally ill: empirical support for the common man's response. *American Journal of Psychiatry*, **134**, 1134–1137.

Levine, D. (1970). Criminal behavior and mental institutionalization. *Journal of Clinical Psychology*, **26**, 279–284.

Lion, J. R. (1978). Outpatient treatment of psychopaths, in *The Psychopath: A Comprehensive Study of Antisocial Disorders and Behaviors* (Ed. W. H. Reid). New York: Brunner/Mazel, pp. 286–300.

McClintock, F. H. (1963). *Crimes of Violence*, London: Macmillan.

McClintock, F. H. (1980). Criminal careers of sexual offenders: sexual recidivism, criminal justice and politics, in *Sex Offenders in the Criminal Justic System* (Ed. D. J. West). Cambridge: Institute of Criminology (Cropwood Publications), pp. 1–5.

McGurk, B. J. (1978). Personality types among 'normal' homicides. *British Journal of Criminology*, **18**, 146–161.

McGurk, B. J., and McGurk, R. E. (1979). Personality types among prisoners and prison officers. *British Journal of Criminology*, **19**, 31–49.

McKnight, C. K., Mohr, J. W., Quincey, R. E., and Erochko, J. (1966). Mental illness and homicide. *Canadian Psychiatric Association Journal*, **11**, 91–98.

Martinson, R. (1974). What works? Questions and answers about prison reform. *The Public Interest*, **35**, 22–54.

Megargee, E. I. (1966). Under-controlled and over-controlled personality types in extreme antisocial aggression. *Psychological Monographs*, **80**, No. 611.

Megargee, E. I. (1971). The role of inhibition in the assessment and understanding of violence, in *The Control of Aggression and Violence: Cognitive and Physiological Factors* (Ed. J. E. Singer). London: Academic Press, pp. 125–147.

Mesnikoff, A. M., and Lauterbach, C. G. (1976). The association of violent dangerous behaviour with psychiatric disorders: a review of the research literature. *Journal of Psychiatry and Law*, **3**, 415–445.

Molof, M. J. (1967). Differences between assaultive and non-assaultive juvenile offenders in the California Youth Authority. *California Department of Youth Authority, Division of Research Report*, No. 41.

Mowat, R. R. (1966). *Morbid Jealousy and Murder*. London: Tavistock.

Mulvihill, D. J., Tumin, M. M., and Curtis, L. A. (1969). *Crimes of Violence: A Staff Report to the National Commission on the Causes and Prevention of Violence*, Vols 11, 12, and 13. Washington D.C.: US Government Printing Office.

Nasby, W., Hayden, B., and De Paulo, B. M. (1980). Attributional bias among aggressive boys to interpret unambiguous social stimuli as displays of hostility. *Journal of Abnormal Psychology*, **89**, 459–468.

Nickel, T. W. (1974). The attribution of intention as a critical factor in the relation between frustration and aggression. *Journal of Personality*, **42**, 482–492.

Novaco, R. W. (1975). *Anger Control: The Development and Evaluation of an Experimental Treatment*. Lexington, Mass.: D. C. Heath.

Novaco, R. W. (1976*a*). The functions and regulation of the arousal of anger. *American Journal of Psychiatry*, **133**, 1124–1128.

Novaco, R. W. (1976*b*). Treatment of chronic anger through cognitive and relaxation controls. *Journal of Consulting and Clinical Psychology*, **44**, 681.

Novaco, R. W. (1977*a*). Stress inoculation: a cognitive therapy for anger and its application to a case of depression. *Journal of Consulting and Clinical Psychology*, **45**, 600–608.

Novaco, R. W. (1977*b*). A stress inoculation approach to anger management in the training of law enforcement officers. *American Journal of Community Psychology*, **5**, 327–346.

Novaco, R. W. (1978). Anger and coping with stress, in *Cognitive Behaviour Therapy* (Eds J. P. Foreyt and D. P. Rathjen). New York: Plenum, pp. 135–174.

Orr, J. H. (1978). The imprisonment of mentally disordered offenders. *British Journal of Psychiatry*, **133**, 194–199.

Pichot, P. (1978). Psychopathic behaviour: a historical overview, in *Psychopathic Behaviour: Approaches to Research* (Eds R. D. Hare and D. Schalling). Chichester: John Wiley, pp. 55–70.

Pinel, P. (1806). *A Treatise on Sanity*. Sheffield.

Planansky, K., and Johnston, R. (1977). Homicidal aggression in schizophrenic men. *Acta Psychiatrica Scandinavica*, **55**, 65–73.

Prichard, J. C. (1835). *Treatise on Insanity and Other Disorders Affecting the Mind.* London: Sherwood, Gilbert and Piper.

Prins, H. (1980). *Offenders, Deviants or Patients? An Introduction to the Study of Socio-forensic Problems.* London: Tavistock.

Quanty, M. B. (1976). Aggression catharsis: experimental investigations and implications, in *Perspectives on Aggression* (Eds R. G. Geen and E. C. O'Neal). London: Academic Press, pp. 99–132.

Quinsey, U. L. (1975). Psychiatric staff conferences of dangerous mentally disordered offenders. *Canadian Journal of Behavioural Science*, **7**, 60–69.

Rabkin, J. G. (1979). Criminal behavior of discharged mental patients: a critical appraisal of the research. *Psychological Bulletin*, **86**, 1–27.

Rada, R. T. (Ed.) (1978). *Clinical Aspects of the Rapist.* New York: Grune and Stratton.

Rappeport, J., and Lassen, G. (1965). Dangerousness—arrest rate comparisons of discharged patients and the general population. *American Journal of Psychiatry*, **71**, 776–783.

Rappeport, J., and Lassen, G. (1966). The dangerousness of female patients: a comparison of the arrest rate of discharged psychiatric patients and the general population. *American Journal of Psychiatry*, **123**, 413–419.

Rappeport, J., and Lassen, G. (1967). Dangerousness—arrest rate comparisons of discharged patients and the general population, in *Evaluation of the Dangerousness of the Mentally Ill* (Ed. J. R. Rappeport). Springfield, Ill.: Charles C. Thomas, pp. 97–105.

Rappeport, J. R., Lassen, G., and Hay, N. B. (1967). A review of the literature on the dangerousness of the mentally ill, in *Evaluation of the Dangerousness of the Mentally Ill* (Ed. J. R. Rappeport). Springfield, Ill.: Charles C. Thomas, pp. 72–80.

Reid, W. H. (Ed.) (1978). *The Psychopath: A Comprehensive Study of Antisocial Disorders and Behaviours.* New York: Brunner/Mazel.

Robins, L. (1966). *Deviant Children Grow Up: A Sociological and Psychiatric Study of Sociopathic Personality*. Baltimore: Williams and Wilkins.

Robins, L. N. (1978). Aetiological implications in studies of childhood histories relating to antisocial personality, in *Psychopathic Behavior: Approaches to Research* (Eds R. D. Hare and D. Schalling). Chichester: John Wiley, pp. 255–272.

Rotenberg, M. (1978). Psychopathy and differential insensitivity, in *Psychopathic Behavior: Approaches to Research* (Eds R. D. Hare and D. Schalling). Chichester: John Wiley, pp. 187–196.

Rutter, M. Yule, W., and Whitmore, K. (1970). *Education, Health and Behaviour.* London: Longmans.

Sarbin, T. R., and Mancuso, J. C. (1980). *Schizophrenia: Medical Diagnosis or Moral Verdict*? New York: Pergamon.

Schalling, D. (1975). Psychopathy and the psychophysiology of socialization. Paper presented to NATO Advanced Study Institute on Psychopathic Behaviour, Les Arcs, France, September 1975.

Scott, P. D. (1964). Approved school success rates. *British Journal of Criminology*, **4**, 525–556.

Smith, R. J. (1978). *The Psychopath in Society*. London: Academic Press.
Sosowsky, L. (1978). Crime and violence amongst mental patients reconsidered in view of the new legal relationship between the State and the mentally ill. *American Journal of Psychiatry*, **135**, 33–42.
Spielberger, C. D., Kling, J. K., and O'Hagan, S. E. J. (1978). Dimensions of psychopathic personality: antisocial behaviour and anxiety, in *Psychopathic Behavior: Approaches to Research* (Eds R. D. Hare and D. Schalling). Chichester: John Wiley, pp. 47–54.
Steadman, H. J., and Cocozza, J. (1978). Selective reporting and the public's misconceptions of the criminally insane. *Public Opinion Quarterly*, **4**, 523–533.
Suedfield, P., and Landon, P. B. (1978). Approaches to treatment, in *Psychopathic Behavior: Approaches to Research* (Eds R. D. Hare and D. Schalling). Chichester: John Wiley, pp. 347–376.
Sutker, P. B., Archer, R. P., and Kilpatrick, D. G. (1981). Sociopathy and antisocial behavior: theory and treatment, in *Handbook of Clinical Behavior Therapy* (Eds S. M. Turner, K. S. Calhoun and H. E. Adams). New York: John Wiley, pp. 665–712.
Swanson, D. W. (1968). Adult sexual abuse of children: the man and circumstances. *Diseases of the Nervous System*, **29**, 677–683.
Szasz, T. S. (1968). *Law, Liberty and Psychiatry*. New York: Collier Books.
Taylor, P. (1982). Schizophrenia and violence, in *Abnormal Offenders and the Criminal Justice System* (Eds J. Gunn and D. P. Farrington). Chichester: John Wiley, pp. 269–284.
Tennent, G., Parker, E., McGrath, P., and Street, D. (1980). Male admissions to the English Special Hospitals. *British Journal of Psychiatry*, **136**, 181–190.
Topp, D. O. (1979). Suicide in prison. *British Journal of Psychiatry*, **134**, 24–27.
Treves-Brown, C. (1977). Who is the psychopath? *Medicine, Science and the Law*, **17**, 56–63.
Walker, M. J., and Brodsky, S. L. (Eds) (1976). *Sexual Assault: The Victim and the Rapist. London: Lexington.*
Walker, N., and McCabe, S. (1973). Crime and Insanity in England, Vols I and II. Edinburgh: Edinburgh University Press.
West, D. J. (1965). *Murder Followed by Suicide*. London: Heinemann.
West, D. J. (1968). A note on murders in Manhattan. *Medicine, Science and the Law*, **8**, 249–255.
West, D. J. (1980). The clinical approach to criminology. *Psychological Medicine*, **10**, 619–631.
West, D. J., and Farrington, D. P. (1973). *Who Becomes Delinquent*? London: Heinemann.
West, D. J., and Farrington, D. P. (1977). *The Delinquent Way of Life*. London: Heinemann.
West, D. J., Roy, C., and Nichols, F. (1978). *Understanding Sexual Attacks*. London: Heinemann.
Widom, C. S. (1978). An empirical classification of female offenders. *Criminal Justice and Behavior*, **5**, 35–52.
Williams, D. (1969). Neural factors related to habitual aggression. *Brain*, **92**, 503–520.
Williams, J. B. W. (ed) (1980). *Diagnostic and Statistical Manual of Mental Disorders*, 3rd edn. Washington: American Psychiatric Association.
Woodman, D., and Hinton, J. W. (1978). Catecholamine balance during stress anticipation: an abnormality in maximum security hospital patients. *Journal of Psychosomatic Research*, **22**, 477–483.
Woodman, D. D., Hinton, J. W., and O'Neill, M. T. (1978). Plasma catecholamines, stress and aggression in maximum security patients. *Biological Psychology*, **6**, 147–154.

Wootton, B. (1959). *Social Science and Social Pathology.* London: Allen and Unwin.
Wootton, B. (1980). Psychiatry, ethics and the criminal law. *British Journal of Psychiatry*, **136**, 525–532.
Wright, R. (1980). Rape and physical violence, in *Sex Offenders in the Criminal Justice System* (Ed. D. J. West). Cambridge: Institute of Criminology (Cropwood Publications), pp. 100–113.
Zillman, D. (1979). *Hostility and Aggression.* Hillsdale, N. J.: Lawrence Erlbaum.
Zitrin, A., Hardasty, A. S., and Burdock, E. I. (1976). Crime and violence among mental patients. *American Journal of Psychiatry*, **133**, 142–149.

Developments in the Study of Criminal Behaviour. Volume 2: Violence
Edited by Philip Feldman

8

'Dangerousness'—ascription or description?

JILL PEAY

> 'There is no foreseeable time when there will not be some people from whom the rest of us will want to feel protected, and to this extend all other sentencing aims are overshadowed by a quite unambiguous one, to achieve as effectively as possible the protection of innocent victims from serious physical assault and harm. Too much emphasis on the justice of imprisonment is not appropriate where there is a high risk that another offence will result in serious injury or death, *so long, that is, as it can be accurately decided who should be regarded as genuinely dangerous and who not.*'
>
> Brody and Tarling (1980, p. 2; italics added)

Introduction

The recent publicity surrounding a series of bizarre murders in the north of England and the fear engendered in the local community are illustrative of a prevalent misconception that danger to the public can be equated largely with unpredictable acts of personal violence perpetrated by one individual upon another. The extent of the relief experienced when a man, identified in the press as 'the Yorkshire Ripper', was charged with one of the murders, further reflects confidence in the belief that the public's safety can be assured through measures directed at specific individuals.

This narrow perspective, ignoring as it does other forms of threat—see, for example, the article by Monahan *et al.* (1979) advocating research into the effects of corporate violence—becomes even more specific with reference to the types of interpersonal violence by which society feels peculiarly threatened. In 1979, 136 individuals (Home Office, 1980) were found guilty of murder; in contrast 186 individuals were found guilty of causing death by reckless driving. However, the response to these acts with comparable outcomes varied: the former group attracted mandatory sentences of life imprisonment; of the latter group only 29.5% were awarded sentences of immediate imprisonment. It is also ironic that, despite the death of 6831 people on the roads in the previous year (Central Statistical Office, 1981), some forms of behaviour which constitute an obvious threat are not only tolerated, but actively encouraged in certain social situations, e.g. 'beating the breathalyser'. (It should also be noted that, of the 502 individuals found guilty of 'driving or in charge of a motor vehicle while unfit through drink or drugs', only 8.5% were sentenced to immediate imprisonment. The fact that reconvictions for violent offences are rarer than for traffic offences further adds weight to the argument that specific kinds of behaviour receive discriminatory sentences.)

This chapter will review the development of the concept of dangerousness and assess its current importance for both criminal justice systems and civil commitment procedures. The implications of the concept for those groups against whom it is specifically invoked, namely mentally abnormal and normal offenders and the mentally disordered non-offender, will also be outlined. Attention will be directed to the influence that assessments of dangerousness have on decisions to intervene in individuals' lives, primarily in the form of detention on either a fixed or an indeterminate basis, and will focus on both the selection of the form of intervention and its duration. Finally, the chapter will review the two major justifications for intervention on the basis of perceived dangerousness—restraint and treatment—and, if the concept is to continue to form a basis for decisions concerning individual liberty, to make suggestions for a more effective and just usage.

'Dangerousness', the law and the mentally disordered

In 1972 Rubin noted that 50 000 people are preventively detained each year in the USA, having committed no criminal act, on the basis that they are dangerous to themselves or others and are in need of treatment. This figure illustrates an acceptance of the imposition of involuntary confinement on the mentally disordered, an acceptance which is believed to have its basis in Roman law. Thus, 'guards or keepers are appointed for madmen, not only to look that they do not do mischief to themselves, but also that they be not destructive to others'. However, it is possible that this assumption of a relationship between mental disorder and dangerousness is based on a misconception. This misconception, as Rubin (1972, p. 398) notes, may be encouraged by

> 'certain mental disorders being characterized by some kind of confused, bizarre, agitated, threatening, frightened, panicked, paranoid or impulsive behaviour. That and the view that impulse (i.e. ideation) and action are interchangeable support the belief that all mental disorder must of necessity lead to inappropriate, anti-social or dangerous actions'.

Hence, the beginnings of an explanation for the fear that is often associated with the mentally disordered.

Whatever the underlying causes and veracity of the relationship are, it is apparent that the concept of dangerousness and its corollary, the ability to identify potentially dangerous individuals, have acquired explicit recognition in mental health legislation. The first Act in the UK to permit the indefinite confinement of 'furiously mad and dangerous lunatics' was passed in 1743. A lay authority continued to form the basis for initial detention in the 1890 Lunacy Act, although it is interesting that the onus for the renewal of detention became the prerogative of the medical profession. Under the terms of the 1890 Act, a patient would be discharged automatically after a specified period unless a doctor issued a barring certificate stating that the patient was 'dangerous and unfit to be at large'. Thus, not only did the medical profession assert their control over the treatment of insanity during the nineteenth century, but they were also ascribed expertise in the identification and prediction of dangerousness. The striking similarity of the phraseology in the 1890 Act with the provisions included in existing mental health legislation (Mental Health Act 1959, Sections 43(2) and 44(2)) should also be noted.

Detailed analyses of the 1959 Act and its operation have been undertaken elsewhere (Gostin, 1975, 1977). However, the specific provisions relating to the concept of dangerousness will be reviewed, as an illustration of its pre-eminence in decisions concerning the detention of mentally disordered individuals.

First, the criteria for compulsory admission for treatment include the provision that detention be 'necessary in the interests of the patient's health or safety or for the protection of other persons' (Section 26(2)(b)); similar criteria apply to the renewal of detention (Section 43(3)). For certain categories of patient prolonged detention can only be justified on the stricter criterion that the patient's responsible medical officer believes that the patient, if released, 'would be likely to act in a manner dangerous to other persons or to himself' (e.g. Sections 33(2) and 48(2)). This stricter criterion applies to patients over the age of 25 years who are diagnosed as suffering from either psychopathic disorder or subnormality and to any civilly committed patient whose nearest relative wishes them discharged from the order against the wishes of the patient's responsible medical officer. Approximately 20 000 compulsory admissions to mental hospitals occur annually (DHSS and Office of Population Census, 1976).

Further compulsory admissions take place under Part V of the 1959 Act for those who have been involved in criminal proceedings. In 1979 (Home Office, 1980), 906 individuals were compulsorily admitted and of these 25% had restrictions attached to their discharge, normally under Section 65 of the Mental Health Act. Such a restriction is applied to patients who are considered to be so dangerous that the power to discharge them is removed from their responsible medical officer and vested solely with the Home Secretary because it is thought 'necessary for the protection of the public so to do' (Section 65(1)). Although the 1959 Act was largely based on the recommendations of the Royal Commission, who clearly stated their preference for such restrictions only to follow the commission of a serious offence, the Act actually permits such an order to be made following conviction for *any* offence punishable on summary conviction with imprisonment (other than for an offence where the sentence is fixed by law). Thus, a mentally disordered individual may be confined indefinitely on the basis of his predicted dangerousness, even though that individual may never have committed a dangerous act. Abuses of this provision have been well documented (Gostin, 1975; Gostin and Rassaby, 1980); furthermore, the Crown Court has been criticized for imposing unwarranted restriction orders (*R. v. Gardiner*, 1967). It should also be noted that admission to a Special Hospital (formerly hospitals for the criminally insane, which provide 'treatment' under conditions of special security) is governed by criteria in Section 4 of the National Health Service Act 1977, which permit the confinement of individuals with 'dangerous, violent or criminal *propensities*'. Television documentaries (BBC Television, 1981) concerning Special Hospitals have highlighted the plight of some of the individuals detained in these institutions for inordinately long periods on the basis of questionable evidence about their potential dangerousness.

In the USA a trend has been noted (Fagin, 1976) towards making 'dangerousness to self or others' the *only* grounds for involuntary commitment; in 1974 38 out of 45 jurisdictions restricted emergency commitment to individuals with this requirement and 24 jurisdictions further specified that the threat of harm be immediate (Harvard Law Review, 1974). Similar proposals have been made in the UK; for example, MIND's recommendations on the Mental Health Act (see Gostin, 1975, p. 33) included the proposal that admission under Section 26 should be restricted to the criterion of 'dangerousness to self or others or to grave disablement' (DHSS *et al.*, 1978, para. 2.41).

As Pfohl (1979) has pointed out, such reforms may well be related to the current concern for the rights of the involuntarily institutionalized, necessitating the identification of the truly dangerous in order to facilitate the depopulation of mental hospitals and prisons of those not requiring such secure confinement. However, the law has, in general, acquiesced in the large scale involuntary confinement of the mentally disordered for preventive and therapeutic purposes. As will become evident, such trends as can be identified in mental health legislation may serve to bolster the dubious association between mental disorder and dangerousness.

The offender, 'dangerousness' and the law

Although intervention in the lives of individuals on the basis of who they are and what they might do is an accepted approach in mental health legislation, the traditional approach in the criminal law has been that of intervention justified on the basis of an individual's past actions. Thus, the confinement on an indefinite basis of mentally normal offenders who are perceived as dangerous is legislatively more problematic. Although the concept is pervasive in Western criminal law with Classical, Oriental and Moslem law also being heavily reliant on notions of dangerousness (Ancel, 1965), it is rare for the law specifically to embody the concept of 'dangerousness'. Attempts to give the concept legislative recognition in the USA and Canada have been reviewed by Sleffel (1977) and Greenland (1976), respectively. It is more common, however, for the special problems created by the 'dangerous' offender to be solved through the differential application of existing legislative mechanisms—with some of these processes being primarily covert in operation.

Foucault (1978) has traced the development during the nineteenth century of the tendency to focus attention on the criminal rather than on the crime. He suggests that this resulted from attempts to explain a series of murders which could be accounted for by neither insanity nor rational motives. Initially such behaviour, termed 'homicidal monomania' was believed to be a special kind of insanity manifesting itself only in outrageous crimes and remaining otherwise invisible—except, of course, to the expert eye (the parallels with both 'dangerousness' *per se* and psychopathic disorders are striking). Since these crimes were apparently motiveless, punishment was considered inappropriate. However, the risk that such personalities were felt to pose to society justified intervention on preventive and reductive bases. Foucault termed this the 'psychiatrization of criminal danger' and noted that the dangerous individual increasingly, and in an ever broadening sense, became the principal target for punitive intervention:

> 'In the course of the past century, penal law did not evolve from an ethic of freedom to a science of psychic determinism; rather it enlarged, organized and codified the suspicion and the locating of dangerous individuals, from the rare and monstrous figure of the monomaniac to the common everyday figure of the degenerate, of the pervert, of the constitutionally unbalanced, of the immature etc.' (Foucault, 1978, p. 19).

Bottoms (1977) also parallels the development of the concept of dangerousness and the use of preventive confinement with the rise of positivism, a school of criminal jurisprudence geared primarily to such practical aims as the elimination of antisocial conduct. Positivism's concept of dangerousness is forward looking and 'based on a clear faith in the success of scientific prediction of the future of dangerous individuals, who must then be treated or, if untreatable, confined' (Bottoms, 1977, p. 75).

Bottoms believes there to be a renaissance of interest in this approach, particularly with regard to the mentally abnormal offender and habitual offenders. He cites the recommendations of both the Scottish Council on Crime (1975) and the Butler committee (DHSS and Home Office, 1975) for some new form of indeterminate sentence in support of his argument. Similarly, the report of the Floud committee (Floud and Young, 1981) advocates the introduction of a special protective sentence for the 'dangerous' offender, but *only* within the context of a substantial reduction in the length of sentences of imprisonment for ordinary offenders.

The trend in the USA is somewhat different. There, the prominence of the therapeutic approach in criminology, with its implicit suggestion that criminals—and in particular violent offenders—must have some form of 'illness' and be amenable to cure, has been challenged. The growth of the justice model in sentencing (American Friends Service Committee, 1971; von Hirsch, 1976: Singer, 1979), with its basic premise that punishment should be allocated in proportion to the seriousness of the offence committed ('commensurate deserts'), returns the focus of attention from the criminal primarily to the crime. Certainly, the stream of publications under the Ohio Dangerous Offenders Project (e.g. Sleffel, 1977; Van Dine *et al.*, 1979), the movement to abolish parole, and the guidelines approach in sentencing (Wilkins *et al.*, 1976) all seem to favour a return to an ostensibly utilitarian view of the value of imprisonment and a move away from the use of indeterminate confinement. Although, as Monahan and Ruggiero (1980) have noted, defining harm and culpability (the components of 'seriousness') can become an arena for expert assessment, this need not necessarily be so. It is possible for the assumed importance of 'mental elements' in crime to be reduced, through the mechanism of directing attention to more observable events, thereby resulting in a demystification of the whole process (Blackman, 1980).

There is another trend, termed 'bifurcation' (Bottoms, 1977), associated with both the current crisis of overcrowding in prisons in the UK and with the decline of the rehabilitative ideal. This trend, which Bottoms believes is emerging in sentencing practices, reflects a desire to limit long terms of imprisonment to the truly dangerous, whilst favouring the use of non-custodial or short terms of imprisonment for petty offenders (Home Office, 1977). Although there is political recognition of this policy (Lord Chancellor, 1976; Whitelaw, 1981), the trend has apparently not yet been implemented in a statistically observable manner and remains at the level of 'political rhetoric' (Vagg, 1981). It is still possible that such exhortations may come to inform the actions of sentencers when dealing with potentially dangerous offenders, and, as such, the 'trend' is important. It should also be stressed that the Advisory Council on the Penal System (Home Office, 1978) has already advocated the introduction of a two-tier sentencing structure, embodying lower maximum penalties for 'ordinary' offenders and exceptional sentences, of any length, specifically for the protection of the public.

The approaches adopted by the criminal justice system for dealing with potentially dangerous offenders can be categorized in two ways: special measures directed at specific groups and the use of existing procedures in novel ways. Both approaches have disadvantages; their utility should be assessed in the context of the assertion that 'there was in fact no evidence to show that determinate sentencing had actually resulted in serious harm which could have been prevented by the delayed release of certain offenders' (Floud and Young, 1981, p. 108).

First, special legislation. The use of preventive detention, introduced in the UK in the Criminal Justice Act 1948, was one such special measure designed to cope with habitual (dangerous) offenders. Its abolition in the Criminal Justice Act 1967 reflects the difficulties of framing legislation precisely enough to ensure that it is applied only to those for whom it is intended. Preventive detention was, in practice, used by the courts to deal with habitual petty criminals, whose offences did not justify long confinement. The courts had not experienced problems confining serious offenders for long periods, since these offences invariably permitted the use of high maximum penalties. (It is interesting that the measure which replaced preventive detention in the 1967 Act, the extended sentence, was designed specifically for the habitual petty criminal whose offences did not merit long confinement. These sentences have been used rarely (Cross, 1975).)

Another problem which special legislation encounters is that of individuals being diverted away from such protective measures during prosecution. Sleffel (1977) reports that habitual criminal laws exist in 40 jurisdictions in the USA, generally permitting the imposition of a long sentence (or even a mandatory life sentence) for the third conviction for the same felony—commonly known as the 'three times loser' state. In practice, however, individuals, through charge and plea bargaining, often avoid the imposition of special legislative measures. Since such procedures may pressurize a defendant into pleading guilty to a lesser charge in preference to standing trial (Baldwin and McConville, 1977), the quality of justice may be lessened. The value of any legislation which has this result must be seriously questioned.

Special legislation also demands the introduction of special measures to ensure that the rights of the person against whom such legislation is invoked are protected; for example, Canada's legislation directed against 'dangerous offenders' requires regular review by the National Parole Board of individuals detained under its auspices (Manning, 1980). The problems associated with this form of review will be discussed in detail later; at this stage it should simply be noted that, as applied by the decision-makers, the criteria associated with a decision to release an individual from special forms of confinement are often stricter than the criteria applied to the initial decision to confine.

The alternative approach to special legislation, and that primarily adopted in the UK, is to use existing procedures in novel ways. For those offenders who are considered potentially dangerous, but who are not eligible for either life sentences or detention under the Mental Health Act, release is inevitable at the end of a determinate sentence. Sentences can only be 'prolonged' through the loss of normal remission or the failure to be granted parole. As Thomas (1979) illustrates, the length of a determinate sentence must be proportional to the gravity of the offence committed and must not exceed the appropriate bracket for that class of offence (*R. v. Coombes*, 1972). However, the Court of Appeal has established that considerations of an offender's 'dangerousness' may permit the sentencer to ignore mitigating factors (*R. v. Wren*, 1974) and to take likely remission into account when fixing the length of the sentence. Thus, sentences may be lengthened covertly for potentially dangerous offenders.

As has been explored previously, offenders who are mentally disordered within the terms of the 1959 Act can be confined indefinitely in hospital. It is possible that, where offenders are perceived as dangerous, these criteria are applied more liberally with a view to ensuring that the offender receives treatment under secure and prolonged confinement. Similarly, offenders who become mentally disordered whilst in prison may be transferred to hospital (Section 72, Mental Health Act 1959) and their release may then become subject to restrictions (Section 74) if they are considered dangerous. It has also been alleged (Gostin, 1978) that these provisions permit the removal from prison of those offenders nearing their release dates who are perceived as dangerous or disruptive, thereby circumventing the assumed limitations of the penal system.

Finally, there is the sentence of life imprisonment. This sentence was not introduced as a special measure for dangerous offenders. It is the mandatory sentence for convicted murderers and a statutory maximum for a few serious crimes (e.g. manslaughter, rape, arson, wounding with intent). Its indeterminacy means that the sentence can be used either compassionately (most people receiving life sentences are domestic murderers, (see Sapsford and Banks (1979)) and punitively. Its distinctive use as a preventive sentence resulted from judicial initiative (Cross, 1975) following the enactment of provisions which made an offender's release subject to recommendations from a number of sources (Home Secretary, Parole Board, Lord Chief Justice and the sentencing judge). The life sentence is reserved for offenders with some degree of mental instability who have committed offences of substantial gravity and who are thought likely to commit further similar offences, if prematurely released.

Brody and Tarling (1980), following their study of dangerous offenders, concluded that the judiciary seemed well able to award ostensibly dangerous offenders lengthy terms of detention on the basis of the actions which they had committed. Similarly, Sapsford and Banks (1979) suggest that the flexibility that the existing system provides appears to work reasonably successfully, since those offenders receiving life sentences for the murder of women and children, and who have histories of violence, sexual assault or mental instability, serve proportionately much longer sentences than domestic murderers, for whom the sentence is compassionately applied. However, there has been criticism of the discretionary use of the life sentence as a protective device (Floud and Young, 1981) on the basis that the criteria justifying its imposition have never been clearly explained. Although Thomas (1979) makes it clear that a *fixed* term is appropriate where the risk of further offences is one which the public ought to bear, it remains possible that the recent increase in the use of the life sentence for non-homicidal offences derives from a widening judicial application of the sentence, facilitated by a lack of legal prescription.

In contrast, the Butler committee (DHSS and Home Office, 1975) did not feel that the existing system provided *sufficient* protection for society from dangerous offenders. Although the report did recognize that 'there is no way which would be acceptable in a civilised society by which the public can be absolutely assured that no one released from an institution will ever commit a violent offence subsequently'—(DHSS and Home Office, 1975, para 4.3). The committee proposed a new form of indeterminate sentence, the reviewable sentence, to compensate for what they felt were the inadequacies of the existing system with respect to dangerous offenders. Release from detention for those individuals given the new form of sentence was to be governed solely by considerations of 'dangerousness', unlike the life sentence which they believed was influenced by retributive and deterrent considerations. They suggested that the reviewable sentence should be applicable not only to those offences currently open for life sentences but also to some other offences (DHSS and Home Office, 1975, Schedule B in Appendix A) provided that the individual had previously been convicted of a life-carrying offence. The proposal which has the most worrying implications is that contained in paragraph 4.41: 'It is consistent with our aim that not only the scheduled offences themselves but also attempts, and incitements to commit them, and threats to commit them where they are made an offence by statute, should attract a reviewable sentence'. A cursory glance at the suicide literature (Beck *et al.*, 1974) would have indicated that motives and aims may often be at variance with those expressed; indeterminate confinement on the basis of such criteria appear indefensible.

Unfortunately, this approach is common to other reports dealing with potentially dangerous offenders. The Advisory Council on the Penal System (Home Office, 1978) advocated the introduction of a new sentence—the exceptional sentence—as a special sanction designed for the protection of the public and potential victims:

> 'An offence which is very likely to cause such harm, even though by good fortune it has not done so in the present instance, should be regarded in the same light as an offence which has. So should an attempt, a threat or a conspiracy to do serious harm' (Home Office, 1978, para. 198).

Similarly, the Floud committee recommended that individuals should be eligible for protective sentences if they had 'done, attempted, risked, threatened or conspired to do grave harm' (Floud and Young, 1981, p. 155).

It should be stressed that the bodies recommending the introduction of special sentences for 'dangerous' offenders share a common desire to ensure that these measures are not abused. However, the special safeguards they suggest—usually some form of quasi-judicial review—have a number of drawbacks which have been highlighted by research by the present author (Peay, 1981). This research concerned the operation of the Mental Health Review Tribunal system. These tribunals constitute an independent body which review the necessity for the continued compulsory detention of patients in hospital under the terms of the Mental Health Act 1959. The tribunals apply the concept of potential dangerousness to their decisions (Mental Health Act 1959, Section 123); the predicted level of dangerousness varies according to the type of application, with some cases demanding a high degree of confidence in the prediction of dangerousness. Thus, the nature of their decisions is comparable to that of those which would be required of any body reviewing protective sentences; the problems illustrated by the research are likely to bedevil their operation also.

First, the Floud committee stresses that 'release on licence from a protective sentence... is not a privilege to be earned but a right to be claimed' (Floud and Young, 1981, p. 132) and the Scottish Council on Crime similarly recommend that detention should only be permissible beyond a 2 year period if 'a positive case were established that such continuation is necessary for the protection of the public' (Scottish Council on Crime, 1975, para. 134). Continued detention under the terms of the 1959 Act is currently legally permissible if the detaining authority makes out a positive case for such detention. However, the criteria that tribunal members apply in practice reflect their desire to ensure that only individuals whom they consider to be no threat are discharged (Peay, 1981). As such, members were attempting to identify the non-dangerous rather than potentially dangerous individuals. Of the members taking part in the research, 62% of them agreed with the statement that 'patients who have committed dangerous acts should be released from secure conditions only when it is *absolutely certain* that they no longer represent a danger'. This response should be contrasted with the approach adopted in the report of the Butler committee (see above).

Secondly, the research indicated that members' definitions of behaviour that constituted a threat to the public did not appear to be shared by the public, who were prepared to tolerate bizarre forms of behaviour that tribunal members believed were an indication of potential dangerousness.

Finally, and this is an issue that will be discussed further, there was even little agreement amongst these experts as to the kinds of behaviour that constituted evidence of potential dangerousness. Given an identical case to assess (members were shown a film of a hypothetical tribunal) the patient was variously described, with the range being reflected by the following psychiatric opinions: the patient was in one case described as 'placid and ineffectual' and in a second opinion as 'prime Park Lane material' (i.e. in need of Special Hospital care). This level of disagreement indicates the injustice and inefficacy of such safeguards and makes questionable the acceptability of any special measures for 'dangerous' individuals. In fact, Radzinowicz and Hood (1978), following their discussion of the 'plasticity' of the concept of dangerousness, conclude with reference to the proposals of the Advisory Council: 'we believe that the concept of "dangerousness" is so insidious that it should never be introduced in penal legislation, let alone under such a broad canopy' (Radzinowicz and Hood, 1978, p. 722).

Definitions of 'dangerousness'

One explanation for the less than satisfactory application of the concept of dangerousness concerns the lack of an adequate definition of both the concept and the nature of the behaviour that justifies its employment in individual cases.

Presumably, a strict definition of 'dangerousness' would prevent the current extension of special measures to the non-dangerous.

The first problem hampering the attainment of an acceptable definition concerns the tendency, certainly reflected in the tenor of the discussion so far, to assume that dangerousness is some form of personality trait that is both stable and readily identifiable. As Walker (1978) points out, dangerousness is not an objective quality like obesity or brown eyes, rather it is an ascribed quality like trustworthiness. Shah (1977) has highlighted the manner in which a 'conceptual short-cut' allows the transition from describing aspects of an individual's behaviour as dangerous to describing that individual as dangerous, Behaviour, however, should rather be viewed as an interaction between individuals and particular physical and social environments. Labelling an individual as dangerous 'may be misleading and also unnecessarily stigmatizing since physically violent or other dangerous acts are usually rather infrequent, occur in specific situational contexts, and may not be representative of the individual's customary behaviour'—(Shah, 1977, p. 105). Indeed, in their recent study of a sample of 811 prisoners Brody and Tarling (1980) noted that 52% of the sample had at some time in their careers been convicted of robbery, violence or sexual offences. It is rare to find an individual's criminal behaviour being consistently of one type; indeed none of Brody and Tarling's sample had records exclusively of violence or robbery. They concurred with the view that 'the dangerous individual' is something of an illusion. Tanay (1976, p. 787) has cogently summarized: 'Dangerous is an adjective describing a person as harmful from a classifer's frame of reference, not a clinical state in itself . . . . Danger is an appraisal of a prospective relationship between two or more entities. It is not an inherent property of an entity itself.'

It is apparent that the approach adopted by legislation does not share this understanding of 'dangerousness'. The logic which underpins the tendency to give Section 65 restriction orders without limit of time (in 1979, of 102 restriction orders, 98 were without time limits—see Home Office (1980)) is derived from the pronouncement of Lord Chief Justice Parker in *R. v. Gardiner* (1967) that restriction orders should be indefinite unless 'doctors are able to assert confidently that recovery will take place within a fixed period'. Thus, an individual made subject to a restriction order will have reinstated all the restrictions associated with a Section 65 order if he ever re-enters hospital—even if as an informal patient. Although Walker (1980) may not object to individuals being described in terms that reflect only aspects of their behaviour, for those labelled as dangerous the law's approach has disturbing consequences.

Not only have there been definitional problems concerning who should be labelled dangerous, but there has also been considerable debate about the nature of the behaviours that are dangerous. One 'solution' to this problem has been that of the Advisory Council on the Penal System—to avoid defining the behaviours at all 'because we felt that an over-specific formula ran the risk of excluding relevant cases by mischance' (Home Office, 1978, p. 207). Others, like the Butler committee (DHSS and Home Office, 1975), which equated dangerousness with 'a propensity to cause serious physical injury or lasting psychological harm' (para. 4.10), have employed further terms (e.g. serious, lasting) which they have failed to define. Similarly, the *Review of the Mental Health Act 1959* (DHSS *et al.*, 1978) redefined dangerousness in terms of 'grave incapacity' and 'a likelihood that the patient will cause serious harm to others' (para. 2.44).

Perhaps the reluctance to come to grips with the issue results from a similar failure in the USA to achieve definitional consensus. Monahan (1975) reviewed the operational definitions of 'dangerousness' and found a considerable disparity. Some definitions limited themselves to injury or death to persons (Rubin, 1972); others included the destruction of property (Mulvihill and Tumin, 1969); some included psychological harm in the form of fear or distress, and in *Overholzer v. Russell* (1960) a federal court equated writing a bad cheque with dangerous behaviour, the rationale being that non-violent acts which may elicit violent responses makes those acts dangerous in themselves: 'There is always the additional possible danger—not to be discounted even if remote—that a non-violent criminal act may expose the perpetrator to violent retaliatory acts by the victim of the crime'.

Megargee (1969) has demonstrated that problems concerning legality and intentionality have further confounded the attainment of an acceptable definition. Focusing on the nature of the act can result in some legally acceptable actions (e.g. injury in the pursuit of sport) being defined as dangerous; ignoring the intention behind the act and focusing primarily on its legality can result in the exclusion of behaviours which would generally be accepted as dangerous, e.g. the activities of such extreme political groups as the National Front or of companies causing some forms of environmental pollution.

Finally, definitions of 'dangerousness' tend to avoid specifying the probability of the occurrence of the behaviour that will justify the application of the label. Shah's (1977) identification of the Rhode Island Mental Health law as including an improved definition of the dangerousness criterion is questionable, since the definition still fails to cope with the problem of probability and includes threats. Shah blames 'a lack of interest, sensitivity and judicial prodding' for the non-emergence of an acceptable definition of dangerousness. In my view the problems are even more intractable.

'Dangerousness' and restraint

Morris (1974) has suggested that our inability to distinguish the dangerous from the non-dangerous and to provide a strict definition of dangerousness that would not be subject to 'criteria stretching' should lead to a rejection of dangerousness as a principle guiding imprisonment. An inadequately defined and inappropriately applied concept will permit the punitively minded to include within its ambit many for whom detention cannot otherwise be justified.

Nevertheless, one of the major publicly supported justifications for imprisonment is the restraint of the activities of individuals from whom the public believes it needs protecting. The assumption presupposes a capacity to identify dangerous individuals and to predict future dangerous acts which Morris (1974) described as 'quite beyond our present technical ability'. The demonstration that the notion of the dangerous individual is something of an illusion and the random quality of dangerous acts would seem to indicate the futility of attempting to predict dangerous behaviour.

A number of other problems are likely to confound accurate prediction. The first of these concerns the very rare occurrence of dangerous behaviour. When an event has such a low base rate, the errors that result from the use of any kind of predictive device with less than 100% accuracy will be predominantly false positives (individuals incorrectly predicted to display the relevant behaviour—in this case dangerous behaviour). In contrast, the low base rate minimizes the occurrence of the other type of error—false negatives (individuals incorrectly identified as non-dangerous). Thus, as Livermore *et al.* (1968) illustrate, prevention of dangerous behaviour through policies of incapacitation will necessitate the restraint of many more non-dangerous than dangerous individuals. Walker (1980) has described these as 'fallacious arithmetic arguments' on the basis that the costs associated with false positive and false negative type errors are not comparable, since society values its safety so highly. Certainly, the possibility that an individual will cause serious harm is a more urgent consideration than the statistical likelihood of his doing so, and the relative weighting of the cost of the two types of error should be debated openly. However, if restraint is to form the primary justification for intervention, then the existing predominance of false positive type errors cannot easily be ignored.

The present limited ability to predict dangerous behaviour has been reviewed extensively (Monahan, 1975, 1976) with false positive rates reported as varying from 54 to 99%. The essence of these empirical findings will be presented here as an illustration of the theoretical problems already outlined.

First, McGrath (1968) reported a recall rate to Broadmoor Special Hospital of 4% out of 293 murderers discharged and 1200 transferred. It might be suggested that despite the fact that little is known about assessing dangerousness beyond intuitive feelings and general statistics that cover certain types of crime, perhaps those in charge of determining discharge are highly competent at assessing dangerousness.

An alternative explanation, that the figures reflect very cautious discharge polices, appears more likely. Although it is difficult to make assessments of the potential dangerousness of individuals who continue to be detained in a secure environment, two opportunities for naturalistic observation that lend support to the latter explanation occurred in the USA: the Baxstrom case and the Menard 17, reviewed respectively by Steadman and Cocozza (1974) and Schwitzgebel (1977). In both cases, court rulings resulted in the discharge from secure confinement of a number of individuals who had been assessed by their psychiatrists as too dangerous to release. Although subject to a number of methodological flaws, follow-up of those discharged indicated that potential dangerousness had been vastly over-predicted.

Brody and Tarling's (1980) study similarly encountered difficulties in their attempt to identify individuals who could legitimately be described as dangerous in the sense that they seemed likely to cause harm again. Despite access to detailed records and staff assessments, of 52 prisoners who had been identified as dangerous, only 13 of them were reconvicted for acts of violence within 5 years of their release; of these offences only nine could be described as dangerous. Of the 648 non-dangerous prisoners, 54 were reconvicted for acts of violence, with nine of these attracting the label of dangerous, i.e. as many as for the 'dangerous' offenders. Thus, if all the dangerous prisoners had been confined for an extra 5 years, only nine dangerous acts would have been prevented whilst 39 individuals would have been needlessly confined. Even though Brody and Tarling recognized that their predictive abilities may have been artificially reduced because of the high percentage of life prisoners who were predicted as dangerous, but who were not released, they still concluded that there was no practical way in which the preventive function of prisons could be generally exploited. They stated that predictions of dangerousness, regardless of what indices were used, were too fallible for incapacitative policies to be based on them.

Attempts to identify the dangerous individual by means of personality tests have been similarly unsuccessful (Wilkins, 1975). An extensive review of the use of psychological tests to predict violent behaviour was undertaken by Megargee (1970). His conclusion that no test could predict violent behaviour in the individual case remains valid.

Incapacitation studies in the USA (Blumstein *et al.*, 1978) appear to have reached similar conclusions to those of Brody and Tarling (1980)—that incapacitation serves neither an important protective nor an important preventive function (Monahan, 1978). Van Dine *et al.* (1979), following their major study, described incapacitation as the 'strategy of failure'. The inability to predict dangerous behaviour with any degree of accuracy will result in incapacitative policies, leading to the need to confine large numbers of non-dangerous individuals at considerable cost in order to have any realistic effect on the incidence of violent behaviour. Cohen (1978) estimated that to achieve a reduction of 10% in the incidence of violent crime in selected states, the prison population would have to be increased by between 8.4 and 57%, with the commonest increase needing to be in the middle of the range. Although Boland (1978) has questioned the accuracy of such figures, on the basis of her belief that a large proportion of offences are committed by offenders who are never caught, this criticism seems less valid with specific reference to violent crime, where clear-up rates are generally high. To Palmer and Salimbene's (1978) conclusion that incapacitation may be a useful tool in reducing crime, but not pre-eminent, could be added the proviso that selective incapacitation for dangerous offenders will continue to be ineffective as a preventive device if, and until, predictive abilities improve.

Apart from the infrequency of occurrence of dangerous behaviour, a number of factors contribute to the current inability to predict accurately (Monahan, 1975). First, there is the problem of lack of corrective feedback. The decision-maker who erroneously predicts dangerousness and, as a result, does not release the individual concerned rarely has the chance to learn about his mistake. Prevention by detention is a self-denying prediction. In contrast, when released individuals have been incorrectly assessed as non-dangerous, the publicity their cases receive is disproportionate. A tendency to err on the side of caution when making release decisions is understandable, but, with the resulting lack of corrective feedback, the accuracy of decisions is unlikely to improve. As Fagin (1976) has stated, 'the unknown mistake of the past becomes the foundation for a confident, but erroneous, prediction of the future'.

It is often asserted that predictive abilities could be improved through an increase in the use of clinical as opposed statistical methods of prediction. Meehl's (1954) extensive analysis of the clinical statistical controversy lent no support to the assumption that the introduction of the human element 'insight' in any way improves predictive abilities. In the light of Pfohl's (1977) transcripts of assessment methods used by psychologists and psychiatrists in a maximum security hospital, the precise nature of the clinical skills being employed might be questioned. Similarly, the rapidity of the decisions made by psychiatrists and other mental health professionals in Bean's (1978) study of emergency commitment procedures raises considerable doubts about their efficacy. Furthermore, Bean (1978) reports that of 58 compulsory admissions to hospital, 31 were made against the rules or spirit of the 1959 Mental Health Act. This may be illustrative of Monahan's assertion that, 'Over prediction . . . may be less a comment on any lack of scientific acumen and more a testimony to the ability of officials to subvert the intent of the law to accomplish what they think is "best" for the patient' (Monahan, 1977, p. 23).

'Dangerousness' and treatment

The second major justification for intervention in the lives of individuals in the form of detention is that of treatment or rehabilitation. The suggestion above that a finding of dangerousness may be no more than a convention to ensure treatment has resulted from unjustifiable assumptions about the nature of both the mentally abnormal offender and the mentally normal offender. Dangerousness and mental disorder are commonly believed to be related; as such, is there any evidence that treatment for mental disorder can reduce the incidence of dangerous behaviour? In addition, is there any support for the alternative assumption that it is possible to treat 'dangerousness' *per se*?

It has been suggested that the relationship between mental disorder and dangerousness may be no more than an illusory correlation (Sweetland, 1972). This apparent correlation persists partially because the processes of selective attention permit evidence to be isolated which supports stereotypic prior expectations as to what constitutes a reliable predictor of dangerousness. The correlation also persists because the individuals to whom the label is applied are relatively powerless to resist its application (Geis and Monahan, 1976). This prevalent misconception has not been dissipated by the historical and continuing isolation of the mentally disordered and a tendency to ascribe mental disorder to those who engage in violent activities. Even amongst mental health professionals (Peay, 1981) a belief in the association between mental disorder and violent crime persists.

There appears, however, to be no empirical evidence that any particular psychiatric diagnosis can be used reliably to identify the potentially dangerous (Diamond, 1975). Indeed, Guze's (1976) study found no significant relationship between any specific mental illness and the propensity to engage in violent crime. The only disorders which he found to be even marginally associated with serious crime were psychopathy, alcoholism and drug dependence—the latter two being questionable psychiatric disorders and the former having been identified as psychiatrically untreatable: 'control is all that medicine has to offer' (DHSS and Home Office, 1975, para. 5.34).

Similarly, Rabkin's (1979) review of the relationship between mental disorder and criminal arrest rate noted that the most reliable predictor of future criminality was evidence of a prior arrest record and not a record of hospitalization. The Home Office study commissioned by the Butler committee found that after release mentally abnormal offenders were no more likely than normal offenders to commit violent or sexual offences. Furthermore, indicators of possible future dangerousness are the same for the abnormal as the normal offender, namely previous convictions and type and severity of the most recent offence and *not* diagnosis or other clinical information. Walker *et al.* (1967) report that even after a third conviction for a violent offence the individual offender was more likely not to be convicted for a further violent offence than convicted. As Gurevich and Bourne (1970, p. 323) point out, 'it is fair to conclude that an individual with a label of mental illness is quite capable of committing any act of violence known to man, but probably does not do so with any greater frequency than his neighbor in the general population'. As such, it seems unlikely that treatment for mental disorder will have any direct effect on the incidence of dangerous behaviour.

The conceptual association has had the effect of involving psychiatrists in judicial determinations of 'dangerousness' and also has resulted in a heavy judicial reliance upon such expert evidence. Steadman (1973) reports a concurrence rate of 87% between psychiatric recommendations and judicial determinations of dangerousness. Similarly, Simon and Cockerham (1977) report that judges were willing to commit individuals to mental hospitals, given evidence of dangerousness, with a lesser degree of certainty than they would apply in other criminal or civil cases. The involvement of the psychiatric profession in the judicial process may be resulting in an unacceptable standard of justice and, as Gunn (1979) stresses, 'justice is justice whether the recipient is bad, mad or both'.

The ability to treat dangerous behaviour *per se* also appears doubtful. Although Kozol *et al.* (1972) claimed that 'dangerousness can be reliably diagnosed and effectively treated', a re-analysis of their data by Evenson and Altman (1975) questions the validity of this claim. As a result of using a battery of techniques and extensive multidisciplinary case work, Kozol *et al.* (1972) reported that the incidence of assaultive behaviour in patients released from the Bridgewater State Hospital against their advice was five times that of those patients released on their advice. However, Evenson and Altman (1975) demonstrated that most of the staff's predictive accuracy came from correctly identifying the larger numbers of patients who were not recidivists. In addition, 65% of the patients released by the courts against staff advice did not subsequently commit serious assaultive acts; as such, the staff's predictive accuracy required the detention of two false positives for every truly dangerous individual detained. Grendon Underwood, Britain's progressive institution for convicted prisoners in need of psychiatric observation or treatment, has similarly had little success in reducing conviction rates (Newton, 1972). The Patuxent Institution in Maryland, employing a medical treatment approach since 1955, has had its 'success' reviewed by Wilkins (1975), who concluded, 'it is possible and even probable that the Patuxent success rate does not exceed those for comparable groups who have served time in ordinary prisons or jails under determinate sentences or who were subject to normal parole procedures' (Wilkins, 1975, p. 42). Thus, there seems currently to exist no available treatment that is even minimally effective in reducing dangerous behaviour in excess of spontaneous remission rates.

The confused conceptualization by therapists and others of 'dangerousness' as a state other than as a description of past events may have contributed to their over-optimistic attempts to treat 'dangerousness'. It is also likely that a secure environment may be incompatible with treatment success and that an offender/patient's compliance with therapy may be less than genuine when his release date is dependent on his co-operation and response to treatment (Gostin, 1976). Martinson's (1974) finding that prisons rarely rehabilitate is not surprising in view of the capacity of such environments to manufacture harmful behaviour. Thus, some weight must be attached to Kittrie's (1971) assertion that 'dangerousness' may be being invoked primarily for covert retributive purposes; calling preventive detention 'treatment' does not alter its nature for those who experience such detention.

Conclusions

Steadman (1973) concluded his article on the inadequacy of the concept and determination of dangerousness in law and psychiatry thus: 'The indications of significant discrepancies among statutes on dangerousness and the literature and research data presented here suggest a serious gap in the theory, data and practice of psychiatry and law.' (Steadman, 1973, p. 424). His conclusions are equally applicable to this chapter. It is apparent that only limited progress has been made towards achieving a better understanding of the concept of dangerousness whilst policy-orientated reports and legislation have continued, without regard, to utilize the concept. The reliance of the law on this concept and advocacy for its wider use have reflected the law's failure to recognize the demonstrated limitations of 'dangerousness'. This failure has resulted in decision-makers finding themselves in the unenviable position of having to make decisions about individual liberty based on a concept that is ill-defined, misunderstood and often inapplicable to the cases with which they are faced. It is understandable that decisions have been made which reflect an apparent abuse of legislative intent.

Whether pertinent legal statutes are capable of being developed is, however, a secondary consideration in comparison with the question, asked by Floud (1978), of whether the concept of dangerousness is either valid or necessary. If the answer to neither of these questions is in the affirmative, then considerable doubt is cast upon the advisability of treading 'this thorny road' (Radzinowicz and Hood, 1981). There is an inherent danger that by pursuing such an elusive concept not only does it acquire spurious respectability, but also that it detracts from efforts to improve on the existing system of decision-making. Thus, although the Floud committee recommended that their protective sentence should only be introduced in the context of changes in the whole sentencing structure, the fact that their deliberations have resulted in a framework for a protective sentence may ultimately have unintended consequences.

Nonetheless, it is worth exploring briefly whether any real progress could be made with the concept of dangerousness. First, our understanding has been hampered by a tendency, possibly attributable to the influence of psychiatric models, to examine the concept within an individual context. The significance of the persistently violent offender has been exaggerated. Dangerous behaviour occurs in a context and results from an interaction between individuals and their social and economic environment. To assume that 'dangerousness' is a permanent feature of an individual is to ignore these situational and contextual factors. As Pfohl (1979*a*, pp. 39–40) indicates, violence suggests a world of meaningful human action: 'To ignore this world is to ignore those who benefit and those who suffer by it, to ignore the experience of inequality and resultant frustration, of sensed repression and resultant agression, of dangerous conditions rather than dangerous people.' Or, as Yoko Ono, subject to the most obvious form of individually based dangerous behaviour, has stated rather more succinctly: 'Guilt is not in the one who pulls the trigger, but in each of us who allows it' (Ono, 1981). If these environmental factors are ultimately demonstrated to have explanatory pre-eminence, it is conceivable that those 'dangerous individuals' incapacitated by current and proposed sentencing policies will merely be replaced by other 'dangerous individuals', whose actions are governed by external conditions and do not result from some defect of personality peculiar to those individuals against whom incapacitative policies are directed.

Individualizing dangerousness will also have the effect of focusing society's attention and resultant action on only certain types of dangerous behaviour—which in turn bolsters individualized views of dangerous behaviour. Such an approach may in addition make society less sensitive to dangerous practices employed by governments and industrial concerns.

However, since the concept of the dangerous individual is likely to remain a continuing cause for concern and an impetus to legislation, it is also important that the problem of the dangerous individual should not be ignored. As Monahan (1975, p. 28) has pointed out, an individual 'has as much right to remain unmurdered, unmugged and unraped as he or she does to avoid unjust incarceration as a falsely positive case of dangerousness'. More effective strategies for coping with dangerous behaviour might be developed as a result of an improved understanding of dangerous behaviour in terms of its situational determinants, and through policies aimed at modifying *those* determinants.

Studies of the factors which trigger or influence violent behaviour, supplemented by studies of situations where dangerous behaviour might be expected to occur, but does not, might assist in the development of policies which reduce the likelihood of occurrence of dangerous behaviour. Such violence de-escalation techniques are particularly important in situations in which dangerous behaviour may occur partially because of the nature of the response it elicits, e.g. the attention-seeking nature of many outbursts within institutions for the mentally disordered. It is unfortunate that the recent Boynton report (DHSS, 1980), reviewing conditions in Rampton Special Hospital, UK, made no reference in its chapter on handling disturbed and violent behaviour to techniques whereby staff could prevent or reduce the likelihood of violent behaviour. Education has a valuable role, not only for those in daily contact with individuals whom society has deemed dangerous, but also for the general public who are sheltered from contact with such individuals. Access to those 'secret places' where such individuals are detained can only help to foster an improved understanding of 'the dangerous individual' and sympathy for his plight.

Morris (1974) has suggested that as a matter of *justice* we should never take power over the convicted criminal on the basis of unreliable predictions of his dangerousness. He maintains that 'fairness and justice in the individual case and not a generalized cost–benefit utilitarian weighting dictate the choice'. Whether or not individuals should be detained for periods longer than can be justified on grounds other than preventive ones is a major question. Perhaps an answer could be approached through a clarification of the kinds of behaviour for which society is prepared to tolerate intervention in the lives of its citizens on an essentially predictive basis; detaining someone for an action they have not yet, and may never, commit.

An attempt to achieve such definitional clarification might be facilitated through a study of the processes whereby individuals are labelled dangerous and the factors which underlie such decisions. An emphasis on visible classification criteria during the labelling process may similarly help to attain greater consistency in the use of the term. As such, Pfohl (1979*a*) should be applauded for his advocacy of the use of behavioural models with their emphasis on an individual's past behaviour in assessing dangerousness, in preference to psychiatric models which stress the nature of the individual. Such an approach will help to limit the application of the concept of dangerousness to situations of demonstrated dangerous behaviour, and preferably to situations where there is evidence that such behaviour is recurrent. Research indicates that such a limited application will maximize the chances of the label being applied appropriately (in a predictive sense). Similarly, Bottoms and Brownsword (1981) recommend that an individual's right *not* to be detained (on protective bases) should not be overridden unless he satisfies the criterion of 'vivid danger', and thereby substantially threatens the rights of others. The factors which make up 'vivid danger'—seriousness, temporality, frequency and certainty—focus attention on evidence of 'past very serious harm'. Since studies of parole decision-making (Gottfredson *et al.*, 1978) have demonstrated that it is possible for decisions apparently based on a complex of elusive factors to be represented by variables that can be evaluated objectively, it makes such an approach feasible. Also, it is possible that the predictive efficacy of such decisions would increase because they would be based on the only criteria which have any demonstrated predictive efficacy, namely the nature of past behaviour. Most importantly, an emphasis on the use of the term only on evidence of *past* dangerous behaviour will permit the concept's use primarily as a *descriptive* rather than a *predictive* label (i.e. this individual has committed dangerous acts in the past, which in turn makes it more likely that he will do so in the future) and substantially decrease the likelihood of its use on individuals who have never committed dangerous acts. Intervention could then be justified on the basis of the description rather than the prediction, on the basis of retributive preconditions (what an individual has done) rather than rehabilitative ones (need for treatment for dangerousness etc.).

The Floud committee adopted this approach in so far as they recommended that their protective sentence should be limited to those individuals previously convicted of an act of grave harm. However, their proposals failed to include objective controls over the judge's assessment of the nature of the acts that would satisfy the 'past grave harm' criterion, thus leaving judicial discretion relatively unfettered.

In their evidence to the Floud committee (Floud and Young, 1981) the Home Office suggested that 'dangerousness' was not a justiciable issue since the facts could not be ascertained with as much certainty as the issue of guilt. However, if the concept of dangerousness were to be transformed in the manner outlined, it would be possible for the behavioural criteria on which such assessments were made, to be evaluated independently by the courts. The role of 'arbiters of dangerousness', a role that psychiatrists are currently expected to play, but one for which they are particularly ill equipped, would then become the preserve of the legal profession. Thus, it would be possible for such standards as the 'beyond reasonable doubt' criterion to be applied to those individuals perceived as dangerous in much the same manner as they are applied to other transgressors of the criminal law.

The efficacy and justice of decisions made by individuals and groups who are given the responsibility for terminating periods of confinement could also be improved through clarification of the term 'dangerousness' and also of the legislative intent behind its application. Such clarification could help to avoid the position whereby decisions are based on the decision-maker's conception of what action the law requires, which may in turn be influenced by conceptions of what is in the 'best interests' of the individual. The relative attractiveness of a therapeutic environment to some decision-makers, combined with the influence of a natural fear of those who have committed serious acts, can interfere with an equitable application of the law. Providing decision-makers with more precise guidelines and relevant information upon which to base their decisions could increase not only the confidence of the decision-makers, but also the efficacy of their decisions. Similarly, a more imaginative use of both parole and conditional discharge could facilitate the individual's resocialization, whilst retaining some control over his behaviour in the community.

The present application of the concept of dangerousness through mental health statutes is particularly invidious since it results in the anomalous position wherein the mentally abnormal offender can be detained for considerably longer periods than a normal offender who has committed the equivalent offence. The justification for such discriminatory action is traditionally couched in terms of the offender's need for treatment and his potential 'dangerousness'—both questionable assumptions. It seems likely that this approach will continue to attract official support; for example from the *Review of the Mental Health Act 1959* (DHSS, 1978, para. 5.26), 'In the Government's view the law should continue to enable society to protect itself from certain dangerous mentally disordered offenders by detaining them in hospital for a period longer than would be justified by the gravity of their offence.' Thus, detention may be indefinite under a Section 65 order even though there may be no prospect of benefit from treatment (e.g. for those adults with psychopathic disorders).

Two cases illustrating this point were highlighted by '*Special Hospital—Moss Side* (BBC Television, 1981): one was that of a patient with a diagnosis of mental illness and psychopathic disorder detained in mental hospitals since 1924 following the theft of £2; another was that of a patient detained for 28 years in Moss Side, also following petty theft. The likely benefit from further treatment for such people is minimal; detention is justified on the basis of predicted dangerousness. Such predictions cannot be derived from the nature of the original offence and can only relate to institutional behaviour. The opportunities for individuals to refute these assumptions will be limited.

Although it is further recognized that 'it would be wrong to provide what would be no more than preventive detention' (para. 2.45), exceptions are to be made for the perceived 'dangerous' offender. However, this 'assessment' can follow the commission of a non-dangerous offence—and be based on potentially misleading information about the nature of the offender. Since the special safeguards against abuse of these provisions have been demonstrated to be ineffective, the mentally disordered offender who is perceived as dangerous is in a doubly unpalatable situation.

It is apparent that if detention is to be justified on therapeutic grounds, then there is a need for some means of assessing both when treatment has succeeded and when it is deemed to have failed. Since there are currently no means of assessing either of these with respect to dangerousness, the proposals of MIND (National Association for Mental Health) are particularly pertinent. They have suggested a move away from the routinized use of restriction orders without time limits and suggested instead that, where an offender *chooses* a psychiatric rather than a penal disposal, the length of the restriction order should be related to the gravity of the offence committed—life if necessary. On the expiry of the restriction order, if further treatment was still warranted, then the individual could be treated voluntarily or, if justifiable, under civil statutes. Thus, their approach prefers the mentally abnormal offender to be treated primarily as a lawbreaker rather than as an individual who is 'sick' (Gostin, 1977).

The criminal justice process, before embarking on a course that welcomes discriminatory legislation against perceived dangerous offenders, would do well to study the realities of the application of such legislation within mental health statutes. The major problem appears to be not that special legislation is abused consciously, but that its very existence results, from a variety of motives, in its over-use. If, as all the evidence in this chapter indicates, it is problematic trying to identify, beyond the obvious examples, individuals who are a danger, then it is preferable that 'dangerousness' sentences should not be passed 'except on one who has already committed an act of really extreme severity, such as murder or attempted murder' (Bottoms, 1977, pp. 80–81). If this is to be the case, then the disadvantages of introducing special legislation may well outweigh the advantages—since only a tiny minority of offenders would be eligible, with the majority of those who would be perceived as dangerous receiving life sentences.

Judges are capable of giving long sentences to recidivist violent offenders, based on evidence of harmful behaviour proved beyond reasonable doubt and subject to appeal if disproportionate. That these sentences may be imposed in a 'covert, irrational and arbitrary manner' (Dean, 1981) is not a justification for formalizing those practices, but an indication of the pressing need for their clarification. Furthermore, there is no reason to suppose that the existence of special legislation would deter the judiciary from giving longer sentences in those cases not qualifying for a protective sentence, but perceived as meriting a longer than average sentence. Thus, a re-evaluation of current sentencing practices and the values underlying them is required as a means of clarifying ideas about from whom society needs protecting and what measures society is prepared to tolerate to deal with such threats.

However, the situation at present, with our inability to distinguish the dangerous from the non-dangerous, does not justify the continuing use of the concept of dangerousness. Thus, although subjectively attractive when applied to certain individuals, the term 'dangerous' can appropriately be applied to only aspects of some individuals' behaviour, and for some individuals the term will never prove to be appropriate. Since we remain unable to identify which individuals fall into which groups, the usage of the term is primarily ascriptive rather than descriptive. The conclusions of Went *et al.* (1972, p. 402) remain valid:

'Confidence in the ability to predict violence serves to legitimate instrusive types of social control. Out demonstration of the *futility* of such prediction should have consequences as great for the protection of individual liberty as a demonstration of the *utility* of violence prediction would have for the protection of society.'

References

American Friends Service Committee (1971). *Struggle for Justice: A Report on Crime and Justice in America.* New York: Hill and Wang.

Ancel, M. (1965). *Social Defence.* London: Routledge and Kegan Paul.

Baldwin, J., and McConville, M. (1977). *Negotiated Justice—Pressures on Defendants to Plead Guilty.* London: Martin Robertson and Co.

BBC Television (1981). *Special Hospital—Moss Side* (broadcast 15 March 1981); *Special Hospital—Park Lane* (broadcast 17 March 1981).

Bean, P. (1978). Are the mental health guardians abusing their power? *The Times,* 3 January 1978.

Beck, A. T., Harvey, L., Resnik, P., and Lettieri, D. J. (Eds) (1974). *The Prediction of Suicide.* Bowie, Md: Charles Press Publishers.

Blackman, D. E. (1980). On mental elements and their place in psychology and law. Paper given to the British Psychological Society conference 'Lawyers and Psychologists—The way Forward', 15 November 1980.

Blumstein, A., Cohen, J., and Nagin, D. (Eds) (1978). *Deterrence and Incapacitation: Estimating the Effects of Criminal Sanctions on Crime Rates.* Washington, D. C.: National Academy of Sciences.

Boland, B. (1978). Incapacitation of the dangerous offender: the arithmetic is not so simple. *Journal of Research in Crime and Delinquency*, **15**, 126–129.

Bottoms, A. E. (1977). Reflections on the renaissance of dangerousness. *Howard Journal for Penal Reform*, **16**, 70–96.

Bottoms, A. E., and Brownsword, R. (1983). Dangerousness and rights, in *Dangerousness Problems of Assessment and Prediction* (ED. J. Hinton). London: Allen and Unwin.

Brody, S., and Tarling, R. (1980). *Taking Offenders Out of Circulation* (Home Office Research Study No. 64). London: HMSO.

Brown, C. Worth, J., Sapsford, R., and Banks, C. (1979). *Life Sentence Prisoners* (Home Office Research Study No. 51). London: HMSO.

Central Statistical Office (1981). *Annual Abstract of Statistics* (Ed. E. Lawrence). London: HMSO.

Cocozza, J., and Steadman, H. (1976). Community fear of the mentally ill: an unsolved obstacle for the community mental health movement. Paper presented at the conference on 'Community and Policy Research', Albany, New York, April 1976.

Cohen, J. (1978). The incapacitative effect of imprisonment: a critical review of the literature, in *Deterrence and Incapacitations: Estimating the Effects of Criminal Sanctions on Crime Rates* (Eds A. Blumstein, J. Cohen and D. Nagin). Washington, D. C.: National Academy of Sciences, pp. 187–243.

Cross, R. (1975). *The English Sentencing System*. London: Butterworth.

Dean, M. (1981). Living with danger. *The Guardian*, 25 October 1981.

DHSS (1980). *Report of the Review of Rampton Hospital. Cmnd 8073*. London: HMSO.

DHSS and Home Office (1975). *Report of the Committee on Mentally Abnormal Offenders. Cmnd 6244*. London: HMSO.

DHSS and Office of Population Census (1976). *In-patient Statistics from the Mental Health Enquiry for England*. London: HMSO.

DHSS, Home Office, Welsh Office and Lord Chancellor's Department (1978). *Review of the Mental Health Act 1959. Cmnd 7320*. London: HMSO.

Diamond, B. L. (1975). The psychiatric prediction of dangerousness. *University of Pennsylvania Law Review*, **123**, 439–452.

Evenson, R. C., and Altman, H. (1975). A re-evaluation of 'The diagnosis and treatment of dangerousness'. Unpublished paper, Missouri Institute of Psychiatry, University of Missouri School of Medicine.

Fagin, A. (1976). The policy implications of predictive decision-making: 'likelihood' and 'dangerousness' in civil commitment proceedings. *Public Policy*, **24**, 491–528.

Floud, J. (1978). 'Dangerousness': it is a valid and necessary concept? Paper given to the British Psychological Society conference 'Symposium on Dangerousness', 9 April 1978.

Floud, J., and Young, W. (1981). *Dangerousness and Criminal Justice*. London: Heinemann.

Foucault, M. (1978). About the concept of the 'dangerous individual' in 19th Century legal psychiatry. *International Journal of Law and Psychiatry*, **1**, 1–18.

Geis, G., and Monahan, J. (1976). The social ecology of violence, in *Morality: Theory, Research and Social Issues* (Ed. T. Lickona). New York: Holt, Rinehart and Winson, pp. 342–356.

Gostin, L. O. (1975). *A Human Condition*, Vol. 1, *The Mental Health Act from 1959 to 1975* (MIND Special Report). London: National Association for Mental Health.

Gostin, L. O. (1976). Regional secure units. Unpublished article, MIND.

Gostin, L. O. (1977). *A Human Condition*, Vol. 2, *The Law Relating to Mentally Abnormal Offenders* (MIND Special Report). London: National Association for Mental Health.

Gostin, L. O. (1978). *The Mental Health Act 1959. Is It Fair*? (MIND Special Report). London: National Association for Mental Health.

Gostin, L. O., and Rassaby, E. (1980). *Representing the Mentally Ill and Handicapped. A Guide to Mental Health Review Tribunals.* London: National Association for Mental Health and The Legal Action Group.
Gottfredson, D. M., Cosgrove, C. A., Wilkins L. T., Wallerstein, J., and Rauh, C. (1978). *Classification for Parole Decision Policy.* London: National Institute of Law Enforcement and Criminal Justice.
Greenland C. (1976). Dangerous sexual offenders in Canada, in *Studies on Imprisonment.* Ottawa: Law Reform Commission of Canada, pp. 247–281.
Gunn, J. (1979). The law and the mentally abnormal offender in England and Wales. *International Journal of Law and Psychiatry*, **2**, 199–214.
Gurevich, G. D., and Bourne, P. G. (1970). Mental illness and violence, in *Violence and the Struggle for Existence* (Eds D. Daniels, M. Gilula and F. Ochberg). Boston: Little Brown & Co., pp. 309–326.
Guze, S. B. (1976). *Criminality and Psychiatric Disorders.* Oxford: Oxford University Press.
Harvard Law Review (1974). Developments in the law—civil commitment of the mentally ill. *Harvard Law Review*, **87**, 1190–1406.
Home Office (1977). *Prisons and the Prisoner.* London: HMSO.
Home Office (1977). *Review of Criminal Justice Policy 1976.* London: HMSO.
Home Office (1978). *Sentences of Imprisonment: A Review of Maximum Penalities* (A report of the Advisory Council on the Penal System). London: HMSO.
Home Office (1980). *Criminal Statistics, England and Wales, 1979. Cmnd 8098.* London: HMSO.
Kittrie, N. (1971). *The Right to be Different.* Baltimore: Johns Hopkins University Press.
Kozol, H. L., Boucher, R. J., and Garofalo, R. F. (1972). The diagnosis and treatment of dangerousness. *Crime and Delinquency*, **18**, 371–392.
Livermore, J., Malmquist, C., and Meehl, P. (1968). On the justifications for civil commitment. *University Pennsylvania Law Review*, **117**, 75–96.
Lord Chancellor (1976). Speech reported in *The Magistrate*, **1976**, 187.
McGrath, P. G. (1968). Custody and release of dangerous offenders, in *The Mentally Abnormal Offender* (Eds A. de Reuch and R. Porter). Boston: Little Brown, pp. 121–129.
Manning, M. (1980). Sentencing laws: a practitioner's view, in *New Directions in Sentencing* (Ed. B. Grossman). Toronto: Butterworth, pp. 273–292.
Martinson, R. (1974). What works? Questions and answers about prison reform. *The Public Interest*, **35**, 22–54.
Meehl, P. (1954). *Clinical versus Statistical Prediction.* Minneapolis: University of Minnesota Press.
Megargee, E. (1969). The psychology of violence, in *Crimes of Violence: A Staff Report Submitted to the National Commission on the Causes and Prevention of Violence* (Eds D. Mulvihill and M. Tumin). Washington, D.C.: US Government Printing Office, pp. 1037–1116.
Megargee, E. (1970). The prediction of violence with psychological tests, in *Current Topics in Clinical and Community Psychology*, Vol. 2 (Ed. C. D. Spielberger). New York: Academic Press, pp. 98–156.
Mental Health Act 1959. London: HMSO.
Monahan, J. (1975). The prediction of violence, in *Violence and Criminal Justice* (Eds D. Chappell and J. Monahan). Lexington, Mass.: Lexington Books, pp. 15–31.
Monahan, J. (1976). The prevention of violence, in *Community Mental Health and the Criminal Justice System* (Ed. J. Monahan). New York: Pergamon Press, pp. 13–34.
Monahan, J. (1978). 'The prediction of violent criminal behaviour; a methodological critique and prospectus', in *Deterrence and Incapacitation: Estimating the Effects of*

Criminal Sanctions on Crime Rates (Eds A. Blumstein, J. Cohen and D. Nagin). Washington D. C.: National Acadamy of Sciences, pp. 244–269.

Monahan, J., and Ruggiero, M. (1980). Psychological and psychiatric aspects of determinate criminal sentencing. *International Journal of Law and Psychiatry*, **3**, 143–154.

Monahan, J., Novaco, R., and Geis, G. (1979). 'Corporate violence: research strategies for community psychology, in *Challenges to the Criminal Justice System: The Perspectives of Community Psychology* (Eds D. Adelson and T. Sarbin). New York: Human Sciences Press.

Morris, N. (1974). *The Future of Imprisonment*. Chicago: University of Chicago Press.

Mulvihill, D., and Tumin, M. (Eds) (1969). *Crimes of Violence: A Staff Report Submitted to the National Commission on the Causes and Prevention of Violence*. Washington, D. C.: US Government Printing Office.

National Health Service Act 1977. London: HMSO.

Newton, M. (1972). Reconvictions after treatment at Grendon. *The Prison Service Journal*, **1972**, 12–13.

Ono, Y. (1981). In gratitude. *The Sunday Times*, 18 January 1981.

Overholzer v. Russell (1960). 238F.2d 195.

Palmer, J., and Salimbene, J. (1978). The incapacitation of the dangerous offender: a second look. *Journal of Research in Crime and Delinquency*, **1978**, 130–134.

Peay, J. (1981). Mental Health Review Tribunals—just or efficacious safeguards? *Journal of Law and Human Behaviour*, **5**, 161–186.

Pfohl, S. (1977). The psychiatric assessment of dangerousness: practical problems and political implications, in *In Fear of Each Other* (Eds J. P. Conrad and S. Dinitz). Lexington, Mass.: Lexington Books, pp. 77–101.

Pfohl, S. (1979*a*). Deciding on dangerousness: prediction of violence as social control. *Crime and Social Justice*, **11**, 28–40.

Pfohl, S. (1979*b*). From whom will we be protected? Comparative approaches to the assessment of dangerousness. *International Journal of Law and Psychiatry*, **2**, 55–78.

Rabkin, J. (1979). Criminal behavior of discharged mental patients: a critical appraisal of the research. *Psychological Bulletin*, **86**, 1–27.

Radzinowicz, L., and Hood, R. (1978). A dangerous direction for sentencing reform. *Criminal Law Review*, **1978**, 713–724.

Radzinowicz, L., and Hood, R. (1981). Dangerousness and criminal justice: a few reflections. *Criminal Law Review*, **1981**, 756–761.

Rubin, B. (1972). Prediction of dangerousness in mentally ill criminals. *Archives of General Psychiatry*, **27**, 397–407.

R. v. Coombes (1972). *Criminal Law Review*, **1973**, 65 (627/A/72).

R. v. Gardiner (1967). *1 ALL ER* 895

R. v. Wren (1974). *Criminal Law Review*, **1974**, 322 (4701/C/73).

Sapsford, R., and Banks, C. (1979). A synopsis of some Home Office research, in *Life Sentence Prisoners* (Ed. D. Smith) (Home Office Research Study No. 51). London: HMSO, pp. 20–47.

Schwitzgebel R. K. (1977). *Professional accountability in the treatment and release of dangerous persons*, in *Perspectives in Law and Psychology*, Vol. 1, *The Criminal Justice System* (Ed. B. D. Sales). New York: Plenum Press, pp. 139–149.

Scottish Council on Crime (1975). *Crime and the Prevention of Crime*. London: HMSO.

Shah, S. A. (1977). Dangerousness: some definitional, conceptual and public policy issues, in *Perspectives in Law and Psychology*, Vol. 1, *The Criminal Justice System* (Ed. B. D. Sales). New York: Plenum Press, pp. 91–119.

Simon, R. J., and Cockerham W. (1977). Civil commitment, burden of proof and dangerous acts: a comparison of the perspectives of judges and psychiatrists. *Journal of Psychiatry and Law*, **5**, 571–594.

Singer, R. G. (1979). *Justs Deserts: Sentencing Based on Equality and Desert.* Boston: Ballinger.

Sleffel, L. (1977). *Law and the Dangerous Criminal—Statutory Attempts at Definition and Control.* Lexington, Mass.: D. C. Heath and Co.

Steadman, H. (1973). Some evidence on the inadequacy of the concept and determination of dangerousness in law and psychiatry. *Journal of Psychiatry and Law*, **1**, 409–426.

Steadman, H., and Cocozza, J. (1974). *Careers of the Criminally Insane.* Lexington, Mass.: Lexington Books.

Sweetland, J. (1972). Illusory correlation and the estimation of 'dangerous' behaviour. Unpublished dissertation, Indiana University.

Tanay, E. (1976). Law and the mentally ill. *Wayne Law Review*, **22**, 781–813.

Thomas, D. A. (1979). *Principles of Sentencing.* London: Heinemann.

Vagg, J. (1981). Trends in sentencing statistics. unpublished article, Centre for Criminological Research, Oxford.

Van Dine, S., Conrad, J., and Dinitz, S. (1979). *Restraining the Wicked—The Incapacitation of the Dangerous Criminal.* Lexington, Mass.: Lexington Books.

von Hirsch, A. (1976). *Doing Justice.* New York: Hill and Wang.

Walker, N. (1978). Dangerous people. *International Journal of Law and Psychiatry*, **1**, 37–50.

Walker, N. (1980). *Punishment, Danger and Stigma. The Morality of Criminal Justice.* Oxford: Blackwells.

Walker, N., Hammond, W., and Steer, D. (1967). Repeated violence. *Criminal Law Review*, **1967**, 465–472.

Wenk, E., Robinson, J. C., and Smith, G. W. (1972). Can violence be predicted? *Crime and Delinquency*, **18**, 393–402.

Whitelaw, W. (1981). Speech to Leicestershire magistrates. *The Guardian*, 14 February 1981.

Wilkins, L. T. (1975). Putting 'treatment' on trial. *Hastings Center Report*, **5**, 35–48.

Wilkins, L. T., Kress, J. M., Gottfredson, D. M., Calpin, J. C., and Gelman, A. M. (1976). *Sentencing Guidelines: Structuring Judicial Discretion—A Report of the Feasibility Study.* Criminal Justice Research Center.

Working Party on the Dangerous Offender (Floud committee) (1977). *The Dangerous Offender. A Consultative Document.* London: Howard League for Penal Reform and NACRO.

Developments in the Study of Criminal Behaviour. Volume 2: Violence
Edited by Philip Feldman

9

Overview

PHILIP FELDMAN

Introduction

The field of violence is obviously very large. From it I have selected eight topics. Three are concerned with violence between 'private' individuals—parents and children, spouses, and rapist and victim. Two dealt with violent behaviour in public institutions—mental hospitals and prisons—involving major disparities of power between staff and inmates, who are often there for long periods. One chapter involved the topic of vandalism—violence against property—usually ignored in the psychological literature, but of great public importance, particularly in crowded settings such as housing estates and mass transportation. Finally, two chapters covered different aspects of the 'mentally abnormal violent offender'.

Why this particular selection, rather than more traditional topics such as murder and general assault? The first reason is that they *are* non-traditional and hence have aroused the interests of psychology only relatively recently—as can be seen from the lists of references following each chapter. Yet all are problems of great public concern and some occur on a very large scale, involving substantial sections of the population and/or great financial loss, to the public purse and to private persons, as well as much individual distress.

The material reported indicates that psychology has already made a useful contribution to describing and accounting for the behaviours concerned. There is also the possibility of using psychological methods in prevention or intervention and social learning theory provides a valuable general framework within which to conduct future research into the control of violence. It is a theory which has generated much valuable work on laboratory analogues of real life aggression and has influenced most of the chapters in this book. The time is now ripe for social scientists to apply the results of such studies to real life problems of violence.

Descriptive findings

Difficulties of obtaining accurate figures

For a particular act to be included in the statistics of violence it has to be observed, reported and recorded. Most importantly, the class of behaviours, of which the particular instance is an example, has to receive the social designation of 'violent'. As a working definition of violence I shall adopt that given by Bandura (1973, p. 8) as applied to aggression: 'injurious and destructive behaviour that is socially defined as violent on the basis of a variety of factors, some of which reside in the evaluator rather than in the performer'. This definition can be expanded in two important ways:

(1) Violent acts damage victims and also have consequences for the assailant, both positive and negative.

(2) Social judgements of what is labelled violent are very important. They depend upon the following: the intensity of the assailant's responses; the level of the display of pain or injury by the victim; the intentions attributed to the assailant; and the characteristics of the assailant—sex, age, social class, and so on. Finally, the characteristics of an observer—the person who is making the social judgement—will determine to some extent the attribution he makes. For example, people interpret observed behaviours in terms of what they might do themselves in a similar situation. To some extent, violence, like beauty, is in the eye of the beholder.

Several of the chapters in this book provide further support for this relativistic view of violence. Gardner and Gray point out that child abuse is far from new—on the contrary, it has been widespread for a very long time. What is new is public disapproval, consequent legislation and publicly or privately provided help for both victim and assailant. Similarly, Minchin indicates that in many homes a certain amount of violence between husband and wife has been regarded as normal, even possibly desirable, as part of a general climate of violence in several aspects of family life.

Public concern about the violence of males against spouses can be traced back over a hundred years, but it has increased sharply in the last decade. Family violence is now much less likely to be seen as a 'normal right' of a husband. Similarly, the courts and public opinion seem less likely than in the recent past to assume that a rape victim might have been 'asking for it'—or even have enjoyed the assault. There has also been recognition of the fact that some attempts by prison officers or mental hospital or mental handicap nurses to control their charges go beyond the bounds of reasonable 'restraint' and constitute assault.

The fact that much violence occurs in the privacy of the home or in institutions away from the public eye sharply reduces the likelihood of a complaint. Many assaulted wives fail to complain because of fears of reprisal, as do some prisoners or patients. Rape victims fear the distress caused by police and medical examinations and the subsequent court appearance—many to such an extent that up to 90% of all rapes may go unreported. Young children are not physically capable of complaining and neighbours hesitate to do so because it is thought undesirable to interfere. The assaulting parents may genuinely wish for help, but fail to seek it, because of the possible penalties resulting from self-incrimination. Violence in public settings also requires a complainant, or at least a reporter. This seems more likely when the victim is a member of staff than a prisoner or patient, particularly when the assailant is a member of staff. While the public is more supportive of patients than of prisoners, this tends to wane between scandals—and it can be surmised that the number of institutions meriting public enquiry considerably exceeds the number that have so far received it.

Instances of vandalism are vastly under-reported, either because those who notice it do not consider it their business, as the property is public, or do not believe reporting will result in effective police action. Finally, the violent behaviours carried out by the 'mentally abnormal violent offender' are not usually different from those carried out by offenders not labelled in this way, and so require no special discussion concerning the difficulties of arriving at accurate figures.

Filling in the 'dark figure'

There are two classical methods of arriving at a more accurate picture, both of which require representative samples of the population of interest: self-reports of offending and self-reports of being a victim. There are considerable technical problems involved but the importance of the data obtained for the development both of sound psychological theory and of effective social policy fully justify the efforts required to overcome them. The results of such studies to date amply confirm the theoretically expected massive under-reporting discussed above.

Current descriptive data

Several pieces of quantitative data, however imperfect, demonstrate the widespread and serious nature of the problems reviewed in this book. The estimates which follow almost certainly vastly understate their true size.

Incidence and frequency. The best available American data suggest that wife beating occurs in nearly one couple in 25 at a frequency of nearly twice per year. In the child abuse field the incidence seems at least as high, possibly even higher. So far as rape is concerned under-reporting is particularly massive, as indicated; possibly only 10% of rapes are actually notified to the police. The true American figure is likely to be at least one woman in 600 per year. British figures are even less sure, as no satisfactory survey has been attempted, but seem unlikely to be markedly lower.

Data for prisons and for mental and mental handicap hospitals are even less satisfactory, as the chapters by Davies and Drinkwater make clear. We may suggest that the intermittent scandals which are uncovered from time to time by investigative journalists or brave employees present only the tip of the iceberg, but we cannot be sure.

There are no useful data for the number of incidents of property damage, but we know something about costs. In Britain these amount to several hundreds of millions of pounds per year—making it easily the most costly crime of all. Even more dramatic is the American estimate that more is spent on repairing the results of school vandalism than on buying text-books. There seem to be no data on the financial costs of medical or psychological help for the victims of marital, or child assault, or rape, but they are clearly very large. Nor are the costs confined to the short term. The damaging effects of such experiences are likely to reverberate down the years, even as far as the next generation—there is a strong suggestion that parents who were assaulted as children are more likely to assault their own children.

The nature of violent incidents

More than half of all assaults on marital partners result in physical injury and half of these require medical care. Similarly, assaults on children often cause severe physical injury, sometimes death. Rape victims who attempt to resist their assailant—even many who do not—may also received physical injury. The same picture of more than occasional injury is found in the institutions. In general, we are not talking about the odd bruise or black eye, but about broken bones and severely damaged tissues.

The nature of the victim

The risks of assault are not equally distributed. Wives who have black belts in karate and children looked after by trained 'nannies' in physically comfortable surroundings are at relatively little risk. The same is true of private property looked after by security guards and of patients in fee-paying mental hospitals who receive frequent visits from concerned families. Conversely, for example, the children most at risk are those who are particularly difficult to rear, who live in physically restricted circumstances, who are members of large families and who have parents who were themselves beaten as children and are lacking in even elementary child rearing skills. The women who are most likely to be rape victims are adolescents and students, those who are black, those who are single and those who work in the helping professions.

Longer term effects on victims

In addition to the immediate physical damage, many victims suffer longer term consequences. For rape victims these may include an increased difficulty in forming and maintaining trusting relationships with males. Assaulted wives are often faced with the grim choice of remaining to face further assault or finding alternative accommodation for themselves and their children as well as a major reorientation of their lives, often in reduced material circumstances. Assaulted children who remain in their own homes face further assaults during their early years. The alternative may be placement in a foster home or in a child care institution, both of inevitably variable quality.

Concluding comment

This very brief selection of the grim tale told in detail throughout this book makes clear the vast importance of the problems concerned, both to individuals and to society, and the urgency of the need to develop methods of intervention and prevention. In turn, these will depend on explanatory theories which do full justice to the available descriptive data and also make clear-cut and practicable proposals for improving the situation.

Explanations

Introduction

In the field of crime in general, theory construction has run well ahead of reliable data collection. Theories have been built to account for findings from biased samples. They tend to fall into two groups: personological and sociological. The former suggest that criminals are almost a separate type of person from the rest of humanity—based on research conducted on long term prisoners whose 'disturbed personalities' may be the result of their incarceration and not its cause. The latter blame crime on the social disadvantages against which young working-class males react by carrying out offences. It is indeed true that such individuals are heavily over-represented among convicted offenders. But this is partially the result of the lengthy sequence from offence to punishement. At each stage of the sequence the same process operates whereby an initially discernible but not massive over-representation is inflated into a very large one indeed (see Feldman, 1977, Chapter 1). Sociological theories are then constructed to 'explain' the differences. Self-report studies indicate a rather different picture: crime is far from confined to young working-class males. It follows that we need a theory to account for criminal behaviour by people in general, not just by those who are disturbed or deprived. Exactly the same argument applies to crimes of violence, whether against persons or property. As we shall see, neither the personal attributes of assailants or the social distress to which they may have been exposed takes us far enough. The attributes of certain potential victims does add something, but much more in the sense of vulnerability to assault than some kind of 'special' precipitating features of their behaviour vis à vis their assailants. As the contributors have shown, social learning theory makes a most helpful explanatory contribution to the acquisition, performance and maintenance of violent behaviours, as it does to criminal behaviour in general. Moreover, it suggests practicable and testable methods of prevention and intervention; the other explanatory approaches are much less helpful in these respects.

Attributes of offenders

It seems true in all the areas of violence surveyed that while some offenders suffer from marked psychological problems, the majority do not. Moreover, the majority of those who are psychologically disturbed do not behave violently. For example, Howell's review of the mentally abnormal offender found no special link between psychosis and violence, with the possible exception of the paranoid forms of schizophrenia. Peay's chapter supports the lack of a special link between mental illness and 'dangerousness'. Minchin's review of battering husbands came to a similar conclusion, although sexual jealousy did play an important part, possibly a more likely occurrence in those with a general tendency to be suspicious of others. Howells found evidence that prisoners with similar pre-prison records of violence had different records of violence *during* imprisonment. Moreover, when prison conditions improved, violence within prison decreased. Both findings suggest the importance of situational, rather than personality variables. However, Osborne and Howells both report data on convicted rapists which suggest that many, possibly a majority, do not rape in order to obtain sexual gratification. Instead, they do so to express a desire for power over women, or to cause them actual physical and psychological harm. Other than the fact that most vandals are young males, the special attributes of offenders contributes little to this area. This is also the case with assaulting parents, as indicated by Gardner and Gray's review. In all, personality variables cannot be dismissed entirely, but they are very far from the whole story.

Attributes of victims

Minchin and Osborne pour cold water on the view that victims of marital or sexual assault are in some way 'responsible' for their injuries. For example, many women who remain with battering husbands do so not because of some underlying desire to be assaulted, rather because they lack financial resources and the available material alternatives seem even worse. The assertion that certain features of dress or appearance 'trigger off' rape ignores the fact that the majority of males do not assault women, irrespective of what they wear or how attractive they are. Moreover, the 'trigger' theory ignores the fact that many rape victims are known to their assailants and that the rapes are often planned. However, victims seen as more helpless, in the sense of being unable to retaliate effectively because of lack of physical strength or an unwillingness to use what they have, appear more likely to be assaulted. This is as true in violent crime as it is in international relations.

Victim helplessness is important in assaults on all dependent persons, from hospital patients to children. Gardner and Gray also produce some evidence for the view that certain children are more difficult than others for parents to bring up. A combination of such children with unskilled parents and inadequate living conditions seems a fairly sure recipe for child battering.

Social distress

Only two of the contributors devote much attention to this variable. Gardner and Gray point out that by no means all poorly off parents batter their children, and many parents do so despite good living conditions. Parents are more prone to assault if they are deficient in parenting skills, although such shortcomings are compounded by poverty.

Mayhew and Clarke found that acts of property damage are carried out against certain targets rather than others (those which are easy of access, are in areas with large numbers of children, and are unlikely to be detected and punished). Social disadvantage does not explain such findings.

Catharsis

A frequent approach to the explanation of aggressive behaviour in general has been that it enables the discharge of unwelcome tensions said to be consequent, typically, on frustration. Those experimental studies which have been well controlled (e.g. Geen *et al.*, 1975) have failed to support the theory—which predicts a reduced degree of aggression at a second opportunity shortly after the first. Instead, subsequent aggression has been shown to be related both to the actual outcome of the first opportunity and the instigating circumstances of the second. Moreover, aggression is only one possible outcome of frustration; others include withdrawal from the situation or passive acquiescence, depending on the outcomes of similar situations in the past.

Social learning theory

Introduction. Full accounts of the theory, as it applies to aggression and to violent crime, are provided by Bandura (1973) and Feldman (1977). It is convenient to divide behaviour into the phases of acquisition, performance and maintenance. The acquisition phase emphasizes antecedent or setting events in the social context within which behaviour is first learned, as well as the processes of acquisition. The major learning processes concern classical and instrumental learning and people acquire new behaviours or lose existing ones through their own direct experiences and also through those of observed others. Once acquired, whether or not a behaviour will be performed depends upon a number of situational variables. Finally, the consequences of behaviours, particularly over a series of occasions, will determine the extent to which they are maintained or diminished.

Acquisition. In the context of child assault by parents, *setting events* include the following: a child that is biologically predisposed to be much harder to rear than the average; a child who was unwanted, or of the 'wrong' sex; parents who were themselves battered as children; parents who are socially isolated, living in poverty, or who are severely deficient in child management skills. Violent incidents in hospitals are increased by staff shortages, and by a lack of staff–patient interaction, irrespective of the number of staff. Damage occurs more frequently against publicly owned property.

The basis for observational learning is an exposure to social models of violence seen by observers to be positively reinforced for their violent behaviour. Property damage by children who are then copied by others is an obvious example of this; another is sexual assault described by young males to their friends. Much research and public attention has been focused on televised violence as a key source of observational learning, but there is no shortage of violently behaving social models in real life settings which people can see for themselves.

Performance. Of all the situational variables which determine the performance of a violent act, simple opportunity may be the most important—as the Home Office studies on vandalism indicate. The presence of a model already carrying out a violent act will increase the probability of copying, as does the absence of surveillance by those who might intervene. Prior emotional arousal makes a violent act both more likely and more severe; hence the advice sometimes given to women not to resist their attackers—unless they are very likely to do so effectively. Prior aversive experiences, whether verbal or physical, enhance aggression, as does the withdrawal of well established reinforcers. Examples of both are provided in the chapters on prison and hospital violence by Davies and Drinkwater, respectively. In institutional settings we may expect to find examples of aggression in response to orders by superiors, so well demonstrated in laboratory studies (e.g. Milgram, 1974). It is characteristic of many categories of the victims of assault that they lack the capacity for effective retaliation against their assailant, and hence he may act with relative impunity. Nor are aggressors likely to be punished by the legal authorities. The great majority of assaults of all kinds go unreported.

Maintenance. Behaviours, including violent ones, are maintained by their consequences and particularly by the long term balance between positive and negative outcomes. Negative consequences for an aggressor are somewhat unlikely. For example, even if a rape is reported to the police the chances of detection and punishment are fairly low, unless the assailant is known to the victim and the evidence is unequivocal. In contrast, positive outcomes for the assailant have a high probability: an assaulted wife obeys her husband more slavishly; the rape victim is visibly humiliated; the friends of the child destroying property congratulate him on his stone-throwing ability; and so on.

Control

Introduction

In the field of crime in general, attention is moving towards prevention, rather than intervention designed to reduce re-offending by those who have already begun. Because of the serious consequences for victims, which are particularly severe in the case of violent crime, the bulk of the very limited work on control has focused on intervention, and prevention exercises are still largely in the planning or research stages. Help is given to the victims of assaults as well as to some of those who have carried them out but would prefer not to do so in the future.

The three major explanatory theories of violence which have been mentioned throughout this book are the dispositional (personality), the social stress and the social learning approaches. Dispositional theories have no consequences for prevention and only limited ones for intervention. There is little evidence, for example, that providing psychiatric help for parents who injure their children will make them more effective parents. In principle, the social stress approach has implications for prevention but, in practice, beyond pious assertions of the need to end poverty, it does not take us very far. It is also the case that far from the increase in prosperity over the past 40 years reducing crime, most property crimes have sharply increased. We cannot be optimistic that material advances alone will reduce the incidence of assaults of all kinds.

In contrast, the social learning approach is more helpful, with its emphasis on the detail of setting events and of individual learning experiences and on often manipulable performance variables. Nevertheless, social learning programmes of intervention and prevention, however well planned, often require the context of a supportive public policy, perhaps on a large scale.

Intervention

Gardner and Gray set out guidelines for training programmes for parents who have assaulted their children. These require an initial stage of observation and analysis of antecedent events, behaviours and consequences as they relate to the current management of the child, followed by training in methods which will produce more positive consequences for both parent and child. In her chapter Osborne focuses mainly on the help given to the victims of rape, often by volunteers, rather than by professional agencies. The companion volume to this (Feldman, 1982) includes a chapter by Perkins (1982) on sex offences which deals in part with his interesting work in a prison setting (Birmingham) with a number of categories of sex offenders, including rapists. He lays much emphasis on training in social skills. In this volume, Howells refers to work carried out at Broadmoor with the offenders labelled mentally abnormal and indicates the difficulties faced by programmes working in such a restrictive setting. Minchin again emphasizes help for the victim, but also mentions the possibility for both partners of marital therapy and of training in spotting and resolving the early stages of conflict. Otherwise, the wife departs, permanently or temporarily. In either case, the problems are practical, involving finances and accommodation.

At present intervention methods for patients involved in violent incidents are poorly thought out and inconsistently applied. They include seclusion, physical and mechanical restraint and, more rarely, the use of electro-convulsive shock. Social learning-based research suggests that violent incidents arise from ineffective ward management techniques, pointing the way to prevention by more carefully designed and executed ones. Davies draws similar conclusions concerning the important role of prevention in controlling prison violence. So far as intervention in the prison context is concerned, this means mainly methods of terminating hostage or riot incidents, without serious injury, and has led to the development of special training programmes for senior staff.

Prevention

Osborne lists some immediate practical steps to reduce the possibility of a woman being a rape victim, including protecting her environment by requiring strangers to identify themselves and using only well lit entrances. Self-defence might extend to formal training in unarmed combat. Measures which require changes in legal practice include making it easier to secure convictions and increased levels of penalty, both of which might help to deter potential rapists.

On a much more ambitious level, and likely only in the very long term, is much better education in male—female relationships, particularly for males. Minchin adds other possibilities, such as measures to improve the social status of women and to reduce media emphasis on violence against them. She points out that while such changes are desirable in themselves, they may have little direct effect on sexual or marital violence.

Gardner and Gray discuss primary and secondary levels in preventing assaults on children. The former means training parents in child management before the children are born or in the very early days of parenthood. Much preliminary research is needed on exactly what is meant by parenting skills and on how to teach them effectively. Primary prevention is at present speculative. It involves teaching children general problem-solving skills which they can then apply to a range of specific situations, including child management, when they eventually become parents.

Mayhew and Clarke suggest that major social policy initiatives might help prevent vandalism. However, they go on to point out that, for example, publicity campaigns to date have been relatively ineffective. Basic changes in the design of public housing schemes, such as an emphasis on 'defensible space', might help, as would increased employee surveillance. But neither is a panacea. The provision of alternative social activities for children might also be helpful, but only if they were substantial, available for long periods and combined with the immediate practical measures for prevention, embodied in the phrase 'target hardening'. There is good evidence that substantial reductions in vandalism can be achieved through the use of stronger materials, putting breakable objects out of reach and immediately repairing breakages.

In the prison context prevention of major violent incidents such as riots would be assisted by improved design of buildings, and a sharp reduction in overcrowding, both of which have possible financial implications. It is much simpler and less expensive to establish a rapid informal grievance procedure, improve the attractiveness of the prison diet, and encourage a continued high level of public interest and knowledge.

The Birmingham research (Drinkwater) has considerable implications for the prevention of violent incidents in psychiatric hospitals. A combination of properly planned ward management strategies and associated nurse training programmes would be needed to increase staff–patient interactions and staff reinforcement for appropriate patient activities. Such changes in well established staff attitudes and behaviours will be difficult to achieve. There is ample evidence of the detailed planning needed before implementing complex change programmes in institutions (see Reid, 1982, in the companion volume).

Public policy

So far most of the discussion on improvements in control has been at the level of the individual person or family, or of the individual institution. Suggestions for more high level changes involving major shifts in society are much less easy to envisage happening, except in the very long term, although there has been progress in the social status of women which might eventually reduce assaults on them, whether by husbands or strangers.

However, there is one specific area, that of the 'dangerous', mentally abnormal offender, in which there is a close interaction between public policy and the fate of individuals so labelled, as Peay's chapter makes clear. On the one hand, it is important for the public to be protected from further assaults by those who have already carried out violent crimes. On the other hand, it is wrong to presume an inevitable repetition and then to avoid it by an indeterminant period of confinement *in advance*, with potential ill effects on those confined.

This is particularly so when, as is the case at present, treatment is either unavailable or ineffective and predictions of further violence are extremely inaccurate. Peay argues for the ending of indeterminate periods of confinement, and a move away from labelling *persons* as dangerous, to the specification of the *situations* in which violent behaviours are more likely (the general approach of this book) as well as a considerable tightening up of legal safeguards for the rights of the 'dangerous' patient. Coupled with these changes should be a much more thorough preparation for effective social functioning after discharge and increased monitoring and support in the initial stages of return to the community.

In general, her chapter is an important example of the rapidly developing interplay between law and the behavioural sciences. Such contacts will have to increase if psychologists are to make their fullest possible contribution to the explanation and control of violence. Some of the implications of the social learning approach, particularly as they concern prevention, take psychologists right outside their usual settings and require a breaking down of the traditional boundaries between social science disciplines. Social scientists, from sociologists to economists, will need to have a much greater appreciation than at present of what they can borrow from each other. It is an effort which will have to be made if the present distressing levels of personal violence are to be reduced.

References

Bandura, A. (1973). *Aggression: A Social Learning Analysis*. New York: Prentice-Hall.

Feldman, M. P. (1977). *Criminal Behaviour*. Chichester: John Wiley.

Feldman, M. P. (1982). *Developments in the Study of Criminal Behaviour*, Vol. 1, *The Prevention and Control of Offending*. Chichester: John Wiley.

Geen, R. G., Stonner, D., and Shope, G. L. (1975). The facilitation of aggression by aggression: evidence against the catharsis hypothesis. *Journal of Personality and Social Psychology*, **25**, 721–726.

Milgram, S. (1974). *Obedience to Authority*. London: Tavistock.

Perkins, D. E. (1982). The treatment of sex offenders, in *Developments in the Study of Criminal Behaviour*, Vol. 1, *The Prevention and Control of Offending* (Ed. M. P. Feldman). Chichester: John Wiley, pp. 91–214.

Reid, I. D. (1982). The development and maintenance of a behavioural regime in a secure youth treatment centre, in *Developments in the Study of Criminal Behaviour*, Vol. 1, *The Prevention and Control of Offending* (Ed. M. P. Feldman). Chichester: John Wiley, pp. 79–106.

Author Index

Subject Index